Myth
and
Philosophy

# Myth and Philosophy

## A CONTEST OF TRUTHS

# Lawrence J. Hatab

OPEN ❁ COURT

La Salle, Illinois

✵

OPEN COURT and the above logo are registered in the U.S. Patent and
Trademark Office.

©1990 by Open Court Publishing Company

First Printing 1990

Printed and bound in the United States of America.

Hatab, Lawrence J., 1946–
    Myth and philosophy : a contest of truths / Lawrence J. Hatab.
        p.   c.m.
    Includes bibliographical references and index.
    ISBN 0-8126-9115-6. — ISBN 0-8126-9116-4 (pbk.)
    1. Myth.   2. Philosophy, Ancient.   I. Title.
  BL304.H37   1990
  291.1'3'01—dc20

                                                    90-40804
                                                    CIP

*To John Tich*
*Who started me thinking about such things*

# CONTENTS

# PREFACE

This book is an interpretive study of the historical relationship between myth and philosophy in ancient Greece from Homer to Aristotle. A number of conclusions are drawn which go beyond the historical treatment, however, and which speak to the general question of truth by defending the intelligibility of myth against an exclusively rational or objective view of the world. I argue for a pluralistic conception of truth, one which can permit different forms of understanding and which surrenders the need for a uniform, or even a hierarchical, conception of truth. The historical displacement of myth at the hands of philosophy is the setting for this argument. Rationality and science emerged as a revolutionary overthrow of myth, but that insurrection is not beyond criticism because myth presented a meaningful expression of the world which was different from, and not always commensurate with, the kind of understanding sought by philosophers. Consequently, the idea that philosophy "corrected" the ignorance of the past or represented "progress" is unwarranted. Furthermore, philosophy developed *out of* mythical origins and continued to exhibit elements of myth. One important conclusion will be that although myth and rationality are not identical, they often overlap; and even when they do not overlap, it is not an either-or situation. Much truth is shown in myth, and the historical connection between rationality and myth only adds to the need for a conception of truth that goes beyond traditional philosophical assumptions.

This investigation has some relevance for contemporary thought, both inside and outside of the discipline of philosophy. The historical study is meant to address current intellectual and cultural problems and to complement some recent responses to those problems. Within the bounds of this study such implications are tentative and provisional; some are threaded throughout the text or prepared more deliberately at the end of the book. Here I can offer some hints which are meant to stimulate further inquiry after the book makes its case. For philosophers and students of philosophy this study offers an analysis which relates philosophy to prephilosophical culture; such analysis provides a supplementary background for important trends in contemporary thought. In particular I am referring to trends which challenge strict distinctions between fact and value, fact and interpretation, science and nonscience, philosophy and literature, and philosophy and rhetoric. I am also referring to the "post-modern" problem of foundations in knowledge. That problem, in the eyes of many, is not *which* foundation for knowledge is to be identified but *whether* a foundation is possible; or more deliberately, the radical claim that our knowledge of the world does *not* have an objective foundation or rational justification.

Nietzsche and Heidegger in the continental tradition, and Wittgenstein in the analytic tradition, are major figures who have challenged philosophy's traditional agenda of discovering certain bedrock truths which can measure and secure other forms of inquiry. What Heidegger called "the end of philosophy" and what Wittgenstein called the "dissolving" of philosophical problems have been guiding themes in various recent attacks against the foundational aims of philosophy. I support these developments, and yet my study of myth and philosophy, which is inspired in part by the later thought of Heidegger, harbors a *positive* consequence of such attacks rather than simply a negative dismantling of traditional philosophy.

For the general reader or persons in other academic disciplines this book offers a fresh entry into the intellectual and cultural background of philosophy and a discussion of philosophy's relation to a broad complex of human concerns. Such an approach, I hope, will make philosophical issues more accessible and modify the sometimes forbidding esoterica of contemporary specialties. Indeed, this study is by nature interdisciplinary. A number of issues are discussed that will be of interest to the disciplines of history, literature, linguistics, art, classics, history of religions, psychology, sociology, philosophy of science, and cultural anthropology.

With regard to the overall implications of my book, I offer readers the following clue (which is admittedly a little cryptic at this point). Contemporary problems in philosophy and other disciplines stem, in part, from a misunderstanding of myth and an exiling or demoting of mythical meaning. Modern "crises"—alienation; intellectual, social, and personal rootlessness; threats from technology; worries about "regressive" antirational developments; and the conflict between science and religious/moral/aesthetic values—*are* crises owing to a "demythification" of thought and an overconfidence in rationality and science. Accordingly, any solution to such problems would include a restoration of myth or mythical meaning. I hasten to add that I leave open the question of what form this development should take, and I say this not simply out of reticence. I only want to argue for a kind of pluralism which can negotiate between "competing" forms of understanding (e.g., science, religion, and values), and not only between but also *within* such areas (a uniform conception *of* science, religion, or values is just as problematic as a reduction of thought *to* any of them). The connection between myth and pluralism will take shape in due course.

I believe that the following study is especially helpful regarding the issues mentioned here, because it provides a specific historical analysis which shows these issues emerging for the first time in the Greek world. Since the Greek tradition is accepted as the origin of our intellectual life, we can prepare a more focused treatment of current concerns by first addressing how and why the Greeks developed the setting for these concerns.

I should add that I am not a specialist in some of the fields that pertain to this investigation, such as classics and the history of religions. Much of my analysis is a gathering of work by scholars in such fields. At times I felt that I might be in over my head. I hope not. I am sure that I have not avoided errors of omission or commission. This study is not meant to be specialized, however, but rather synthetic, interpretive, and somewhat adventurous. It does not pretend to be a definitive or thorough analysis of the various topics involved. This is not the kind of book a specialist would want to write, but there is a value in gathering this vast historical material into one piece, despite the inevitable thinness in the treatment of the parts. I hope I have been able to provide an accessible entry point for nonspecialists, contribute a broad overview to the material, introduce a perspective which can illuminate the material in an innovative way, and evoke insights that may not have been recognized before when narrower interests were being served. Even though my work depends on many influences, I have tried to avoid jargon or adherence to the standard vocabulary and agenda of any particular movement. For better or worse I did not want to press this material into any particular academic mold. I ask, then, for the reader's indulgence in letting the work speak for itself, since it might be hard to classify (which I think is one of its chief virtues).

I would like to thank Old Dominion University, the College of Arts and Letters, and the Philosophy Department for various grants and opportunities for release time that helped me research and produce this book. I also want to thank the friends, colleagues, and students who have given helpful suggestions, criticisms, and moral support. My thanks also to Elaine Dawson for her help in the preparation of the manuscript.

# INTRODUCTION

In the *Theaetetus*, Socrates recounts the following anecdote about Thales, the first of the Greek philosophers:

> . . . a witty and attractive servant-girl is said to have mocked Thales for falling into a well while he was observing the stars and gazing upwards; declaring that he was eager to know the things in the sky, but that what was behind him and just by his feet escaped his notice (174a).[1]

Socrates goes on to say that a philosopher should always expect such mockery because philosophy pursues essential and universal knowledge at the expense of immediate things and will always seem foolish to people pursuing the ways of the world. That anecdote may be the first example of the "absent-minded intellectual" theme which has become quite familiar. Philosophy has traditionally defended that kind of absent-mindedness as a necessary by-product of its own mindfulness of abstract knowledge. One should not expect a philosopher to be completely immersed in everyday activities; the very nature of intellectual reflection requires a kind of detachment from, or suspension of, immediate engagement.

But there may be a degree of wisdom hidden in the servant-girl's mockery—not simply with respect to *how* a philosopher engages the world but more importantly with respect to *what* philosophy has produced, or how philosophy has *understood* the world. Since the practice of philosophy involves a detached analysis of fundamental issues behind the everyday commerce of life, questions can arise regarding problems of "distance," not simply the distance between intellectuals and people absorbed in everyday passions and practices, but also a problematic distance from lived experience reflected in philosophical systems themselves. In other words, one might ask whether the first type of distance can create an absent-mindedness not simply in philosophers as human beings but in the results of philosophy too, to the point where it falls into error about the world.

These questions have been the mark of what can loosely be called existential philosophy, which has walked a tightrope of ambiguity by pursuing philosophical inquiry while at the same time engaging in a critique of traditional philosophy, by calling abstract reason back to the "lived world" and away from certain tendencies that have held philosophy at a distorting distance. Metaphysical and theological systems, and rationalist, empiricist, and positivist philosophies, all exhibit a kind of remoteness from everyday life because of certain traditional standards of truth. Those standards indicate that truth requires some kind of "correction" or resolution of immediate lived experience, affective concerns, passionate engagement, and emotional responses to the world. Such areas are judged to be a kind of chaos, confusion, or contingency, an obstacle to be overcome in the path toward truth, or at most they are deemed "subjective" occasions outside the realm of "objective" truth.

Existential philosophy has attempted to liberate thought from a kind of abstract, objective imperialism and from far too-exclusive interpretations of truth. It aims to give thought to the concrete situations and challenges that claim human existence and that are not susceptible to rational or abstract formulas—matters of life and death, success and failure, limits and uncertainties, and the struggle to find meaning in a world that can block human aspirations.[2] Traditional philosophy has exhibited various strains of rational, empirical, and scientific assumptions and methods ever since its inception in ancient Greece. Abstract reason and scientific thinking are certainly important, but they tend to pass over other important forms of experience and understanding.

Friedrich Nietzsche and Martin Heidegger stand as the most profound and penetrating figures in existential thought, for at least two reasons. First, rather than simply rebeling against traditional philosophy or indulging in some kind of reactionary romanticism, they pursued an *internal* critique of philosophy to show how and why it developed an alienated stance and consequently ran astray in seeking answers to fundamental questions. Secondly, both Nietzsche and Heidegger recognized that such a critique demanded a *historical* analysis. If philosophy itself is problematic, then a return to its historical emergence in Greek culture would offer the most telling clues about its nature and its relation to other forms of culture *external* to philosophy. Both thinkers saw in Greek culture a rich atmosphere in which philosophy could be properly analyzed in terms of its own character and whatever important elements it may have laid aside.

In effect this amounts to saying that there were (and are) certain important elements of culture which traditional philosophy had overlooked, rejected, or pushed aside, and which should not have been so dismissed. In ancient Greece this distinction and conflict is clearly seen in the contest between philosophy and myth, beginning around the sixth century B.C. when philosophers began to challenge traditional religious forms of understanding. Both Nietzsche and Heidegger recognized in Greek poetry and myth many important features which could be *defended* against philosophical criticism and which consequently would prepare a countercriticism of philosophy.

Therefore, comprehending the relation between myth and philosophy would be essential for a proper understanding of intellectual history and the nature of philosophy. In exploring this historical relationship my analysis assumes that myth in a general sense can be understood in the light of an existential critique of traditional philosophy. If existential thought has called philosophy to task for abandoning or misinterpreting certain important elements of culture, then perhaps prephilosophical culture (myth) can be understood as having presented those elements in an authentic manner. If something like rationalism or positivism can be called into question, then perhaps the cultural forms which Greek reason and science tried to displace can be defended in view of the questionable character of traditional philosophy. In other words, what is said to have been missing in philosophy may have been present in a certain way and to some degree in mythical culture.

One question in this study involves the extent to which Greek myth can be understood as a prephilosophical "mirror" of existential thought, and thus the extent to which the history of thought displays a certain symmetry, in that a modern critique of traditional philosophy may stem from preconceptual, mythical soil and thereby may involve an echo of something ancient. Accordingly, I am undertaking an analysis of myth which is animated by many of the assumptions of existential thought. Since I believe that the existential critique of traditional philosophy has merit and tells us something true, I aim to analyze myth in terms of its *truth* and its legitimate role in culture.

Of course we thus abandon a common meaning of the term "myth," namely, something false or fictional. That meaning is in fact a historical consequence of *philosophy*'s response to myth and is not indicative of its original meaning. We need to understand the ways in which myth is a form of truth. Therefore the reader must ignore the conventional meaning of the term and hear the word in a new way. We will also engage the term "primitive," which likewise should not connote a derogatory meaning or a sense of backwardness. Rather, the term should be taken to mean "primal," that is to say, something original and essential. Both the

mythical and the primitive will have to be understood in a positive
light. Indeed, I have not said anything new here. Much work has been
done in analyzing primitive experience and mythical culture in a serious and positive way, but I hope that my overview of Greek culture can
add to this work by extending its scope, clarifying the important issues,
and drawing out certain implications that may have been missed or
underdeveloped.

In order to set the stage for an analysis of myth, I want to identify four
themes from Heidegger's thought, each of which represents a radical
challenge to traditional philosophical assumptions and which will be
mirrored in certain ways in Greek mythical imagery. The first is the notion of being-in-the-world.

**Being-in-the-world.**    In *Being and Time*,[3] Heidegger prepares his reflections on Being with an existential analysis of "world." The starting
point of this analysis is the rejection of traditional ontologies which
ground the being of the world in objective characteristics independent
of human involvement. For Heidegger, Being is first given as meaning,
disclosed in existential situations and moods. World is characterized as
being-in-the-world, a unified configuration meant to express the correlation of human existence and its environment. The world is not first
disclosed as objects merely present before us, but in the light of our existential involvement, our concern for the world and our place in it. The
unified term for this involvement is "care," which itself emerges out of
the primal mood of angst, or the concrete awareness of the possibility of
death and nonbeing. The existential tension of life and death, being and
nonbeing, and the subsequent concerns and projects into which we are
thrust to withstand this tension of finitude constitute what is meant by
"world."

The world therefore cannot be grounded in objective explanations
because it is first disclosed in a nonobjective, existential context of relations stemming from primal care as a consequence of finitude. But this
does not mean that the world is then grounded in "subjective" states.
The notion of an isolated or interiorized subject would preclude real involvement, and subjectivistic accounts would not suit the ways in
which the world *claims* us. For Heidegger our sense of self is disclosed
only in and out of a world-situation. And when we care for and about the
world, this is not an "internal" state separate from the world. We *dwell*
in care and *are* in-the-world. One way of putting this is that the movement from angst to world-involvement is not a subjective "decision."

**The finitude of Being.** Care for the world is rooted in angst, which Heidegger explicates in terms of being-toward-death. Human awareness of death in the midst of life, of nonexistence in the midst of existence, is that which allows the meaning of the world and of Being to show itself. Angst reveals the Nothing, which, however, is not the same as sheer nothingness or the opposite of Being. Being and Nothing belong together. As the visibility of the moon is inseparable from the dark sky, the Being of beings is inseparable from the Nothing. Only out of the Nothing can it be shown that beings *are* (i.e., are *not* nothing). What follows from the Being–Nothing correlation is that human existence and Being itself are essentially finite in nature, because at a fundamental level beings are understood *as* beings only in relation to a negative limit. So the Being of beings is not itself a positive condition, but rather a process of emergence from nonbeing to being. For Heidegger it is this inseparable correlation of negative and positive, absence and presence, that so strains our object-oriented language and makes the issue of Being so elusive.

**Unconcealment and truth.** In connection with Being as the process of emergence, Heidegger distinguishes between ordinary truth and primordial truth, or representational and presentational truth.[4] In representational truth, a statement must correspond to a state of affairs. The statement "A tree stands in the field" is true if in fact the tree is in the field. All well and good. But Heidegger argues that before this correspondence takes effect, "something" must first be presented, come to be, or show itself as a phenomenon.[5] Indeed, a good deal must first show itself—the meaning of tree and field; their relation; the context of relations and meanings into which tree and field fit; statements; the relatedness of statements and states of affairs; a criterion of empirical verification; and primarily the meaning of Being itself. So before representational correspondence, before the operation of empirical verification, a primal presentation shows itself. Presentational truth refers to this primal showing or emergence, which Heidegger calls unconcealment, based on an etymological interpretation of the Greek word for truth, *alētheia* (literally, unhiddenness).[6] Such primordial truth is prior to *what* is disclosed by naming the *process* of disclosure itself, emergence out of concealment. That process as such cannot be disclosed, since any disclosure presupposes the process. The only thing prior to unconcealment is not some other condition or state of affairs, but, as the word suggests, concealment. Here something "negative" shows a priority, which more than anything else is emblematic of Heidegger's challenge to traditional philosophy. When pursuing an "origin" at a fundamental level, thinking must acknowledge a mystery.

**Granting.** Although human existence is the entry point for the inquiry into Being, for Heidegger nothing in human nature can serve as a foundation for Being, any more than any other designation can. Even human self-discovery implies the prior process of unconcealment. In his later thought, Heidegger gives maximum focus to the extra-human features of Being. The process of disclosure is not something that comes "from" human thinking but rather "to" human thinking, as an arrival, which Heidegger often expresses as a granting or a giving. Being itself is the process of arrival which simply "gives." Heidegger eventually subordinated even the term Being to the "it gives" which grants Being (playing on the German *es gibt Sein*).

> In the beginning of Western thinking, Being is thought, but not the "It gives" as such. The latter withdraws in favor of the gift which It gives. That gift is thought and conceptualized from then on exclusively as Being with regard to beings.[7]

Now the early correlation of Being and Nothing is described as a process of emergence involving a simultaneous arrival and withdrawal. But in addition, the language of giving or granting adds to the image of arrival all the attendant existential meanings that gather around a gift— significance, appropriateness, receptiveness, wonderment, gratitude, care.

There are some significant implications of Heidegger's thinking for our analysis. By refusing to trace Being to some fixed or describable "ground," Heidegger renounces the "foundational" character of western philosophy. Any proposed foundation of beings will have already been given in a prior process of unconcealment, which itself cannot be "founded." So no "explanation" of the world can claim to be fundamental, if explanation means a representational reduction to some state of affairs. What *is* fundamental is the *process* of unconcealment as such. Since the process of unconcealment itself has priority, however, then no one state of affairs or *product* of unconcealment can stand as a "measure" for something which shows itself in a different way. What is shown in the world are phenomena such as numbers, emotions, empirical facts, ideas, material states, moral values, art forms, religious beliefs, myths, and scientific explanations. An attempt to "explain" certain basic phenomena in terms of others (i.e., reduce one to some other) would violate the priority of unconcealment. In other words, Heidegger's analysis permits the coexistence of different forms of unconcealment, different forms of truth—a kind of pluralism. Since primordial truth does not involve a standing ground or standard by which various forms of understanding can be "measured," then those forms are permitted a kind of internal autonomy and protection from external judgment.

In our age, science is said to present the facts. The term "fact" has a meaningful use except when tending toward a metaphysical reduction, when "fact" tends to connote a fixed truth by which other forms of disclosure can be measured rather than that which is shown in accordance with the criteria and methodological assumptions of science. Within contemporary philosophy of science, many writers have argued that facts are theory-laden, that the way the world is shown is not independent of the method of approach. If there is no free-standing or purely objective reference point for scientific facts, then it is nothing wild to argue for the "incommensurability" of scientific and nonscientific forms of disclosure. Assumptions of uniformity, predictability, and objective verification cannot themselves be justified scientifically since they are the conditions for such justification. And if there is another form of disclosure for which these assumptions are inappropriate (e.g., myth), then as long as it is not pretending to be a scientific explanation, it cannot be judged "untrue" by science without begging the question of scientific requirements.

From a Heideggerian standpoint, how the objects of science come to be (i.e., become unconcealed) as scientific objects is a metascientific question. If scientific reason cannot be its own object, then the positivistic tendency to view "science" as the proper account of "the world" is an argument with a smuggled premise. The full meaning of the world cannot and should not be an object for science, since science itself cannot be objectified as an ultimate reference point. According to Heidegger there always remains a preobjective meaning of the world which precedes, and makes possible, objectivity.

That which precedes objectivity at the most fundamental level is the primal process of unconcealment. The priority of unconcealment limits the authority of any particular product of unconcealment. And, in general, the world as such cannot be explained, since it runs up against an ultimate limit of concealment. For Heidegger, it is something like being-toward-death that permits the unconcealment of the world to take place, since human awareness of the Nothing shows the Being of the world against the background of that negative limit. Consequently, human existence exhibits an essential "transcendence" of the world (of entities, facts) which allows by contrast the disclosure of the world.

In the light of this analysis, we can begin to approach the significance of myth as distinguished from objective explanations. Myths are meant to express, among other things, the limit of the world, the world as such. Creation stories speak to the element of "transcendence" limiting the world, unconcealment itself (i.e., how the world first comes to be). The nonobjective character of mythical imagery is no threat to its truth, since the issue at hand is essentially nonobjective. No objective reference *within* the world (e.g., matter, causal relations) can ever account for the world as such, since any such reference already presupposes the unconcealment of the world. A central point which will require elucidation in the ensuing chapters is as follows. A myth is not *meant* to be an explanation but rather a presentation of something which can *not* be explained (in the sense of an objective account). Certain irreducible *limits* to objective explanation will constitute the *truth* of mythical disclosure. Of course, myths are often taken by some to be a kind of explanation or establishment of facts, as in the case of religious fundamentalism; but such a viewpoint not only runs up against scientific criticism, it also undermines the very meaning of myth as a cultural phenomenon.

Science, too, is susceptible to its own brand of fundamentalism, but we must question the positivistic overpromotion of science and demotion of nonscientific, nonobjective thinking. Even scientists should wince when a "high priest" like Carl Sagan declares on television: "Science is applicable to everything; with it we vanquish the impossible." Although science is in principle incompatible with dogmatism, there is a tendency toward a methodological dogmatism. Science is not a reportorial account of "the facts." Facts are defined by scientific *methods*. But there are elements of the world that are unavailable to or resist scientific methods or rational explanations. In addition to the issue of primal unconcealment, I would include the phenomenon of culture.

A certain limit to explanation becomes evident when we consider the cultural aspects of human existence. By culture I mean those features which seem to distinguish us from other animals and express our *human* nature: art, religion, morality, technology, abstract thinking, language. I would suggest that the meaning of culture is incommensurable with something like empirical facts. In making this point, I am sustaining a Heideggerian outlook. I am not referring to cultural institutions, specific beliefs, or products of culture, but rather to the background meaning of cultural phenomena. Religion and philosophy stem from a sense of a limit to the world, hence the wonder and questions about its origin or nature. Art goes beyond a brute encounter with things to create new images of things. Morality proposes a reformation or modification of unattended human behavior. Technology transforms physical nature. And abstract thinking, one consequence of which is science, involves looking beyond immediate experience.

The point to be made here aims behind the products of such phenomena to the *way* in which the world is engaged therein. It is evident that such cultural activities all presuppose a *transcendence* of the brute given, the simply "there," a transcendence of "empirical data." Accordingly, if questioning, creating, evaluating, and other such cultural phenomena involve a transcendence of empirical objective data, then accounting for the presence of culture by means of such data (e.g., as a special organization of material, environmental, or biological states) makes no sense. More generally speaking, culture cannot be accounted for since "giving an account" is a cultural phenomenon. The *way* culture discloses the world (and not just the products of culture) cannot be meaningfully expressed by or translated from empirical facts or objective explanations. The phenomenon of questioning, for example, which animates much cultural activity, is essentially inexplicable. There is something peculiar about the question "Why do we ask questions?" The query presupposes and cannot ever capture the phenomenon in question. Science runs up against similar circularities. Science as such is a cultural phenomenon which transcends the brute given. *Seeing the world as* an empirical set requiring experimental verification cannot itself be derived from empirical facts or experiments.

So, with respect to "entities," "facts," and "explanations," the phenomenon of culture displays a qualitative and inexplicable "leap." That leap is the clue to the phenomenological meaning (and truth) of *mythical* language. Just as there is a qualitative and incommensurable difference between the physics of sound and music, with respect to culture there is a differential leap shown in the world; and mythical words such as "soul," "spirit," and "god" are meant to *express* that difference. Mythical images which tell of mysterious origins should be seen to express something true about the world; the same holds for stories telling of the special character of human beings compared to other entities. (Religious objections to evolution should not be taken as an alternative explanation or as a refutation of biological links with other animals but rather as an expression of the extrabiological aspects of a *cultural* animal.)

Myth can be seen as presenting a form of truth. So, just as much as we should resist the *rejection* of mythical and other nonobjective forms of disclosure, we should also resist the imperial "toleration" of these forms (as mere "edification," for example). We will see that rationality and science are not purely "objective," and that myth is not merely "subjective." Although neither side can claim exclusive possession of truth, both disclose important elements of the world. Truth is not always an explanation. Explanation is one way of comprehending things (tracing one thing to another thing, from a lesser known to a greater known). Truth as unconcealment allows a pluralistic embrace of various aspects of the world which are *shown* but which resist reduction to other things. Even prior to an explanatory reduction, the elements to be explained have to be unconcealed, and the notion of the reduction itself has to be unconcealed.

The transcendence shown in culture and certain inexplicable elements of thought usher in the phenomenon of myth. Mythical notions such as "divine origin" present this inexplicable transcendence and express its phenomenological *meaning*. At such a point, neither science nor any other form of disclosure can do any better than myth, except perhaps by renouncing mythical imagery and simply acknowledging a limit to explanation. But that is not inconsistent with the phenomenological meaning of myth, and mythical or poetical formulations might still be possible, even desirable, since they can express something that the mere renunciation of explanation would miss, namely the existential meaning of certain inexplicable matters (i.e., the claim they make on our lives). Moreover, the atmosphere of extrahuman (e.g., divine) imagery in myths can express the sense that such matters and meanings are not just *our* constructions.

In the end I want to say that certain fundamental aspects of culture and forms of understanding, *science included*, exhibit irreducible, unjustifiable, and yet indispensable notions, which, though perhaps different from traditional mythical presentations, nevertheless share the underlying existential meaning and unverifiability of myths. At this point I anticipate certain later conclusions. First we must examine mythical disclosure and elucidate its complex meaning and structure.

Our historical study cannot go back in time to engage the actual experiences that generated the cultural forms we will be analyzing. For the most part we can only engage the linguistic documents that have survived, but that is not a limitation so long as we attend to the importance of language as a cultural phenomenon. At this point I am borrowing one final Heideggerian assumption, namely the phenomenological priority of language.[8] For Heidegger, the disclosure of the world is accomplished essentially through language. Disclosure cannot be reduced to the human mind or to things in the world, since "mind" and "thing" are linguistic events. Consequently, when seeking the "essence" of something, we should attend to linguistic meaning and use rather than some ultimate reduction to "cause," "explanation," "entity," or "faculty," all of which beg the question of language. Language is an essential cultural phenomenon which, in fact, gathers the inexplicability of unconcealment. Any attempt to explain language must employ language (e.g., language as a label for "things" or as an expression of "ideas"). In effect, outside of language there is "nothing," or concealment. What could one *say* about a nonlinguistic foundation of language, or something "outside" of language? The world, therefore, is disclosed or unconcealed through language, a phenomenological point against which it would seem odd to *speak*.

The phenomenological priority of language has significant consequences, both for the specific questions of this study and for philosophy in general. If language establishes its own irreducible "authority," then a sense for linguistic pluralism will follow, since language mirrors and in fact executes the process of unconcealment (by not being traceable to "entities"). The coexistence of different linguistic presentations is in principle protected, so that mythical and scientific language, for example, need not be in competition. For instance, the notion of "soul" can be seen as a form of *language*, disclosing elements of human experience that physical language cannot. This need *not* mean that a soul is an "entity" separate from the "body." *Reification* on both ends, as opposed to phenomenological unconcealment, accounts for philosophical dilemmas like the mind-body problem (How are they joined? "Where" is the mind?). Reification, or the insistence that reality be grounded in "entities" or "objects," rather than the disclosure of different meanings through language, causes such problems.

Moreover, language differences are not simply "different ways of talking" but different ways in which the *world* is disclosed. If a materialist says that an idea is "really" a brain state or that mental language is simply another way of talking about neurological events, he is implying a phenomenologically impossible world. Even if one could translate the "ideas" in this book into brain-state language (e.g., a description of my neural firings), such a translation would render the book meaningless. Brain surgery and intellectual discussions demand different linguistic contexts suitable for each, which are mutually untranslatable. In the same way I am suggesting a coexistence of mythical and rational language. There is a deep meaning in mythical language which expresses what cannot be expressed in rational or scientific language. If a myth presents the world through a story and not "the facts," and if, as I have argued, facts are not the end of the matter, then mythical language fits certain matters well. Such matters include, among other things, existential meaning, the lived world, and primal origins.

We aim to engage the often contentious relationship between myth and philosophy by returning to the Greek periods in which that relationship took shape. Our first step is to apprehend the mythical period which preceded the advent of philosophy. Only then can we properly understand the differences between myth and philosophy, the nature of their contest, and the relative status of each. Moreover, if language is the key to meaning, we must listen to the language of a mythical age to gather its meaning as opposed to interpretations through postmythical terminology. We will try to let myth show itself through its language. Obviously we have to *interpret* (we cannot simply recount the myths as such), but we must attempt to be faithful by at least screening out extramythical assumptions. Accordingly, we aim to show the autonomy and meaningfulness of a mythical age on its own terms, thereby undermining the prevalence of certain "progressive" interpretations of ancient history (i.e., the view that mythical culture was backward or even prerational).

> The historian of an epoch must therefore not regard it as a preparation for what is to come. How an epoch influenced the future, and how it was constituted and understood itself, are very different things.[9]

Such an outlook will help us understand the movement from myth to philosophy *not* as a progression from ignorance to truth but as a series of *revolutions*, a cultural contest which was and still is an exchange between equally meaningful elements. Although we will work through the historical development from myth to philosophy, which demands our drawing *distinctions* between them, nevertheless we must guard against a strict *separation* of myth and philosophy. In other words, we will discover why it is wrong to say that myth has nothing in common with philosophy or that philosophy has nothing in common with myth.

In order to give the reader adequate preparation for discerning the points I have mentioned, I will offer a two-part overview of the basic themes of this investigation, themes relating to the historical treatment and to the issue of pluralism. After a general discussion of mythical disclosure in the first chapter, the chapters on Greek myth and philosophy will develop in detail a number of key themes that will serve to shape the historical analysis.

1. Greek myth presents the world in terms of existential meaning. It presents the lived world, which is shown to be finite, temporal, variable, value-laden, affective, and uncertain. The sacred imagery in myth expresses these aspects of existence, and the form of disclosure will be seen as a process of unconcealment.

2. The path of philosophy turns away from the sacred imagery of myth toward empirical and conceptual models of thought. This entails a turn from the existential lived world toward abstract representations of the world. Now the world is measured according to principles of unity, universality, and constancy, and the mind aims for empirical and conceptual foundations which permit a kind of certainty. Thus disclosure of the world moves from a process of unconcealment toward a kind of foundationalism, where thought is reduced to a knowable, fixed form and structure.

3. In all the different periods of Greek thought, the way in which the world is understood is inseparable from the way in which the human self is understood. The world and human self each influence the shape and nature of the other.

4. In early Greek myth and poetry, the human self is shown to be noncentralized (not autonomous but subject to divine control), contextual (not internalized but imbedded in world situations and relations to other selves), receptive (not self-contained or self-knowing but passive in a process of disclosure from extraconscious origins), and pluralized (not a unity but a complex of distinct functions). Such a form of selfhood will be seen to mirror the form of the world in mythical disclosure.

5. The development from a mythical to a philosophical understanding of the world is matched and made possible by changing contours of selfhood, that is, in the direction of a unified, individuated, interiorized, active, self-conscious, reflective self. The key feature here is the detachment of the self from immediate immersion in the lived world.

These historical themes will help reveal another set of themes related to the notion of pluralism, such as the defense of myth against rational criticism and the subsequent call for a coexistence of different forms of understanding (e.g., myth, art, philosophy, and science). The historical emergence of philosophy in the context sketched above might be seen by some as a progressive development from ignorance to knowledge, from an inadequate to a more adequate picture of the world. Although the emergence of philosophy and science is important, assumptions about strict progress and the restriction of truth to rationality are problematic. The themes that will speak to this question and shape an argument for pluralism are as follows:

1. The critique of myth on the part of Greek philosophers is rigged, because it assumes that myth can be corrected by rational methods when, in fact, the essence of myth is something *different* from the aims of rationality and science. Mythical disclosure presents an intelligible picture of the lived world and the form of human involvement with the lived world, whereas rational models depart, in some sense, from that context. The key distinction here is that between existential form and abstract form, with a certain degree of incommensurability between the two.

2. The analysis of different forms of selfhood in the periods of Greek thought is important for a defense of pluralism, because one of the preconditions for a rational critique of myth has been, I think, the assumption of a "timeless" model for human selfhood (reflective self-consciousness) against which a mythical world does not make sense. But rational models of understanding depend upon a particular conception of selfhood which is not timeless but historical and situational. The detailed treatment of "world" and "self" in the different periods of Greek poetry and philosophy is a survey of evidence for the thesis that self-understanding and world-understanding are two sides of the same coin. If this thesis is correct, then a sensitivity to the historical and "relative" nature of this matter and an appreciation of the "sense" of a mythical self and world will undermine the dogmatic *reduction* of thought to rational models of understanding.

3. Attention to the human self as a factor in the form of the world will reveal many nonobjective features in the turn to philosophy. There are certain psychological aspects within the critique of myth. When Greek philosophers (especially Plato and Aristotle) criticized traditional myths in the light of rationality, at a certain level this was not so

much a refutation as it was an *evaluation*, an objection to the lived world exhibited in myth (its negativity and uncertainty) and a preference for order, constancy, and self-control. The connection between the advent of philosophy and certain moral and evaluative concerns will undermine the idea that the turn from myth to rationality was a purely "objective" matter.

4. Philosophical discoveries and the related contours of human selfhood will be seen growing *out of* mythical disclosure (especially the changing shape of the self in the periods of epic, lyric, and tragic poetry). Moreover, we will see that a mythical sense of self and world does not entirely disappear with the coming of philosophy. Mythical meanings remain a part of philosophy (more strongly in the pre-Socratics but to a significant degree later as well). The historical relationship between myth and rationality and the overlap factor will undermine a complete rejection of myth.

5. The foundationalist tendencies in philosophy will show shortcomings and an inability to escape the sense of uncertainty and existential meaning expressed in mythical disclosure. Rationality, at a certain level, will be shown to need the kinds of meanings (especially the idea of unconcealment and its implicit sense of mystery) for which myth is an appropriate (perhaps *the* appropriate) form of expression.

The importance of this historical study should not be underestimated. Seeing philosophy *itself* as a historical phenomenon (which is something different from the history of philosophy), realizing that philosophical assumptions had to come forth in the midst of nonphilosophical thinking, will serve two purposes. First, the notion that philosophy corrected the mistakes of myth is an assumption that depends on the near-mythical idea of an ahistorical truth. A historical perspective, on the other hand, would reveal the relationships between philosophy and its nonphilosophical antecedents. That might help bridge the gap between so-called rational inquiry and so-called nonrational or prerational disclosure. Secondly, with respect to perennial problems in philosophy (e.g., mind and body, freedom, goodness, and truth), a prerequisite for engaging such matters should be attention to the historical emergence of philosophy, to how and why these matters *became* problems. We may realize that one reason why such problems *remain* problems is the failure to include prephilosophical meanings against which Greek philosophy *rebelled*. That rebellion may not always have been justified, and accordingly, certain clues to the solution of philosophical problems might be at hand.[10]

A historical/phenomenological/linguistic approach to myth and philosophy, which avoids interpreting myth through postmythical developments, will show the continuing significance of this matter. That is to say, it speaks to ever-present cultural issues. The notion that myth is only a historical matter, that its day has passed, is, on the one hand, a consequence of a philosophical bias concerning the "correction" of myth, and, on the other hand, a distortion of cultural history since the Greek period, wherein myth and rationality have continued their relationship. Historical periods are never really "exchanges" or movements entirely "from" one set of ideas "to" another. At most, historical periods reflect different *emphases* of ever-present elements of disclosure which continue to show themselves in the different periods. The discipline of history tends to veil this fact by creating "ages" with different attributes (e.g., the age of religion, the age of reason, the age of science, and the age of anxiety). I hope I can convince the reader in the pages to come that the "history" of myth and philosophy in the Greek period has always been, and always will be, reenacted in certain ways.

# I

## A Phenomenological Analysis of Myth

### The General Framework

How can we begin to interpret the countless tales of gods, heroes, and sacred forces that mark the beginnings of human culture? Perhaps nothing is more difficult to define than myth. One reason for this difficulty is the great variability of themes, images, and meanings within myth. Nevertheless there have been many theoretical attempts to define myth from the standpoint of some common feature, set of features, or structure which would allow an organization of the great variety of myths. Such attempts have generally taken two directions, either classification or explanation. That is to say, *either* one may look for common references or themes within myths themselves (e.g., slaying monsters, incest, family killings, quests), *or* try to explain myths by reducing or tracing them to certain conditions which are external to the specific imagery of myths but which would account for their origin (e.g., nature, social functions, historical events, the human psyche) or render them intelligible in terms of some underlying abstract scheme (e.g., ritual patterns, linguistic or cognitive structures). I will not give a survey of such theories here.[1] In my view, however, these approaches are highly questionable for two basic reasons. First, an attempt at classification will be frustrated by counterexamples because of the great variety of mythical references. Second, an attempt at explanation is subject to the same frustration and, in addition, is limited by being *external* to the phenomenon in question.

At the outset I can agree, therefore, with G. S. Kirk when he rejects typical definitions because "the attempt to isolate some central specific quality of myths is misdirected. There are too many obvious exceptions."[2] The best we can do, he tells us, is to call a myth a "traditional tale." A myth is a tale in that it is a dramatic narrative; it is traditional in the sense that it takes hold in a society and is found important enough to be passed on because of a communal, functional, and authoritative quality which distinguishes it from a mere "entertaining story."[3] This is a good beginning, but I would like to go further by approaching myth from the existential and phenomenological perspective we have prepared. Although I agree with Kirk that proposed theories all disclose some relevant aspect of myth but fall short by being reductionistic, nevertheless I think it is possible to give a general analysis of mythical disclosure per se. In other words, I do not think the task is to explain myths, to reduce them to objective, abstract references, because such references are antithetical to mythical disclosure; rather, the task is to adopt a phenomenological attitude ("to the myths themselves") and attend to the way in which myths disclose the world and human existence. The hope is that one can give adequate generalizations from this angle which are appropriate for various types of myths and specific mythical traditions.

One way to set the stage for our approach is to recognize a key difficulty in such an enterprise. If we are to take myth seriously, we must also take seriously the fact that people have taken their myths seriously—people have believed in myths and their lives have been guided and shaped by myths. There is an inevitable difference between "interpreting myth" and "living a myth." It is not that living a myth is the only way to understand it; rather, the best interpretation of myth is one that least violates what it means to live a myth. Many theories which take myth seriously, which do not see it as a form of ignorance, nevertheless explain myth in terms of objective references or abstract structures which miss the existential significance of myth as something *lived*. What is needed is an internal hermeneutics, that is to say, an interpretation which at least begins by acknowledging that myths originally involve sincere beliefs and commitments and which begins to shape its generalizations in the light of that lived atmosphere.

We must resist the assumption that if a myth is to be properly understood, it must be translated into some scientific or objective model (whether natural, biological, social, psychological, cognitive, or linguistic). Doing so fails to acknowledge that a myth presents nonobjective, existential meanings, that it can reflect a form of life that is *followed* (not just analyzed). It is not that such models are wrong—they can tell us a great deal about myth—but they must acknowledge their limits and the inevitable distortions that accompany their analyses. Ultimately we must go beyond trying to explain a myth in terms of something else, something "outside the tale."[4] We need an orientation which can open up the way a myth discloses the world and shapes human existence *on its own terms*. Even though we will be seeking general meanings behind the imagery of specific myths, we must arrive at those meanings by passing *through* the imagery, by considering what is shown for those living a myth and how the world is given meaning therein. In this way we will be able to talk of *truth* in myth (but in a general sense as a legitimate form of disclosure and *not* in the sense of defending a particular myth as an accurate description of "the truth"). The problem with various explanatory models is that they are susceptible to the following difficulty. If, for example, a myth about a deity is explained simply in terms of social structures, then we seem forced to say that for people who live the myth and worship the deity, their immediate experiences have nothing to do with the "true" nature or function of the myth, or are at best distinct from the "real" meaning of the myth. Such an interpretive outcome is at least questionable.

What we will see as we proceed is that the general problem with various accounts of myth is that they construct an objective explanation for a phenomenon which in its *own* atmosphere involves something nonobjective and inexplicable. Of course, we are in a precarious position here because our analysis must step outside myth to draw out the general meaning of mythical disclosure, but acknowledging this distance can be part of the interpretation. In addition, I think that the best strategy for illuminating mythical disclosure is to *contrast* it with postmythical developments which specifically attempted to displace myth with a different form of understanding. The *tension* between the explicable and the inexplicable will therefore be an interpretive tool. Such illumination-by-contrast is one of the central tasks of our historical investigation.

Let us begin our analysis of mythical disclosure with the following generalization: *A myth is a narrative which discloses a sacred world.* To understand the implications of such a notion the following specific characteristics will be discussed: (1) origins, (2) lived world, (3) culture, (4) sacred and profane, (5) mystery, and (6) existential transcendence.

## ORIGINS

According to Eliade, myths tell a sacred history, how the world or important features of the world came *to be* when sacred powers came forth to establish the world.[5] In other words, a myth expresses the *presence* of a sacred meaning through a narrative which depicts its emergence. A myth of origins shows the world as a limit and fills in the void with primal occurrences. To talk of myths as historical, however, can be misleading since the cultural *function* of myths makes it very difficult to distinguish between the "telling" and the "origin." It would be a mistake to assume that the telling of origins refers to an irretrievable past cut off from the present, because such an assumption ignores the way in which myths are part of a culture. The cultural function of a myth can best be shown by recognizing the relationship between myth and action. The Greek word *mythos* did not originally mean a fictional account or even a story, but rather something spoken or uttered by the mouth. Moreover, there is evidence that the Greeks considered a myth not to be a detached account but the spoken (*to legomenon*) correlate of an acted rite, a thing done (*to dromenon*).[6] One could call a myth the "plot" of an action, since such a connection was expressed even by Aristotle (in the *Poetics* the term *mythos* meant the plot of a *drama*, which in Greek literally means a deed or an action). The relationship between myth and ritual along with the phenomenon of ritual "identification" suggest that to some extent a myth is a retelling/reenacting of a sacred origin. Kerenyi tells us that a ritual cult repeats and identifies with a sacred beginning. Gods and humans come together and behavior is "archaized."[7] Myth is therefore nontheoretical in the sense that it is not detached from *praxis*; it is originally a *lived* reality.

## LIVED WORLD

Walter F. Otto says that a myth and a cult are each the "mirror image of the other."[8] Such a correlation prevents the reduction of one to the other. But if this relationship between myth and ritual is to be significant, it would have to refer to the barely clear archaic origins of myths, since there are many classical Greek myths, for example, which seem to have no reference to rituals.[9] The most fruitful use of the myth-ritual correlation would be to understand myths in the broader sense of the coincidence of thought and action, or "lived world." A myth's narrative aspect is itself a direct expression of a lived world, an existential setting with living images, actions, situations, and temporal movements. Myths were not intended as "speculation" or even mere stories because they were *functional*, woven into the concrete lives of a people. Myths established social and educational values; prescribed daily tasks and ceremonial responses; inspired painting, sculpture, music, dance, poetry, and architecture; gave meaning to birth, maturation, marriage, and death—in other words, myths shaped the cultural life of a society.[10]

## CULTURE

Myth is therefore another way of saying culture. The word culture is derived from cult; in Latin, *cultus* means adoration or worship and comes from the verb *colere*, to cultivate. The connection between myth and cult thus tells us much about the religious and formative aspects of myths. To see myth as merely literature, for example, betrays the tail (art) wagging the dog (culture). Myths are expressions of religious *experiences* which take shape in cult, and cult is the expression of awe at the immediate presence of the sacred, involving the whole being of the self.[11] In other words, myths should be seen in the light of lived experiences (ecstasy, devotion, exaltation, epiphany). Culture begins with "primal appearances" where the world is shown as a "plenitude of divine configurations."[12]

At this level, meaning is not invented but rather *revealed*. It is questionable to explain myths as an expression of human goals and purposes, because it may be that myths give human goals and purposes their first shape. Archaic experience did not see myths as coming "from" human agency but "to" humans.[13] If we can avoid looking at mythical culture externally and take seriously the phenomenon of sacrifice, we can learn much from considering that myth and cult originate in a revelation of such power as to compel a community to devotion. If myths were "really" inventions or based on utility or curiosity, how could one account for the lasting devotion they inspired or their pervasive and uncontested authority in every facet of the life and practice of a people? Too often moderns try to explain (away) myths through human motives which are either subsequent to, or phenomenologically unsuited for, the *formative* nature of myth and the way in which myth functioned and was experienced.

## SACRED AND PROFANE

We must try to avoid explaining myths—where they come from, what they are based on—and penetrate the way in which myths show the world in a general sense, and thus include the many things to which some have tried to *reduce* myth. What are the general phenomenological features of a mythical world? We must begin with the basic distinction between the sacred and the profane, following the characterization of this distinction given by Cassirer.[14] The sacred does not mean exclusively the supernatural or otherworldly, but simply the *extraordinary*, the uncommon, both wondrous and terrifying. The profane, therefore, does not mean something sacrilegious but simply the *ordinary*, the common. This distinction does not speak of two worlds but rather a single, two-dimensional world. The sacred is shown whenever something affects an existential situation in important ways— exciting terror, hope, joy, or awe or displaying pragmatic efficacy. Given the limit conditions in life, the sacred expresses the various meanings arising from these conditions, the powers and fortunes that arrive and withdraw in circumstances involving success and failure, quests and struggles, life and death.

The world's capacity for uncommon power can be summed up by the general idea of "mana," an impersonal, even pre-theistic notion which refers not to a "thing" but to the shaping of existential meaning *within which* things can first be located.[15] Consequently, the sacred means the presence of mana, while the profane simply means the absence of mana. Moreover, the sacred is not separate from the profane; it lies dormant within the profane and can show itself at any time or be invoked through a ritual. For example, a river is a body of moving water, but a river suddenly overflowing or drying up shows a sacred power. In general, strokes of fortune breaking through the normal course of things are sacred occurrences.

The sacred-profane distinction can be seen in the Latin word *profanum*, literally "before the sanctuary," i.e., the ordinary ground at the limit of a sacred place. The profane is simply the not, or not yet, or no-longer sacred, and defining the profane in the negative indicates the priority of the sacred in determining what is real or meaningful. Perhaps one could say that in archaic experience the profane (the simply "there") is an "intermission" between advents of the sacred. Again, there are not two worlds.

Something important must be said here. The notion of the profane indicates that primitive people were well aware of what *we* call common sense, the ordinary experience of things describable in what we call empirical terms, without a mythical reference. But the so-called empirical facts were not the standard of what was real. Actually, the term "real" is misleading, because this does *not* mean the profane was unreal. It would be better to say that primitive experience did not find the profane (things simply "there") *important*. The "thing" alone, the ordinary encounter, was not the realm of significance; as profane it *awaits* the sacred, through which its value, its meaning, is shown. To the mythical mind, therefore, the profane is that which is meaningless, the sacred that which is meaningful.[16] And if we define "world" as a context of meaning, then we can say that the sacred shows the profane as a world. To sum up thus far, myth expresses this arrival/withdrawal of existential meaning which establishes a world.

## MYSTERY

Because of its arrival/withdrawal character and the notion of extraordinary and therefore unpredictable occurrences, the sacred is ultimately a mystery, that is to say, beyond human control and complete comprehension. Many myths express this sense of mystery and limits on complete disclosure—e.g., the priority of night and darkness in some myths, prohibitions against humans having total access to the divine, and motifs of hiding and concealing.[17] There is as much a sense of absence as there is presence in mythical disclosure, which can be called a telling which tells of something ultimately beyond all telling (as Plato put it in the *Timaeus*, 28–29).

For this reason it is wrong to interpret myth as a form of explanation, because explanation intends what myth does not exhibit, namely the elimination of mystery in the light of verifiable causes or rational principles clearly known by the human mind. Perhaps this point can be put in the following way. Explanation answers the question *why* or *how* something is by discovering a prior cause, tracing the cause of a thing back to another (profane) thing. Myths, on the other hand, should be seen to disclose *that* something is, the *first* meaningful form a world takes, the background of which is hidden. Myth is therefore not explanation but *presentation* of the arrival/withdrawal of existential meaning. The shift from mythical disclosure to rational and scientific thinking cannot be seen as a correction of myth because it was a shift to a *new* intention—the reduction of beings to the explanatory capacities of the human mind or verifiable natural causes. To see a myth as an error (a wrong explanation) is an anachronistic misunderstanding of the function of myth. Myth presents more than natural things alone (the profane); it presents the arrival/withdrawal of sacred meaning within the world.

One might object: If a primitive man believes that a demon makes him fly into a rage, surely this is (for him) an explanation for his rage. That might seem obvious enough. However, the fuzziness of such a view can be shown by realizing that *how* the demon induces the rage is not known, is not even an issue, and therefore it would hardly count as an explanation in our sense of the term. What is at issue is simply *that* the rage occurs, as a sacred phenomenon. And by "sacred" is meant, therefore, something which *cannot* be explained, but which emerges as an uncommon though compelling eruption and which must simply be acknowledged.

But again, it would be a mistake to assume that primitive people knew nothing of what we call common sense and empirical facts. Certainly primitive language allows empirical statements, generalizations, and factual claims ("the sun is hot"), and certainly primitive thought had some understanding of cause and effect (seeds must be planted for crops to grow). But the way in which the *complete* picture of human involvement with the world was understood and seen as meaningful was not on the *basis* of empirical facts but rather sacred meanings (one must say a prayer before planting; the growth of crops is a gift from a sacred power). Primitive experience does not deny what we call facts; rather, it finds them culturally unimportant, or, better, less important. There is evidence that primitive thinking knows well and often attends to natural causes and classifications, but such notions are ultimately subordinated to, or distinguished from, powers which must be approached in nonempirical (nonprofane) ways.[18]

An interesting example of this was shown on a PBS *Odyssey* program about the present-day Sakkudei of Indonesia. The Sakkudei see the world animistically and believe in ritual healing, where medicine men go into or induce trances to exorcise spirits. The Indonesian government is trying to bring the Sakkudei into modern life because, as one official said, "medicine men impede progress." But one of the tribesmen was interviewed and said quite coolly that if they have stomach aches, the medicine man can't cure that; they go to the clinic. But the clinic can't cure ills which the spirits cause; they go to the medicine man for that. The point here is that the mythical mind is not ignorant of empirical, natural causes. There is, however, the priority of the sacred which requires people to yield to forces beyond their immediate (profane) control. In *relation*, therefore, to what we call natural or rational explanation, mythical disclosure reflects a sacred mystery.

## EXISTENTIAL TRANSCENDENCE

In order to draw out the contours of a mythical "world," I am adopting the admittedly clumsy phrase "existential transcendence." Its clumsiness is due to the matter at hand, namely that myth cannot be understood from the standpoint of modern categories of objectivity or subjectivity, because myth is prior to both terms, a priority both historical and phenomenological.

First, let us rehearse what is meant by "world." In myth the world is shown in the light of existential involvement, or what was earlier termed a lived world—affective and pragmatic situations, purposes, values, life and death, success and failure. "World," therefore, is not synonymous with "earth." When we say someone has lost their whole world or speak of the art world, it signifies a *context of meaning*. In a general sense, world is therefore synonymous with *culture*. In the Introduction, culture was connected with transcendence, meaning transcendence of the brute given, the simply there, the mere perceptual encounter or animal functions. Human awareness of death and limitation figures deeply into cultural phenomena like religion, morality, technology, and language, all of which render the world in terms of a metafactual meaning. In other words, culture is not simply living, but living-for, coming-from, heading-toward, living-in-the-midst-of-death-and-limits—all of which are "more" than and therefore limit the brute given. The "more than" implies the sacred-profane distinction sketched earlier. The sense of limit is a fundamental human dimension lying behind all wonder, all the questions, all the fears and hopes of the race. Myths express the limits of the profane and speak to human limits through sacred meanings.[19] Furthermore, the limit of the world as such is expressed through creation myths and myths of origins.

In sum, "world" is equivalent to culture and meaning, that is, to purposes, destinies, origins, models, and guidelines, all "more" than the profane. Myths *present* such sacred, transcending elements and express the entire range of experiences relating to these elements, a lived world where the fate of human beings situated-in-the-world counts as "reality." Another way of saying this is that in myth existential meaning precedes "objectivity." Too often, certain theories of myth assume or interject the category of objectivity in explaining (away) myths. But objectivity is phenomenologically alien to myth. Since the world "is" only insofar as it affects humans existentially, explaining myth as, for example, the personification of nature may make sense for us, but it is not appropriate for myth.[20] Such an explanation is a retrospective anachronism. There are no prior "natural objects" (as a discrete notion *independent* of the sacred or as a *standard* of reality) to which meaning is attached.[21] Things come *to be* meaningful things first through relation and involvement. Disinterested reflection, detached objectivity, is a subsequent historical development. For this reason, myths take the form of living beings and narratives, not objects or abstractions.[22]

Furthermore, if we want to let myth speak for itself, we also must recognize that the existential context is *not* seen in terms of subjectivity either. In other words, the view that myths are inventions or even projections meant to portray human emotions or needs is also phenomenologically suspect. Primitive experience does not "project" the sacred, it *finds* the world infused with the sacred; it does not view what I have called the existential setting as coming "from" but rather "to" humans, as something more than human (a deity), or in the case of mana, as an impersonal power. The sacred is experienced as an "other." Moreover, humans see themselves *controlled* by these forces. In fact, we will see later that the very idea of a subjective self is a historical development not evident in primitive culture, where selfhood is understood in relation to a form of divine transcendence. The sacred is experienced as "given" to humans. What can therefore be called *givenness* is an essential feature of mythical disclosure, and it will be quite significant when we examine postmythical developments.

If we want to understand the phenomenon of myth internally, free of postmythical assumptions, we must conclude the following: The imagery of myth shows that objectivity is out of place (since myth is an existential story); furthermore, subjectivity is out of place (since the center of attention is a human-transcending element). In other words, myth *shows* that the world is disclosed through the human existential situation, but at the same time it is not human-centered—that is, the world is an existential transcendence. Since objectivity and subjectivity strictly speaking are not a factor in mythical disclosure, it would be phenomenologically unsound to talk about something like a subjective projection upon an objective world.

Myth is therefore a nontheoretical expression of what could be called a self-world circle, since "human" and "world" cannot be delineated discretely into subject and object. Perhaps an example would help. Consider one of the Demeter myths in which the Greeks accounted for seasonal change. Demeter (a vegetation goddess) lost her daughter Persephone to Hades in the underworld. In her grief,

Demeter withheld warm weather and plant growth. Persephone's release was negotiated by the gods, but because she partook of food in the underworld, she was obligated to return there for one portion of every year. Therefore, part of every year was warm and fruitful; the other part, cold and barren. The crucial factor in the story is the joy and grief of the goddess. How are the seasons understood here? Not, of course, in terms of objective criteria such as the earth's axis and position in relation to the sun, but in terms of an existential *response* to seasonal change. The *moods* of spring and winter, the sense of revitalization and joy followed by the sad closure of the winter months— these are what present the existential meaning of the seasons. Furthermore, the joy and grief in the myth are the moods of a goddess, which suggests that this is an element of the *world* (note the vegetation reference) and not simply a human, subjective state. In this way, the mythical meaning of the seasons is neither objective nor subjective.

Such an atmosphere is not at all strange, even to us. Of course the position of the earth is part of the objective explanation of seasonal change, but this is not relevant to what the myth is disclosing, and we can easily understand this if we look at ourselves phenomenologically. If someone said, "it's almost spring," I am quite sure the first thing in your mind would *not* be the earth's axis. Also, when we experience the moods of spring, we do not sense ourselves "hurling out" subjective feelings to the smells of the moist earth, the blooming trees, the singing birds, the erotic energy, thus "adding" joy to the scene. Phenomenologically speaking, the *world* presents the mood; we dwell in it. Even our language shows us something here; we never "have" a mood, but are always "in" a mood. We do not project or "decide" to experience basic moods, they simply happen, they "come over" us—hence the aptness of the mythical "other."

So, the Demeter myth is neither a mistaken objective account nor a subjective projection, nor is it a replacement for an objective account. It simply discloses a nonobjective meaning that is phenomenologically intelligible. Mythical narratives present the world in the light of living beings, situations, interactions, and functions that show the concrete meaningfulness and imprecise richness of human existence. But with the sacred, these meanings are shown to be *there*, in the *world*, and not just a human concoction.

The world is *first* shown existentially, not objectively (children, of course, are the purest examples). Myth presents the world as such a context of existential meanings. For this reason, scientific objectivity is possible only *subsequent* to the meanings found in myth. Objectivity is a continuing active *disengagement* from the affective setting in which we first find ourselves (and which only *then* becomes subjective). But in myth, such distinctions are not found. A myth cannot be seen as "added to" or "taken from" a world of experience, since myth *establishes* what "experience of a world" *is*. It is this "transcendental" character of myth that prompted Cassirer to reject any attempt to explain it in terms of some realm of objects or subjective experience (e.g., nature, dreams, or social settings), because myth is a precondition for the disclosure of such realms (e.g., myth *defines* a social setting for a group).[23] In myth, the being of the world and the human forms a circle.

Another approach to the meaning of this mythical circle is the often-mentioned distinction between an I-it relation and an I-thou relation.[24] An I-it relation is the subject-object relation familiar to modern thought. Here the mind is active and can manipulate the object in terms of its abstract relation to other objects; being a member of a group or series ruled by universal laws, the object is rendered predictable; and such an operation is emotionally indifferent. An I-thou relation is a person-person relation. Here the mind is passive and receptive; the thou reveals *itself* as a unique, unpredictable presence; and there persists an emotional reciprocity. A frequent modern critique of myth maintains that it falsely projects a "thou" upon an "it." The problem, however, is that the primitive mind does not *know* a discrete "it"; the world is revealed *as* a "thou." Consequently, the world is founded in a story (for the same reasons why, when we want to know a person, we would not want an account of cells, muscles, and body chemistry, but rather a life story). This analysis, especially the active-receptive distinction, helps us understand why myths in the prephilosophical period were not subjected to skeptical criticism but were taken as given. Furthermore, we can better see why it would be improper to call a myth an error. An error is the misapplication of a rule (e.g., a mistaken calculation in mathematics). But since the rules of the subject-object relation were not part of the world in myth, then it would seem odd to talk of a mistake (just as it would be odd to accuse Picasso of depicting mistaken perceptions).

Thus it would be an anachronistic "category mistake" to see myth as a primitive form of science or a pseudoscience (e.g., Frazer in *The Golden Bough*).[25] It is not a characteristic of myth to make hypotheses or propose theories, to test a notion against an already given and assumed objective reality to discover verifiable causes. Rather, myth discloses a meaning in the lived experience of a people, that is, it discloses what reality is for them. For myth to be a primitive form of science, what would be required is the a priori assumption that an empirical test discloses reality. But this is not the case *in* myth; sacred meanings, not what we call empirical facts, are what is real.

It should be clear that mythical disclosure is not thoughtless or chaotic. It has a form and shows a form of truth, and should not be judged by scientific objectivity. But then two questions must be clarified: (1) How is it that myth is not "irrational"? (2) How and to what degree is myth different from scientific objectivity and conceptual reason?

## Myth and Sense

Although we will address the differences between myth and conceptual reason, such a distinction cannot be turned into a strict separation or opposition. Myth displays a form of thinking, namely, a concern for issues transcending immediate data (e.g., origins, aims, justice), which could be seen as forerunners of the later abstract treatment of such matters.[26] There are also mythical notions of cause[27] and of time and space (which will be discussed later), although these notions are not abstracted from the lived world of experience ("abstraction" comes from the Latin *abtrahere*, to pull away from); rather, they are disclosed solely in the light of an existential context.

A strict separation between myth and logic is ultimately untenable. There is a logic in myth, namely a coherence within which the world is organized and understood and through which the form of whole societies and sets of practices can be defined, guided, supported, and transmitted. A key distinction between myth and modern logic is that mythical coherence follows an existential form while conceptual logic follows an abstract form, but the fact that there *is* form in myth—that there is culture, communication, and agreement—undermines the accusation of irrationality often leveled against myth.

When the term "irrational" is used, usually one of two senses is meant: (1) a contradiction or inconsistency (e.g., "I am a married bachelor"); or (2) the denial of an evident truth (e.g., "it is irrational to believe that a god makes the plants grow"). The first sense refers to the meaning of terms or the relation of propositions, but since avoiding contradiction is a precondition for communication in *any* society, this kind of rationality is at work even in primitive cultures. For example, rituals follow certain rules which must not be broken; terms like "warrior" will have a meaning calling for a proper use; objections against lying imply the value of consistency; or if someone were to say that Zeus is a slave to man he could be "refuted."[28]

The second sense of irrationality refers not simply to the meaning of terms or relation of propositions but to the *truth* of propositions, arising when different cultures or assumptions confront each other. Moderns cannot call mythical culture irrational in the first sense, so it is evidently the second sense which is meant. But, as this chapter has attempted to show, such a charge of irrationality is fraught with difficulties and is more rhetorical than anything else. Once we understand the meaning of mythical language and the cultural shape it engenders, along with realizing that modern objective assumptions are not even a factor, then the charge of irrationality indicates a paradigm clash rather than a successful critique.

If a primitive culture displays a social order, if there is communication, if life makes sense, if children are educated, if people can distinguish a right way from a wrong way, then there is a *form* to a mythical world. For this reason some writers have called for the extension of the term "rational" to include primitive mentality. There is much to be said for this.[29] My only objection to the extension of the term is that "reason" and "logic" in general use do mean *something* different from "myth," because myth is so often called irrational. It may be that this is unwarranted, but we cannot overlook that our sense of the terms "reason" and "logic" arose historically in *opposition* to mythical disclosure (as we shall see), and that mythical language never used such terms (e.g., *logos*) in the way we understand them.[30] I would therefore nominate "sense" rather than "reason." Consequently, in calling myth or the primitive mind rational we imply different kinds of sense (and also similar kinds of sense, as indicated in the notion of consistency). With this in mind, we can now move on to distinguish mythical sense from conceptual reason, an important preparation for the coming chapters on Greek thought.

## Myth and Conceptual Reason

### MYTHS EXPRESS WHAT IS UNIQUE WHILE CONCEPTS EXPRESS WHAT IS COMMON

Snell tells us that in Homer verbs and virtually all terms refer to specific, unique functions.[31] For example, there was no common term "body" referring to physical life. (The word *soma* referred to a corpse.) References were only to specific parts, such as arms, legs, and chest, and only particular movements described actions. For example, a body does not run, legs run. Only later in Greek thought did concepts of essence develop, namely, that which is *common* to bodily parts, body as such. Conceptualization co-emerged with objectification—determining "what" a thing is in general, abstracted from the direct, lived experience of things, which is a series of unique functions and encounters.

Myth does not subsume particular occurrences under general laws or abstract classifications. Each significant event has a specific source (e.g., the will of a god). For instance, myth would not account for the death of a person through biological laws but through a narration telling why *this* man died at this particular time.[32] In other words, myth expresses the immediate specificity and variety of lived experience which concepts must filter out in favor of abstraction. It is for this reason that myth is inherently pluralistic and nonreductive. Events do not follow universal, regular laws, and the world is not unified or reduced to a common essence. Consequently, we might want to say that a purely mythical view is always polytheistic, in a manner of speaking.[33] The world is presented as a multifarious context of existential meanings, a constellation of sacred powers, and not as a system of laws or manifestations of a primal being.

### IN MYTH, THERE IS NO SEPARATION OF FORM AND CONTENT, THOUGHT AND SENSATION

When we moderns look back at a mythical world, we naturally assume that its form is inadequate to the content of sense experience. It is simply wrong to explain thunder, for example, as divine anger; myth errs by attaching psychological features to the influx of sounds, which are better explained as air masses, wave frequencies, and the like. There is no such thing as "sensation" in myth, however, at least not in the modern empiricist sense of the term. Myth does not abstract its form from what it "senses." It is only when conceptual abstraction is introduced that concrete awareness is *then* called sensation, that is to say, bare impressions (sound) to which concepts give form (thunder). The forming of experience in myth is not an abstract process but the immediate formation of existential meaning. Sensation, as such, follows from and is itself a theoretical *abstraction*. From what is sensation an abstraction? Precisely from lived experience, existential meaning. For mythical thought, thunder *is* the anger of a god, not a bare, neutral sound to which a form (anger) is added.

In fact, a certain case can be made for the phenomenological aptness of such mythical expressions. If I jump at a sudden clap of thunder, it is certainly not the bare sound that elicits this reaction, but *fear* (anticipating the sound could change the reaction). At the same time I do not see myself processing external data and then projecting an inner state of fear "out" to the sound either. That would seem to be a very dubious dissection and polarization of what is simply a fearful phenomenon. If someone shouts angrily at me, I will not think of sense data, sound waves, and air masses. One need not argue for the literal existence of a god to appreciate the phenomenological sense of a myth. Mythical experience did not hear "sounds" but meanings. Thunder *is* wrath. Therefore a myth is *not* an empirical error, because it is not assuming objective criteria but rather something preobjective. *First* there is existential meaning, which only then can be subjected to abstraction.[34]

Because of existential immediacy, primitive experience is completely absorbed in the presence of events. Again, things are not subsumed under abstract laws but are presented as unique advents of meaning. For example, Cassirer argues that change in myth is not a process that a unitary thing undergoes but rather two unique states affecting each other; not the "how" of change (from one state into another state according to an overriding law) but the "what" (the succession of two distinct states).[35] Examples include Homeric heroes, where a change of mind is divine intervention, and the primitive belief that disease is not a physiological process but possession by a demon.[36] Myth is therefore nonreflective and nontheoretical in that it does not strictly distinguish between thing and attribute, universal and particular, and consequently does not employ logical classification as we know it.

If we remember that existential significance is the basis of mythical form, then certain primitive beliefs will begin to make more sense. For example, mythical "identities," which seem so strange to us, are not based on conceptual classification or empirical similarity but rather on affective, situational, and functional similarities. Some examples of mythical identity include ritual identification, where the performer *becomes* the deity simply by acting out its story; magical sympathy, where different things pertaining to a certain magical practice are identified;[37] the identity of nature and deities, where an affective response shapes the world in personal terms; the identity of a human being with certain objects, where an overall functional complex creates connections (e.g., the belief that capturing a man's weapon gives one power over him); totemistic identity, where affective, functional, or situational similarities create connections between man and nature (e.g., linkages born of the dependence upon animals for food and clothing, and certain behavioral similarities, as in the case of so-called Homeric similes, where the connection between a warrior and a lion stems not from physical appearance or external properties but from power and effect).

The point of all this is that there *is* mythical form, but it is one with and shifts with its content—the ever-varied and often conflicting realm of existential concerns. Conceptual form abstracts from (existential) content and subsequently *measures* content from that position of abstraction. In other words, the criteria of systematic consistency and order, conceptual organization of differences, and "impersonal" analysis do *not* represent the introduction of form into a world of disorder but the introduction of a *different kind* of form—abstract form. Conceptual reason becomes selective, in favor of a complete, overarching stabilization of experience, allowing "only those data of experience which can be controlled by thought, which satisfy the tests of repeatability, of identification by comprehension, and of non-contradiction."[38]

Myth simply displays the various and varying forms of the existential field in all their profusion. It is only from the standpoint of detached, disinterested abstraction that a clear distinction between form and content can be drawn, making possible conceptual judgment. Myth does not apply its form *to* the world, nor does it measure the world *by* its form; rather we should say that the world first *takes* form in myth. Consequently, we should also be wary about talk of myth and symbol, if the symbolic suggests that there is some content behind the mythical form. Such a notion emerged historically only after the advent of philosophy. Myth itself does not "re-present" the world, it presents the world.

## MYTH IS PASSIVE AND RECEPTIVE WHILE CONCEPTUAL REASON IS ACTIVE

Because of the processes of abstraction, analysis, synthesis, and judgment, conceptual reason must actively work on what is immediately given. In this way the world is re-presented from the "control center" of the mind. Myth, on the other hand, does not "work on" anything. Since it is original presentation, mythical disclosure must be seen to be essentially receptive, uncritical, even enthralled by its imagery. Snell suggests that mythical forms come forth in much the same way that dreams come forth—already formed and simply "taken in."[39] The notion of receptivity and the "givenness" of myth will become significant later in this investigation. Receptivity may be the most illuminating characteristic of mythical thought in that it shapes both the form of the world and the human response to it. So little does primitive experience see itself in control that not only is the general course of the world seen to be bestowed and guided by sacred powers but even such mundane things as tools and skills are venerated, even worshipped, or seen as gifts grounded in sacred origins.[40]

## IN MYTH, LANGUAGE AND WORLD ARE COEXTENSIVE

With conceptual reason, language is the vehicle for an "expanding synthesis" which re-presents a being in terms of its inclusion among other, similar beings by way of a law or classification. In mythical disclosure, although certain rudiments of classification can be found in profane designations, as far as the sacred is concerned, since a unique singularity dominates, language does not aim beyond the being; it *presents* the being, there is nothing "else."[41] Now we can begin to understand the countless examples of word-thing identities and the sacred power of words described in primitive cultures. In many mythical cosmogonies, words have power, are sacred, and are even the very source of creation.[42] Often the *name* of a god is a source of power, the power to invoke the force of the deity and in some ways even power over the deity.[43] Such word-thing or name-essence identities form the basis of many mythical practices and beliefs, especially word magic, divination, and ritual identification.[44] All this can be read in terms of the phenomenological priority of language sketched in the Introduction.

In general, then, the immediacy of response to a singular and unique phenomenon implies an original language-world correlation that in postmythical developments becomes sectioned off, where words become "signs" for things. Such a development can be attributed to the very procedures of conceptual reasoning—overcoming singularity, abstracting from things and differences, and the synthesis of the particular into the universal. Then language itself takes on the character of abstraction, which results in a representational theory of language.[45] To the primitive mind, however, a word is not a sign for a thing but is often the sacred power of a thing's very being. Language is woven into the fabric of a mythical world.[46] And drawing together what we have seen thus far, we can summarily indicate that it is the *coextensiveness* of language, world, and existential response that gives mythical disclosure its form and content—the telling of the world's story through living imagery.

## IN MYTH THERE IS NO CONCEPTUAL DISTINCTION
## BETWEEN ILLUSION AND TRUTH

For conceptual reason the mark of truth is consistency, that is, the conforming of a thing to a general law, classification, or empirical regularity. The utterly unique is a kind of outlaw and comes to be dubbed an illusion. But in myth, truth and illusion in this sense find no place. As we have seen, existential meaning animates mythical disclosure. Therefore *anything* of existential significance or displaying affective power is important and hence real. For example, dreams are considered real events, and the emotional impact of dreams about deceased persons accounts for the absence of a strict separation between the living and the dead.

Since the extraordinary is a mark of the sacred, then an uncommon or unique event becomes its own law, a compelling presence. The world is not measured by consistency but by existential import. In fact, in relation to the status of regularity in conceptual thinking, mythical disclosure presents a kind of inversion. The sacred is more important than the profane (the ordinary). An interesting example of this is the shaman figure, about which we will say more later. The trances, visions, and general behavior of a shaman have all the marks of what we would call insanity. Yet in primitive culture the shaman is revered, respected, even trained, and he becomes an *authority* because of his access to the sacred which ordinary people do not have. Therefore, since it might be said that mythical meanings are the *reverse* of modern assumptions about "truth," we have another indication of how inappropriate it is to render an internal critique of mythical "illusions."

But it is important not to overemphasize the differences between myth and conceptual truth, because of our earlier discussion of mythical sense. The world in myth is not a chaotic spray of disconnected particulars. Connections *are* drawn (e.g., genealogies, theogonies, and patterns of divine relationships), but such connections are existential, not systematic. Moreover, the world can even be said to be unified, though not in terms of some conceptual scheme, single being, or principle, but rather in the mystery of the sacred. Such a unity can be recognized, as I think it was by the Greeks when they acknowledged the priority of a generalized fate. But this dimension is essentially a mystery eluding comprehension. It is simply recognized in the continuing arrival and withdrawal of power in the various moments of existential significance. So a mythical world can be said to have coherence, though it should be distinguished from the *kind* of structure demanded by formal logic since the time of Aristotle.

Snell has said that logic is implicit in myth.[47] This is an important point because it helps us to see that conceptual logic was not a sheer *de novo* invention, invading myth, so to speak, from alien territory. There were implicit rudiments of conceptual form in myth, and the recognition of patterns, relationships, comparisons, and structures beyond the brute given should be seen as the precursors of conceptualization. But when conceptual logic became *explicit* and a standard, there developed an alteration of assumptions about what counted as real. Mythical form has an existential specificity, as we have seen, but once such patterns as causing and comparing became explicated as such, and hence abstracted, then the localization and variations of mythical form became a problem.

Let me give an example. Zeus commands a sacrifice. Zeus is a particular god with a particular history and shape. He is known to have certain interests and domains. A certain kind of knowledge follows from dealing with him. A form of consistency and purpose is also implied in his command. Obedience is due him "because" he is a god. "If" he is disobeyed, "then" humans will be punished. In other words, causes and inferences are implicit. But here the form is identical with the content (the command of a particular god). As the Greeks knew well, the command of one god can be inconsistent with that of another god, but the fact that a different content carried a different form was seen to be "in order." As we shall see, the early Greeks acknowledged that conflicting existential aims (the ways of the gods) were beyond resolution, that the outcomes of life were *in principle* unpredictable and therefore beyond the overall comprehension of mortals. But with the advent of conceptual logic, the form of consistency, for example, becomes abstracted from lived content. Only now can there arise the notion of consistency per se, the notion of *universal* consistency; and only *now* can the mythical (existential) field be seen as chaotic.

All of this further supports my objections to talk of mythical logic. Such claims, though not entirely mistaken, become very ambiguous unless the notions of abstraction and universality are brought in to distinguish mythical logic from philosophical logic. Since abstraction, consistency, and universality marked the historical emergence of the term "logic," it seems more appropriate not to connect myth and logic, but to employ a term like "sense." I have no problem when Kirk, for example, criticizes the strict separation of myth and philosophy, but we must also attend to important *distinctions*, because the advent of abstraction and the universal ordering of meaning *was* a change. It is true that there arose in Greek myth the notion of Zeus's "universal" justice, but it is also true that its overall nature eluded the human mind.[48]

At this point perhaps it would help to offer a brief discussion of certain specific examples of mythical sense, so that the preceding general discussion of myth and reason can be clarified somewhat. Let us see how the notions of space and time show themselves in myth. The following analysis is, to a large extent, drawn from Cassirer's insightful treatment of the subject.[49]

## MYTHICAL SPACE

Mythical space must be distinguished from the abstract space of geometry because in myth the designation of a space does not distinguish between position and content. Position is not "pure" or detachable from what is taking place in the world. Space is therefore really a "place" which is disclosed only insofar as it is filled with a certain significance. The mythical "here" is not an abstract "here" applicable anywhere, but a *significant* "here," for example, a god dwells here (a sacred place) or a god is not here (a profane place). We can get a feel for such a demarcation of space by considering the Greek word *temenos*, from the verbal root *tem* meaning "to cut." Originally the word meant a sacred precinct marked off for a god (hence "temple") and later took on a more extended spatial meaning referring to any piece of land marked off, as to show ownership. Even early Greek mathematicians felt this original relationship between marking off a precinct and sacred meaning; witness Pythagoras's designation of limit (*peras*) as good and unlimited (*apeiron*) as evil.

The opposition of day and night, light and darkness, also figures into mythical spatial designations. The existential meaning of light and dark leads to certain divine or demonic characteristics of space. For example, East (the origin of light) is the source of life; West (where the sun sets) is the origin of death. The point is that mythical space is embedded in the world of experience and practice, filled with meaning. For this reason the notion of uniform space is not in evidence. It is only in an existential context that the world takes shape and in which human beings begin to know their way around.

> Every mythically significant content, every circumstance of life that is raised out of the sphere of the indifferent and commonplace, forms its own ring of existence, a walled-in zone separated from its surroundings by fixed limits. . . . All movement into and out of this ring are governed by very definite sacral regulations. Transition from one mythical-religious sphere to another involves *rites of passage* which must be carefully observed. . . . The barriers which man sets himself in his basic feeling of the sacred are the starting point from which begins his setting of boundaries in space and from which, by a progressive process of organization and articulation, the process spreads over the whole of the physical cosmos.[50]

## MYTHICAL TIME

Similarly, mythical time is not a measurement according to abstract units of minutes and hours which are applicable to any event, but is imprecise stretches bound to practices, daily life, or momentous occasions. In Homer, for example, the time designation is "day," which is inseparable from meaningful situations such as the day of fate, the day of homecoming, and the day of enslavement.[51] Time is always time *for* something: harvest time, war time, the time of worship, the time of death. Mythical time, therefore—and this is also true for space—is qualitative and not quantitative. Time is always disclosed in some particular context of a significant coming or going. It is more akin to biological time, the rhythmic ebb and flow of life forms. For this reason cosmic time in myth usually mirrors the life process, where the periodicity of nature is seen in terms of life and death.[52]

The temporal forms of before and after are disclosed in the mythical concern for sacred origins and the "historical" narratives about the gods. But just as myth does not reflect anything resembling Newtonian absolute time, so too it is not comparable to our sense of historical time, with its fixed chronology and irreversible past, present, and future, where a thing can hold only one position on this line. We have seen that mythical relations and identities allow empirically different things to merge or intermingle if they exhibit affective, functional, or situational similarities. Since there is no thing-attribute distinction, then changes in quality or external influences are perceived as substantial transformations or identifications. The same is true of mythical time relations. The mythical "now" is "laden with the past and pregnant with the future."[53] The past and future are not separated or distant from the present. Such "loops" of time are disclosed in ritual identification, poetic vision, divination, and prophecy. Also, the affective import of dreams and memories collapses the strict distinction between past and present for the mythical mind.

Mythical time so described cannot be considered a mistake, because the context in which it is shown has nothing to do with the purposes and methods of abstract time or strict historical time. It is also not an alternative replacement for abstract time measurement. Its meaning is "lived time" which is phenomenologically prior to "clock time" and which is evident every day in our experience as well.[54] The general meaning of lived time as concrete, situational, imprecise "stretches" is certainly shown in our experience: I have no time; I had a good time; these are hard times; I recall my early days. Moreover, the *lived* present is certainly not separable from a sense of past and future. What I am and do now follows from and therefore pulls along my past experiences; also, my actions now are shaped and therefore pulled along by my future aims. Every human present is laden with the past and pregnant with the future. Such is the general phenomenological meaning of mythical time.

# General Themes

To conclude this chapter, I will sketch a number of themes which summarize some of the basic points presented thus far and also forecast some of the issues that will be central to the ensuing discussion of Greek myth and the advent of philosophy.

## MYTH AND THE ESTABLISHMENT OF WORLD

There are both phenomenological and historical reasons for proposing myth as the origin of "world." We have discussed the precedence of existential meaning over objectivity and therefore the phenomenological priority of mythical disclosure. The historical precedence of myth is shown in the fact that all cultures begin with myth. Mythical paradigms, therefore, are the forms in which a world and human situation (as opposed to the brute given or the mere reactive/behavioral situation of animals) are *first* presented. Greek myths, for example, told the story of Greek existence, disclosing to the Greeks who they were and where meaning and value were to be found.

It may seem trivial to stress the historical precedence of myth, since this is hardly a debatable point, but in the analysis to come much more will be made out of this precedence. A very common view holds that ancient culture was lost in the darkness of ignorance until "liberated" by the advent of philosophy. Although the birth of philosophy was a momentous and important event in human history, the notions of ignorance and liberation are nevertheless highly problematic. This chapter, of course, has argued against the view that myth is a form of ignorance. In addition, our analysis of Greek philosophy will show that its development was slow and gradual, and in fact never a complete break with myth. Rather, philosophy first grew *out of* a mythical heritage and continued to exhibit elements of that tradition up through Plato and even to a certain degree in Aristotle. Greek philosophy was never completely free of myth, it simply re-formed much of its mythical origins. Of course, that re-formation did break with tradition in many respects, but not in all respects, as we shall see.

If I may briefly forecast one of the conclusions I hope the reader will draw from this study, *no* form of thought, science included, is ever completely free of a certain mythical sense. Myth does not explain the world; it is the "worlding" of the world, its unconcealment. Prior to myth the world, as a context of meaning, is "not there" (concealment). Conceptual reason interprets a world already there. In other words, some context of meaning, which conceptual reason *serves*, must first be in place. *Before* the world can be objectified (detached from the existential situation) it has to *have* existential significance. A *mythos* is the first telling (*logos*) of the human story in a world situation, where existential meaning is embedded in the world. Only *then* is something like scientific objectivity possible. No culture, and no person, *first* comes across the world objectively. Moreover, there is never such a thing as a purely detached state of mind.[55] Even the scientist must be motivated, attracted to, and excited by science. The *value* of science, both personal and collective, the spirit of the search, the draw of the unknown—these are all preobjective animations which are inseparable from the scientific enterprise. In other words, science must first *matter*, and this is a prescientific matter. Here we can notice echoes of the mythical. Ultimately the meaning of myth should not be limited to specific images of gods, heroes, and the like. The absence of such imagery does not mean that a general mythical sense is absent from a culture. Even our age of extensive objectification, quantification, and mechanization can be seen to be guided by certain mythical motifs (e.g., "mastery of the earth").

## THE EXISTENTIAL CIRCLE

When considering human experience and the world in myth, subjectivity and objectivity are out of place. Scientific reason sees itself as objective (dealing in the "real facts") and tends to call myth "merely" subjective (providing fiction or edification). But *this* sense of subjectivity is possible *only* with the advent of objectivity, that which filters out the subjective (existential) elements. Objectivity (in the world) and subjectivity (in us) are in fact mutually delimiting terms which arise together as two sides of the same coin. In the process of abstraction the subject pulls back from direct existential involvement with the world (reserving the existential for its own sphere) so that the world is thrust into objectivity (i.e., de-existentialized). But since objectivity is not a factor in myth, neither is the idea of subjectivity.

*We* can speak of objective and subjective elements in myth (e.g., nature and the personal imagery), but, as we have seen, since the mythical world first appears only as an existential matrix, objectivity is misplaced. And, as we will see, what we mean by subjectivity, namely an interiorized self distinct from the world and seen as the center of experience, is *not* in evidence in mythical culture. Therefore, since "self" is first shown to be within and controlled by an extrahuman, sacred dimension, and since "world" is first shown in an existential, preobjective dimension, then myth exhibits a self-world circularity that undermines a strict subject-object distinction. Such circularity helps us understand the primitive sense of kinship with other life forms.[56]

It is preferable to understand myth as an irreducible circle of world-and-self presentation, out of which world and self are later separated and objectivity and subjectivity become an issue. *We* might naturally analyze myth according to objective and subjective accents, but that cannot justify explaining myth in the light of these terms. Then the attempt to explain myths anthropomorphically or even anthropologically must also be questioned, since myths themselves disclose a *world*, and one *within which* humans are placed (in a position of subordination). An anthropological account follows from our assumptions, but regarding myths themselves, reducing them to functions of the human mind, psyche, or social structures would be phenomenologically inaccurate.

## CONSCIOUSNESS AND THE SELF

The question of consciousness and the self will help us clarify the nonsubjective character of myth and will also be of continuing importance when we examine developments in Greek poetry and philosophy. I have argued that before myth there is no "world." We should also recognize that before myth there is no "self" which could "invent" myths either. When we think of a self we usually mean self-consciousness, but as we shall see, self-consciousness as the mark of human identity is a late, historical development. Early mythical forms always seem to take the shape of an arrival, an emergence from something nonconscious *to* consciousness. Entire communities were guided by prophetic and poetic revelations, the source of which was not thought to be human consciousness. This, together with the sense of *subjection* to the gods, indicates that an internal analysis of myth should adopt the category of givenness. We can say that myth takes shape "through" the human self (cf. the role of poets), but always in relation to a sacred "other." The tension between humans and a powerful other brings forth a spontaneous creation to give shape to this meeting. The basis of myth is neither the human self nor the objective world but a sacred, extraconscious *mystery which arrives*.

Cassirer argues that myth cannot begin in a "self" or a "world" since the delimitation of these regions is first determined *by* myth.[57] The modern view of self-identity can roughly be summarized as: (1) self-consciousness, or the internal sense of separation from the external world and other selves; (2) independence as the initiator and center of thought and action; and (3) continuity through time. But this notion of a subjective, personal self-consciousness—i.e., *inwardness, autonomy*, and *unity*—developed only gradually in human history. As we shall see, in archaic experience the presence of such a self cannot be inferred.[58] The primitive self is immediately fused with a feeling of community.[59] As we shall see, in mythical thought there is no private self but rather a social self. But even this sense of a human collective grew out of a deeper sense of the total community of humans and nature.[60] And as far as continuity is concerned, just as archaic experience does not see the world as a unified continuum but rather as extraordinary advents of crucial (existential) interruptions, intervals, and transformations, so too the self which experiences such a world is not a unified continuum. It is common for primitives to speak of a new self with each new phase of life (hence initiations and name changes). The immediate, existential response to life's radical changes does not permit an abstract notion of a unified self.[61]

The mythical self, therefore, can be characterized in the following (admittedly clumsy) way: self-in-the-midst-of-nature, self-in-the-midst-of-community, self-in-the-claim-of-a-sacred-other. In myth, human thought and action were not based in a private internal center, but were placed in a larger context, as in the case of divine possession or intervention. Again we must keep in mind the phenomenological aptness of such beliefs. If existential effect and response in a lived world or group situation is the *sole* criterion of meaning, then the idea of a detached autonomous self is impossible.[62] Later we will see how the advent of philosophical reflection and the detached self are inextricably connected. Modern forms of thought and the modern view of self are interdependent. But then we would have just as much trouble passing judgment on the mythical idea of self as we would the mythical view of the world.

## MYTH, ART, AND APPEARANCE

It is common to view myth as a form of art, that is to say, an aesthetic or literary creation and not a rational or empirical "truth." From what we have seen so far, the only questionable part of such a view is the notion of truth. Since myth is in principle nonobjective and nonempirical, and since it takes a narrative and not an abstract form, we can readily call myth an artistic creation, as long as this does not connote anything fictional or subjective, or confine myth to a single cultural category ("the arts"). If it is true that the world first takes form in myth, then the idea of creation (bringing-forth) is quite appropriate. And since the background of mythical disclosure is a sense of mystery—i.e., the arriving-withdrawing character of the sacred, which "gives" its form from hiddenness, which is ever more than ordinary, profane objectivity—then the phenomenal (nonsubstantial) character of artistic creations is consonant with the meaning of myth, since it expresses the world without a presumption of ultimate truth. There is a certain transparency in myth in that it speaks while acknowledging an unspeakable mystery in the background.

Perhaps we should say that myth is not truth but appearance. Measured by postmythical thought this may be the case, but such a distinction can only imply a shortcoming in myth. As we have seen, the notion of truth as a reduction to and conformity with conceptual principles or empirical facts is problematic. Heidegger speaks of a more primordial form of truth, unconcealment, a primal "appearing," before any conceptual or empirical reductions can take place. Here we can find a deep sense of truth in mythical "appearance," and therefore circumvent any sense of deficiency. Mythical appearance is positive and presentational (cf. the actor appearing on stage), rather than something which hides the truth (cf. he only appears to be kind). Myth, like art, must "come forth." Its truth is not in some existing condition simply waiting to be described; its truth is found only in the creative coming-forth itself. The point here is that the connection between artistic creation and myth is no deficiency, and in fact it raises many questions about the relation between art and truth.[63]

We will see that the western rational tradition began in large part with objections to the multiplicity, elusiveness, and affective character of myth in favor of a more unified truth which could be gathered in the conceptual forms of the human mind. In other words, it wanted to *secure* a formative power within the human mind, apart from the mythical sense of emergence from a mysterious "beyond" and abstracted from the aesthetic, affective, and existential variability in myth. Such securing of form in the human mind's capacity for abstraction naturally led to seeing myth as unfounded, as a fiction or merely entertaining story. But if we can show that mythical disclosure has an intelligible structure and that the first philosophers were in some respects cultural *rebels*, then at least we can question philosophy's criticism of myth and subsequently see myth and art in a new light.

## MYTH AND REFLECTION

To conclude this chapter, something important needs to be said. An analysis of mythical disclosure is possible only by stepping out of myth. As our study of the tragedians and some of the first philosophers will show, an understanding of the general meaning of myth does not emerge explicitly within myth itself. So not only do we understand myth by contrasting it with postmythical developments, we also *need* reflection to gain a sense for the intelligibility of myth, and this is indeed a gain. What we want to avoid is a strict opposition between myth and reflection. Our look at Greek intellectual history will show that a kind of dialectic between myth and reflection is possible. We simply want to understand what was disclosed in myth, and then what was gained and what was lost with the advent of philosophy. If there is anything to retrieve from myth, this will not entail a return to the mythical past but rather a deeper reflection upon what disclosure of a world *means*, one that can *include* reason and myth, science and art, and a sense for a certain confluence of such forms.

Such inclusiveness is a pluralistic sense of truth. If there is one problem to be found in the advent of philosophy, it is its tendency toward exclusivity and its banishment of certain forms of disclosure. If we can establish that existential meaning precedes objectivity and that lived involvement precedes abstraction in important ways, then the tendency of conceptual reason to demote art because of its resistance to abstraction, uniformity, and objectivity, and the subsequent tendency to demote myth to a "mere art form" because its existential imagery offers a comparable resistance—then these tendencies can be considered a highly questionable inversion. If abstraction can be grounded in a pluralistic, existential world, then perhaps we can be dissuaded from the most problematic tendency in abstract thinking— a kind of imperialistic uniformity. Perhaps we can come to see that the world is disclosed in many ways, with no ultimate reduction, common essence, or absolute truth other than a pluralized, irreducible coexistence of cultural perspectives, each of which can tell *a* truth. Truth per se would have to mean, in Heideggerian terms, the *process* of unconcealment itself rather than any particular *product* of unconcealment.

# II

## Greek Myth and Religion

### General Characteristics

We usually encounter Greek myths as a form of literature. The reasons for this may become clear as we proceed, but at the outset we must realize that Greek myths reflected a form of religion and were not simply poetic inventions. Greek myths embody a full cultural life and stem from genuine experiences of the sacred. One reason why Greek mythology has become demoted to mere literature is that its character does not fit the model we have come to reserve for religion, a model which is primarily Middle Eastern and Asian and which assumes a form of other-worldliness not evident in Greek religion. Yet the early Greeks experienced the presence and force of the sacred, which engendered cults and rituals as serious as any world religion. No religion can *begin* with mere stories or "faith," but with what Kerenyi calls "arresting evidence" of some kind.[1]

In Greece, poetry was a prime vehicle for cultivating this religious experience. The poets transmitted and adapted traditional religious myths. They provided a sacred content with an ever-creative form, a continual telling (*legein*) of a sacred *mythos* (which becomes *mythologia*). Their role, as Plato put it, was to transmit stories "about gods and divine beings and heroes and all that the underworld contains" (*Republic*, 392a). But again, poetry was far from being simply "literature." It was the formation of Greek culture.

One point to be drawn from the preceding chapter is a warning against an anthropomorphic interpretation of Greek myth. Greek deities are powers which blend cosmic, social, and human features in such a way that these features cannot be strictly distinguished.[2] Moreover, historically speaking, the manifestation of a divine form seems to *precede* the development of a distinct human self-image as we know it. Otto has said that the human form is rooted in and derives from the divine form.[3] It is true that what we call the human form dominates Greek mythology in an incomparable way. But if the human so dominates Greek myth, and if we can show that the modern conception of human form grew historically *out of* this mythology, then how do we know that the "human" did not first *take shape* through Greek myths? Perhaps the human is the *result* and not the cause of these myths. Could it be said that Greek "man" was a "theomorphic" development? I leave these questions aside for now. The point here is to underscore the genuine and compelling religious significance that animates Greek myth. Let us now outline the general features of the early Greek world, an overall sketch which will be developed in more detail in the next three chapters.

## RELIGION OF THE EARTH

When we visit Athens and the many historical sites throughout Greece, we are struck by the worldliness of ancient Greek culture. Compared with the other-worldliness of Christianity, here is a religious atmosphere thoroughly rooted in the earth, with its expression of nobility, beauty, and excellence, with humans, beasts, and gods dwelling together and reflecting the sacred elements of *this* world. Nothing shows this better than the Parthenon. Compared with the Christian cathedrals of Europe—soaring skyward, their dim interiors sheltering the sacred from the outside world—the effect of the Parthenon is striking. Meant to overlook and gather the focus of the city, elegant and simple, completely earthward in its thrust and at home on the hillside, bright and dazzling in the incredible Greek light—the Parthenon alone is enough to show what Otto meant when he said that Greek culture "overwhelms us by its uniqueness" because it was able to "see the brilliance of life with an eye more luminous than the rest of mankind."[4]

In Greek religion, and this is especially true of Homer, a deity is not a power above the world and nature. Important events in the world and nature present themselves *as* sacred. Again we must realize why the notion of symbol misses the point. Ares, for example, is not called the god *of* war, but simply the god war; in other words, the quality of war itself is deified.[5] What characterizes Greek religion is "seeing the world in the light of the divine,"[6] not yearning for another world or seeing the divine "behind" or "above" the world. *This* world was divine for the Greeks. It is perhaps such a rootedness in the world that more than anything else accounts for the Greek, of all the world cultures, being the only one to develop "natural philosophy." But it is important to recognize that in early Greek religion a god was not identical with a natural element but was rather the sacred dimension of that element. Consider Poseidon and the sea. When Homer tells us of Poseidon riding over the waves (*Iliad*, XIII. 21ff.) we witness an example of the sacred-profane distinction.[7]

In Homer, "every state, every capacity, every mood, every thought, every act and experience was mirrored in the deity."[8] As long as we keep in mind that there were profane states too, we can see the point: Every existentially important event was sacred. An interesting example comes from a later source, Euripides, where something is said that seems odd unless we attend to the meaning of the sacred sketched in the first chapter: "to recognize one's friend is god" (*Helen*, 560). The word *theos* can refer to any extraordinary occurrence and not just a deity.[9]

Greek religion does not explain, justify, or interrupt the course of the world but simply presents and exalts the various features of existence, never reduced to one form, one god, or one universal idea. Greek religion is not only polytheistic, even individual gods have more than a single form or essence. They manifest their power in many ways, and so, for example, there are many Zeuses, each with his own epithet.[10] It is this inherent *pluralism* of the sacred that accounts for the so-called immoral behavior of the gods. But since both the benign and the terrible have existential import, we should see that Greek polytheism simply reflects a sacralization of the fact that existential concerns vary and that human aims are often thwarted by other forces in the world.

Early Greeks were not only subjected to the gods but also to the conflicting aims of different gods. Furthermore, the gods were capable of deception, and their actions often were the result of arbitrary whims. Consequently, even though the world made sense for the Greeks, even though they knew their place in the world, they nevertheless did not possess certainty about, control over, or responsibility for their overall fate. In other words, the immediate existential matrix, most of which resists prediction, engendered the kind of *religious* fatalism characteristic of the early Greeks. The extraordinary, unpredictable features of the lived world took *divine* form. Whatever worship Greeks performed, they could never be *sure* of fate or the gods.[11] Perhaps we could say that the Greeks were sure of one thing: The gods *are* unpredictable and capable of the unexpected; life is a mysterious fluctuation of blessings and curses; one can simply hope for the best, but ruin is also "in order." It is this fatalism which culminates in tragedy and contrasts sharply with the later search for constancy in rational laws. Nevertheless, early Greek fatalism reflected a *kind* of order in the world which dictated what should and should not be possible for human beings. So there *is* a moral and structural sense in early Greek religion, but not moral perfection or universal regularity. The flux and contest of forces in the world are not eliminated but rather apportioned and celebrated as such, thereby implying an affirmation of the whole of life.[12]

The pluralism of Greek myths expresses the acute sense of worldliness reflected in early Greek culture. Perhaps we can understand this contrasted with Christian transcendence and the Greek philosophical development of rational abstraction from the lived world. The historical link between these traditions (e.g., in Medieval philosophy) becomes easier to understand when we notice their common dissatisfaction with sensuous immediacy and the disorder of the lived world, the negativity of which both traditions try to resolve. It is also easier to understand why monotheism and rationalism historically share a common ethical form. In other words, both developments represent a *reform* of the lived world, the contentious plurality of sensuous experience and existential concerns. For this reason both traditions will maintain that there is something flawed in the way we first encounter the world, which is in need of correction by either spiritual transcendence or rational abstraction. And since the Greek myths are nothing more than a presentation of the lived world, both traditions did battle with these myths. The subsequent demythification of the world resulted in a secularization (or profaning) of the world, which had two significant consequences: Christian dualism and scientific naturalism. In contrast to these developments, we can recognize the kind of worldliness that is expressed in Greek religion: The lived world *is* sacred.

Since it presented all the varying features of the world as an irreducible plurality, Greek religion was essentially fluid, dynamic, and undogmatic. There was no fixed doctrine, no rigid cult formula, no organized canon, and no priestly class with cultural authority over worshipers.[13] There was great flexibility of interpretation and adaptation. Perhaps this doctrinal and social pluralism explains why the critical spirit of philosophy grew out of Greek soil, and, moreover, why Greek philosophers did not entirely abandon the idea of divinity but rather revised it.

## MORTALITY

The crucial feature of the lived world is the horizon of death which presents the ultimate limit. When one compares the way early Greek religion responded to death with the way other religions offer some kind of everlasting compensation for human demise, one is struck by something quite remarkable. Although, as we shall see, there are compensations for death in Homer, these compensations are fully worldly and in no way resolve or overcome human mortality. Greek religion saw death as an unavoidable fate. Human beings are called mortals, death is their ultimate destiny, for only the gods are immortal.[14]

But what about Hades, the place of the dead in the underworld? Is this not an afterlife? I think we would have to say no. Consider the curious nature of Hades depicted in Book XI of the *Odyssey*. It is really a shadow-world with none of the features of the lived world, a kind of ghostly sleep which held no attraction for the Greeks (beginning at line 485 Achilles says he would rather be a laborer on earth than king of all the shades in the underworld). Hades would not seem to count as an afterlife or a realm of personal existence (Hesiod, in *Works and Days* 154, calls the dead in Hades "nameless"). And yet the Greeks spoke of this place Hades, in which departed souls were located. What are we to make of this place which is not a form of life?

An answer to this question is given by Kerenyi.[15] We have seen that the mythical mind gives a sacred form to any state which has existential significance. The Greeks were practically obsessed with giving form to everything. Kerenyi says that the Greek mind simply *acknowledged* nonexistence and gave it the *form* of Hades. The image of Hades therefore *presents* nonexistence as a necessary part of the world, not as an alternative world or afterlife. The existential import of death demanded a sacred form. With Hades the Greeks deified even death.

Furthermore, the form of nonexistence helps bring the counterform of existence into sharper relief. Such a sacred contrast which dominated early Greek thought perhaps can help unravel one of the more perplexing enigmas which anyone encountering Greek culture has to ponder. Never have a people been more vital, life-loving, and worldly in their cultural existence than the Greeks; *at the same time* they possessed a deeply fatalistic resignation to death which we might expect to have a debilitating effect. Perhaps this will not seem so puzzling after we witness Nietzsche's interpretation of Greek tragedy, below. Just as the value of loved ones becomes magnified when they are lost to us, perhaps the degree of life's attraction is proportionate to one's sense for its finitude.

For the early Greeks, therefore, death was an acknowledged counterpart of life and was usually associated with a return to the earth, hence the form of Hades. Since death was given a sacred *form*, it was not perceived as a void. Absence was given a cultural presence. Death fit in with and consequently animated and accentuated the Greek *world*. The form of death offered a continuing and pervasive illumination of the form of life.

The Greek view of death is well illustrated by some of their grave reliefs. One such sculpture shows a deceased woman sitting in a chair while a servant holds out the woman's infant child so that she can have a last look before departing from life. The look on the woman's face and her bodily posture show a half-detached, serene, and noble bearing, a love for her life and yet an acquiescence to her fate. That a scene such as this should be chosen for a grave is quite startling when you compare it with other images of death. There are no skeletons or demons, no scenes of lamentation; we are shown no ascension to heavenly perfection, no lying in state, but simply a last look at life. And that we are shown an image at all again indicates that death fits in with the form of the world.[16] The Greek response to death displays a sad yet noble resignation to an inevitable fate, not a welcomed release from life (as in some Oriental religions) or a transition to another life (as in Christianity). The recognition of mortality highlights the deep sense of limit and finitude that characterizes early Greek culture, so much so that the idea of a positive infinity is absent and at times even deliberately rejected.

## GODS AND HUMANS

The immortality of the gods limits and thus defines the mortality of humans, but the notion of limit also figures into every aspect of the divine-human relation and consequently every aspect of life. Through the power of the gods the Greeks acknowledged the essential ambiguity of the human condition, that there is a cost for every gift. Birth and death, achievement and toil, success and failure, happiness and sorrow are inexorably linked and mixed in the world.[17] What is remarkable, however, is the positive response of the Greeks. Instead of a cowering subordination or a debilitating surrender, the early Greeks saw limitation as a challenge. This is best exemplified by the heroic ideal which animates Homeric poetry and about which we will have more to say shortly. Presently we can say that the heroic ideal generally represents the achievement of excellence through adversity, and more specifically the pursuit of worldly glory in the midst of and *despite* inevitable doom. Regardless of the overriding limitations of divine management, fate, and death, the hero acts to fulfill whatever degree of excellence is allotted him. Both gods and men admire most the hero. Humans give the hero honor, reward, and station, while the gods spend much of their time devising tasks and situations to test the skill and courage of the heroes (in addition to making sure mortals do not overstep their bounds). Failure is sometimes preordained, and death always so. Often, because of divine competition, outcomes are a gamble, even for the gods. But for the hero a sense of uncertainty and futility does not inhibit the pursuit of excellence.

One of the primary features of Greek religion, therefore, is the heroic pursuit of excellence, in the cultivation of which both gods and humans cooperate. Consequently, the relationship between gods and humans is not one of master and slave or judge and sinner, but rather one of friendship, mutual admiration, and respectful competition. The gods challenge mortals to achieve excellence. Since competition figures into the *religious* life of the early Greeks, we should not be surprised about the coexistence of religion and sport in their culture. The major centers of worship (e.g., Delphi) have a temple, a theater, and a stadium. We should not be swayed into thinking that sport was simply a sidelight to religion, that it was nothing more than entertainment and recreation. Competitive sport was the theatrical analogue of the more crucial competition between warriors and between gods that generated the cultural ideals of Greek mythology.

The Olympic games, for example, were considered a spectacle for men *and* gods; they represented what could be called a ritualized performance of a *religious* ideal which included victory, physical beauty, and prowess. This is why the victory odes of Pindar praised the athlete in the light of traditional heroic and divine exemplars. If we have a hard time understanding the connection between sport and religion (few of us today even see any *cultural* significance in sport), then again we must realize how unique and worldly Greek religion was.

This notion of a tension between opposite forces and a competitive response to these limit conditions continued to be a pervasive and dominating feature of the Greek world. The *agōn*, or the contest for excellence, showed itself in every important aspect of Greek culture, even in later periods. This is clear enough in military and athletic ideals and in the myths of heroic tasks and divine competition, but there were contests even in the arts (e.g., dramatic competitions). Furthermore, the Greeks took great delight in political debates, to such an extent that rhetorical skills alone were often admired. Indeed, the contest of political speeches was an essential aspect in the evolution of democracy (as opposed to uncontested authority). I think one can also make the case that a hallmark in the development of philosophy and science, namely argumentation, is traceable to the agonistic element in Greek culture. Perhaps this can add to our understanding of why such revolutions, which fought off the complacency of traditionalism, arose in Greece and nowhere else.[18]

Another noteworthy feature of Greek religion which is also connected with the idea of limitation is the curious phenomenon of divine laughter.[19] Especially in Homer we find that the gods laugh at humans and at themselves; humans can even laugh at the gods. Certainly this is a remarkable thing compared to the seriousness of the major world religions, but again I think it is a reflection of the distinctive sense of limit we find in Greek religion.[20] I will develop this point in the chapter on tragedy, but presently I will propose that laughter stems from the recognition of a limit and is therefore in a way linked to the tragic. Humanity, though kin to the gods, is separated from them by mortality and the degree of powerlessness. Gods too have limitations on their power. Whenever gods or humans try to overstep the limits of their power, they appear comical and are subject to laughter. But only humans are subject to mortality, and the death of a hero can prompt even a god to weep, because the pursuit of glory with a reward of death is a tragic thing. We can see, then, how the idea of limitation, the central element of Greek religion, could generate the two luminous art forms, comedy and tragedy, for which the Greeks deserve our everlasting gratitude.

## FESTIVITY

We have noticed in Greek religion its surprisingly positive, life-affirming response in the midst of divine control, limits, and mortality. We can see more of this vitality in the markedly festive atmosphere surrounding the interaction between gods and humans.[21] The Greeks seemed to delight in celebrating sacred meetings and feasts, which could reflect either joy or sadness, although joy seems to have been the predominant mood.[22] There are even times when lamentation or sorrow, for example, is associated with a kind of joy and satisfaction (*Odyssey*, IV.102–105; *Iliad*, XXIV.513–14). The presence of joy even in times of sadness will become important later when we try to understand the religious significance of tragedy, but for now we can simply appreciate that the intermingling of gods and humans in Greek religion had an aura of joyful celebration, serious yet playful, filled with sensuous pleasure, beauty, and camaraderie.

If the gods come to share a feast with humans, again we notice that their relationship is not that of master and slave. In fact the Greeks believed they had a common origin: "the gods and mortals spring from one source" (Hesiod, *Erga*, 108); "the origin of men and gods is one and the same; from the same mother we draw our breath" (Pindar, *Nemean Odes*, 6.1). If we recall the existential meaning of the sacred in a mythical world, we can well understand such a form of intimacy— but the preoccupation with beauty and joy, visual and sensual delight, is perhaps nowhere so pronounced as in Greek religion. So embedded in the bright Mediterranean world is Greek myth that beauty and visual form take on an unprecedented importance and continue to do so throughout the periods of Greek culture. When Plato did not seem to distinguish between beauty and the good, he was simply continuing a Greek heritage which could use the same word (*kalos*) for both beautiful and good. Moreover, the connection between knowing and seeing is deeply rooted in the Greek language. *Eidenai* (to know) and *eidos* (form) stem from an original meaning which is entirely concrete, namely seeing or catching sight of. For the early Greeks, knowing the gods meant *seeing* them. For this reason Kerenyi calls Greek religion a "religion of show."[23] In Greek, *thea* can mean a goddess and also something seen, and the later developments of tragic drama find their religious roots in this earlier sense of a *theatron*, a spectacle for divine onlookers. Therefore the festive scenes of divine and human gatherings have a serious religious significance. We should not think of the feasts and sacrifices of the Greek cults as primarily utilitarian requests or appeasement but rather a form of convocation. Religious references are always filled with invitations, summonings, and songs of advent, so that the gods can become present (unconcealed), *seen*, and therefore known.

With the advent of the sacred, an atmosphere of awe also pervades the Greek festival. If we recall the connection between the sacred and the extraordinary, then awe and wonderment would constitute a mythical religious response. Indeed, Greek poetry and cult references abound with feelings of awe, astonishment, and wonder. Rather than fear or slavelike subservience, the Greek form of worship arose out of a sense of amazement at the sight of a sacred marvel. The Greek word *eusebeia*, meaning piety or religion, is better rendered more precisely as an awe-struck reverence for the gods, since it is rooted in the word *sebein*, meaning to step back from something with awe.[24]

## THE OLYMPIAN–TITAN DISTINCTION

Perhaps the most important element in early Greek thought is the demarcation of the world into two divine realms, Olympus and the Underworld. The Titans were the gods of the dark underworld, the *chthonic* gods (gods of the earth), who were prone to violence, brutishness, and excessive passion (the name "titan" literally means stretcher or strainer). The Olympians, ruled by Zeus, were the radiant gods of the sky and exhibited beauty, intelligence, and moderation. If we consider a certain pattern regarding masculine and feminine archetypes in world mythologies, where "masculine" represents brightness, intelligence, and order, and where "feminine" represents darkness, instinct, and excess, then we can call the Olympian gods masculine and the Underworld gods feminine. As we will see later, such a distinction does not refer primarily to sexual gender but rather to a kind of cosmic duality.

Mortals, whose place is the earth's surface, find themselves in between these divine regions and are subject to the power of both realms. The two realms complement each other, and both are honored with rituals, sometimes conjointly. Olympian gods can also have a chthonic counterpart.[25] Humans therefore continually dwell in the midst of a sacred duality, the tension of which represents all the conflicting elements of the lived world: passion and moderation, chaos and order, animal drives and culture, malevolence and benevolence, death and life. We will later witness how this mythical image of a tension of opposites not only constituted central themes of Greek poetry but also characterized other cultural forms, including philosophy.

# The Nonrational and Nonconscious in Greek Religion

When Aristotle said that "he who exercises his reason and cultivates it seems to be both in the best state of mind and most dear to the gods" (*Nicomachean Ethics*, X.8.1179a, 23–25), he was proposing something quite alien to earlier Greek culture, which he would have had to say was dominated by irrational states of mind. We have already discussed the problematic nature of "irrationality" in such a context. If earlier cultural forms were not assuming rational criteria, they could hardly be accused of violating them—hence my preference for something like "nonrational sense."

But we did not mention another connotation of irrationality, one that will help us further develop the assumptions underlying this paradigm clash. That connotation refers to insanity. We call the madman irrational when he is visited by uncontrollable eruptions that violate normal consciousness, such as visual or auditory hallucinations, an imaginary world that does not conform to the so-called empirical field or logical consistency or common practice. We could say that a mythical world of sacred imagery and much of primitive experience might easily be called irrational in this sense. And yet one would not be prone to call primitives insane (one might say they were ignorant). Why? Well, for one thing, if an entire culture operated in that way, a demarcation between sane and insane could not be found. Furthermore, *they* saw themselves as all right. Perhaps we mean to say that sanity is a cultural and social matter, as many have come to recognize. In other words, the way a person fits into a culture determines sanity, and that is why we cannot judge primitive experience as being pathological. But perhaps the reader has noticed the trap here. If we connect the term "irrational" with insanity, then maybe we find here further evidence of the pitfalls inherent in calling primitive cultures irrational from any standpoint. Perhaps rationality too is a social, historical, and relative matter.

The early Greeks recognized an unbalanced state of mind as a form of madness (*mania*), but the important point is that *mania* was not always a derogatory or pathological term; often it was a phenomenon of utmost cultural importance, to the extent that it was usually a source of authority. The reason for introducing the question of madness at this point is as follows. If we are to understand the differences between rational and nonrational forms of disclosure and the cultural assumptions involved, one extremely helpful question is that of mental "disorder," helpful because it brings to light many of the social, behavioral, psychological, and cultural elements found behind the revolutionary development of rationality, and more specifically because it focuses on what I think is the single most important factor in the story of myth and philosophy, namely the nature and status of consciousness.

## SACRED MADNESS

The Greeks experienced *mania* as an uncontrollable invasion of ordinary states of mind, where powerful forces would take over or radically alter the personality. Such invasions could be called the wakeful analogue of dream experiences. To use modern terminology we can say that in these eruptions, ordinary consciousness is invaded by extraconscious imagery (a voice, vision, or feeling) and can become either the receptacle for this imagery or possessed by it, thus losing conscious control altogether. We can see here a psychological context within which the sacred-profane distinction finds further illustration. Ordinary consciousness of self and the surrounding world is the profane, while extraordinary disruptions of consciousness are sacred advents. And this is precisely how the Greeks usually perceived *mania*, as a sacred phenomenon.

The following discussion of sacred madness is drawn to a large extent from E. R. Dodds's classic work on the subject.[26] Oddly enough it is the philosopher Plato who has Socrates say in the *Phaedrus*: "the greatest blessings come by way of madness" (244a). By this is meant a sacred madness, to be distinguished from madness through disease, although Dodds thinks it is doubtful that such a distinction was made in earlier times, since all extraordinary mental states seem to have been attributed to divine intervention. The connection between sacred powers and mental disorder was generally quite common in the Greek world.[27] In any case, Plato gives us access to this phenomenon by distinguishing four types of sacred madness: prophecy, ritual healing, poetry (244b–245b), and love (265b).

**Prophetic mania.** Prophecy was a culturally prominent phenomenon in the Greek world. Apollo was the god who bestowed sacred messages through his oracles, the most famous of which was at Delphi. Prophecy required that the oracle become *entheos*, or taken over by a divine voice. Answers came spontaneously and immediately, often accompanied by frenzy and severe contortions of the body. The oracle was most often a young female from a poor background.[28] Why were such oracles not thought to be pathologically mad? Well, not thinking them so made it not so. Cultural support is perhaps the key factor in preventing such mental disruptions from becoming pathological. The oracles were not always mantic. There were ritual preparations, a managed environment, techniques for trance inducement, and group support, all of which contributed to the socialization of these experiences. These oracles were looked upon with awe and respect, and were considered authorities. Moreover, since such experiences were managed and ritualized, normal states of mind were not lost forever but regained after the ceremony. Even today many people are prone to "hearing voices." The way in which such people would fit into their culture would largely determine the degree of their pathology. The most striking evidence for the cultural support and subsequent cultural meaning of such psychic states in the Greek world is that the oracles had to be *trained*. Children with a propensity to hear voices were "apprenticed" by temple priests and shown techniques to help induce and manage such experiences. In other words, training, positive expectation, techniques, and group support all contributed to *promoting* mantic processes and also to minimizing the possibility of what we would call dysfunctional insanity.[29]

The authority of the oracle was uncontested in the early Greek world and was taken seriously even in the Classical period up to the Roman period. The extent of its sacred authority is evident in that often the oracle sided with the enemy of a city but did not seem to diminish in influence. Even Socrates respected the Delphic voice, as we shall see. Nevertheless, through time, the oracle became less and less clear, in need of obscure interpretation, fitful, erratic, and finally incomprehensible, until Apollo declared that he would never speak again. Such a withdrawal was, of course, matched and prompted by cultural changes which made its deauthorization inevitable.

**Ritual mania.** While Apollo's cult was more individual and aristocratic, there were other cults given to group worship. The most famous of these more-communal cults was that of Dionysus. The manic process in Dionysian worship was the inducement of ecstasy, the meaning of which is shown in the Greek word *ekstasis*, literally "standing out of." Ecstatic worshipers would perform uninhibited rituals which resulted in a loss of the conventional self and an invasion of the god's personality or power. Dionysian and Corybantic rites involving unrestrained music and dance were known to bring about a cathartic cure for anxiety (*deimata*). The effectiveness of such cures was not doubted in the Greek world. Even Plato and Aristotle recognized their value and success.[30] We notice that ecstatic cures illustrate the issues raised when we considered the mythical and primitive sense of self. If it is true that individual ego-consciousness is derivative of a more primal social or contextual self, then it is no surprise that Greek religion would discover that the tension and alienation stemming from the fragmentation of ego development could be eased by a ritualized loss of ego consciousness. Of course we are no less aware today of the power and attraction of group identification or ecstatic intoxication.

**Poetic mania.**   We should not think that when Greek poets spoke of hearing the muse or began their poems with invocations to the muses, they were engaging nothing more than literary devices or formalities. The evidence indicates that the ancient Greeks experienced creative activity as an arrival from beyond the boundaries of the conscious self. In other words, poetry was not thought to be "invented" by the poet but rather "given" to the poet, sometimes whole cloth, at other times as raw material to which the poet would add a form. Inspiration would range from simply a calm hearing of the muse's voice to actual frenzied possession in later times. In any case the poet was, as Plato tells us, "not in his senses but is like a fountain giving free course to the water which keeps flowing on" (*Laws*, 719c). The poet therefore had to lose his conscious, profane self, or the fixation thereon, so that sacred imagery could pass through. The result was the religious conviction that poetry was not human but divine in origin.

Aside from the religious question, even today we hear poets and artists talk of the creative process as a not entirely conscious activity. We hear of inspiration, of works with a life of their own, of the artist as a receptacle. We know of poets (e.g., Milton, Blake, Yeats, Rilke) who often "heard" their poems dictated to them whole cloth. Of course the creative process is not divorced from conscious training and formative skills, but when we hear of the extraconscious dimensions of artistic activity, we hear an echo from the ancient past where such phenomena took a sacred form.[31]

**Erotic mania.**   The early Greeks saw the passion of love as a form of possession, associated with Aphrodite and Eros. Love was a loss or disorder of the conscious self and was thought to come from "beyond." We have already spoken of the phenomenological meaning of such a sacred reference, and we will have more to say on the subject later when we discuss the lyric poets.

## THE SHAMAN

The phenomena of divine apparitions and voices which would reveal or command culturally important matters were common in Greek antiquity. An example of the institutionalization of such experiences is the cult of Asclepius, which was prominent in Greece and which was built around the notion of a divine cure for disease. Incubation techniques were employed to induce a trance and the dream visitation of the deity whose voice would prescribe a cure. There are many records of successful cures. Though the Greeks attributed such cures to divine intervention, we may still be able to take this phenomenon seriously because of what we know about the healing role the unconscious can play in certain maladies. Nevertheless it must be kept in mind that such talk of the unconscious would be out of place in early Greece. Dreams, for example, were not thought to be a subliminal dimension of the human mind. The mythical criteria of efficacy and extraordinariness gave dreams a "real" status. In fact their subsequent sacred nature often made them *more* important than conscious experiences. In Homer, for example, dreams are events in the world like any other, which happen *to* the sleeper and which usually disclose crucial information. For the early Greeks, therefore, one does not "have" a dream, one *sees* a dream. And, as in the case of the Asclepius cult, dreams played a significant role in forming the world and practice of that time. For this reason Dodds is right when he says that the divine dream should not be interpreted as a psychic or literary image but as a "culture pattern."[32]

The general conclusion to be drawn is that in early Greek culture (as in mythical culture generally) extraordinary states of mind and disruptions of normal consciousness were *standards of meaning*. A summary designation for such cultural authority can be found in the so-called shaman figure, a term which, like mana, has found a general use in naming certain common features of primitive cultures. Eliade has summarized the following characteristics of the shaman: (1) an initiation comprising his symbolic dismemberment, death, and resurrection, (2) ecstatic journeys as a healer and psychopomp, where, for example, sick souls are conducted to the underworld or the soul of a sick man which had been stolen by demons is recaptured and restored to the body, (3) the conquest of pain, as in, for example, the mastery of fire, (4) the ability to assume animal forms, fly, and become invisible.[33] The essential element underlying these characteristics is the phenomenon of *ekstasis*, or the departure from the conscious mind and ordinary experience. Throughout ancient Europe and Asia such inspired seers were of the utmost importance to their communities. It was the shaman who *established* values and tasks by reporting sacred truths from out of his possessed state.

Cornford indicates that the same situation was to be found in ancient Greece.[34] There the shaman figure embodied a triple function which was sometimes seen as separated, sometimes united in a single individual. That triple function was differentiated in the following way: (1) the *poet*, who experienced visions of the past, (2) the *sage*, who possessed sacred knowledge of the present, and (3) the *seer*, who had prophetic visions of the future. Cornford maintains that although the functions of the poet, sage, and prophet later became separable and specialized, nevertheless they originated in a single, mantic, en-thused figure—the shaman. The Greek shaman, like his counterparts in other areas of the world, was considered a gifted, special individual who, after showing mantic tendencies in his youth, was trained in the cultivation of visionary skills. His specialty was a disembodied journey into sacred regions. Ceremonies inducing such experiences were usually accompanied by music, song, and dance, which were at times quite unrestrained and frenetic. In his possessed state he issued dramatic speeches which disclosed messages for the community, which eagerly awaited his directives. Such states of possession were typically followed by complete mental and physical exhaustion.

We can summarize the preceding sections of this chapter in the following way. In Greek antiquity, knowing the world was in principle a form of revelation, that is to say, formulations which would "arrive" from beyond the conscious mind *to* consciousness, or which would at times reside outside self-consciousness altogether. Knowledge therefore always had to acknowledge and embrace this conscious-nonconscious *field*. Now we are in a position to understand the enduring, authoritative, and uncontested role of poets, muses, oracles, and their like in early Greek culture (and, for that matter, to a significant degree in later periods as well). Moreover, in the light of our phenomenological analysis of mythical disclosure, we cannot attribute these phenomena to ignorance, invention, or such things as manipulation of the masses. Such phenomena presented the *world* of that age, the way in which the world was disclosed to the Greeks.

# Hesiod's *Theogony*

One of the most important stories in Greek mythology is Hesiod's *Theogony*, since it presents an organization of the Greek view of the world by telling how the gods first came into being and what their relationships were.[35] Although the aim of the poem seems to be the praising of Zeus and his establishment of divine justice, we also find a wealth of imagery concerning the primal form of the cosmos. Furthermore, in the Prologue we discover a number of references to the nature of poetic inspiration and the cultural role of the poet, which can confirm some of our previous observations.

From the Heliconian muses let us begin to sing (1). . . . one day they taught Hesiod glorious song while he was shepherding his lambs (22) . . . . breathed into me a divine voice to celebrate things that shall be and things that were aforetime; and they bade me sing of the race of the blessed gods that are eternally, but ever to sing of themselves both first and last (31–34). . . . let us begin with the Muses who gladden the great spirit of their father Zeus in Olympus with their songs, telling of things that are and that shall be and that were aforetime with consenting voice. Unwearying flows the sweet sound from their lips (36–40). . . . whomsoever of heaven-nourished princes the daughters of Great Zeus honor, and behold him at his birth, they pour sweet dew upon his tongue, and from his lips flow gracious words. All the people look towards him while he settles causes with true judgments: and he, speaking surely, would soon make wise end of a great quarrel;(81–87) . . . And when he passes through a gathering, they greet him as a god with gentle reverence, and he is conspicuous amongst the assembled: such is the holy gift of the Muses to men. For it is through the Muses and far-shooting Apollo that there are singers and harpers on the earth;(91–95) . . . though a man have sorrow and grief in his newly-troubled soul and live in dread because his heart is distressed, yet, when a singer, the servant of the Muses, chants the glorious deeds of men of old and the blessed gods who inhabit Olympus, at once he forgets his heaviness and remembers not his sorrows at all; but the gifts of the goddesses soon turn him away from these. Hail, children of Zeus! Grant lovely song and celebrate the holy race of the deathless gods. . . . Tell how at the first gods and earth came to be(98–108).[36]

The poet then proceeds to sing of the generation of the gods and consequently the first form of the world, the story of which can be summarized as follows. The first god to emerge is Chaos, then Gaia

(Earth) and Eros. Chaos brings forth Darkness and Night, who unite through the power of Eros and bring forth Aether and Day. Earth brings forth Uranus (Sky) and Pontus (Sea). Gaia and Uranus bring forth the Titans, who are hated and oppressed by their father. At the instigation of Gaia, the Titans revolt against Uranus. They are led by Kronos, who castrates his father. Kronos and Rhea unite and generate Hestia, Demeter, Poseidon, Hera, Hades, and Zeus. But Kronos, knowing he is to be overthrown by his children, devours them. Zeus, however, hidden in secret, grows to overthrow Kronos and the Titans, who are cast into the Underworld. Thus begins the Olympian rule of Zeus that dominates Greek mythology.

We must now explicate some of the important notions which lie within this mythical presentation. At the outset we are told that the first gods simply "came into being" (*genonto*). There is no mention of any prior cause. Consequently the *Theogony* is not strictly speaking a creation myth; the first gods simply *appear*; we are not told from where. For this reason the poem is better read as an expression of unconcealment rather than creation. The Greek sense of creation is never *ex nihilo* since the cosmos is never thought to have an absolute beginning. Rather, the artistic sense of creation, where form and order are brought forth from a formless state, better illustrates how the Greeks dealt with origins.[37]

We can speak to this point by considering the first of the sacred appearances in Hesiod's poem: Chaos. In this early mythical context, Chaos does not connote anything like disorder. It derives from the verb *chainō*, meaning to yawn or gape, and is best rendered as "yawning gap." In the setting of the poem Chaos presents a primal event, namely the original separation of Heaven and Earth, a mythical theme which is found throughout the world. But a connection can be found between the earlier and later meanings of the word chaos. The original separation of Heaven and Earth implies a primal state of unity before that demarcation. When we examine some of the first philosophers, we will see that this primal separation, which creates the distinction and relation between forms, has some connection with chaos in later usage. This is evident as long as we realize that chaos will not refer to a kind of anarchistic confusion of forms (i.e., disorder), but rather to a primal indeterminacy *preceding* the demarcation of forms as such. In this context we get a better reading of the chaos-cosmos distinction in Greek thought.

Next we must give some attention to important priorities disclosed in the sacred generations in Hesiod's poem. Earth appears before Heaven, and Night appears before Day. The priority of Earth is something that reflects the worldliness of Greek religion, but it will also become important when we try to understand the relation between, and status of, sacred forces in the Greek world. There is also something very significant which is implied in the priority of Night. If Night precedes and in fact gives birth to Day, we can see here the priority of the negative. In early Greek thought one theme that will be repeated is the precedence of negativity. We notice in Hesiod's poem—both in a general sense (the emergence of the first gods from something undetermined) and in specific instances like the priority of Night—that "non-being precedes being."[38]

But what are we to make of this precedence? Is it simply chronological? No. What comes first in the generations is also an origin. For the Greeks, beginnings and origins were identical, and origins were also responsible for and related to their progeny, as part of their maintenance. The Greek word embodying this point is *archē*, which can mean origin or beginning, but also sovereignty, dominion, and rule. Consequently the precedence of the negative would also be constitutive of the positive in some way. In the *Theogony* we find an interesting example in the description of the underworld. There (736ff.) we hear of a great empty gulf (*chasma*, related in meaning to *chaos*), in which no direction or bearing can be found, but which gives the "springs and limits" of all things. We can speak in the abstract of the notion of a negative limit which allows, by contrast, the boundaries of forms to take shape. As we have seen and will see, the positive role of a limit in the constitution of form was prominent in Greek thought. Here in the poem the implicit negativity of limit, of finitude as such, is given the sacred image of an *origin* (spring).

As a corollary to this issue, we should take notice of the other offspring of the goddess Night. We hear (211–12) that Night also gave birth to Doom, Fate, Death, Sleep, and Dreams. Furthermore (217–18) she bore the "ruthless, avenging Fates": Clotho (the spinner), Lachesis (the disposer of lots), and Atropos (the unturnable), who "give men at their birth both evil and good to have, and they pursue the transgressions of men and of gods" (219–20). Here we realize that both mortals *and* gods are subordinate to the terrible force of fate, which limits and thus determines the regions of all things through its destructive power. Greek gods are not omnipotent or omniscient; they can suffer and be deceived. Greek myth does not reflect any sense of unlimited power but rather a balance of powers.

A number of other important themes emerge in the *Theogony* when the relationships between the gods are considered as prefigurations of later developments in Greek thought. In general it can be said that these relationships present a primal tension between heaven and earth after their separation. With the castration of Uranus at the hands of Kronos, the devouring of Kronos's offspring, and the rebellion of Zeus against his Titan father, we witness the fundamental contest and alternation of power between Chthonic and Olympian forces that continued to animate Greek myth.

The theme of family killings and savage, bloody acts will form the basis of much of Greek poetry, especially tragedy, but myths of family strife should not be read as mere literary, psychological, or social allusions. The cosmic dimension of such imagery can be recognized if we generalize its implications into the following notion which will become prominent even in Greek philosophy, namely, the *opposition of related pairs*. The tension between and the balance of opposing forces (with balance stemming from some common bond) marks more than anything else the spirit of Greek thought and is exemplified in many different cultural forms.

Consider Zeus's victory over the earth-bound Titans. After a ten-year battle the forces of Zeus defeated Kronos and his followers, who were hurled into the underworld (Tartarus). Afterwards, Zeus sets up a trinity of power: Zeus (Olympus), Poseidon (Sea), and Hades (Underworld), each with his own domain to be respected by the others. Here we find mythical expression for the idea of justice as a balance and a cooperative recognition of limits that will characterize political, moral, and philosophical developments up through the Classical period.

And what of the Titans? Is Zeus completely victorious? Not really. His victory in fact simply creates a demarcation which will continue to exhibit a tension between opposing, though related, forces. It is true that the victory of the Olympian gods over the Titans represents what we often take to be the classic form of Greek culture, namely the victory of beauty, form, and moderation over animal brutishness. But the Olympians are a *second* generation. The force and influence of the Chthonic gods will always remain in the background. At times the powers of the underworld earth deities will even come to the foreground, as in the case of tragedy. We can say in a generalized way, therefore, that the tension between nature and culture continued to be seen as an alternation of *sacred* elements in the world, each with its authority and importance. These elements did not represent separate forces, since there was continuing interpenetration between them. The balance between nature and culture did begin to come apart somewhat in later philosophical developments, but the familial nature of this relationship was rarely, if ever, lost to the Greeks.[39]

# III

## Epic Poetry

In this chapter we will be dealing primarily with Homer's *Iliad*.[1] I am not going to engage the so-called Homeric question, namely the problems concerning whether the epic poems are the work of one writer, the relation between the written poems as we have them and earlier oral epics, or the connection between the poems and actual history, among other questions. I say this not because such problems are unimportant but because for the purposes of this study we simply have to deal with the poetry we do have and try to interpret its place in Greek cultural history.[2] In referring to Homer we simply name a poetic complex which at least represents the earliest linguistic documents we have and which can therefore be read in relation to later poetry regarding the development of cultural ideals in Greek history. I do assume, however, a number of conclusions that seem to find general acceptance among classical scholars: We can place Homer in the eighth century B.C., prior to Hesiod; the poetry does display a deep connection with an oral tradition; and the *Odyssey* is in most respects a later poem than the *Iliad*.

## The World in Epic Poetry

The epic world is a lived world with the matrix of man, god, beast, and nature presented as a constellation of sacred powers. We find no judgment, criticism, or justification of the world, but simply the lived environment presented as such, devoid of abstract order or otherworldly control. The best illustration of the epic world can be found in the *Iliad*, XVIII.478–616, where the great shield of Achilles is described, a beautiful depiction of early Greek culture in miniature form. Humans are placed in the natural order of sun, sea, sky, and earth; there are marriage festivals and other celebrations; the gods, larger in scale, display their power over mortals; warriors terrorize shepherds, showing an aristocratic order of power; bloody battles among rival cities are fought; other scenes show the common man farming the earth and shepherds trying to protect their animals from beasts of prey.

Although the epic world is a multifarious world of lived experience, Homeric poetry still displays an order or sense. A mythical structure of existential meaning dominates the *Iliad*. Human beings and events find their place in relation to sacred powers. When we compare Homer to other mythical traditions, we find that the *Iliad* stands somewhere between more primitive cultures and later, more rational developments. For example, there is not much evidence of magical belief and practice in Homer. Sacred forces do not reside utterly beyond the ken of humans, requiring ceremonies to tap dark and mysterious powers. In the *Iliad* the sacred takes the luminous form of gods whose thoughts and actions appear to humans and with whom they can converse and relate. Although epic order is disclosed in a sacred form and therefore not yet solely in the human mind, nevertheless the imagery and accessibility of divine thought and action shows that Homer stands somewhere between the primitive and the rational.[3] The epic view of the world gathers an archaic past and is also *continued* in various ways in postepic developments of thought.

Another important feature of the epic world, therefore, is the specific form that the sacred takes. Here we face the question of how Homeric poetry reflects the Olympian-Titan distinction sketched earlier. It is evident that the *Iliad* represents the predominance of Olympian gods over the earth-bound Titans. If we recall the distinction between Chthonic and Olympian deities in terms of certain archetypal dualities—earth and sky, death and immortality, excess and moderation, feminine and masculine—then the Olympian emphasis in Homer is clear. Dionysus, an important Chthonic god, is mentioned but does not figure in the Homeric world. We find there no excess of passion or madness in its deities, and no "dying gods." Only moderation, luminosity, and the ideal of intelligence seem to predominate. Archetypally, the atmosphere is generally masculine; even some of the goddesses are primarily masculine in nature. Consider Athena. She has no mother; her epithet is *Parthenos* or Virgin; she is marked by her intelligence and serves to inspire courage and skill in battle.

But it is a mistake to assume that the Chthonic influence is absent in the *Iliad* or that Homeric religion is a complete repudiation of the earth deities. Homer's poem no more eliminates them than his tale of the heroes eliminates the common man. Olympian immortality and the subsequent demarcation of human mortality, and thus the fateful horizon of death which accounts for the dramatic and religious tension in the epic, reflect the fundamental Greek experience of an opposition of life and death which is personified in the Olympian-Chthonic distinction. The forceful presence of death, over which the Olympian gods have no power, represents the continuing and pervasive authority of the Chthonic earth religion, even though its deities do not appear on the epic stage.

We can develop this point by addressing the question of fate and its status in Homeric poetry. Fate in Greek is *moira*, derived from the verb *meirō*, meaning to allot or apportion. Versenyi tells us that what makes allotment so fateful is that the Greeks conceived it in the past perfect. In other words, fate has already been set and irrevocably so.[4] But it would be wrong to think of fate in Homer as a form of predestination similar to later notions of religious determinism, where every detail of life is preconceived in the mind of God. First of all, fate is impersonal in Homer. Secondly, fate does not generally refer to specific circumstances and their details but rather to a general sense of inevitability. In this regard fate in Homer is usually connected with death or catastrophe, though it can be seen in a larger sense as encompassing all *limits*. In general, then, fate is an impersonal power which seems to designate the force of *negativity* in the world. It arises almost always as a constraint, a "slayer," and even when it brings good fortune it is often still described in the negative ("it was not yet his fate to fall").[5]

Fate implies a kind of order in the world, which could be considered a preconceptual version of a regulative order which later came to be seen as rational or natural "law." The differences, of course, are many. Fate presents itself only in existentially significant events and therefore is not an abstract order applicable to all events as such. Fate is always a specific apportionment (the "whole" of fate is never named[6]), but that it is a kind of impersonal necessity over which humans have no control shows at least an analogous connection with later conceptions of law. The workings of fate, even retributions for its violation, exhibit no volition or conscious motivation but rather, so to speak, an automatic regulative balance in the world.

The impersonal and negative character of fate helps us understand the ambiguous relationship between the gods and fate in Homer. At times the gods are seen as the disposers of fate, especially when they control or direct the lives of men. They also have the power to prevent that which seeks to go beyond fate. But in other respects, the gods appear to have no power over fate, especially when it comes to death. We can generalize and say that in matters of life and action the gods seem to embody the forces of fate; but as far as death is concerned, even the gods acknowledge a limit to their power.[7] Thus it would seem that the tension between the Olympian immortals and the fated mortality of human beings indicates that a negative fate has a certain priority in epic poetry, which therefore displays the authority of Chthonic forces even in the midst of Olympian rule.

Moreover, the power of fate can be applied to one of my remarks in the first chapter: that despite mythical pluralism a certain feel for an overall, mysterious unity can be implicit. If even the gods must yield to a dark, negative force which appears impersonal, then perhaps we can recognize a sense for an inchoate unity, even though it is never explicitly articulated and epic visibility breaks it up into pluralized appearances of particular fates. To conclude, the phenomenon of fate in epic poetry allows us to establish two significant assumptions that will remain important for our understanding of Greek culture: (1) the priority of a negative force in the world, and (2) the implicit sense of a unified, impersonal order.

# The Self in Epic Poetry

After considering the Homeric world, we now need to understand how human beings fit into that world. Many of the clues regarding their nature and place have already been established because, as we have remarked earlier, a mythical world and human nature do not represent a strict demarcation but rather an interpenetrative field. There are three aspects of Homeric poetry that can give us access to the epic sense of human nature: the heroic ideal, the noncentralized self, and the god-man relation. Our treatment of these features will show that the epic self is essentially social, noninteriorized, and finite.

## THE HEROIC IDEAL

Even though there has come to light much evidence that there actually was a Troy and that therefore the *Iliad* has some connection with historical events, nevertheless it must be realized that the primary aim of the epic is not a historical account of the Trojan War. The *Iliad*, as myth, is meant to disclose a sacred meaning. It does not begin with the initiation of the war, nor does it end with the completion of the war. In fact, if we stay strictly within the parameters of the poem, there seems to be no fundamental change from its beginning to the middle and end.[8] The reason is that the Trojan War is only a setting for something larger and more sacred, namely, the fate of Achilles. Achilles represents a primary cultural ideal of the time, the heroic life. It is the sacred dimension of heroism and the forms of the hero that dominate the *Iliad*, not profane, objective events. Only one character, Thersites, is given what could be called a direct, realistic description (II.215–220); but he is the antithesis of heroic stature. The heroes are always presented as larger than life, through similes and exalted comparisons; we never hear ordinary, matter-of-fact descriptions. But the presence of Thersites shows that the poet is well aware of ordinary, commonsense matters (the profane). His aim, however, is to bring forth the sacred dimension of heroism, which represents the only *culturally* significant matter.

If we want to know why heroism is a sacred phenomenon, we have to understand its existential context and its "extraordinary" character. Taking Achilles as an exemplar, it can generally be said that the hero faces a crucial paradox: the pursuit of glory leads to death, which thus precludes a long life. This was the dilemma Achilles faced; he knew he was fated to die in battle and yet his accomplishments in war were the very meaning of his life and the source of his stature. With this as a background let us now try to delineate the specific features of the hero and his situation.

The hero complex can be characterized by the following sequence of cultural assumptions: (1) Human beings are essentially mortal and subject to fate: "As is the generation of leaves, so is that of humanity" (VI.146); ". . . as for fate [*moira*], I think no man yet has escaped it once it has taken its first form, neither brave man nor coward" (VI.488–489). (2) Although a man's ultimate fate is death, he can receive the worldly compensation of honor and a kind of immortality through glory and fame. (3) Honor, glory, and fame can be achieved only by risking one's life and facing death on the battlefield. (4) The courage to face death and risk one's life isolates and alienates the hero from the normal course of life, but it also elevates the hero above the rest of humanity, giving him his station and status as protector, defender, and noble exemplar.

It is evident that this sequence in the heroic complex contains an existential paradox: heroic values are incongruous with that which is *normally* most desirable—life and comfort. Cultural excellence in the Homeric world demands that the hero risk and sacrifice that which is normally most dear to humans. In sum, then, the heroic ideal represents the achievement of excellence (specifically warrior values) *despite* death and other terrible limits. It is the paradox of the hero that makes the *Iliad* tragic in some respects, and later we will address the links between epic poetry and tragic drama.

The best illustration of the heroic response to this existential paradox can be found in Book XII. At one point (244) Hektor asks a hesitant warrior: "Why are you so afraid of war and hostility?" For us that is surely a strange question, but the heroic rationale for such a question is given a short time later (310–328), when Sarpedon speaks to Glaukos before engaging in battle. His speech is actually a form of encouragement to stand fast in the midst of the paradox. Why, he asks, are we honored above all men and rewarded with wealth, station, land, and even "the choice meats"? Because the mass of men appreciate and pay homage to the courage and sacrifice of the warrior, defender of home and country. The hero's risk is therefore the source of his nobility and subsequent privilege. Thus if they wish to uphold their claim to nobility and its rewards, it is their *duty* to fight. But what about death? Sarpedon's speech discloses the positive aspects of the heroic paradox with surprising insight. He says that nobility and mortality are of one piece. He asks, suppose we were immortal? But then we would not *strive* for glory which is the source of our station. In other words, it is mortality which constitutes the *value* of courage, honor, and glory in battle, i.e., noble values. Sarpedon makes a lot of sense. In a world where no one died, the need for protection and the subsequent rewards for heroic risk would be absent. All people would be on a common footing and noble privilege would disappear. So a true hero would face death with a kind of fatalistic willingness. Listen to the stirring conclusion of Sarpedon's speech:

> *But now, seeing that the spirits of death stand close about us*
> *in their thousands, no man can turn aside or escape them,*
> *let us go on and win glory for ourselves, or yield it to others.*

(326–328)[9]

Glory and fame supply the epic compensations for mortality.[10] In fact mortality prompts these noble aims. Since life cannot endure, fame is the only form of endurance which fills in the void of meaninglessness that death represents. So the only alternative to meaninglessness is glory, the rewards of which are both temporary (privilege) and lasting (fame). The ordinary man cannot achieve such compensation, and therefore his life is ultimately meaningless, which accounts for the sense of pride, rank, and distaste for the common typical of aristocratic cultures like that depicted in the *Iliad*. But again, nobility is constituted by a paradox: to acquire compensations for the meaninglessness of death one must *face* death; to live the noble life one must *risk* one's life.

Heroism thus defines the cultural values of the epic period. The Greek word *aretē* referred to this noble complex of excellence. The later meaning of *aretē* as "virtue" does not do justice to this original meaning because of certain moralistic connotations which came to repudiate many heroic values. But we can retain the term virtue if we realize that the epic period represented a different sense of virtue—values associated with war, violence, and death. Even today we recognize that in many respects the wartime virtues of the soldier are the vices of peacetime.

In any case, *aretē* is better rendered as "excellence" because it captures the uncommon achievement and aristocratic rewards, like honor, which characterize the values of the epic world. Jaeger claims that not only Greek culture but all culture begins with some kind of aristocratic ideal.[11] One way of understanding this is through the connection between culture and myth. If myth forms a culture by presenting the sacred, and if the sacred is characterized by uncommonness, then in the social sphere those who live close to the sacred will take their cultural place above common people. In this regard, it should be recognized that the *Iliad* does not represent the entire life of the epic period but rather its cultural *ideals*. The heroic aristocracy was therefore a form of selection. The common man certainly existed, but off on the sidelines, culturally insignificant at this point.[12] It will become evident later that one important factor in the cultural changes of the Greek world was the ascendancy of the common man, with a subsequently different set of values leading to a different sense of culture.

## THE NONCENTRALIZED SELF

If we recall the previously mentioned criteria for the modern view of self-identity—unity, interiority, and autonomy—we must say that epic heroes are in many respects alien beings. The language of the *Iliad* gives us little evidence for what we would call self-consciousness. It might be easy to conclude that there is no self at all in epic poetry, but that would be misleading. One thing is certain, however. Whatever sense of self there is in Homer must initially be understood in *contrast* to modern criteria for self-identity. I think that in some loose way we can call the Homeric hero a self, but in a markedly different sense than certain modern assumptions about selfhood.

With regard to the notion of unity, we find in Homer no abstract concepts expressing a common essence, since lived experience is the measure, preceding abstraction and requiring a pluralized response. We have already mentioned Snell's comments about body references being an aggregate of distinct functions and not an abstract whole.[13] Here are some examples: ". . . I knew easily as he went away the form of his feet, the legs' form from behind him" (XIII.70–72); ". . . my feet underneath me are eager and hands above them" (XIII.75); ". . . he saw that these were enemy men, and moved his knees rapidly to run away" (X.358). One might argue that a reference to "his" knees implies a bodily whole. I tend to agree. Such a reference implies *something* other than sheer discontinuity. But there is no explicit use of an abstract concept of "body" with all that *that* implies about whole-part relations, essence-function distinctions, and so on.

Turning to soul or mind references, which would better serve a discussion of self, we also find no mention in Homer of a common faculty to unite mental functions. We find instead distinct words referring to distinct functions: *psychē* as "life force," *thymos* as the source of emotion and agitation, *noos* as the receptacle of ideas and images, these being the more frequent and important words.[14] *Psychē*, *thymos*, and *noos* appear as separate organs, so to speak, and not as aspects of a common soul. I agree with Snell that the notion of organ often used to designate such functions is highly misleading. There is some justification for this usage in that the analogy between physical organs and Homeric mental functions reveals a good deal. Each function has a distinct place and effect in the overall complex of experience. There is no one soul which lives, thinks, and feels. Rather, *psychē* lives, *noos* thinks, and *thymos* feels.[15] And just as physical organs do not encroach upon each other's limits, there is no unitary mind with divided aims or mixed feelings, but rather two different units presenting a conflict.[16]

But to assume that these functions *are* physical organs is going too far, because the way such words are used (e.g., the *psychē* leaving the body at death, the *thymos* being filled with joy) clearly indicates something other than a physical object. But often we hear of the breast and heart, for example, in such contexts. What then? I think the best answer draws on the sacred-profane distinction. The *thymos*, seemingly located in the chest, neither is nor is not a physical object. In the lived context of the sacred there is neither a departure from the physical world nor a concern with mere profane objects, but rather the disclosure of existential *meaning* within the world. So the excitation of the *thymos* both is and is not in the chest. One can feel the physical palpitations of joy, but as the phenomenon of *joy* it is not something to be found by opening the chest. Only the sacred-profane distinction can help us here. The abstract concepts of "physical" and "mental" are not yet a factor in the Homeric world. Since the sacred is the extraordinary, revealed in lived experience and not yet abstracted from the concrete, it can have both a physical and nonphysical tone. Therefore I would say that the so-called mental organs in Homer refer to distinct existential advents such as emotions, surges of energy, ideas, and life, each of which has its own significance and is consequently localized in language: *psychē, thymos, noos*, and so on.

To sum up thus far, in Homer there is no evidence for the general distinction between soul and body, each distinct from the other and uniform in nature. Such notions were discovered and developed after Homer. Later writers will begin to talk of the soul as something separate from the body. Later poets will describe different feelings as different aspects of a unified self. But in Homer we find nothing more than different functions of lived experience. For instance, joy is not described in terms of a person who experiences joy as an "attribute" of a unified self. Rather, joy is the excitation of the *thymos*. Furthermore, we often hear a man addressing one of the organs as if it were a separate person (e.g., Achilles speaks to his own heart, XVIII.5). Consequently there seems to be no abstract sense of unity in the Homeric self.[17]

The next criterion of self-identity not exhibited in Homer is autonomy. Any extraordinary augmentation of physical or mental power is presented as divine intervention. Some examples: "not without god does he rage so" (V.185); "Ares the dangerous war god entered him, so that the inward body [*hoi mele' entos*: the limbs within] was packed full of force and fighting strength" (XVII.210–12); "Poseidon . . . striking both of them with his staff filled them with powerful valour" (XIII.59–60). There seems to be no self-willed change in Homer. Or better put, the cause of any *important* change is a deity. Any bewilderment of normal awareness, which is how Dodds interprets *ate*,[18] is attributed to a god. Once again the sacred-profane distinction helps us avoid a lot of confusion about the absence of autonomy in Homeric he-

roes. In *extraordinary* advents of feeling or thought we find a disruption of either normal consciousness or awareness of ordinary events
and one's everyday personality or self (i.e., the profane). Dodds gives
an account of the phenomenological sense of such situations:

> The recognition, the insight, the memory, the brilliant or perverse
> idea, have this in common, that they come suddenly, as we say, "into a
> man's head." Often he is conscious of no observation or reasoning
> which has led up to them. But in that case, how can he call them "his"?
> A moment ago they were not in his mind; now they are there. Some-
> thing has put them there, and that something is other than himself.
> More than this he does not know. So he speaks of it non-committally as
> "the gods," or more often (especially when its prompting has turned
> out to be bad) as a daemon.[19]

The important point here is that the Homeric heroes were not au-
tomatons (their heroic risk, for example, is freely chosen). Although
the idea of divine intervention is unfamiliar to us, the phenomenon of
something coming into one's mind from who-knows-where is not.
Agamemnon is not entirely different from us, but what *is* different is
that the modern conception and feeling of self-consciousness is not in
place there as a criterion for understanding experience. The cultural
meaning of human experience is not *centered* in a conscious self or interpreted according to assumptions about abstract unity, interiority, or
autonomy (assumptions which make *our* view of the self fuzzy when
something like a sudden insight occurs). Whatever sense of self can be
found in Homer, it is not limited to consciousness. The primary meaning of experience is found in *disruptions* of normal consciousness,
culturally presented as sacred intervention.

One can certainly imagine the following exchange among Homeric
heroes: "Are you Achilles?" "Yes, I am." This surely implies some sense
of self-awareness. Achilles was not a robot with no degree of control
over his actions or sense of identity. At the same time, however, if a
modern observer entered the epic scene and suggested to Achilles that
the full range of his experience was centered in his own identity, he
might reply: "But that is not what my life is like!" His life is experienced as frequent disruptions of his Achilles-identity in crucial
situations.

Nonetheless, one may easily raise the following objection. Can we
not assume that the real-life heroes of the epic age experienced the
world just as we do? Perhaps Homer simply introduced poetic embel-

lishments for dramatic or religious purposes, or simply used poetic analogies to dress up natural situations of compulsion and overwhelming emotion that we describe in a less figurative way. There is no way to absolutely prove this objection wrong, but I think there are good reasons for laying it aside. First of all, the language of Homer is the only access we have to the epic world. Homeric poetry presents disruptions of consciousness as real events in the lives of its heroes. There is no evidence for the use of analogy or poetic invention in the description of the heroes' behavior and reactions. Although, as I have tried to show, there are some ways in which the epic self is similar to the modern self, nevertheless the phenomenon of compulsion by a sacred power beyond the self so pervades the *Iliad* that the nonsacred phenomena required to measure the proposed analogous nature of Homer's imagery are not at hand. We often use poetic analogies, metaphors, or personalizations to describe phenomena, but we also recognize them as such by using terms such as "like," "as if," and so on. But Homer does not say Achilles flew into a rage "as if" possessed by a god; he says a god filled Achilles with rage. At least with regard to extraordinary phenomena, Homeric language presents no alternative to divine intervention as a genuine form of experience. To call it a mere figure of speech would betray an external interpretation of the *Iliad*.

Of course it is hard for us to imagine human experience actually being the way it is described in the poem, but the alternative view raised in the objection seems to me more speculative than attending to epic language as it is.[20] The objection would imply that there always has been a unified, interiorized, autonomous human self, but for some reason Homer either could not or would not express it. This seems rather strange. If there is no linguistic expression of some cultural phenomenon, on what grounds can we infer its existence? Surely, later in Greek history, linguistic references to a form of self-identity more familiar to us did find expression. But not so in Homer. The wealth of divine intervention references indicates that in the epic age, the self was most often experienced in the midst of extraconscious, sacred invasions.

The last criterion for self-identity not evident in Homer is interiority. There seems to be no private, internal self underlying the varying aspects of experience. The epic shows a man always in *relation* to others and the world situations in which he acts, never isolated in pure privacy behind his actions. Fränkel sums this up by calling the Homeric self a "field of energy."[21] The absence of interiority helps us make much better sense out of certain aspects of heroic behavior in the *Iliad*. The heroes are not shown to have secrets, concealed motives, or emotions. Whatever feelings arise are immediately expressed.[22] They fly into a rage, cry, or rejoice at the drop of a hat. They do not practice deception, which would require a distinction between inner thoughts and outward behavior.[23] Furthermore, the heroes remain fundamentally unchanged and thus exhibit no "growth of character," which would imply a hidden, though present, potential.[24] But the most significant element of the *Iliad* which is rendered more comprehensible in this way is the almost obsessive concern with honor (*timē*) in the context of praise and reward. With no interior self, the hero cannot be satisfied with his "own" sense of accomplishment. Honor must be externalized, hence all the worry over tangible prizes and payment (even among the gods). The excessive competitiveness of Homeric heroes follows quite naturally, since *aretē* can be measured only in relation to others and public action. It might be said that the withdrawal of Achilles and his refusal to fight represents an exception to the proposed lack of interiority in epic heroes. But what brought on his withdrawal was Agamemnon's seizure of Briseis, Achilles's concubine. What would seem relatively trivial to us was a serious threat to the Homeric sense of honor, which is thoroughly immersed in the public and tangible realm. It would do no good to ask Achilles to "swallow" his pride or realize his worth despite the loss of his prize. For Achilles there is no internal compensation. The public event *constitutes* his sense of self.

We find in Homer, therefore, not a private but a *social* self, which continued to be an important mark of Greek culture. It could even be said that the Homeric self represents a primitive analogue of modern interpersonal models of the self.[25] In any case, Homeric values are defined by "publicity, surface visibility, and disclosure, the outer image rather than a hidden substance."[26] Epic morality is shown in its standards for *aretē*, which include honor, beauty, pride, courage, and fame. Such values reflect physical form, worldly achievement, and, most importantly, interpersonal recognition. For this reason epic heroes were subject only to shame as a form of moral enforcement. Just as one's honor is constituted by recognition from others, so too the possibility of recognition is enough to dissuade one from an ignoble deed. But without publicity there is no evaluation; hence "guilt" is an alien phenomenon in the epic world. Guilt implies an internal experience of values independent of what you do in the world or what other people think.

Guilt also carries a number of assumptions about where value is to be found. In other words, guilt is not only an internal perception, it also implies an internal standard of values. It is for this reason that later forms of morality would find heroic behavior and attitudes immoral in many respects, or at least misguided. Pride and a desire for fame become vices in later moralities. Preoccupation with beauty becomes an obstacle to true moral worth. Medieval writers could not understand why Aristotle, who in some ways inherited epic values, considered courage a virtue and pride the prerogative of the good man. What we have here is not a moral versus an immoral world but two different standards of value and meaning, one more internalized and spiritualized, the other completely embedded in the lived world of visibility, action, accomplishment, and social relationships. Otto even goes so far as to chide us for our denigration of mythical values in epic poetry:

> If in the old conception of existence inward man had no myth to himself, this means that he was entirely integrated, in a single and complete configuration, with the warp and woof of the myth of the world. His experiences are no property of his soul, anchored in deep solitude or in a formless beyond kindred to the soul, but a portion of the world which has its place and its meaning in the great myth of the world. Hence there is no lack of depth, as we may like to think. For here the sensitivity with which we scrutinize the soul's depths is directed to the world and its configurations. . . .[27]

The relative merits of these different notions of the self and its place in the world will become a significant issue as the course of this investigation proceeds.

Concerning the noncentralized self, I think it would be wrong to say that Homeric heroes exhibit *no* unity, autonomy, or interiority at any time or in any way. There are some instances in the *Iliad* where action displays a combination of self-effort and divine intervention. For example: "He will fight again, whenever the heart in his body [*thymos*] urges him to, and the god drives him" (IX.702–703). Also, there is an occasion where Odysseus ponders two courses of action within himself (V.671). And at one point we hear of Paris being shaken by fear, with no apparent divine intervention (III.30–35). But a few remarks are in order. These instances still do not explicitly portray a unified self: The "heart in his *thymos*" prompts courage; Odysseus's pondering is between his *noos* and *thymos*; Paris's heart is shaken. Furthermore,

Odysseus's divided course of action is resolved not by himself, but by Athene (V.676).

But we should conclude that the gods are not behind every action and event, only those of highest value and importance. Epic life seems to be a mixture of human and metahuman forces, the latter being of greater importance and presented as divine. Once again, the sacred-profane distinction illuminates the extent to which the epic self is or is not the measure of action. The heroes are not puppets but vehicles for sacred intervention when the situation calls for it. When something extraordinary occurs, it presents itself as something extraconscious and supraindividual. So far as autonomy is concerned, there may be degrees of self-effort in the profane dimension,[28] but the sacred is shown as a disruption of self-effort.

As for interiority, I think it is the attribute for which little or no evidence can be found in Homer, at least not for the kind of interiority implied in the notion of a private, subjective self. But some sense of interiority is displayed when we hear of the *thymos* or the *noos* "within" him. There are obvious connections between Homeric language and later developments of self-consciousness. For example, the visual function of *noos* can be found in the later visual metaphors that figure in our mental language (seeing the point, being bright, clarity of mind, and so forth). Also, the many examples of emotions or thoughts being put "in" *noos*, *thymos*, and the like, can be seen as forerunners of the interior mind "space" of modern consciousness. But again, we find in Homer no overall unity or complete interiority comparable to the modern self.

When we hear about the *noos* "within him" and "his" *thymos*, however, we should recoil from the suggestion that the epic self was an utterly fragmented, disconnected set of functions. Such linguistic references are not simply grammatical in nature. The form of life and behavior in the epic indicates that *some* form of unity and wholeness is present there, if only in the fact that the heroes were named and distinguished from one another. Therefore we must conclude that the Homeric self was some sort of whole, but *not* in the pure sense of modern, highly abstract assumptions about a unified self "behind" its actions or functions. Rather, we can see epic selfhood as an *existential* whole, which even we recognize without concerning ourselves with a metaphysical unity behind the multifarious display of human behavior and experience. The epic self is a *lived matrix*, not an abstract unity distinct from its functions. So we can talk of selfhood in Homer, but as an existential self it presents itself phenomenologically as contextual and pluralized.

Perhaps I can complete this point by returning to my example of Achilles and name recognition. I argued that Achilles's response to and use of his name indicates some form of self-awareness. But we cannot go too far and claim that naming can suggest a unitary self in the modern sense. If we stick to the context of Homeric poetry, we find that names still suggest a contextual self because of the ever-present epithets accompanying names: I am X the swift, the sacker of cities. I am X the leader of A, the son of B, the favorite of god C, the doer of such and such. I believe that the fixed epithets are not simply metrical devices or formalities. Rather they show in another way the contextual and pluralized shape of human experience in the epic period, a time in which a man's sense of himself was deeply embedded in and constituted by the lived world and the phenomenon of the sacred.

There are good reasons for focusing only on the *Iliad* in this discussion of the Homeric self. The *Odyssey* exhibits much more self-willed activity as well as the first recognizable contours of interiority. The character of Odysseus is the key here. His display of craft and deception, which, as we have noted, implies a distinction between inner thoughts and external appearance, gives Odysseus a form of internal detachment from the world matrix not found in the *Iliad*. Furthermore, the following passage from the *Odyssey* indicates the embryonic shape of autonomy in the making: "I do not know whether some god moved him, or whether his own mind had the impulse to go to Pylos" (IV.712–13). But since the *Odyssey* is generally considered to be a later composition than the *Iliad*, we can conclude that the relationship between the two poems represents among other things a transition from a noncentralized self to a more centralized self.[29]

## THE DIVINE–HUMAN RELATION

Among mortals, the heroes are the closest to the gods. They move within a god-directed field, and to ordinary men they appear most godlike. The gods invite and appreciate the risks and challenges that constitute heroic action. Even though the heroes are subjected to fate and death, the beauty and power of the gods transform epic fatalism into a world redeemed by sacred values. The gods, therefore, represent centers of power and value to which mortals are subjected and within which epic sacrifices become a positive *integration* into a larger, sacred world. In other words, within the context of selfhood, the gods and fate characterize the following view in epic poetry. Human beings exist in the midst of a suprahuman field, and the highest ideals are shaped in terms of a disruption or dissipation of the normal, profane self. Both the hero's willingness for death and his "transparency" to sacred intervention show that epic cultural ideals involve the continuing sacrifice of the "human" as well as certain fixed limits to human aspiration and power.[30]

The mark of sacred value in the epic world is power. The degrees of and limits to human power present another perspective from which we can understand the human relation to the sacred. Versenyi sums it up well:

> The words *theos, dios, theios* in the *Iliad* are not synonymous with our word divine; they mean powerful, mighty, excellent, awful, marvelous. This is why not only gods but also men and even animals and inanimate objects can be "divine" insofar as they exhibit a more-than-usual excellence in their particular function. The difference between gods and men, and everything else, with respect to divinity, is by no means absolute. It is merely a difference of degree. The gods are more powerful than men, and the more powerful, the more divine.[31]

It is in the light of such a power principle that we can appreciate the later charges of immorality or amorality with respect to epic behavior. But as we have said, the power principle does not represent an absence or violation of moral values, only a different morality. In the epic world, whatever displays power is sacred and therefore worthy of respect; whatever enhances power is good. For this reason, even terrible things in the epic are divine; and a show of mercy by a god can even be considered unjust if it would result in a diminution of power. Furthermore, the power principle is generic, which helps us understand the typical heroic respect for the enemy:

> Father Zeus, watching over us from Ida, most high, most honored, grant that Ajax win the vaunt of renown and the victory; but if truly you love Hektor and are careful for him, give to both of them equal strength, make equal their honor. (VII.202–205)

Later (285–300), Hektor and Ajax stop their fight and agree to a postponement, so that they can "fight again until the divinity chooses between us" (291–92). Then they exchange gifts! The battle, therefore, does not seem to be personal or fought out of hatred. The contest for power and excellence itself seems to motivate the heroes. The causes of the war and personal antagonisms seem incidental and can easily be suspended in favor of mutual respect. Combat represents an opportunity for glory, and glory does not seem to be a selfish pursuit since the heroes are so easily able to defer and yield honor to an enemy.

We see here another example of the noncentralized character of epic experience and the noninternalization of values. The soundness of such a model can be further illustrated by attending to the emotional behavior of Homeric heroes. In general emotional responses are completely embedded in world circumstances and therefore have a decidedly outward direction, as opposed to internalized emotions which can live on independent of their situational origin. For example, anger is displayed but does not seem to be internalized into hatred; there is sorrow, but not its internalization into despair; fear, but not anxiety. The heroes leap from joy to sorrow as soon as circumstances so dictate. There does not seem to be the lasting presence of emotions which would reside in the person and color his view of the world from that standpoint. True, Achilles lingers in anger, but this is because of the lasting circumstance of his loss to Agamemnon. Homeric heroes do not appear to be psychologically constituted to carry a grudge beyond the settlement of a dispute.

But I think the most significant example of this noninternalization model is to be found in the response to defeat. The heroes are continually subjected to failure, not to mention the ultimate defeat of death, yet if there is one quality entirely absent in the *Iliad*, it is a sense of wretchedness. Though much is said of the limits of human power, helplessness, and suffering, this is never taken to the extreme of despising life or declaring the baseness of humanity. We find the hero proud even in defeat and disaster. This might seem startling except that the noncentralization of experience renders such a response to defeat quite fitting. With divine control, human action is part of a larger order; in the midst of that action *field*, suffering cannot be internalized, or at least cannot be sealed off from the outer world matrix. Seeing his life compelled by sacred, extrahuman forces, a hero's downfall is in the order of things and is not therefore internalized so as to be a measure of ultimate worth. Hence there can be pride even in defeat, and, as we have seen, honor for one's victorious enemy.

As a result, the use of the term "failure" is really misplaced. It would seem that failure presupposes the possibility of success (it would be odd to say that one failed to walk through a brick wall). It is better to stay with the terms "victory" and "defeat," which, because of divine management, are not ultimately in human control and therefore not a sign of human failure. It would be wrong, however, to say there is no sense of responsibility in the epic. There is responsibility in the sense of accountability, accepting the consequences of one's actions. But responsibility here is purely circumstantial and is measured simply by participation in events. There is no sense of personal responsibility, implying an *internal* placement of causality. For this reason guilt finds no place in the *Iliad*, nor the subsequent sense of wretchedness or self-denigration. Here we find a clear link with tragedy, in that a classic tragic theme will involve suffering the consequences of something over which one has no control (i.e., justified punishment without guilt). At any rate, our model for epic selfhood, namely a noncentralized, sacred "field," enables us to uncover the cultural sense of and structural rationale for perhaps the most striking quality of the epic attitude—the noble acceptance of fate without rebellion, despair, or resentment.

Consequently, a fatalistic view of the world need not entail a depressive form of life denial. The atmosphere of a *positive* fatalism can readily be found in many aspects of epic poetry. We have seen that the immortality of the gods sharpens the sense of human mortality, which can consequently magnify the urgent importance and value of human pursuits. The Greeks seem to display a peculiarly affirmative response to fatalism, where a tragic sense of mortality promotes a heightened appreciation for life. An interesting example can be found in the *Iliad* (III.437–446). Paris has just confronted death through a duel with Menelaus, and will soon have to do so again. In the interim he speaks to Helen, who begs him to give up the fight. Paris rebukes his wife but asks her to go to bed with him, saying: "Never before as now has passion enmeshed my senses," never more "did I love you and sweet desire seize me." There are countless examples in human life of such a response in times of danger or war, but I think the Greeks more than any other culture were inclined to such a positive appropriation of life's terrible negativity.

To conclude this section, I would like to make two observations which have a bearing on succeeding material. We have seen that the epic self is enmeshed in a sacred field; this does not make mortals, as such, divine; it simply shows human dependency on sacred forces. The *distinction* between the human and the divine is constantly maintained, especially in the separation of mortality and immortality. Furthermore, Homeric religion presents a divine "command" that mortals stay within their limits, as in Apollo's admonition:

Take care, give back, son of Tydeus, and strive no longer to make yourself like the gods in mind (*phroneein*), since never the same is the breed of gods, who are immortal, and men who walk groundling. (V.440–43)

Humans err if they try to penetrate the divine realm by denying their fatedness or seeking complete control over their life.[32] But we should notice something here. Homeric religion commands that we stay within our bounds and limit our energy and understanding to ourselves. Should we not detect here a clear link between early Greek religion and Greek "humanism"? The Greek emphasis on humans in the natural world gave birth to the disciplines of science, politics, literature, and philosophy in the way we have come to understand them, that is, not as a revelation from or expectations of another world, but the human cultivation of this world. But it is Greek *religion* which sets the stage through its strict demarcation of the human and the divine, and the imperative that we not cross that boundary.

It should also be pointed out that such a demarcation did not suggest a complete separation of man and god. There were not two utterly different worlds, one human, another divine, but rather one world with two dimensions. Human form and divine form were not dissimilar, and human life was enmeshed in sacred powers. The point is that when Greek culture did turn from religion toward its so-called humanistic developments, even then the break was not complete, because certain links with past cultural forms are evident. When the Greeks discovered the human mind as such, and the shape of self-consciousness and rationality began to crystallize, there was at least an analogous relationship between the new self and the old god-man complex. The self emerged as a unitary whole to be distinguished from its different functions as well as its physical neighbor, the body. The modern concept of mind involves certain qualities—responsibility for decisions and actions, internal debate with itself, ethical and rational "commands" which direct other facets of the person—qualities which can be seen as the *internalization* of a previous god-man relation. The new self in relation to the epic self could be described as man becoming his own god.[33] Plato and Aristotle continued to view mind and/or soul as divine, though in a different form, of course, than Homer. The conclusion to be drawn is this: Mythical structure was not obliterated by philosophy but rather reconstituted according to certain new assumptions. Specifically, the relationship between Homer and later philosophy is not one of complete opposition but rather transition. The philosophers presented a new formulation of certain cultural patterns that were first *established* in Homeric mythology.

## The Beginnings of a Break
## with the Epic World

At some point in the eighth century B.C., writing entered the Greek cultural scene. The impact of writing had more than an incidental effect. The change from an oral to a written medium was not simply a transference of speech to written signs. That transfer made possible, or perhaps even generated to some extent, new ways of thinking which marked a shift from mythical paradigms and the beginnings of a break with mythical disclosure as heretofore analyzed. To begin the discussion we must establish that Homeric poetry reflects an oral tradition which preceded the first written form of the *Iliad* and *Odyssey*. That tradition was built around the social role of the singer-poets who would enter into inspired states beyond their normal consciousness and spontaneously recite sacred stories, in part from memory but also embellished anew with each telling. It was through these poets that a community would receive its cultural education as well as delight in reliving such great and exciting events.[34]

Not only did the material of epic poetry reflect the cultural assumptions we have described thus far, its form of composition was also part of that complex. In the context of epic selfhood both behavior in and the composition of the *Iliad* were not centered in a subjective state of interior self-consciousness. A helpful summary of this point is offered by Simon in the following set of five parallels between oral poetry and Homeric models of mind.[35] (1) In oral poetry the bard receives and transmits the poem. He does not invent the poem from a subjective state but rather receives it from the muses, his teacher, and tradition. In the Homeric mind, mental activity is initiated externally by a god, another person, or part of the person. (2) In oral poetry the poem arises in the context of an interchange among poet, audience, and traditional material. In the Homeric mind, mental life is shown to be a personified interchange rather than a purely internal activity. (3) In oral poetry the poem consists of traditional, common material expressed in traditional ways. In the Homeric mind, mental activity is presented as visible, public, and common rather than private and idiosyncratic. (4) In oral poetry there is no distinction between composition and performance. In the Homeric mind there is no distinction between structure and function, that is, no clear distinction between the mental organs, their activity, and the products of those activities. (5) In oral poetry the blurring of boundaries between poet, audience, and characters in the poem is constitutive of the performance. In the Homeric mind the self is set within a field of forces or in a series of interchanges with other persons.

With the advent of writing, a number of important consequences follow which begin to disrupt this complex of traditional epic paradigms. For one thing the figure of the singer-poet becomes less important with respect to his cultural role. Consequently, the notion of a continual openness to the extraconscious also becomes less important. Furthermore, with the absence of a live performance, the sense of a historical distance between the sacred material and its depiction begins to emerge, as opposed to the sense of identification inherent in an oral reenactment (recall the correlation of myth, action, and telling in Chapter I).

But perhaps the most important consequence is that *fixing* the poem in time and space overcomes the irreversible flow of an oral transmission which constantly sweeps the mind along with ever-new advents and surprises, transfixing the mind and maintaining its transparency to sacred forces and embeddedness in a sacred world. The written word breaks this enthrallment and brings about conditions allowing an emphasis on profane, ordinary awareness. At this point the conscious self can become the measure of the poem, and what follows are many forms of thinking which, as we have seen, are not characteristic of oral or mythical traditions. Writing facilitates (if it does not itself generate or come from) an emphasis on consciousness and subsequent forms of thinking which will usher in a new set of cultural and intellectual assumptions. I think Versenyi summarizes these conditions quite well, so I will simply quote in full a passage from his treatment of the subject.

Writing, with its fixity and permanence, allows the reader to range back and forth over the text, to compare its parts and become aware of inconsistencies, to follow a long line of gradual development and growth, to see general patterns slowly emerging through particular incidents, to see, synoptically, the whole of what is revealed through the parts. As such, writing brings with it a wholly new type of thought: one demanding coherence, unity, harmony, organic wholeness, and logical connection in all diversity. This type of thought is fully aware of the tension between surface and depth, potentiality and actuality, and it can conceive of a hidden order, a not immediately apparent connection, an underlying law. It fosters a new sense of time: real differences between past, present and future become visible, as well as the overarching, unchanging pattern. It asks for a new truth: not surface visibility (*aletheia*), but the vision of something not immediately visible, the form or idea that transcends the particular and is yet immanent in it. It has a new concept of reality: the real is not what appears to sight but precisely that which does not and cannot be seen except by the reflective intellect. And it brings with itself a new responsibility. To the individual who is no longer spellbound by his own unconscious absorption of the oral tradition, an explicit deviation from that tradition is no longer an anathema. But the possibility of deliberate innovation lays the burden of justifying what tradition no longer hallows on the innovator himself. Critical thinking, unsupported by tradition, must henceforth provide its own justification and be its own primary foundation and support.[36]

But at this point we are jumping ahead quite a bit. The forms of thinking identified here took centuries to develop through a long and gradual transformation of mythical assumptions. We are here simply emphasizing one significant factor in that development—the advent of writing as a catalyst for the conscious mind becoming the measure of thought and culture. Writing is one way in which consciousness can be emphasized and consequently detached from the traditional cultural matrix of myth, specifically the intrinsic absorption in the extraconscious and the lived world.[37]

In regard to the emergence of self-consciousness, Hesiod's *Works and Days* exhibits in many ways the first documented break with the epic tradition. Here we find an emphasis on ordinary consciousness as well as a call for moral reform which speaks against some of the epic values we have analyzed. Furthermore, the seeds of criticism are born in Hesiod's poetry, where the immediate authority of mythical disclosure begins to decline. We should keep in mind, however, that Hesiod does not represent the discovery of selfhood, morality, and truth but rather *new forms* of selfhood, morality, and truth which will usher in a cultural revolution.

Historically, Hesiod does something unusual in his poetry—he ends the anonymity of previous poets. With his personal references and first-person standpoint, Hesiod represents the first cultural example of a self-conscious individual. The dispute with his brother, Perses, is an important part of his motivation to tell the story of Zeus's justice.[38] Moreover, the reader is always aware that the mythical account is transmitted through the poet's own reflection, no longer the immediate presentation of a mythical world. We notice here a new attitude toward myth, one that anticipates later doctrines of truth. At the very outset of the poem (10) Hesiod promises to tell of "true things." Mythical "truth" is never so explicated. Myth discloses a sacred world with immediate presentation (unconcealment, *alētheia*). Mythical truth is not behind its imagery, rather the form of the world is presented *in* its imagery. But Hesiod does a number of things which indicate a departure from myth. His mythical references no longer have the kind of lived immediacy found in Homer. Hesiod introduces a sense of distance between the myth and the world. The story of Zeus seems to serve only a heuristic purpose; the god is no longer really a person but rather the force of justice which is enlisted to rectify certain transgressions (specifically those of his brother) and the general immoral climate of his day. In other words, Zeus becomes more a "symbol" than an actual sacred presence.

There is also a form of distance created for the reader. When Hesiod proceeds to tell about how humanity came to its present troubles, he does something new. He gives two different mythical accounts, the story of Pandora and then the five ages of humanity (90–201). There are important consequences which follow from relating two versions of one subject. First of all readers can no longer remain passive. Since they are placed between the accounts in relation to the subject at hand, readers are naturally prompted to compare, reflect, and choose.[39] Furthermore, the subject of humanity's lot cannot be immediately connected to the mythical form since there are two different forms here. Consequently, mythical truth can no longer be its immediate presentation but something "behind" the myths themselves.

> If there is any truth to them at all, this must be a new type, a hidden, underlying truth rather than the immediate surface revelation of the Homeric epic. Seeming and being, the phenomenal and the real, the mythical and the nonmythical are beginning to be separated. . . .[40]

In his myth of the five ages Hesiod depicts the origin and gradual degeneration of the race from a golden age, where people lived in har-

mony with the gods and each other, to the present age, where they pursue selfish aims and abuse each other. We find here a sense of historical
change which departs from the kind of timeless presence found in
Homer, where the characters, gods, and the form of the world seem
fundamentally fixed in terms of the immediate presentation of sacred
meanings. The idea of fundamental change in Hesiod introduces another form of distance which not only undermines the lasting presence
of mythical forms but also subverts the unquestioned authority of traditional paradigms. Such a disruption of the passive, receptive attitude
that characterized the mythical mind opens the door for something like
moral reform, which requires that distance from the cultural matrix on
the part of the reflective individual.

Hesiod himself represents just such a reflective distance from tradition and culture. Although he declares his task to be a restoration of sacred truths, his tale of a golden age introduces a new element into the
mythical world, namely, cultural criticism. Hesiod is a self-conscious
reformer who proposes a new set of values which were not part of the
previous cultural tradition. His call for justice and moral reform can in
many ways be understood as a specific rejection of Homeric values
which characterized the preceding age. *Works and Days* presents
those forms of life which were off on the sidelines in the *Iliad*. As a depiction of agricultural labor and everyday activities, it stresses the life
and values of the common man. For Hesiod, *aretē* is represented by
hard work and the farmer's success, not the warrior's deeds. As we have
seen, heroic ideals were correlated with a social aristocracy and the
subsequent "amoral" character of the heroes, especially regarding
their privilege and power over ordinary men. Since power was the
measure of value, the victim had no "rights"; indeed, the victim's defeat represented a positive demonstration of *aretē* in the victor and was
considered "in order" or just.

To whom is Hesiod's accusation of injustice addressed? Specifically
to his brother, Perses, who finagled a larger share of inherited property
and then idly squandered away his wealth. More generally, Hesiod addresses the princes, those lords whom Perses bribed to obtain his share
and whose power permitted such inequities. More generally still,
Hesiod attacks the aristocratic notion of hierarchical power and the
subsequent abuse of the common person's interests. At one point
Hesiod tells a tale about a hawk and a nightingale which graphically depicts the power principle:

And now I will tell a fable for princes who themselves understand. Thus said the hawk to the nightingale with speckled neck, while he carried her high up among the clouds, gripped fast in his talons, and she, pierced by his crooked talons, cried pitifully. To her he spoke disdainfully: "Miserable thing, why do you cry out? One far stronger than you now holds you fast, and you must go wherever I take you, songstress as you are. And if I please I will make my meal of you, or let you go. He is a fool who tries to withstand the stronger, for he does not get the mastery and suffers pain besides his shame." So said the swiftly flying hawk, the long-winged bird. (202–212)

In many ways the Homeric heroes are well represented by the hawk, but Hesiod wishes to attack the power and violence of warrior ideals as they pertain to ordinary life. One might say that heroic values reflect a wartime situation and that Hesiod's values pertain to peacetime. But since Homeric values represented *cultural* ideals, there was a spillover effect such that the aristocracy of the princes maintained power over the ordinary person. Hesiod is not just attacking the misplacement of warrior ideals, he is introducing a new *cultural* ideal which opposes aristocratic power *in principle* so as to elevate the standing of the powerless.[41]

Here I want to sort out the various factors that have emerged in this discussion of Hesiod, factors which can be read quite beyond the text of the poem but which I think are implicit in *Works and Days*. We have mentioned heroic ideals, which stem from the cultural assumptions delineated in this chapter. We have seen how the emergence of self-consciousness is at work in Hesiod's poetry, which therefore in several ways departs from earlier cultural paradigms. Finally, we have noted Hesiod's concern for social justice and his rejection of aristocratic power. There is a subtle connection between Hesiod's social program and the larger question of self-consciousness and its departure from the noncentralized self of epic poetry. This connection will become explicit only in later intellectual developments, but I think it can be forecasted on the basis of an overview of Hesiod's poetry.

We should recall that the aristocratic position of Homeric heroes had its sacred "justification." In other words, the sacred presented itself as an uncommon disruption of ordinary consciousness, and those who were so favored by the sacred, namely the heroes, were naturally elevated above the more profane types. If that social hierarchy is to be rejected, then so too must its sacred justification. What is required is a notion of equality which abstracts from differences and uncommon

traits. If the profane is characterized by commonness, then the repudiation of the Homeric aristocracy would be coincidental with a cultural
elevation of profane, ordinary awareness. We have seen that ordinary
awareness in Homer was continually open to the sacred. In Hesiod,
consciousness begins to distance itself from the sacred. In other words,
the new model of the self implied in Hesiod's poetry and his social
aims can be seen as two sides of the same coin. The rejection of aristocracy demands a model of equality which demands some notion of commonness. Such a model is the basis of Hesiod's conception of justice,
which advocates law over power. The law of Zeus's justice must abstract from differences and the immediate lived context of the earlier
sacred matrix. And, as we have seen, Hesiod's poetry indicates the
emergence of the self's detachment from the sacred matrix. It is in such
an atmosphere that the abstraction required for the formulation of a
law can take place.

In other words, Hesiod represents a reform that is simultaneously
social and intellectual. *Works and Days* displays the advent of self-
consciousness, its detachment from the sacred, and a concurrent emphasis on the profane, ordinary self (the common person). Consequently, there follows a repudiation of the special individual favored
by extraordinary forces, and so the promotion of an egalitarian morality and the call for protection of the ordinary man. Justice, for Hesiod,
is the displacement of the power principle by the rule of law which ap-
plies to strong and weak alike. We have seen how epic justice was simply the various gods' exercise of power. It is no surprise that Hesiod's
gods become quite depersonalized. Zeus now embodies a universal
justice and not a particular position among other sacred powers. Reward and punishment are no longer the whim of a deity but the consequences of an unswerving law. And human transgression is no longer
attributed to divine infatuation; Hesiod's myth depicting the ages of
humanity puts the blame for misdeeds squarely on human beings
alone.

What we see here is the beginning of a detachment from the sacred
matrix, so that cultural ideals can become formulated from that standpoint of the reflective mind. For Hesiod, justice is a universal law
which must abstract from epic pluralism and judge those favored types
who embodied the heroic ideal, with the aim of protecting the interests of ordinary people. So the new sense of justice is both dependent
on self-conscious detachment from the lived world and meant to protect the ordinary self (the common person) in its social circumstances.

Hesiod's abstractions, namely "law" and "humanity," depart from both the content of epic poetry (*special* individuals) and its form (sacred pluralism).

I am trying to establish here a complex set of relationships that will characterize the movement from mythical culture to rational thought. We find in Hesiod an egalitarian morality challenging the heroic ideal, as well as abstraction beginning to displace poetry. In my view, the pivotal factor in these developments is the emergence of the self-conscious mind and its detachment from the lived world of myth and the extraconscious forces therein. With that detachment comes the power of abstraction and also an abstract view of human nature which can introduce a common notion of humanity on the basis of that distance from the lived world's inherent plurality. Ordinary consciousness, common to all, now becomes the *measure* of human existence and judges all those disruptions of consciousness that constituted the sacred, mythical world.

Here we are only anticipating later developments of the rational mind and a demythification of the world, but by focusing now on self-consciousness as the key element in these matters we can begin our survey with one advantage. Greek cultural developments represent a rich fabric with many interwoven strands. We have to recognize that Greek philosophy, science, art, politics, and morality were all interrelated and shared many overlapping interests and assumptions, which undermines the notion that Greek philosophy emerged in some kind of pure intellectual space and which compels our attention to the psychological, social, and political influences that helped give rise to philosophy.[42]

The relationship between intellectual, moral, and social matters has been indicated in Hesiod's poetry. The way in which these matters overlap has been shown in terms of self-consciousness. Such a complex will remain important in our analysis of the subsequent periods of Greek thought. The turn to abstraction in intellectual matters will continue to be related to moral and social concerns. Moreover, the idea of reform will be exhibited by philosophers in their reactions against myth and poetry, and this idea of reform will involve *similar motives* to those of moral and social reform. Consequently, the turn to philosophy will involve a multidimensional development which is, in some essential way, *evaluative* and not, therefore, purely objective. Such an analysis forces us to rethink the nature and status of philosophical discoveries in relation to other forms of disclosure. The setting of philoso-

phy does not involve timeless or purely objective criteria but rather
historical, social, and psychological developments. The focus for such
a claim is the emergence of the self-conscious mind as the one common element that runs through the various cultural developments
which led the Greeks away from myth. Such a process did not occur
overnight, however; the shape of self-consciousness and a related sense
of the world took a long time to unfold. And we should keep in mind
that even in these developments, the Greeks did not entirely abandon
myth or forms of selfhood found in a mythical world.

# IV

## Lyric Poetry in the Archaic Age

The seventh to the sixth centuries B.C. roughly marks the archaic age in Greek history. Among the many important features of this age we will emphasize the growth of self-consciousness and the beginning of a cultural distinction between self and world, a distinction which breaks apart the integrated complex that characterized a mythical world. We have seen in Hesiod's poetry the embryonic development of self-consciousness. Hesiod still wrote ostensibly in the epic mode, however; his poetry reflected the world at large, though indeed colored by self-consciousness and also directed toward mastery of the world and protection of human interests (which departed, therefore, from epic fatalism). In lyric poetry, self-consciousness becomes more detached from the world and the lived matrix. Poets will now give cultural expression to the inwardness of personal experience, and in doing so they not only sever the self-to-world correlation of the epic period, they also prepare the distancing from the lived world which will become a crucial ingredient in later intellectual developments.

Before beginning a general sketch of the archaic period, I want to offer some remarks about the emergence of self-consciousness. What contributing factors can we find in the background of that emergence? First of all there is the influence of writing, which we have already discussed. Secondly, the known world was growing larger. With the development of trade, different cultures were coming into contact with each other. When confronted with a different culture, the immediacy of one's own is naturally suspended. The awareness of cultural differences can obviously create an intermediate "zone" of self-recognition. Furthermore, the expansion of contact led to an increase of turmoil, disorder, and confusion, the tension of which could disrupt one's sense of being at home in the world and send one "within."[1] Thirdly, many social, political, and economic factors brought about the ascendancy of the common man. The subsequent emphasis on common awareness would naturally play against the traditional model of the noncentralized self in epic culture. Psychologically speaking, the tendency to "secure" ordinary awareness and life began to supplant heroic fatalism and the sacred disruption of consciousness.[2] Finally, with the many causes creating a breakdown of traditional culture, there arose a kind of circular and exponential effect with respect to the role of self-consciousness; circular because it is impossible to know clearly whether cultural changes caused the emergence of self-consciousness or vice versa (actually, the search for a "cause" is inappropriate from a phenomenological standpoint); exponential because, whatever the role of self-consciousness, the breakdown of tradition and the subsequent loss of authority and order demanded more and more of the self-conscious mind to compensate for that loss. In other words, the more humans distinguished themselves from the cultural matrix, the more they were thrust into themselves.

## The Archaic World View

As Dodds has pointed out, much of the literature of the archaic period expresses a feeling of despair, insecurity, and helplessness in the face of an overpowering fate.[3] This is in sharp contrast to the epic notion of heroic action and pride despite the rule of fate. How are we to understand such a change? I think the most significant factor would have to be the changing shape of selfhood. I have argued that the epic heroes could remain proud even in disaster because the self was not clearly separable from the intervening sacred forces that governed the course of events. Consequently, victory and defeat were not a purely personal responsibility. Since the individual as such was not the ultimate criterion of meaning, individual gain and loss could not serve as the complete measure of the world's value. Thus we noticed the curious but now understandable combination of fatalism and life-affirming activism in epic poetry. The heroes were completely integrated into and simply drawn along by the fluctuations of the lived world. Without a strictly interior standpoint, epic feelings were triggered only by the ebb and flow of world situations. Sorrow was strongly felt but completely washed out by joy once the hero's fortune changed. Sorrow was never interiorized, there to linger independent of circumstances, thus becoming despair, a generalized denial of life's positive possibilities.

Once self-consciousness becomes the measure of experience, however, once the human self begins to separate from intervening, extra-conscious forces and destructive world events, then these disruptions of consciousness and safety present themselves as a form of pure negation, without the corresponding *integration* which characterized the epic view. And since the negation of human interests seems continual, generalized feelings of despair, insecurity, and helplessness can begin to shape a new view of the world.

With the internalization of self-consciousness we can also notice in the archaic age certain moral attitudes concerning human character that are much closer to the modern view in contrast to the epic period. The epic hero, ever rooted in sacred powers, never seemed to internalize success into complacency or pride into arrogance. He could never so bathe his self-image in such general ways because of the constant intervention of unpredictable forces. In the archaic period, however, we begin to hear of hybris, a pervasive fault which manifests itself as an overblown pride or arrogant dismissal of fate, which brings about a vengeful punishment.

The heroic situation was not presented in this way, although there appear to be surface similarities. Even though challenging limits was part of the epic complex, the hero never disregarded fate or expected that he was in complete control of his life. Defeat was never thought to be punishment but rather an inevitable consequence of a sacred interplay. Furthermore, the archaic sense of hybris and punishment could easily have a debilitating effect on human motivation ("why strive?"), but we have seen that despite (or rather *because* of) sacred control in the epic world, the hero remained proud and active. This was so because the absence of complete responsibility meant that loss could not be internalized and become an immobilizing loss of confidence.

So the issue of self-consciousness can help us understand the very different responses of these two ages to a fateful world. In the presence of fate, epic individuals remained assertive. In the archaic period, when individuals began to distinguish themselves from fate, that same fate now appears less integral and more negative, less a part of human meaning and more a loss of human meaning. At the same time the notion arises that fateful destruction is due not to sacred intervention, which partly constitutes human action, but to human assertiveness in the first place. Fate is no longer part of the heroic complex but a punishment of human self-assertion. So the advent of self-consciousness from out of the noncentralized epic self brings about a world view which dissembles the epic sense of integration and seems to obviate heroic vitality. The archaic self comes to see the world as a more negative place and, oddly enough, tends to lay the blame on itself. We find evidence for such a view as early as Hesiod, who says that even natural disasters and crop failures are a consequence of human injustice. In the Golden Age, human beings lived in perfect harmony with nature.

All of this can be summarized by saying (with Dodds) that the archaic age represents a shift from a shame pattern to a guilt pattern. What we find now is an internalization of responsibility for the course of human life, the notion of "sin" as opposed to the more primitive notion of "pollution." Such a shift, however, only found its first steps in the archaic age. The transformation was a gradual process which took a long time to crystallize. In any case the two views of human existence are strikingly different. Homeric heroes were never blamed for their misdeeds and defeats. Because of divine intervention and infatuation, personal blame for actions would be just as unthinkable as blame for growing old or getting hungry. Even when the hero was done in by fate, he would never conclude that there was something fundamentally wrong with him personally. Archaic experience, however, begins to interpret terrible cosmic forces as forms of punishment meant to avenge human transgression. The gods (especially Zeus) are no longer competing among each other for power and using mortals as pieces in some divine game. Now the gods, as we have seen in Hesiod, come to be seen more as impersonal agents of justice and punishers of mankind.

It is true that in epic poetry the avenging fates could easily match this function, but the fates were more connected with death in general and were at odds even with the gods at times, and the vengeance of the fates did not seem to be a response to some human flaw. We could say, however, that the epic pattern of avenging fates became generalized into the archaic view of the gods and associated with the new sense of human responsibility and subsequent need for punishment. Thus the epic notion of a controlling fate is retained to some extent in the archaic world. What is new is something which lays the groundwork for a genuine cultural revolution. With the internalization of responsibility, injustice is not only something that requires punishment. If human beings are the cause, then injustice can be rectified by changing human beings. No longer need people simply hope for a divine change of fortune. In dealing with their own deeds and motivation, people now direct appeals for change toward themselves. People can, to some extent, ward off the terrible forces of fate by altering their behavior. What we know as moral reform is now made possible.

But the archaic age did not fully develop such a notion of moral reform—self-consciousness was not yet completely distinguished from sacred forces. Lyric poets, as we shall see, could still speak of extraordinary passions in the epic form of divine intervention, but the difference is that archaic experience saw divine intervention as a form of punishment, which is thoroughly unepic in character. So we find a curious mix in archaic culture: On the one hand, passions are still seen as possession by an external power; on the other hand, there is also a strong sense of personal responsibility, sin, and punishment. We must conclude, therefore, that despite the emerging emphasis on self-consciousness, the epic integration of self and world has not yet been divided.

In this regard we should clarify the moral dimension of archaic culture. We find in that age at one and the same time a sense of human hopelessness and powerlessness along with a sense of moral necessity in the cosmos. We might find it difficult to reconcile two such attitudes (even though, as we have seen, both can be attributed to the advent of self-consciousness). We will find the same juxtaposition in tragic poetry. But when we hear of "justice" in archaic and tragic culture, we should not think that it corresponds to our understanding of moral law. Archaic justice is more akin to the necessity of fate in epic poetry than to the idea of a moral law, because our understanding of morality is much more a function of rational principles than the idea of an extrahuman, cosmic power. Since both rational morality and archaic justice share the notion of subjecting individuals to some higher form of regulation, we might easily come to see them similarly, but the question of *what* human beings are subjected to shows a difference. In later Greek and Christian morality, some form of mind is responsible for moral commands, and the human mind has access to these principles (Kant eventually takes this even further by saying that with the moral law the rational mind is subjected to *itself*), but archaic and tragic "subjection" is not to some set of rational principles discovered in the human mind but rather to an extrahuman fate more comparable to the forces of nature.

I leave this point in a rather vague form for now. When we come to tragedy I will pick it up again and try to show that tragic justice has little to do with morality as we understand the term. Perhaps it is now a little easier to understand how notions of human hopelessness and cosmic justice could coexist in the archaic age. The pessimism felt in that age will begin to evaporate only when the conscious mind becomes marked off from the world matrix and begins itself to define values. In other words, archaic hopelessness will become alleviated in a later age when justice is defined through the values of the conscious mind (i.e., a rational morality). Consequently, the optimism of the classical age depends upon the degree to which the human mind can shape the world and thus break away from both epic fatalism and archaic pessimism.

To conclude my general remarks about the archaic age, as a consequence of the rise of self-consciousness, lyric poetry shows an emphasis on emotional suffering. No longer is the subject of poetry the heroic warrior, but rather ordinary personal feelings. More often than not the lyric "battlefield" is love, but there the threat is no longer physical and the lover can die many deaths. As a result, loss is more frequent and is not given the compensations of epic honor and glory or Hesiod's cosmic law. Such a setting can help us understand the acute sense of the transitoriness and futility of existence expressed by lyric poets. There also developed a new form of compensation which, however, had none of the lastingness of heroic fame. The poets sing of enjoying the moment and indulging in sensual pleasure while one can. Listen to Alcaeus:

> *Zeus rains upon us, and from the sky comes down*
> *enormous winter. Rivers have turned to ice. . . .*
> *Dash down the winter, throw a log on the fire*
> *and mix the flattering wine (do not water it*
> *too much) and bind on round our foreheads*
> *soft ceremonial wreaths of spun fleece.*
> *We must not let our spirits give way to grief.*
> *By being sorry we get no further on,*
> *my Bukchis. Best of all defenses*
> *is to mix plenty of wine, and drink it.*[4]

> *Drink, Melanippus, and be drunk with me.*
> *How can you think that you will ever see,*
> *Once over Acheron, the pure bright day*
> *Again? Come, throw such proud desires away.*
> *Sisyphus, wisest of men, thought he could find*
> *An artifice that should leave death behind,*

*But fate decreed his wisdom should not save*
*Him from twice crossing Acheron's rough wave,*
*And Cronus' son gave him great sufferings*
*Below the dark earth. Hope not for such things,*
*While we are young. Now is the moment, now,*
*To take what happiness the gods allow.*[5]

This so-called hedonistic poetry was the forerunner of a philosophy of life defended by some of the Sophists which inspired the reactionary moral reforms of Socrates and Plato.

We can see that the archaic emphasis on the individual self spawned a different response to a world of change and negativity. What ensued was the bare recognition of the powerlessness and destruction of the individual *without* any of the traditional compensations and integrations (which stemmed from a different notion of selfhood). Archaic experience tended toward three possible reactions: faulting humans for their sufferings, recommending reform, or indulging human desires while life lasted.

## The Emergence of Self-Consciousness in Lyric Poetry

One of the most important aspects of lyric poetry is the expression of personal identity, which becomes a crucial ingredient in the historical development of rational thought. Such a connection may not seem evident at first, but we will soon see the relationship between conceptual reason and self-consciousness—and lyric poetry displays the rudimentary forms of self-consciousness, especially interiority and unity, without which later intellectual developments would not be possible. Let us take a brief look at some of the ways in which lyric poetry begins to break loose from its mythical traditions and consequently anticipates future cultural innovations.[6]

We can note the shift from the epic to the lyric period best by recognizing one of the central themes in lyric poetry: personal love. A perfect example can be found in one of Sappho's poems, which mentions Helen of Troy but which clearly shows a departure from epic interests:

*Some there are who say that the fairest thing seen*
*on the black earth is an array of horsemen;*
*some, men marching; some would say ships; but I say*
*she whom one loves best.*[7]

Rather than the heroic exploits instigated by Helen's love, Sappho thinks the most important thing in life is love. But the passions of love are an individual matter, and so the hero of the lyric poem becomes the individual poet herself. Sappho's poems are usually expressions of her own passion and the object of that passion. Although there are many vestiges of epic assumptions in lyric poetry, nevertheless the poetic content has shifted from world and cosmic events to personal experiences as such. Implicit in this shift are a number of important departures from epic attitudes which prefigure a new view of the human self and the world.

Let us explore this point by considering the phenomenon of love in Sappho's poetry. First of all, love's passion is still experienced as sacred infatuation, an external invasion by Aphrodite:

> *Sweet mother, let the weaving be,*
> *My hand is faint to move.*
> *Frail Aphrodite masters me;*
> *I long for my young love.*[8]

Furthermore, love is expressed as a complete disruption of the normal self:

> *And the sweat breaks running upon me, fever*
> *shakes my body, paler I turn than grass is;*
> *I can feel that I have been changed, I feel that*
> *death has come near me.*[9]

Here we notice a connection with the epic model of human experience, but personal love also brings with it something that introduces an element of interiority lacking in the epic world. Though a deity may possess the self with love, the beloved may not return the feeling. Heroic possession always involved actions in the world, but if one is invaded by love, one cannot *do* anything if the beloved does not respond. The heroic complex continually entailed achievement, and even defeat was at least preceded by a glorious attempt. The spurned lover, however, is overcome by a feeling of passive helplessness. There persists a contradiction between one's intentions and the inability to pursue those intentions. Hovering in this zone of helplessness, the poet has nowhere to turn but within. The deity is not responsible for the feeling of loss, and the outside world can offer no consolation; in fact, someone in that world has caused this feeling. In other words, though love is still a divine intervention, *impediments* to love create a form of self-reference which takes on elements of inwardness and solitude. A singular interiority now distinguishes itself from the active/contextual epic self.

*The Moon is gone and the Pleiads set,*
*Midnight is nigh; time passes on, and passes,*
*Yet alone I lie.*[10]

It is interiority which begins to create a sense of individuality much closer to the modern view of the self. Homer never identified himself in the poem, and his characters were completely relational in nature. But with Sappho, the individual self, the personal "I" becomes the dominant subject of her poetry; she uses the first-person singular pronoun more than any other grammatical form.[11] Moreover, the connection with interiority brings about a number of cleavages in the epic world matrix that will have enormous consequences in later intellectual developments. With the internal and the external becoming more distinct, the world situation becomes thrust out beyond inner experience. Furthermore, surface visibility can become distinguished from a realm behind external appearance.[12] Internal reflection can become separated from action in the world. Factors such as these will become fundamental elements in the process of abstraction, which requires a form of detachment from lived experience.

Another feature of self-consciousness which begins to emerge in lyric poetry is unity. We have seen that in Homer there is no unitary faculty underlying different mental functions. The soul as we understand the term had not yet taken shape. Although the lyric poets do not present the strict concept of a unitary, nonphysical soul that will characterize some later developments, nevertheless we can recognize a turn in that direction if we pay attention to certain implications of the poet's experience.

*Love has unbound my limbs and set me shaking,*
*A monster bitter-sweet and my unmaking.*[13]

Sappho's phrase "bitter-sweet" stands out in marked contrast to epic experience. We saw that conflicting feelings in Homer were presented as an alternating exchange between different mental organs, but Sappho expresses something easily recognized in the experience of personal love. In the case of unrequited love, joy and sorrow can overlap or coexist, and cannot be perceived as mere alternations. "I" can perceive the interweaving of conflicting aspects in a single phenomenon. Anacreon proclaims: "Again I love, and I love not, I rave and do not rave."[14] If the unhappy lover can affirm and deny the same thing, we notice the contours of a unified experience "behind" different perceptions. So the rudiments of a common faculty underlying the various aspects of experience begin to take shape in lyric poetry. Although some feelings are still perceived as divine intervention, obstructions to these feelings create an internal, unitary self-consciousness which gathers in the contextual and pluralized configurations of the epic self, and which therefore prefigures the notion of a soul or mind.[15]

The other essential feature of self-consciousness, namely autonomy, also finds some expression in this period. Autonomy can be understood in two senses—human autonomy as opposed to divine control, and individual autonomy with respect to social relations. Regarding the first form of autonomy, Jaynes points to a line from Terpander which shows a dramatic break from the traditional view of poetry: ". . . come sing to me, O Phrenes!"[16] The *phrenes* is one of the mental organs discussed in the chapter on epic poetry. Although Terpander still displays a more pluralized self than some other lyric poets, nevertheless he introduces a clear sense of autonomy by invoking neither the muses nor a god, but part of his own mental activity. The human mind is beginning to assert itself by separating the thought process from the gods.

An even clearer sign of human autonomy can be found in the writings of Solon (640–560 B.C.), one of the most important figures in ancient Greek culture. More than a poet, Solon established intellectual, moral, and political principles that helped animate the cultural revolutions for which the Greeks are so renowned. Later we will touch upon the moral and political influence of Solon, but at this point I want to highlight his contribution to a form of human self-understanding that we take for granted. Compared to earlier figures, Solon is probably the first thinker we would recognize as like ourselves. He begins to say things we might expect would or could have been said in earlier periods but which were not and could not be said. Solon sounds more familiar to us because he is participating in the *discovery* of human nature in our sense of the term. The best way to approach the innovations of Solon is to focus on his appeal for human self-understanding, self-improvement, and self-regulation.

Solon begins to emphasize the faculty of *noos* with a significant frequency. The way in which he uses the term is also revealing. Rather than a fragmentary part of mental experience with a decidedly visual function, *noos* for Solon begins to take on the quality of wholeness and represents a more generalized foundation of human thought and moral principles.[17] *Noos* is the term that eventually came to designate "mind," and in Solon we witness the mind-space of *noos* replacing divine voices, which in his age are speaking only to special intermediaries, the oracles. Solon does not abandon the gods, but he begins to separate human mental activity from sacred intervention and proposes that humans are responsible for the course of their lives.

Contrary to the fatalism of the epic age and the pessimism of his own age, Solon tells Athenians not to blame the gods but themselves for their misfortune.[18] Responding to the social conflicts of his day, Solon declares that people have brought about their own troubles by failing to moderate their behavior and, more importantly, by failing to reform social and economic patterns, which reform would improve their lot. We have already seen, in our discussion of Hesiod, the relationship between self-consciousness and moral reform. Solon goes one step further by proposing that the rule of law is a necessary component of moral reform. If special interests and social hierarchies are creating abuses, then the power of law to abstract from differences and protect the powerless is needed to enforce justice. The gods will not suffice; human beings must restructure society so that the communal force of law, not the gods, can intervene and change human behavior. For Solon, the laws of the polis will connect the power previously attributed to the gods with the new self-conscious moral aims, that is, connect moral right with political might.[19]

Solon's legal reforms represent an institutionalization of Hesiod's sense of justice. Hesiod had still seen justice in terms of the divine, but Solon sees it as a human social task. Hesiod had thought that human injustice brings about divine punishment in the form of natural disasters, pestilence, and famine. Solon sees injustice as having purely human consequences, as leading to civil strife and a breakdown of social cohesion.[20] All of this shows that Solon has introduced an element of autonomy which begins to dissemble the traditional view of human nature and which fills in one of the crucial features of self-consciousness that will figure prominently in later intellectual developments. We can hear the transformation summed up in the phrase which Greek tradition attributed to Solon: "know thyself."[21]

Attention to Solon in connection with the emergence of self-consciousness is important for the following reason. Historically speaking, the advent of consciousness cannot be understood in isolation from social and political developments. Snell has rightly pointed out that the discovery of individuality *coincides* with the formulation of a *polis*, a community of *individuals* (citizens, not a faceless mass), bound by laws and ideals which protect, respect, and promote individual interests in a social context. The experiences of individuals and social-historical forces are mutually related and intimately bound together.[22]

Even though the lyric poets expressed a self-conscious individuality, this does not mean that they completely exchanged the traditional social self for a strictly "private" self. There is no such thing as a pure monologue in lyric poetry. Although experience is gathering around an individual personality as such, that individual is still to a certain extent relational in nature. Lyric poems are addressed to someone or some public audience; the relationship between the individual and others is still a part of the poet's self-understanding.[23] Although the shape of the epic self clearly becomes changed, the Greeks (even in the classical period) never entirely abandoned the social self which characterized their mythical beginnings. The self, the mind, never becomes something private, sealed off from extra-individual connections, a world unto itself.[24]

The same warning would hold with respect to the second form of autonomy that shows itself in lyric poetry, namely, individual autonomy with respect to social relations. Archilocus is a poet who breaks through the aristocratic sense of rank that characterized the social structure of the epic period. His invective criticisms of public figures and his lampooning style reflected the growing sense of a commonality among men, such that social station was no longer inviolable.[25] The epic atmosphere of praise and honor given to the excellent few, along with a social order in which one deferred to the power of one's betters, was giving way to a liberation of the common man and the subsequent sense of freedom from aristocratic social control. But even though individual autonomy was developing and social criticism began to take a cultural form, this does not mean that an anarchistic individualism was the result. These developments coincided with the advent of new political ideals which would usher in a restructuring rather than a denial of social order.

## Pindar: Heroism's Refrain

Upon viewing the cultural changes in the archaic period, we would do well to consider the poetry of Pindar (518–483 B.C.), which shows that these changes were not a single movement, sweeping everyone along in locked step. There were many convolutions and counterreactions within the cultural developments in ancient Greece, and quite often a cultural form received its most vivid expression when it was about to perish. At the close of the archaic period, when many traditional patterns were in great disarray and decline, came Pindar. In many ways, Pindar represents a reverberation from the epic period and an attempt to retrieve or preserve certain traditional values. Consequently, Pindar presents a reaction against the growing cultural innovations of his time.[26]

Pindar is not so personal a lyric poet. The emphasis on self-consciousness is not evident, either in his own case, since he is not the subject of his poems, or in his subjects. Pindar's lyrics are songs of *praise*, which simply present and glorify human excellence or sacred meanings without thoughts of reform or calls for justice. Much like Homer, Pindar sees the task of the poet to be the immortalization of sacred events, and his many references to the muses indicate that he maintains the traditional view of the poet as an inspired receptacle:

*My Muse, steer me the flight of these my*
*words straight and glorious. For men pass,*
*but the songs and the stories bring back*
*the splendor of their deeds.*[27]

Moreover, Pindar's idea of *aretē* is much more an expression of the epic heroic ideal than some of the values promoted in his own era. Rather than the Solonic maxim "know thyself," which suggests self-reflection and knowledge, Pindar says: *genoi hoios essi*, "become what you are" (*Second Pythian Ode*, 72), which has the ring of action and achievement, or which at least suggests self-*expression* in a lived context more akin to the epic model than the growing interiorization of the self we have noticed in the archaic period. Also, rather than emphasizing the common experience of ordinary people, Pindar sings the praises of special individuals who achieve great deeds.

Pindar does not entirely mirror the epic past, however. He departs from the glorification of war: "War is sweet to those who have not tried it. The experienced man is frightened at the heart to see it advancing."[28] He does uphold an aristocratic, heroic idea, but usually in the nonmilitary arena of athletics. Pindar's praise of the athlete reflects the Greek attitude toward sport. As we have seen, athletic contests had a religious significance. The glory attained in a contest was an analogue of the traditional picture of human existence: Limited by fate, mortal, excluded from the realm of the gods, an individual can nevertheless achieve glory by challenging limitations to whatever degree possible, by risking self and striving for excellence, the uncommonness of which elevates the individual and yields a share of divine power. In light of this, we can better understand why Pindar calls athletic games *hieros*, "sacred" (*Sixth Nemean Ode*, 61). The victor embodies the religious significance of the heroic ideal, and in fact the poet will often identify the athlete with some divine or heroic exemplar. Sport allows a form of compensation in the face of human mortality. The athlete, therefore, is a kind of sacred figure who actualizes the ideals of Greek religion. Mortals may be cut off from divine immortality,

> *but blessed, worthy of the poet's song, is the*
> *man who by excellence of hand and*
> *speed in his feet takes by strength and daring*
> *the highest of prizes. . . . He cannot walk*
> *in the brazen sky, but among those goods*
> *that we of mortality attain to he goes the*
> *whole way.*[29]

The athlete, like the Homeric hero, risks himself and is subject to the unpredictable fate of the contest's outcome, but through courage the athlete can strive to attain a degree of glory. Pindar clearly compares the athlete to the hero and finds in sport a religious significance.[30] Why else would he preface his song to the athlete Alcimidas with the following lofty words?

> One and the same is the origin of men and of gods; from one selfsame mother we breathe, of both kinds, but divided by great difference of power; for what is here is nothing, but the brazen heaven has eternal duration as an unshakable place of abiding. And yet in many things we come near to the great mind or nature of the immortals, although we know not where, according to what the day or the nights bring to us, fate has appointed the end toward which we hasten.[31]

In sum, therefore, Pindar's poetry can be seen as nostalgia for, and yet innovative use of, traditional heroic values, which counterbalances the growing emphasis on the common self and the interiorizing tendencies prevalent in his time. We have seen how aristocratic station was coming under attack, but for Pindar, the achievement of excellence elevates the individual above the crowd, and for that reason he deserves praise and honor. Moreover, Pindar's retrieval of the heroic ideal is not unrelated to his maintenance of epic fatalism and a model of selfhood which seems to continue epic noncentralization. We have seen how many developments in the archaic age reflect a growing emphasis on and protection of ordinary consciousness. Heroic glory was constituted by intervening powers, and the heroic life was characterized by an individual who *risks* himself. The meaning of heroism cannot be dissociated from limitation, fate, and death. Such a complex was beginning to come apart in the archaic period, where preservation was replacing heroic sacrifice, but Pindar seems to bemoan the loss of heroic glory and stature in the face of a general levelling tendency and a withdrawal from the *positive* consequences of epic fatalism, namely, achievement through risk.

I emphasize Pindar's retrieval of a positive fatalism because in many ways the next period of Greek culture, the tragic age, in addition to being a continuation of revolutionary cultural developments, is also a kind of reverberation from the epic past. Although tragedy will reflect changing views of human nature, it will persist in placing human existence within a sacred context that combines both the Olympian and Chthonic forces that defined the epic world. Tragedy will also display the kind of positive fatalism that characterized epic and Pindaric poetry: Despite (or even because of) human mortality and limitation, there is beauty and value in life. In this regard, let Pindar close the chapter.

> He to whom recently great good luck has fallen soars up to the greatest bliss in high self-confidence on the wings of his distinctions; his mind dwells on things better than riches. For a little time our mortal joys blossom. Even so they are cast down and shattered by a turning aside of purpose.

> Creatures of the day: What is man? What is he not? Man is a shadow in a dream. But when glory comes, sent by the gods, then a bright radiance and a happy existence is granted to man. . . .[32]

# V

# Tragic Poetry

Greek tragedy is subject to a good deal of misunderstanding. Usually it is approached as a form of literature at the expense of its dramatic character, but even when Greek tragedy is performed, the presentations are too often colored by modern assumptions. Taking tragic poetry as the first form of drama or tragedy implies that the Greeks simply invented an art form which has been continued in the writings of Shakespeare and other dramatists. Although it is certainly possible to read the plays of Aeschylus and Sophocles merely as a form of literature, and likewise to see in their plays themes which are comparable to other forms of tragedy and which reach across the ages to modern life, nevertheless such a reading overlooks what is uniquely *Greek* about them. There are certain elements of Greek tragedy which are not found in later forms and which cannot be captured by modern assumptions about human existence and the world. More than a mere art form, Greek tragedy shaped the cultural ideals of that time and was deeply rooted in religion. We have the advantage of having prepared an overview of Greek culture and religion, so that we are in a position to read tragic poetry with more of a Greek eye and to understand how tragedy reflects and relates to the various aspects of mythical culture we have been analyzing.

## Tragedy and Greek Religion

### NIETZSCHE ON TRAGEDY

More than any other modern writer, Nietzsche is responsible for initiating the kind of internal analysis which this study presupposes. It was his view that classical studies were marred by non-Greek assumptions which fostered a picture of Greek culture more in line with our own ideals than with anything else. This situation was most acute, he felt,

when it came to interpreting tragedy. Let us take a brief look at
Nietzsche's treatment of Greek tragedy, marked off against some of the
interpretations which held sway up until his time.

Perhaps the most influential interpretation of tragedy was that of
Aristotle. His well known definition is as follows:

> A tragedy, then, is the imitation (*mimesis*) of an action that is serious
> and also, as having magnitude, complete in itself; in language with
> pleasurable accessories, each kind brought in separately in the parts
> of the work; in a dramatic, not in a narrative form; with incidents
> arousing pity and fear, wherewith to accomplish its catharsis of such
> emotions. (*Poetics*, 6.24–28).

Aristotle's definition indicates that however close in time he may be to
tragedy, he nevertheless interprets it as an art form and is much closer
to a modern literary treatment. Nietzsche's objections to such an approach are based on his contention that Aristotle gives, in the main, a
formal analysis of tragedy at the expense of its religious significance.
Although the Aristotelian notion of catharsis discloses a good deal of
what Nietzsche finds important in tragedy, nevertheless Aristotle, because of the demotion of myth in favor of conceptual reason, has
placed tragedy at the fringes of culture rather than at its very heart. For
Nietzsche, tragedy shapes a cultural world, and although formal elements are important, it is the resonance of mythical paradigms that
should take center stage.

Next we should mention the Christian European interpretation of
tragedy, represented by such thinkers as Kant, Schelling, and Lessing.
Generally speaking, here we are told that tragic destruction is precipitated by the moral transgressions of the hero. The idea of a tragic character flaw coupled with the subsequent guilt and responsibility of the
hero brings on irresistible punishment and disaster. But the moral interpretation of *Greek* tragedy runs up against a number of problems.
First of all, the notion of a character flaw cannot be said to mirror exactly even the Aristotelian concept of *hamartia*, which is better rendered "mistake." The idea of "guilt" is highly questionable when it
comes to Greek tragedy. As we shall see, I think we are forced to conclude that Greek tragedy has little if anything to do with morality, at
least in the expected sense of the term.

Finally we should mention Schopenhauer, since his views on tragedy can by contrast illuminate Nietzsche's position most clearly. For
Schopenhauer, tragedy does not represent moral justice; rather, the

paradoxes and irresistible destruction essential to tragedy show the vanity of human life and the inevitable suffering that constitutes existence. Furthermore, the feelings of horror and dread excited by tragedy prompt a pessimistic sense of salvation—the only recourse we have in the midst of inevitable suffering is to deny existence altogether.

> Thus in tragedy the terrible side of life is presented to us, the wailing and lamentation of mankind, the dominion of chance and error, the fall of the righteous, the triumph of the wicked; and so that aspect of the world is brought before our eyes which directly opposes our will. At this sight we feel ourselves urged to turn our will away from life, to give up willing and loving life.[1]

Although Schopenhauer gives a vivid account of the tragic setting, Nietzsche pointed out that he was entirely wrong about the way in which the Greeks responded to tragedy. The true paradox of Greek tragedy is to be found in the notion of positive fatalism. In the midst of inevitable destruction, the Greeks nevertheless affirmed life. Schopenhauer indeed recognizes this but offers a rather presumptuous explanation. Because the Greeks would not surrender the will to live in the face of tragedy, he concludes that they "had not yet reached the summit and goal of tragedy."[2] For that reason he prefers the more pessimistic modern tragedies to those of the ancients. In other words, Greek tragedy was less tragic than modern tragedy. But Nietzsche saw how odd Schopenhauer's interpretation was. Could the Greeks fall short of the essence of tragedy when they themselves invented it? If the Greeks did not display a pessimistic attitude, it is possible that pessimism has little to do with tragedy. Nietzsche was prompted to ask: What, then, *is* tragedy? By emphasizing the religious and cultural context of ancient drama, Nietzsche was able to show that moralism and pessimism are alien to the Greek experience of tragedy. Although the term "tragic" has a negative meaning for us, this does not justify our overlooking elements in Greek tragedy that are not fully compatible with such a meaning. In fact, if we wanted to stick with the *Greek* meaning of tragedy and disallow any equivocal use of the term, one might conclude that there *are* no "tragedies" outside of the Greek form. If we are to understand this, let us begin by drawing out the basic features of Nietzsche's main work on the subject, *The Birth of Tragedy*.[3]

It was Nietzsche's contention that tragedy represented the culmination of Greek mythical culture and served a function analogous to that of philosophy by evoking insights regarding the overall meaning of existence, but that function must be understood in relation to the nontheoretical form of myth. Nietzsche selected two important mythical figures, Apollo and Dionysus, the combination of which would disclose the general meaning of tragedy. It is generally thought that tragic drama had its origins in the dithyramb and the satyr play, both of which were connected with the worship of Dionysus. The satyr was half human, half goat, and was looked upon as a fertility daemon. The goat was seen to be an image of Dionysus and was often sacrificed in Dionysian rituals. The Greek word *tragōdia* literally means "goat song" (*tragos* = goat). So we find that tragedy involves a poetic response to the worship of Dionysus. But Nietzsche recognized that later Attic tragedy introduced other elements, especially mythical references drawn from Homeric religion. He chose Apollo to represent that counterpart to Dionysus and decided that the interplay between these two deities could best disclose the general meaning of Greek tragedy.

According to Nietzsche, Dionysus and Apollo embody two fundamental elements of the Greek spirit which are initially in opposition but which become reconciled in Attic tragedy. Dionysus was a Chthonic deity whose sacred manifestations were found in earth forces, music, dance, revelry, and wine. Apollo, an Olympian deity, was a god of the sky who represented light, beauty, balance, poetry, and prophecy. Nietzsche generalizes these two forces through the analogies of intoxication and dream. Dionysus represents ecstatic self-transcendence, where the personal self is lost, where all boundaries between the self and nature, and between individual selves, are shattered. Here the flow of natural destruction is penetrated, and the amorphous unity of dissolution is given a sacred meaning. Apollo, on the other hand, represents the principle of individuation embodied in poetry and the plastic arts. That principle is meant to counteract the annihilating flux of Dionysus through the construction of boundaries, the introduction of measure and form, with the aim of isolating and preserving the presence of individual entities. Since natural destruction has a kind of priority in that all things are destined for annihilation, Nietzsche proposes that the Apollonian sense of form presents appearances, that is to say, the "dream" of individuation which is only a temporary permanence in the midst of a Dionysian whirl. Generally speaking, then, Apollo and Dionysus embody the principle of form and an underlying formless flux. The Dionysian religion (as we will see) shows how the Greeks embraced the dark, destructive side of existence and gave it a sacred value. It is the priority of negativity that, for

Nietzsche, gives us insight into the Greek meaning of tragedy, namely, a deep sense of fatalism.

Greek tragic fatalism, even though it is obviously not a type of optimism (in other words, the belief that form can be permanent or substantial), nevertheless does not display a Schopenhauerian pessimism either. Greek tragedy, according to Nietzsche, is neither optimistic nor pessimistic and better fits the model of positive fatalism we have previously outlined. When the tragedians propose the inevitable destruction of the hero without any resolution, we recognize a fatalistic, Dionysian attitude. At the same time, Dionysian worship was not a form of sheer destruction. Religious rituals gave to fatality a sacred significance; the *expression* of a Dionysian *mythos* through music and dance prompted a sense of living communion with a sacred force so that sheer negativity would be transformed into a cultural meaning and worshipers could experience a sense of harmony and redemption.

Furthermore, the presence of an Apollonian dimension in Attic drama gave tragedy an even greater degree of cultural form than Dionysian worship alone. In tragedy the terrible truth of Dionysus is wedded to the saving appearances of Apollo. Apollonian art forms gave the Greeks a bearing and a meaning to withstand annihilation and resist self-negation. For this reason tragedy was not purely Dionysian, since it included dance, music, poetry, and characters, the structure of which grants a temporary veil of beauty and the enjoyment of a cultural world. But tragedy retained its Dionysian basis in that its themes reflected the terrible and inevitable destruction of culture. So it is the combination of Apollonian and Dionysian elements that shows us the positive fatalism of tragedy. Beautiful Apollonian forms delight the viewer, but at the same time they portray a dark Dionysian theme. Apollo yields to Dionysus by forming the figure of a hero who is necessarily doomed to destruction.

Contrary to Schopenhauer, Nietzsche maintains that by cultivating and beautifying the tragic, the Greeks were saved from a negation of the will to live. The "comfort" of tragedy is that even though individuation is shattered, life is ever powerful and pleasurable. Even though the ultimate truth is that all is for naught, tragic poetry saves the will by offering joy in appearances, through which human beings can live amidst a terrible truth. The Apollonian mask gives meaning to life. But tragedy also shows that the mask must eventually be torn off. The gradual unfolding of fate in the drama leads the hero to his doom. Nietzsche concludes that the following general world view can be inferred from

Greek tragedy: Individuation and form allow life to be meaningful and beautiful; however, underlying individuation is a formless flux which persists as a continual destruction of forms. The Apollonian expression of Dionysian wisdom indicates that individuation is recognized as an appearance, since form is not substantial and must yield to negativity.

Nietzsche gives us a most insightful treatment of Greek drama because it allows us to see tragedy fitting into the general religious and mythical patterns we have witnessed. Also, Nietzsche's analysis will help us understand certain connections between tragedy and early philosophy, but at this point we simply want to recognize the importance of Nietzsche's contribution regarding the cultural significance of tragedy. The positive elements of tragedy allow us to better understand this significance. There appear to be two levels of affirmation in tragic poetry—first, the Apollonian affirmation of beauty and form, and secondly, the religious affirmation of Dionysian dissolution as *justified* destruction. We will soon discuss these positive elements further, but Nietzsche's analysis gives us the proper direction and starting point for an internal understanding of Greek tragedy. Certainly Nietzsche did not invent the Dionysian angle. The connection between tragedy and Dionysus has always been acknowledged, if only because of the performance of the plays during Dionysian festivals, but Nietzsche was the first to fully penetrate the thematic relationship between tragic drama and Dionysian worship. In other words, he was able to show that the connection between tragedy and Dionysian religion was not simply a historical but an *essential* relation. He was able to draw parallels between the general phenomenon of tragic drama and the dark subterranean forces at work in the cult of Dionysus.

By emphasizing the religious dimension of tragedy, Nietzsche also illuminated those positive aspects that distinguish Greek tragedy from something like pessimism. Because of the element of worship, the terrible force of Dionysus was integrated into people's sense of themselves and of the world, such that negativity was "in order" and part of a sacred matrix. In this way Nietzsche was able to solve the puzzle that would otherwise confound us when we look back at the Greeks: How could such a vital, active, prolific, and life-affirming people present their ultimate cultural expression in the form of tragedy? We can now see that this is a pseudopuzzle resulting from our misunderstanding of tragedy as the Greeks experienced it. It was not a wholly negative phenomenon and was more likely to evoke joy than depression. We know that Greek audiences took great delight in tragic performances and would readily sit through day-long presentations with vociferous demonstrations of pleasure or displeasure, depending on the quality of the play. We have already come a long way toward resolving this apparent incongruity by stressing the positive fatalism of early Greek religion. In many ways tragedy is the explicit presentation and completion of certain elements in the mythical tradition which preceded it.

## THE LINK WITH EPIC POETRY

Although we can posit the connections between tragedy and religious experience (Dionysian worship and ritual), nevertheless its unique Greek development in later stages was in the direction of what we would call an art form. Since classical Attic tragedies incorporate Homeric stories and characters as well as other non-Dionysian mythical elements, one could easily object to a purely Dionysian interpretation of tragedy. Certainly later tragedy presents rich characterizations and plots, and social and political references as well. But that Greek tragedy introduces so much formal structure and embraces such a wide range of cultural issues does not consequently nullify the Dionysian dimension. Rather, we find in tragedy a blend of many different cultural forms, with, however, a Dionysian foundation. Nietzsche has given us a way to uncover the manner in which tragedy maintains its religious character, but he never proposed that Attic drama was a purely Dionysian phenomenon. The Apollonian element was essential to tragedy and contributed to its overall significance.

In the context of our investigation we can approach this point by discussing the relation between epic and tragic poetry. The Homeric epic and Attic tragedy are not two entirely separate tracks in Greek culture. Although there are obvious differences, we should also recognize many overlapping features. Moreover, tragedy can be seen as a continuation and extension of some of the developments we noticed in the transition from epic to lyric poetry.

Classical tragedy differs from its earlier, more religious form by portraying many mythical figures from the Homeric tradition, but tragic poetry does bring to the foreground Chthonic elements which epic poetry held in the background. The Dionysian character of tragedy draws out and emphasizes those non-Olympian forces whose implicit power we recognized in the Homeric world. Generally speaking, we can say that Nietzsche's Apollonian–Dionysian distinction crystallizes the Olympian–Chthonic duality in Greek religion. Consequently, in accordance with Nietzsche's interpretation, we can conclude that mature tragedy represents a blending of Olympian and Chthonic elements. Even though tragedy presents a greater deference to Chthonic forces, we should recall that epic poetry did not ignore them. Although Homeric poetry distinguishes itself by the degree to which the luminosity of immortal forms outshines the Titanic underworld, nevertheless the power of fate and death was a continuing counterweight to Olympian rule. Tragedy simply gives the subterranean dimension a greater thematic weight while still displaying the shapes of Homeric poetry. In other words, tragedy gathers together certain general features of Greek religion but distinguishes itself by its specific Dionysian emphasis.

We were able to recognize in Homer a certain tragic atmosphere. The heroic ideal entailed the paradox of achievement in the midst of death and fate. Thus limitation and negation were built into the positive aspects of heroism. But epic poetry was not fully tragic, even though the hero faced many fatal dilemmas and was subjected to forces beyond his control. One reason can be found in the many compensations available to the hero in the epic world (e.g., glory and social station); another can be found in the epic self, which had not yet fully distinguished itself from sacred forces (recall the absence of internalization and the subsequent lack of "personal" suffering). Hence the key to the difference between epic and tragic poetry is the advent of self-consciousness and individuation, such that the disruptions of consciousness and the threats to the individual are more sharply distinguished and hence more acutely perceived. The tragic self has become more internalized and less embedded in a sacred matrix; negative forces are not as integral to, and are hence more a destruction of, the self; and the lack of social compensations further enhances the degree of negativity felt by the individual. In other words, tragedy presents the heroic paradox of achievement in the midst of death and fate, but now from the perspective of the hero's internalized *suffering* of this tension. Epic fatalism becomes tragic when the hero becomes more starkly aware of fatality from the standpoint of individual consciousness. In tragedy the tension between life and death, self and fate, attains its full force because the life of the individual self is more sharply defined and hence more threatened than in the epic world. Whether we give a cosmic or a social interpretation to tragedy, we shall see that it is the hero's individuation and self-affirmation which create a truly tragic tension.

A certain relationship can now be seen between the cultural periods we have discussed. One could say that tragic poetry makes explicit the tragic implications of epic poetry and does so by way of lyric poetry, which discovered individual self-consciousness and a heightened experience of personal suffering. I should add that this relationship is somewhat dialectical. Even though lyric poetry can be seen as a transition from epic to tragic poetry, tragedy retrieves certain epic elements lost in the lyric period. For example, rather than emphasizing the common man, tragedy retains the epic notion that the hero is the most noble and admirable human type. Also, rather than the tendency toward pessimism in the archaic age, tragedy retains the positive fatalism of the epic period. Tragedy is more reconciled to negativity and suffering because it retains the epic sense of a sacred meaning regarding human limitations (i.e., suffering is necessary, justified, and part of the world order). At this point let us begin to penetrate the sacred dimension of tragedy by turning our attention to the god whose nature animates tragic poetry.

## DIONYSUS

We want to examine Dionysian religion in order to understand its thematic relation to tragic poetry, to see to what extent elements of tragedy echo the myth of Dionysus. To that end let us try to isolate the essential features of Dionysian myth and ritual.[4] One basic characteristic of Dionysus is that he is a god who "arrives." His arrival generally takes three forms which often overlap: (1) various types of epiphany; (2) a divine "epidemic" in which the force of the god evokes a kind of mass hysteria; (3) the god answering a call from his followers.[5] The notion of arrival brings up a historical point. It was usually thought that Dionysus was a foreign god who came to Greece from Asia, but recent scholarship has cast some doubt on this assumption. We have discovered relationships between the early religion of Crete and later Greek religious forms. Many elements of Dionysian religion—nature worship, visionary experiences, female devotees, images like the bull and snake—are found in ancient Cretan religion.[6] Thus the stories of Dionysus's "arrival" suggest more a *revival* than a foreign invasion. I would think that the outbreak of Dionysian worship (around the eighth century B.C.) came to be seen as foreign because the spread of this religion was a threat to conventional life and introduced a profound cultural tension which continued to be a disruptive factor until the Greeks were able to incorporate the growing cult into the general fabric of their institutions. Furthermore, I would read the myths of arrival from a phenomenological perspective. Part of the phenomenology of myth is the arrival-character of the sacred, in that it interrupts the profane and presents a continuing emergence from hiddenness. Aside from their specific features, I would say the Dionysian stories speak to the heart of mythical presentation itself.

The myths of Dionysus disclose the essential message of that religion: The god suffers a cruel death and dismemberment but, in various versions, is restored to life. Dionysian religion can be said to express the Greek experience of an indestructible flow of life underneath passing individual lives, or infinite life (*zōē*) beneath finite life (*bios*).[7] Here we find, personified, Nietzsche's notion of a formless destructive force underlying form. What is distinctive about the Dionysian religion can be shown by contrasting it with Olympian religion with respect to immortality. Olympian immortality meant freedom from death; Dionysian immortality means continual death and rebirth. The myth of Dionysus reflects the cyclic regeneration of nature, the destruction and reconstruction of life forms. There is no evidence that early Dionysian religion was based upon personal immortality; in that regard it shares with Olympian religion the notion of essential human mortality. But Dionysian myths are a stark contrast to Olympian myths in that a god must suffer death. Here we find Chthonic, earth elements deified to such an extent that finitude and destruction are not only acknowledged but given a sacred form. Thus the worship of Dionysus involves not only acknowledging a destructive force but yielding to its sacred power. Dionysian religion embraces the dark side of life in order to receive the blessings that stem from harmonizing the self with a necessary cosmic force. Its essence seems to be the realization that although nature destroys the individual, the *whole* is indestructible and sacred; therefore ecstatic self-transcendence (as opposed to self-containment) grants religious integration.

Against such a background we can better understand the meaning of the unusual rituals associated with Dionysian worship. In general the rites took two basic forms: (1) joyful erotic feasts, which embraced the "positive" side of the life process by throwing off the conventional self and yielding to the passions of sexual regeneration; and (2) somber sacrificial ceremonies which prompted participation in the "negative" side of the life cycle.[8] The latter form of ritual is certainly the most fascinating and troubling aspect of Dionysian religion. Let us try to comprehend the cultural meaning of these practices.

Dionysian religion was originally a cult of women. In the beginning men were deliberately excluded, and the various myths point out the association between Dionysus and women. But beyond any specific gender references, such an association should lead us to conclude that Dionysus represents a feminine archetype which partly characterized the Chthonic dimension of Greek religion.[9] In any case, women were the chief agents and followers of the god. Their rituals presented a startling form of identification with the myth of Dionysus. After a one-year subterranean absence, during which the women would call to him with singing and music, the god became present either in a vision or in a ceremony through which his fate was represented by a sacrificial animal. Such rites involved the women working themselves into a state of frenzy, followed by the infamous rending of the sacrificial victim (*sparagmos*) and devouring it raw (*omophagia*). There is even evidence of occasional human sacrifice. Cult practices were largely kept secret, and it was considered a sacrilege to disclose them to the uninitiated.[10]

The Dionysian women were famous for their uninhibited behavior during these rites—frenetic dances, wild screams, heads flung backward, rigid bodies, overt displays of sexuality, and supposedly limitless physical strength. It is no wonder that Dionysus was called a "mad god" and that his followers were named "maenads," possessed by a sacred *mania*.[11] Recalling our previous discussion of sacred madness we can better appreciate the cultural significance of such experiences. Dionysian rituals were a dramatic example of cultural support for the disruption of the conventional, profane self. The terrible practices of the cult, though mad by ordinary standards, were nevertheless religiously significant in terms of a ritualized participation in a sacred force of destruction. Although the wild exploits of the maenads were a vivid contrast to other, more moderate aspects of Greek life, still Dionysian worship was thought to bring peace and blissful communion with the god. Since it aimed *to cultivate* dark, destructive drives, giving them a ritualized and thus selective outlet, the cult's institutional channel prevented the outbreak of these drives in uncontrollable forms. Furthermore, since the annihilating force was necessary and inevitable (hence its divinization), then *resisting* this sacred power would only invite more terrible destruction. Consequently, embracing such a force in a ceremonial manner resulted in a cathartic kind of peace.[12]

We can summarize the religious significance of Dionysian *mania* by saying that its goal was a form of dynamic self-transcendence by immersion in a natural force of destruction and unrestrained passion. From a psychological standpoint we can surmise several possible attractions of such experiences. First of all, the transcendence of the ego-self can lead to a transcendence of suffering. Even though the Dionysian religion represents a kind of paradox in that suffering is overcome by giving full vent to destruction, the key to its anesthetic effect is the dissolution of self-consciousness. Today we recognize the relationship between consciousness and pain, since distraction can diminish pain and hypnosis can eliminate it. Secondly, the cathartic effects of Dionysian rituals were known to have a therapeutic value even beyond the ceremonial time frame. The rites were said to cure certain diseases and calm many mental disorders. We should notice an analogy between such experiences and modern psychoanalytic methods. The repression of powerful emotions can have a debilitating effect and lead to pathological symptoms. If an analyst recognizes that venting or reliving such emotions is part of a cure, we immediately notice the cultural meaning of Dionysian rituals. Since the Greeks institutionalized such cathartic processes, we can conclude that they recognized the therapeutic value of these rites. By acknowledging and embracing passion and violence as part of the natural order, the Dionysian cult was able to channel such drives, give them their due, and so prevent their pathological "vengeance."[13]

Only against such a background can we fully understand the positive and religious elements of Greek tragedy. In acknowledging the priority of a destructive fate, tragic poetry shows its derivation from the worship of Dionysus. Moreover, since the annihilation of the individual seems to be inevitable in tragedy, we can comprehend its positive dimension only in terms of the *sacred* meaning given to a negative force. The ruin of the hero is the *emergence* of Dionysian power. In fact, it is when the hero *resists* the fatal limit to his individuality that an even more terrible end occurs (the most notable example being the brutal consequences of Pentheus's resistance to Dionysus in *The Bacchae*).

The religion of Dionysus is animated by a profound paradox: The god of life drives his followers to kill; and yet *he* is the victim. Since Dionysus is the source of the sacred mania which spawns ritual violence, and since the sacrificial victim is seen to embody the myth of divine dismemberment and death, then Dionysus is both the slayer and the slain. His followers are driven to participate in the life *and* death of Dionysus. Such a paradox, however, is simply a reflection of the course of nature, the dialectic of *zōē* and *bios*, a life process which persists through the annihilation of individual lives. The natural order shows itself to be a kind of fatal paradox: The constant surge of life involves both self-regeneration and self-destruction; life begets life, and at the same time, life must feed off itself, in that living things must be nourished by consuming other life forms. It is this paradoxical self-relation inherent in nature which is the core of Dionysian religion and which serves to illuminate certain basic themes in tragic poetry.[14]

The notion of indigenous self-destruction would be the proper starting point for understanding the predominance of *family* killings in tragedy. In view of Dionysian origins, certain interpretations of tragedy completely overlook the cosmic dimension of violence among "relatives". This is not to say that sociopsychological readings are unwarranted, but simply that such analyses are quite limited and miss the deep religious resonance that tragic situations had for the Greeks. Their fascination with family violence was part and parcel of an awe in the face of life's paradox—that nature both bears and kills her children. In addition, the theme of self-destruction is evident in individual tragic heroes. But again, rather than reduce such a theme entirely to personal attributes like arrogance, immorality, and ignorance, we should keep in mind the link with the sacred paradox of Dionysus. As lord of eros and death, attraction and repulsion, Dionysus embodies a full range of contradictions displayed in the course of nature. The tragic hero is in many ways, as Nietzsche pointed out, a mask for Dionysian juxtapositions. In *The Bacchae*, for example, Pentheus (whose name means "man of suffering") is punished for denying Dionysus; but he is related to the god (a cousin), and even represents him in the terrible rite at the end of the play when he is torn to pieces by his own mother. We recall that Dionysus is a god who suffers and lets himself be killed. Tragedy presents this sacred paradox in the guise of a man who destroys himself. Thus one of the central themes of tragic poetry, the hero's self-destruction, must be read beyond simply the negation of an individual human being; the tragic paradox unfurls something positive, namely, the sacred nature and power of Dionysus, the meaning of which evokes a religious insight.

Since tragedy is connected with religion, it should not be interpreted as an entirely negative phenomenon. Tragic negation is the advent of a sacred meaning. We can further underscore the positive significance of tragedy by gathering a summary profile of Dionysus. He is the god who combines many apparently contradictory features. He is both terrible and benevolent; he evokes frenzied violence and bestows peace; he is both a destroyer and a healer. We have gone some way toward explaining how such juxtapositions can contain a positive meaning. If the force of the god is a necessary part of the world, then resistance invites retribution, and compliance leads to harmony. Although one might easily balk at this since the sacred force seems to be constituted by negation, nevertheless Dionysian worship *embraces* negation, affirming the disruption and destruction of the individual. Not only does this religion accept finitude, but its experiences of ecstatic self-transcendence offer *immersion* in that formless flow beneath finite forms. In this way the essentially sacrificial nature of Dionysian religion is "justified" in that the followers are *shown* the dissolving power of the god along with its cathartic effects.

The Dionysian rupture of individual form would be *purely* negative only if one considered individual form to be the full limit of reality. But in a clear way the religion of Dionysus maximizes the model of experience which was found to constitute a mythical world. We have seen that the mythical self is embedded in extraconscious and extraindividual forces; the clear separation between self-consciousness and the world process is not evident. If we add in the fatal power of negation which formed a Chthonic background in epic religion, we can conclude that Dionysian practices epitomize the belief that reality is not limited to individual consciousness or form. Both the disruption of consciousness and even the destruction of the body are seen in terms of a sacred "field" and hence not from the standpoint of individual units of life. Again, the annihilation of the individual is the advent of a sacred meaning, hence the positive character of Dionysian religion. But what distinguishes it from epic religion is that the sacred field is not simply a constellation of divine forms but rather the formless power of negation that runs through the passing forms of nature.

Dionysus is essentially a god of becoming; one of his central features is metamorphosis.[15] Since he can take any shape, no one shape can capture his nature, which should be seen to be essentially shapeless. Dionysian religion is a form of nature worship in which the overall process of emergence and passing away of natural forms is deified. Moreover, it can also be called a form of nature mysticism, in that its followers can embrace this field and draw from it an existential meaning—their sense of life is widened beyond their individual selves and bodies. Thus, negation is religiously transformed; suffering is ameliorated because one is *integrated* into one's own negation; loss becomes a sacred whole.

To further understand the positive aspects of Dionysian religion, we should remember that death and dismemberment are only one side of its makeup. As a god of nature, Dionysus is also a god of life; he bestows erotic passion which promotes regeneration. The orgiastic practices of his cult allowed the release of sexuality and carnal pleasure. But one can recognize in eroticism an analogous "dismemberment," in that conventional behavior is disrupted and everyday order is overthrown by surges of passion. In any case, joy and pleasure are just as much a part of the Dionysian complex as natural destruction. We find in this religion a gathering of several subversions of consciousness and form, some somber and fatal, some erotic and hedonistic.

We have been examining the bipolar character of Dionysus in order to comprehend the positive elements of tragedy. We can go further in this direction by addressing the relationship between Dionysian religion and comedy, and consequently the interesting correlation between comedy and tragedy. The somber, violent rites of Dionysian women had a male counterpart in ancient Greece: the *komos*. Here swarming bands of drunken men would engage in dancing, laughter, and witty and mocking language, where all social conventions and inhibitions were stripped away.[16] The association of Dionysus with wine has its origin in these practices. To a large extent the wine cult displaced the severe archaic cult in later periods. Wine allowed a greater degree of popularization in that it permitted access to Dionysian ecstasy in the more accessible and less dramatic form of drunkenness. The *komos* represented a more frolicsome and less grave form of ecstasy in which social conventions were subjected to Dionysian "dismemberment." The etymological connection with comedy can be found in the Greek word *komodia*, "song of the *komos*." The thematic connection should also be clear. The religious phenomenon of disinhibiting revelry, which included mocking attacks against figures of authority that were socially permissible during such celebrations, can easily be considered the forerunner of comic drama.

Consequently, the bipolar character of Dionysian religion shows a single origin for two different but related dramatic forms, comedy and tragedy. On the one hand, the somber ecstasy of the feminine cult promotes the participation in the actual destruction of life and hence reflects the fatal process of nature in which individual life and meaning are subjected to an annihilating force. Here we recognize the roots of tragedy. On the other hand, the frolicsome ecstasy of the masculine cult promotes a disinhibiting intoxication which reflects a "harmless" destruction of social and cultural roles by means of mockery and the temporary subversion of authority. Here we recognize the roots of comedy. The first type of Dionysian worship embraces the actual destruction of life in the fatal dialectic of nature. The second type embraces the destruction of convention to loosen the role-fixation in human nature. Both can be said to share in different ways a common Dionysian insight: Form is insubstantial, and religious meaning can be found by breaking through the fixation on form in favor of the nihilating power of Dionysian ecstasy. We notice in tragedy and comedy, therefore, two forms of Dionysian negation, one having more to do with nature, the other having more to do with culture. Should we not find here an illuminating answer to the often-asked question concerning the relation between tragedy and comedy? From both a historical and a thematic standpoint we find in Dionysian religion clues to Plato's suggestion that "the same man might be capable of writing both comedy and tragedy—that the tragic poet might be a comedian as well" (*Symposium*, 223d).[17]

If a pompous man slips on a banana peel, his pose has been annihilated, and we laugh. If he dies from the fall, we do not laugh. The common element is negation, the insubstantiality of form. Comedic negation is temporary and less harmful; tragic negation involves the annihilation of life or a complete cultural downfall. Both are animated by common elements—the disclosure that our conventional (profane) life is not entirely what it seems to be and the belief that by acknowledging the disruptive negation of life and culture humans can receive the "blessings" of pathos and humor, in that both teach about the necessary limits of form. Pain and laughter can be related in that pain suffers negation while laughter enjoys negation (e.g., mockery, satire, and self-deprecation).

In Dionysian religion, suffering from negation is transformed into a sacred integration, resulting in what we have called a positive fatalism. The Dionysian features of comedy further highlight the positive aspects of Greek drama. Although tragedy and comedy did become two separate art forms in Greek theater, nevertheless their intimate connection is not only indicated by a common religious origin but also by the early history of Greek drama. Originally the performance of tragedy took the form of a tetralogy, a series of three works followed at the end by a satyr play in which heroes and gods from the tragedy were mocked or parodied. Aside from what could be called comic relief, we must recognize the religious function of such a comedic epilogue. Ecstasy and joy were just as much a part of Dionysian worship as fatal destruction. *Embracing* the god was meant to produce a positive response in the midst of negation. The satyr play was an effective means of capturing the mythical rebirth of the god by transforming the solemn destruction of the hero into the joyous recognition of a sacred force underlying that destruction, but because the satyr plays were later dissociated from tragic trilogies, it is easy to miss the positive religious outcome of tragic performances. Although comedy and tragedy may seem to be opposites, in Greek culture they grew from two aspects of a single religious attitude which should be generally characterized as the worship of a nihilating force underlying the forms of life.

Let us summarize the Dionysian religion before turning to its dramatic descendant, tragic poetry. Broadly speaking, it promotes self-transcendence, the disruption of self-consciousness and individuated form. The subsequent breaking of boundaries leads to four forms of integration: (1) integration with a god, or ecstatic identification, which overcomes the Olympian separation between mortals and gods; (2) integration with other humans, where social and personal boundaries give way to a festive, orgiastic, communal merger; (3) integration with nature through ritual identification with animals; and (4) integration with self-negation, where ecstasy turns loss into a positive religious phenomenon.

This religion of self-transcendence can be read as an affirmation of finitude. God and humans are joined in such a way that the epic duality of mortality and immortality is undermined, but not in the sense that humans are delivered over to something like Olympian deathlessness. Dionysus, the dying god, represents the natural dialectic of life *and* death. Here the dark power of fate and death is sacralized to the point where finite limits are no longer deficiencies in comparison with the immortal gods but rather the disruption of life and consciousness is *itself* a divine, sacred meaning. The ecstatic immersion in annihilation indicates that finite limits, and the subsequent loss of finite form, are "in order" *even from the divine side*. We notice here what could be called the sacred affirmation of finitude in that the sacrificial nature of life is *embraced* rather than avoided, stoically tolerated, or simply endured.[18]

We can identify in Dionysian religion a vivid reflection of certain mythical paradigms discussed earlier—the self-world circle, the contextual self, immersion in extraconscious forces, and fatal negativity. Certainly Dionysian religion is an extreme form of mythical integration, but the advent and remarkable spread of Dionysian worship in Greece (even through the classical period) could be considered a counterreaction to a sense of alienation stemming from the growing isolation of self-consciousness and the subsequent "distance" between self and world. Perhaps the degree to which self-consciousness became sharply defined meant that a primal need for integration required a comparably sharp rupture of consciousness. In any case, Dionysian religion expresses and even dramatically exaggerates the cultural paradigms of the Greek mythical world.

## Tragedy and the Dionysian Tradition

The early forms of tragedy, which would supposedly show a clear connection with Dionysus, are unavailable to us. Although later tragic drama contains many elements that make the connection between tragedy and Dionysian religion less evident, we should avoid the assumption that Attic tragedy somehow broke away from its religious origins. It could not have been simply a formality or deference to custom that tragedies were performed during Dionysian festivals. Although many social, political, and psychological themes are evident in mature tragedy, nevertheless deep within these secular surfaces persists a mythico-religious meaning which continues to reflect a Dionysian foundation. Before we examine this point, let us briefly discuss the way in which mature tragedy (from the seventh through the fifth centuries B.C.) transformed the Dionysian into something beyond its original religious tone.

In and of itself, pure Dionysian experience is unrestrained and rather amorphous—the maenads would whirl convulsively either in silence or with wild cries, shrieking and howling. Although there were arranged rituals, their aim was the loss of personal identity in a violent kind of chaos. Dionysian ecstasy is more visceral than cultural; "it establishes community but it communicates nothing."[19] Tragedy introduces something different. Out of its dithyrambic origins, tragic drama converts amorphous experience into a more clearly defined cultural world. The poet gives shape to Dionysian intensity through rhythm, measure, form, and character. The convulsive whirl is transformed into a dance; ecstatic cries are turned into song; sheer chaos is transfigured into a cultural *situation* undone by fateful destruction; and the loss of self becomes a highly characterized self *confronting* that loss (thereby maintaining individuation in the midst of chaos). The result is tragedy, which in fact has a greater depth than pure Dionysian experience in that it emphasizes the tension between form and formlessness rather than one or the other alone. Tragic poetry, therefore, maintains a cultural world in which beauty and form acknowledge the formless, as opposed to the one-sided formlessness of Dionysian abandonment. It is this correlation that lies behind Nietzsche's insistence that Apollonian individuation is just as essential to tragedy as the Dionysian.[20]

The interjection of Apollonian elements could easily lead someone to question the proposal that tragedy retained a Dionysian foundation. As long as we keep in mind something like Nietzsche's "mixture," we can conclude that on the one hand tragedy was not purely Dionysian, but on the other hand thematic and structural considerations show the continued presence of Dionysus underneath an Apollonian superstructure. Since Attic tragedy is the intersection of Dionysian and epic-heroic meanings, the surface content need not explicitly express a Dionysian *mythos*. Nonetheless, the underlying themes of life and death, resistance to a god, punishment and sacrifice, the triumph of a god, and necessary destruction do constitute the Dionysian elements of tragedy.

A Dionysian interpretation can also be given to Aristotle's notion of catharsis, the purgation of pity and fear through recognition (*anagnorisis*) of the great error (*hamartia*). We have seen that Dionysian religion promotes something positive through self-transcendence. Tragic *peripeteia*, the "turning around" of the hero's fate, is *also* the advent of a sacred power. Dionysian myth and ritual presented a *peripeteia* from grief to joy following the god's rebirth after destruction. The purgation of pity for the individual hero and fear of fatal destruction can be understood, then, in the Dionysian sense of catharsis. It is for this reason that Nietzsche spoke of the universal Dionysian theme underlying the specific characters and plots of Greek tragedy. He read tragic "recognition" as a metaspecific insight—seeing the individual hero *as* a mask, that is to say, an appearance of form which had hidden the sacred formlessness of Dionysus. Thus, *hamartia* is not a particular deed but rather individuation as such, the mask of individual form which tragic fate must tear off in favor of the god. Tragedy presents rich configurations and variations of a central theme, the tension between individuation and annihilation. The individual is a beautiful but insubstantial mask which veils a terrible but sacred negativity.

## The Self in Tragic Poetry

We can fill out our final approach toward the tragic poets by retrieving the issue of selfhood and considering how tragedy is related to previous periods of culture. I want to argue that the tragic self bears a kind of dialectical relationship with the epic and archaic self. Tragic poetry both affirms individual self-consciousness *and* acknowledges its limit. This is another way of portraying the coexistence of Apollonian individuation and Dionysian dissolution. In a way, tragedy represents a convolution of epic heroism/fatalism and lyric personalism; but it subsequently carries both notions in a new direction.

In suggesting that tragedy is a blend of heroism and personal consciousness I am trying to overcome certain suppositions about tragic ideals. Given the many examples of choral warnings against self-assertion and hybris, one might easily think that in tragedy the Greeks were turning away from heroic ideals in favor of restraint and moderation, and that tragedy was simply carrying forward the cultural ideals we saw brewing in the archaic age. There the advent of self-consciousness ushered in a breakdown of the epic contextual self and cultural matrix, leading to such things as moral criticism of self-assertion, a sense of personal guilt, pessimism, and passivity. But tragedy is much more complicated than this and is not simply a linear progression from the epic and archaic ages.

Nietzsche's proposal that tragedy is a mixture of Apollonian and Dionysian elements helps us understand its complications. First of all, I do not think the chorus can be sufficiently understood as a "moral" force. If the chorus (being communal) can be connected with the underlying (extra-individual) Dionysian force of destruction (as Nietzsche maintained), we can say that the fate of the hero is not due to any personal fault but rather to the sacred limit of negation. Secondly, if the hero embodies Apollonian individuation, then his form too shows a sacred necessity. This is perhaps an obscure way of saying that tragedy did not entirely abandon the heroic ideal but rather intensified its atmosphere of fatality. But it did so by departing from strict epic selfhood via lyric personalism. Tragic poetry presents the first full recognition of self-directed action in Greek literature. By magnifying the tensions of self-consciousness found in lyric poetry, tragedy puts the human self on center stage with the gods now in the background. But the depicted self is not the lyric personality which showed tendencies toward emotionalism, pessimism, passivity, or hedonism. Rather, the tragic self is the heroic self—noble, active, beautiful, and cultural exemplar. However, tragedy greatly intensifies heroic fatalism by stressing individual self-consciousness and consequently sharpening the suffering from loss. For example, self-consciousness diminishes the contextual, social self of epic poetry; as a result, the tragic hero is no longer fortified by the epic compensations of honor, glory, and fame. Tragic fatality is now a complete loss. In a way tragedy adds Dionysian annihilation to epic heroism and fulfills lyric self-consciousness, which was not found either in epic poetry or in pure Dionysian experience.

I have mentioned a dialectical relationship regarding epic, lyric, and tragic selfhood. Let me outline the dialectic by gathering some of the central ideals of the different periods in the following way:

1. **The epic age** emphasizes the hero; heroic assertion is good in that it leads to fame and honor despite fated destruction.
2. **The archaic age** emphasizes the common man; self-assertion is bad in that it leads to strife and is punished by destruction pure and simple with no compensation.
3. **The tragic age** emphasizes the *tragic* hero; self-assertion is affirmed in the Apollonian beauty of the hero (thereby echoing #1) *and* it is punished by destruction pure and simple (echoing #2).

Tragic poetry in this way represents a rich combination of various cultural elements that constituted the mythical phase of Greek history—heroic nobility, emerging self-consciousness, and fatalism.

We can complete our treatment of the tragic self by considering the notion of choice. In Homer either a hero decides between two possibilities on the basis of profitability or a god intervenes to prompt a decision. In both cases a decision is based upon an external factor. We could not call this choice in the sense of self-direction, coming from an internal weighing of alternatives, distinct from external considerations or influences.[21] But in tragedy, self-direction takes shape. For example, in the *Oresteia*, Orestes is confronted with conflicting divine claims (Apollo orders matricide, which the Furies will avenge). This dilemma forces him to stand alone and decide from within.[22] In tragic drama, characters become markedly distinguished from the overall world order. The heroes seem to act solely from within their own hearts, no longer simply from external stimuli, whether from a god or conditions of outcome.[23] Here, choice in the true sense is evident, since the source of action is located in the conscious human self.[24]

Nevertheless, even though the human self as such emerges in tragedy, it is still to some extent enmeshed in an extrahuman fate. This is particularly true in Aeschylus and also to a significant degree in Sophocles. Orestes's choice is between *divine* alternatives, and the choices of Oedipus secretly play out a preordained fate. We could say that the tragic hero has choice, but the matters chosen are still sacred, extrahuman values. In effect such is the full force of tragedy—the *simultaneous* magnification of human autonomy and fatality.

> The day of destiny (*to morsimon*) waits for the free man as well as for the man enslaved beneath an alien hand. (*Libation Bearers*, 103–104)[25]

The hero *chooses* that which is fated for him, or his own choice accomplishes that which is beyond his control (the ultimate paradox of Oedipus). In the broadest sense, tragic dilemmas embody a primal Dionysian theme—inevitable destruction despite the impetus toward individuation in the life process.

# The Tragic Poets

## AESCHYLUS (525–456 B.C.)

The poetry of Aeschylus reflected a time of cultural crisis in the Greek world. Fifth century Athens was still tied to its mythical traditions, and yet there was growing criticism and skepticism about myths. It was a time of great ambiguity, ambivalence, and confusion, just what one would expect from a mythical age beginning to turn for the first time to the countertraditional phenomenon of reason. There were both intellectual and political developments which had not yet rejected the past but rather were living through a cultural tug of war. The tragedies of Aeschylus, particularly the *Oresteia*, dramatize the deep tension resulting from the *coexistence* of traditional mythical powers and intellectual "enlightenment." In a way, then, the poetry of Aeschylus represents a point of suspension between two forms of culture, the mythical and the rational. Such would account for the ambiguity of his plays and the startling juxtapositions therein—the mixing of beauty, intelligence, and progressive ideas with a truly fearful atmosphere of doom, catastrophe, and blood.

Generally speaking, both the form and content of tragedy speak to this question of cultural ambiguity. Greek tragedians introduced something new to mythical disclosure—a *reinterpretation* of traditional stories to make them relevant to a new age. They did not always follow the specific content of the tales handed down by tradition. In so doing they took up the advent of conscious reflection and departed from the pure "givenness" of earlier mythical presentation. Furthermore, tragic poetry gave a new sense of structure to myth in that the dramas shaped a much clearer and more deliberate pattern of beginning, development, and end. Not unrelated to such a structure was the broadened message of tragedy. Beyond the selective emphases of epic and lyric poetry, the tragedians offered a reflective overview of the complete pattern of human fate—the rise and fall of humans in the world.[26] But even though tragic poets displayed an attitude of reflection, they did not reject myth, as did some of the early philosophers. Rather, their detachment from the immediacy of mythical forms allowed a greater sense of sophistication and depth which continued to maintain mythical disclosure by drawing out a more generalized *meaning*. No longer simply myth and not yet abstract reflection, tragedy mixed a balance in which myth and reflection are almost indistinguishable. Let us turn to Aeschylus's *Oresteia* for a brief look at the way in which tragic poetry can accomplish such a balance.

The general plot of the Oresteian trilogy can be summarized as follows. Agamemnon has just returned to Argos after the Greek victory over the Trojans. While en route to Troy, the Greek ships were stalled by a great calm, and it was prophesied that the Greeks would not make it to Troy unless Agamemnon sacrificed his daughter to the gods, which was done. Upon his return to Greece, Agamemnon is killed by his wife, Clytemnestra, to avenge the sacrificial death of their daughter. The son Orestes is then commanded by Apollo to kill his mother in return. The dark Furies, however, are bound by blood vengeance to kill Orestes. He is pursued by the Furies but later acquitted by a court presided over by Athena. Let us try to unravel the basic themes of this rich and complicated trilogy in the light of our previous discussions.

The most prevalent image in the plays is that of a net or web, indicating the subordination of mortals to an inescapable fate.

*Surely it is a huge*
*and heavy spirit* (daimona) *binding the house you cry;*
*alas, the bitter glory*
*of a doom that shall never be done with;*
*and all through Zeus, Zeus,*
*first cause, prime mover.*
*For what thing without Zeus is done among mortals?*
*What here is without god's blessing? (Agamemnon,* 1481–1488)

Orestes's situation shows how foreign the notion of "personal responsibility" is to tragedy. The individual is truly in a no win position since he is faced with two conflicting *divine* commands. If Orestes disobeys Apollo, he will be punished; if he obeys, he will be punished by the Furies. Our understanding of the tragic has always included the idea of destruction in the context of an inescapable dilemma. What makes *Greek* tragedy so distinctive is that the dilemma cannot be traced back to human traits or social circumstances but rather to sacred forces.[27] It might be easy to suppose that the various prophesies and divine agencies are simply a conventional backdrop to the human situation or a way of symbolizing powerful human drives and conflicting emotions. But in view of our analysis of mythical disclosure, such an interpretation would be external at best. For the Greeks these sacred forces were genuine cultural realities, and if anything can be said to be symbolic in tragedy it would be the individual characters and their circumstances, as a richly specified enactment of a deep, underlying religious meaning—the immersion of humans in a sacred, coercive fatality. In Greek tragedy there does not seem to be anything the character could have done differently. What we find is the unsettling paradox that a *required* action leads to doom. In other words there is accountability without *personal* responsibility or guilt. It is the deed that counts and not the doer; punishment is justified even though the individual had no control over the situation.

Aeschylus of course did not invent this sense of fatality (we have seen it well embedded in earlier mythical forms), but Aeschylus has drawn sharp individual characters, and since he brought about the innovation of adding a second actor (outside the chorus) to dramatic scenes, he introduced individual conflict and thereby individualized fatality to a greater degree. Since Aeschylus highlighted the individual in relation to fate, he consequently magnified the tension and force of human fatedness. In this regard, we can turn to the character of Agamemnon, who embodies a tragic dilemma and also highlights the heroic dimension of tragedy that was mentioned earlier in this chapter. Agamemnon's situation represents a classic tragic paradox with an emphasis on the hero's circumstance: his heroic deed (victory over Troy) required an act (his daughter's sacrifice) which brought about his death. We have seen a comparable sense of paradox in the *Iliad*, and Agamemnon's fate can be considered a new and highly intensified version of heroic doom. The sense of crime or sin in tragedy does introduce a nonepic element, but if we read these terms with too much of a modern eye we miss the tragic point. Agamemnon in a way was compelled to sacrifice his daughter. The fate of the Greek army and the success of the Greek nation were hanging in the balance. In fact his action was a sacrifice of his personal concerns for the good of the community.

In any case we should remember that the heroic ideal had not vanished from the Greek scene. The chorus *welcomes* Agamemnon's great victory and expresses the city's heartfelt joy (*Agamemnon*, 270ff.). As the paragon of heroic achievement and excellence, Agamemnon nevertheless was fated to seal his own demise (the chorus speaks of Agamemnon's doom while in the same breath declaring him blessed and honored by the gods for the capture of Troy: 1331–1342). In order to *be* Agamemnon he had to sacrifice both his daughter and himself (witness the mixture of good and evil in the prophecy aboard ship: 122–159). The only thing to be "blamed" is the heroic situation itself, and I am convinced that this was not the intention of Aeschylus. Rather, the aim of the tragedy is to present the paradoxical juxtapositions at the heart of Greek culture, here portrayed through the heroic dilemma.

I think that Nietzsche's interpretation helps us unravel the ambiguity of the tragedy at hand—the simultaneous elevation and desolation of the hero. The "crime" of Agamemnon is not some particular deed, motive, or mistake, but rather, as Nietzsche proposed, *being* an individual (hero). But heroic individuation remains a Greek ideal. Hence we find in this tragedy the acknowledged coexistence of Apollonian individuation and Dionysian destruction. Agamemnon's deed is a crime, according to Nietzsche, only in the sense that individuation asserts itself over against the formless unity of the Dionysian process and hence it must be punished by reabsorption. But "crime" and "punishment" are metaphors for a cosmic dialectic and are not to be read in a strictly moral sense. The inevitability in the tragedy, together with the presence of contrary authorities, makes a moral interpretation (in the sense of personal responsibility and resolution) subject to frustration.

We should here retrieve a previous interpretation of family killings to further emphasize the mythico-religious substructure of Greek tragedy. The *Oresteia* is a veritable orgy of family violence, with husband and wife, parent and child, killing off each other. Even the curse of Atreus (Agamemnon's father), which forms the fateful background of the trilogy, stemmed from family killings (Thyestes unknowingly ate his own children who were fed to him by his brother, Atreus; and Aegisthus, Clytemnestra's accomplice, was the son of Thyestes). It seems entirely unwarranted to assume that Aeschylus was primarily offering some kind of social commentary on Athenian family strife. And if he were simply speaking to human violence in general, why the preoccupation with the family? I think it is more appropriate to link the troubled family with the deep-seated traditional model of family violence in Greek myth (recall the killing and opposition of related pairs in the *Theogony*), along with the Dionysian notion of a life process feeding on itself. The individual family members in Greek tragedy mask a more primordial tension. Clytemnestra herself proclaims a deeper origin for her actions:

> *Can you claim I have done this?*
> *Speak of me never*
> *more as the wife of Agamemnon.*
> *In the shadow of this corpse's queen*
> *the old stark avenger*
> *of Atreus for his revel of hate*
> *struck down this man,*
> *last blood for the slaughtered children. (Agamemnon, 1497–1504)*

And when he is being killed, her husband, Agamemnon, is called a bull (1125), which is a Dionysian image. The Dionysian notion of an inevitable interplay between life and death, success and ruin, is often generalized in the text (e.g., 1001–1007). And the idea of a common fate underlying the opposing elements is suggested in the lines spoken by Clytemnestra and Orestes (*Libation Bearers*, 909–910). Deep within the familial turmoil are the reverberations of a sacred mythical tradition.

The final feature of the *Oresteia* that should occupy our attention is the obvious confrontation between Olympian and Chthonic forces. The court scene in *The Eumenides* brings face to face the two central elements of Greek mythical culture (which we have generalized in terms of Nietzsche's Apollonian–Dionysian distinction). On the one hand there is Athena's court and Apollo's defense of Orestes. On the other hand the blood-vengeance of the Furies represents an older, darker force which requires automatic punishment and which reflects the instinctive, stark brutality of nature. Aeschylus, however, is not simply repeating the sky-earth, god-fate tension of epic poetry. The juxtaposition has been intensified and sharpened, because the Olympian aspect of the drama is closer to the reasoned sense of justice which had developed in the writings of Hesiod and Solon, while the Chthonic aspect breaks loose from its background epic function to take center stage in a terrifying, wild, and bloody embodiment. The scene presents a debate between reason and passion, culture and nature, freedom and fate, new intellectual patterns and old mythical traditions, all however still presented in the language of myth.

The question arises about the significance of Orestes's acquittal at the end of the play. It would not be unreasonable to suggest that it represents an affirmation of rational law and justice over natural violence and passion, and that Aeschylus was dramatizing the emergence of new intellectual and political developments that were coming to shape Athenian culture. But I think the *Oresteia* is more complicated than that, and in fact the final scene speaks to the point. It is not exactly clear that the acquittal indicates an Apollonian victory. The court is initially deadlocked in a tie vote, and Orestes is freed after Athena breaks the tie, but only after the Furies are "persuaded" to compromise. In a telling speech (*Eumenides*, 848–869), Athena pays homage to the Furies. She admits that they are older and wiser, but she asks them not to disdain her intelligence. She proclaims that the old sacred forces will continue to be honored in religious festivals and asks the Furies to "share our country." In the end they agree, and the atmosphere at the close of the play is one of joyous reconciliation.

It is true that Aeschylus gives voice to developments which will later strive for a victory of reason over passion, civic over natural law, internalized conscious reflection over traditional fate and mythical disclosure. But it seems that Aeschylus gives both sides their due and that the end of the trilogy represents a harmony of Olympian and Chthonic, Apollonian and Dionysian, elements. Aeschylus draws out something consistent with, but nevertheless unprecedented in, the Greek mythical tradition: He deliberately brings together Olympian and Chthonic forces and makes their coexistence no longer implicit but explicit. Furthermore, he seems to present the coexistence of a new-born rationality and traditional myth.

One might think that the acquittal scene undermines the traditional sense of tragic fatalism, but we must remember that a positive outcome is not inconsistent with the *Greek* sense of tragedy. The joyous reconciliation of light and darkness at the drama's end could reflect the positive elements of Dionysian religion we discussed earlier. Moreover, recall Nietzsche's point that tragedy is not purely Dionysian but Apollonian as well. Apollonian beauty and form introduce a cultivated moderation of pure Dionysian instincts and form a *world* out of and within the terror of negativity. The Apollonian spectacle contributes just as much joy as the sacred ecstasy of Dionysian formlessness. I think the end of the *Oresteia* proclaims a joy which stems from the mutual affirmation of two necessary dimensions of the world and which gives clear witness to the sense of *positive* fatalism that characterized the early Greek mind.

## SOPHOCLES (496–405 B.C.)

Sophocles gives tragedy a slightly different direction while still maintaining its basic substructure. The most important feature of his poetry in this regard is the increased emphasis on individual self-consciousness. The chorus, which for Aeschylus played a major role, steps more into the background, thus giving the spotlight to the individual hero. Sophocles also introduced a third main actor to the tragic scene, thus increasing the sense of individual conflict. But the accent on individual consciousness does not lessen the power of fate in Sophocles's world. Human fatedness is still the guiding theme, and in fact, as I have said earlier, a sharper definition of individual existence only intensifies the tension and paradox of human subordination to fate.

We shall focus on Sophocles's treatment of the Oedipus myth in order to penetrate the meaning of his poetry. *Oedipus the King* is a classic example of Greek tragedy. As a work of art it is close to perfection. The beauty and weight of the poetry, the effective use of tension, the symmetrical form shaped by ironic twists in the plot, the noble pathos of the characters, all make the play a marvel. The general plot is as follows: An oracle proclaims that Laius, king of Thebes, will be killed by his son, who will then marry his mother. Dreading such a prophecy, Laius orders his young child Oedipus taken away from the city by a servant and left to die of exposure. Out of pity the servant gives the child to a shepherd, who takes him to his king in Corinth. Oedipus is raised by the king and queen, but upon manhood he hears the prophecy of his fate. Thinking the king and queen to be his parents, Oedipus flees Corinth. On the road Oedipus meets and gets into an angry quarrel with Laius, whom he kills. Oedipus then arrives at Thebes and saves the city from a curse by solving the riddle of the sphinx. In glory Oedipus marries the widowed queen and becomes king of Thebes. The city becomes victim to a plague, and an oracle declares the need to expiate the guilt of Laius's murder. When the truth is learned, the queen kills herself, and Oedipus gouges out his eyes and takes exile from Thebes.

What does the play show us? First and foremost the figure of Oedipus stands out. He is the typically Greek heroic individual, but his individuality is much more pronounced than any other prior cultural figure. With respect to his situation we see Oedipus as someone primarily alone, singled out from his environment. The drama concerns his own confrontation with his particular fate, which ends not in sheer destruction but in isolation from society and loss of meaning with respect to his cultural stature. Oedipus's character is also much closer to the modern sense of self-identity—a fully conscious individual whose actions and decisions are his own. We notice the development of unity and interiority, but the question of autonomy forces us to see Oedipus in the light of Greek tradition.

Sophocles has created a remarkable ambiguity. Despite the full selfhood of Oedipus, fate remains in the background, though hidden in the sense that the hero must destroy *himself*. Sophocles internalizes what for Aeschylus was more a cosmic struggle. Although sacred forces are still implicitly at work, they now seem embodied in or enacted by humans alone. Still, the hero's self-destruction remains a powerful expression of certain tragic themes. The Dionysian notion of a natural dialectic of life and death, where the life process feeds off itself, has been suggested as the subtextual meaning of family killings, an image which continues to be a part of Sophoclean drama. But the idea that reality is simultaneously self-constructive and self-destructive is sharpened even further when family strife is condensed into a single person destroying his own life and stature.

The figure of Oedipus also reveals a good deal about the Apollonian–Dionysian distinction in terms of the juxtaposition of heroic individuation and tragic fate in Sophocles's play. Oedipus is a model of Greek excellence—strong, brave, intelligent, a leader. We can infer no criticism of these traits *per se* within the context of the play. Heroic individuation is affirmed by the noble stature of Oedipus, but at the same time the hero is subjected to an inescapable fate which dismantles individuation and which seems *indigenous* to his heroic position. This is what makes the hero tragic rather than "flawed." In order for

Oedipus to *be* Oedipus he had to act in such a way as to simultaneously
elevate himself and precipitate a terrible downfall.

In a famous choral speech from *Antigone*, Sophocles proclaims the
glory of man, with a typically Greek corrective at the end:

> *Many the wonders but nothing walks stranger than man.*
> *This thing crosses the sea in the winter's storm,*
> *making his path through the roaring waves.*
> *And she, the greatest of gods, the earth—*
> *ageless she is, and unwearied—he wears her away*
> *as the ploughs go up and down from year to year*
> *and his mules turn up the soil.*
> *Gay nations of birds he snares and leads,*
> *wild beast tribes and the salty brood of the sea,*
> *with the twisted mesh of his nets, this clever man.*
> *He controls with craft the beasts of the open air,*
> *walkers on hills. The horse with his shaggy mane*
> *he holds and harnesses, yoked about the neck,*
> *and the strong bull of the mountain.*
> *Language, and thought like the wind*
> *and the feelings that make the town,*
> *he has taught himself, and shelter against the cold,*
> *refuge from rain. He can always help himself.*
> *He faces no future helpless.*[28] *There's only death*
> *that he cannot find an escape from.* (332–360)

With that abrupt switch the chorus goes on to declare that humanity
must not dishonor the sacred powers of the world. Sophocles is here
exploring a theme which was a central feature of Aeschylus's *Prometheus Bound*: the tragic price of human gifts and advancement. For a
man to be the wonder that he is, he must elevate himself above the
world matrix, but in doing so he is destined to be checked and ultimately destroyed by that matrix from which he arose. I am convinced
that the tragic poets were neither demoting nor strictly promoting
human nature. Rather they were simply acknowledging a paradox—
human advancement is coextensive with a fateful limitation. Human
beings dwell in a world which simultaneously supports and undermines their achievements. The tragic view is neither optimistic nor
passively pessimistic but rather a positive fatalism.

The paradox of human life is well captured by a word used twice in
the first line of the choral speech above. That word is *deinon*, which
has an essentially ambiguous meaning: wondrous, awful, dangerous,

skillful, terrible, mighty. Oedipus himself personifies a paradoxical co-incidence of contrary features: construction and destruction (his own advance led inexorably to his decline); knowledge and ignorance (he was not the man he thought he was); success and failure; power and powerlessness; home and homelessness (his home in Corinth was not his true home, and his true home produced his ultimate alienation); familiarity and strangeness (every aspect of his life concealed a terrible aberration); convention and taboo; guilt and innocence.[29] Here we find a full dramatic picture of the existential matrix in which human life is embedded and which displays the positive-negative correlation of the Apollonian–Dionysian dialectic at the heart of tragedy.

Perhaps the most startling paradox in *Oedipus the King* is that his relentless drive for truth (the identity of the murderer) leads to blind darkness. Tragic truth reveals a terrible negativity at the core of culture. Sophocles maintains the traditional belief that individuation is limited by fate. Though Oedipus moves through the play apparently self-directed and independent of divine agency, the oracle maintains an invisible effect. The highest irony of all shows itself when Oedipus's deliberate attempt to *avoid* his fate becomes the very condition for its actualization! Sophocles has turned fate in a new direction. Divine embodiments have left the stage, and fate becomes internalized to the point where Oedipus accepts his guilt and punishes *himself*. Traditional mythical meaning is retained, and the form of presentation remains within a mytho-poetic mode, but divine imagery has withdrawn in favor of the heroic individual's internalization of the traditional complex. The power of an extrahuman fate resounds throughout the drama, but the focus of attention is individual decision within that fate. Sophocles thus approaches the famous dictum of Heraclitus: "Character is man's destiny" (*ēthos anthrōpoi daimōn*). Here a man confronts directly in himself the truth that he cannot control his life, and that self-assertion is matched by doom.

When Oedipus's search for truth culminates in blind darkness, Sophocles has drawn out an implication of the Greek mythical tradition, but in doing so he alters the *way* in which the sacred is presented. With the withdrawal of the gods and the emphasis on humanity, human downfall is no longer ameliorated by the cosmic compensations of a divine epilogue. The negativity of human fate is more fully explicated since it is no longer "filled in" by a display of sacred forms. Sophocles does not deny the gods, he simply no longer *portrays* the divine. The shape of the divine seems to have lost its personality, order, and sense of purpose. For Sophocles the sacred stands as a mystery, dark and even absurd.[30] Consequently he has emphasized the sense of mystery which has been suggested as the background of mythical disclosure, but now we sense a mystery as such, at the expense of sacred forms. And if the sacred is now a sheer mystery, the only form left to *portray* is the human form. Oedipus represents a man confronting a fateful power which is barely visible in the drama and which actually culminates in darkness. I would suggest that this sacred atmosphere in fact reflects the implicit formlessness of the Dionysian.

In conclusion, the sharply drawn character of Oedipus, together with his dark end, presents a heightened intensification of the Apollonian–Dionysian correlation. Again, if we want to steer clear of external interpretations of Greek tragedy, we have to keep in mind the Apollonian element. Although one might sense in Sophocles the lyric/archaic feeling of helplessness and pessimism, a profound modification is evident in *Oedipus at Colonus*, where Oedipus departs from life with peace of mind and noble resignation. The Apollonian element of tragedy is shown in the heroic individual's noble bearing and stature even in the midst of a terrible end. Without heroic affirmation we inevitably misread tragedy as it was experienced by the Greeks. Too often certain moral sensibilities lead us astray. The tragic situation shows itself to be terrible but incorrigible. In order to be who he was, Oedipus had to suffer; human life is wonderful-and-doomed.

For all his innovations Sophocles did not abandon the underlying meaning of that tradition. Even though he turned more to human consciousness than his predecessors, his retention of the idea of a fatal limit prevented him from turning to human understanding as an end in itself (one of the marks of philosophical reason) and kept him within an essentially mythical framework. In a way Oedipus represents a coalition of cultural developments past and future—the sacred meaning of a mythical world together with full self-consciousness and growing demythification. Oedipus is comparable to modern humans, but still embedded in an extrahuman setting; he is the free individual who alone confronts and reconciles himself to the terrible limits of individuation.

## EURIPIDES (484–406 B.C.)

The dramas of Euripides represent in many respects a break with the Greek tragic tradition. Such a position might seem odd, since Euripides wrote tragedies and his plays maintained a treatment of the gods and fate along with what could be called a decidedly greater catastrophic atmosphere than even the dramas of Aeschylus and Sophocles. But I think the claim that Euripides was less tragic than Aeschylus and Sophocles can be supported, and the apparent oddness of the claim only highlights my contention that the tragic in Greek culture has a special meaning which is easily misread. To a modern audience Euripides might appear to be a model tragic writer, but in the context of our analysis of *Greek* myth and tragedy, he does show himself to be departing from original tragic meanings. The point at issue is not the dramatic form as such, or the presence of fate and negativity, but rather the *way* in which human existence is portrayed in such a context and the underlying meaning of the tragic setting.

In this regard Nietzsche's analysis of tragedy helps us approach the question of Euripides' status as a tragic poet. On the basis of his Apollonian–Dionysian model, Nietzsche decides that Euripides abandoned the mythical meaning of tragedy in favor of assumptions more in line with countermythical developments which were emerging at that time. Nietzsche specifically cites Socratic philosophy as the embodiment of these developments which turned Euripides in a new direction. Nietzsche's critique of Euripides to some degree has a historical precedent in the comic poetry of Aristophanes. It was Aristophanes who maintained that Euripides represented not the apex of tragedy but rather its demise. In *The Frogs* tragic poetry is depicted as having decayed under the influence of Euripides and Socrates, who along with the Sophists undermined healthy traditions, dethroned poetry, and ushered in prosaic thinking.[31] According to Aristophanes, old tragedy was "moral" in that it aimed to transform people by teaching religious, cultural, and social values; Euripides and the Sophists were "immoral" in that they encouraged individualism, rational criticism, and the subsequent attack upon tradition.

Nietzsche takes the criticisms of Aristophanes on a somewhat deeper course. The demise of tragedy is a threat not only to cultural institutions and social order; it represents a cultural crisis in which the *meaning* of myth is being displaced by philosophical reason, a displacement which will have a revolutionary effect on history and yet also alienate humans from an indigenous and necessary mythical sense of the world. Furthermore, Nietzsche would not exactly agree that Euripides was immoral but rather that he represented a *new* morality built around rational individualism, a set of values which would create

a new intellectual, moral, and political climate. Finally, it is not that
Euripides explicitly introduces philosophical assumptions into tragic
drama (he continues to work within the bounds of mytho-poetic disclosure); rather, he presents the tragic mythical setting in a new mood
which could be characterized as the self-deprecation of myth, a mythical voice which speaks a traditional language divested of its traditional
meaning.[32] Though Euripides remains a poet, one could infer the implicit influence of nonmythical intellectual developments offstage.
The connection between his tragedies and the emergence of philosophy is therefore indirect but visible nevertheless when we compare
certain philosophical assumptions with the ways in which Euripidean
characters act and think. To that end let us take a brief look at
Nietzsche's analysis of Euripides.[33]

According to Nietzsche's interpretation of tragedy, Apollonian
individuation yields to the background power of Dionysian dissolution. As a consequence we notice two fundamental tragic assumptions:
(1) on the cosmic level there is the priority of a formless unity over individual forms such that form is a nonsubstantial "appearance"; (2)
from the standpoint of human existence there is the priority of the
nonconscious over consciousness such that self-awareness is also not a
fixed "substance." Nietzsche notices in Euripides a tendency, inspired
by Socratic philosophy, to emphasize form and conscious knowledge,
with the result that the Apollonian becomes severed from its Dionysian
background, thus undermining the nature of tragedy. What is unfolding is a switch between Dionysian truth and Apollonian appearance in
that form and conscious individuation are becoming the measure of
truth to fill in the negative mystery of Dionysus and give the world a
more formed, substantial structure.

As we have said, Euripides is a poet, not a philosopher; he does not
construct an intellectual picture of the world according to the conceptual principles of philosophy. What, then, aligns him with a philosopher like Socrates? According to Nietzsche, at least his resistance to and
dissatisfaction with the traditional mytho-tragic atmosphere. If we recall the notions of mystery and sacred arrival from our discussion of
myth we can set the scene here. Nietzsche focuses on Euripides's use of
prologues in his plays. With that device the poet offered a forecast of
the tragedy, giving the background and meaning of upcoming events in
the drama. But in this way the spontaneity of mythical effect (mystery
and arrival) is lost; so too is affective absorption in the dramatic events.
Nietzsche contends that Euripides is here demonstrating that his own

conscious knowledge takes precedence over the nonconscious and nonreflective elements of mythical disclosure. The prologue encourages a form of mental detachment which could be called analogous to the detachment from lived experience exhibited by philosophical reason.

The most telling example of Euripides's departure from tragic myth is the way in which individual characters are portrayed in his plays. In this regard, Nietzsche analyzes a psychological aspect of Euripidean drama which he feels is not unrelated to certain assumptions about human nature in the development of philosophy. That aspect involves the growing isolation of individual consciousness from sacred forces and the subsequent loss of self-transcendence which characterized early tragedy. In Euripides, though fate maintains its power, the relationship between the individual and fate seems to have changed from a dialectical tension and integration into a polarized opposition. No longer does there seem to be a reconciliation with fate but rather an atmosphere of resistance and rebellion. Euripidean heroes tend to defend their actions with arguments and counterarguments; they indulge in heated analyses of their situations from the standpoint of their own subjectivity. An emphasis on individual motivation appears to replace the notion of sacred control in many of the plays (e.g., *Medea*), but even where fate inexorably destroys a hero, the character reveals the extent of his individuation by maintaining resistance to the end, without the noble resignation which characterized Aeschylean and Sophoclean heroes. There is no longer the tragic sense of individuation in the midst of a sacred fate but rather a sense of individuation *versus* fate.

In this regard, Nietzsche says something which would seem rather strange, namely, that Euripides has abandoned tragedy for "optimism." How can this be, when his plays clearly present more failures and catastrophes than those of his predecessors? I think we can clarify what Nietzsche had in mind. The issue is not how the play turns out in the end but the way in which the individual responds to that end and his situation. By "optimism" Nietzsche means something emerging within the development of philosophy, specifically that of Socrates and Plato, something which departs from traditional mythical ideals. On the one hand, optimism would refer to the idea that the human self can control its own life, free itself from negative limitations, or perhaps even survive death; but on the other hand, even short of these possibilities, it would refer to the belief that the human mind has the ability to *know*

the world and free life of its mystery through explanation and reduction to abiding principles. Even if Euripidean heroes are doomed, their
behavior could imply a background optimism, namely, that one should
*strive* for conscious knowledge if one is to express one's true nature.
But according to Nietzsche, optimism undermines tragic wisdom by
isolating Apollonian surfaces without the Dionysian reabsorption of
appearances. The tragic also entails a sense of joy resulting from the
recognition of Dionysus as the underlying unity of life beneath the
masks of Apollonian individuation. Since Euripidean characters have
been sealed within conscious individuation, Dionysian joy is out of
reach. Hence the destructive finale of the drama is really pseudotragic
in that it only presents the loss of individuation and the failure of conscious knowledge and *not* the emergence of Dionysian meaning. The
relation to fate is now one of struggle rather than transformative resignation. So, it is not the negative outcome of the drama as such that indicates its tragic character (we have seen that some tragedies have a
positive atmosphere) but rather the comportment within a fatal
setting.

The sense of fatality and negativity in Euripides can be distinguished from the tragic in the following way. Euripides was a *pessi-
mist*, and pessimism can be rendered as a failed optimism. He could be
seen as valuing the ideals of optimism but denying the possibility of
their realization. Why else the atmosphere of rebellion? Euripidean
"tragedy" thus reflects this negative theme: Humans *should* succeed
but cannot; conscious knowledge *should* succeed but does not. It
ought to be clear, however, that this pessimistic negativity is not equivalent to tragic negativity.[34] The success of the hero was not the issue in
tragedy, but rather inevitable and necessary limitation (hence the
hero's resignation). Tragedy *affirms* both the various checks on the
conscious self and the negativity of the world process. Euripides's re-
bellious hero ushers in a new human model—the free individual guiding his own destiny by means of a faculty peculiar to the conscious self,
namely, unaided reasoning from experience, free of sacred intervention.[35] For this reason Euripidean characters rebel against various
extra-individual forces (fate, the gods, society). The failures of these
characters do not take away from the implicitly optimistic model at
work defining the aims and motivations within the drama.

In old tragedy the hero was never a mere individual as such but a
*special* individual, because he was embedded in extra-individual,
extraconscious forces and became a cultural exemplar by confronting

the sacred fatality of a mythical world. Euripides's turn to individuation as such is shown in the way he portrays the character of heroes and gods. His "heroes" are often presented as weak, imperfect, apologetic, and vulgar.[36] Nobility and the depth of heroic passion seem to be lost. It was Nietzsche's contention that such characterizations indicated Euripides's preference for ordinary consciousness and had the effect of reducing the hero to the level of the common man. In the context of our previous discussions we can designate such a shift as the collapsing of the sacred into the profane. Perhaps we can say that Euripides, the proponent of ordinary consciousness, had abandoned the original meaning of myths and portrayed them in a new way: not as a presentation of sacred, extra-individual meanings but as a representation of the passions, motives, and activities of ordinary men.

Because of the way in which he shapes his plays and characters, Euripides is often thought to be a part of the Greek intellectual "enlightenment." But to be precise we would not want to fall prey to the progressive notion that Euripides's poetry was coming closer to the truth by critically undermining the authority of myth. Euripides more than anyone else shows that the situation was a cultural *struggle* between two significant forms of disclosure. He was still speaking in a mythical voice and yet his tone was echoing certain nonmythical developments. Hence the "demotion" of myth from a sacred to a profane atmosphere could not be accurately called a "critique," since it *abandons* the paradigmatic background of myth. What we have, therefore, is the beginning of a paradigm shift, the advent of a new, nonmythical criterion—the individual, rational self. The Euripidean demotion shows more ambiguity and ambivalence than criticism, and the element of *resistance* suggests that Euripides is not "finally telling the truth about myths," but rather is looking at myth in a *new* way, by means of certain criteria which would be *inappropriate* for the old view. Though speaking through myth, Euripidean tragedy implicitly abandons a mythical world and awaits a more explicit break in the emergence of philosophy, science, and rational morality.

## Tragedy and Myth

Let us summarize the relationship between tragedy and mythical disclosure, again with the help of Nietzsche. It was Nietzsche's contention that tragedy reveals the meaning of myth through myth: "Through tragedy, the myth attains its most profound content."[37] In a general way the Dionysian element of tragedy crystallizes what could be called a fundamental feature of mythical disclosure—that form is an "appearance." We have discussed the background negativity and mystery of the sacred, the "emergent" quality of mythical forms, and the contrast between mythical meaning and rational truth (unified concepts, objective facts, and the like). According to Nietzsche's interpretation, tragedy dramatizes the sense of myth, which in effect is an inversion of modern assumptions about truth and appearance. Tragic myth shows that truth could be called an underlying formless process, while form is an appearance in that it emerges out of formlessness and is not therefore substantial in itself. While form is an appearance, this is not to be taken in the negative sense of illusion. Dionysian formlessness is in itself meaningless; Apollonian individuation presents a world in the midst of this formlessness and hence establishes meaning and structure. But form is simply not the bottom line according to tragic wisdom. Nonetheless, form could be called truth *as* appearance, that is to say, the appearing, emerging of cultural meaning out of formlessness (i.e., unconcealment).[38]

Since the *creative* dimension of myth and poetry entails the emergence of form out of formlessness, mythical disclosure cannot and does not resist the negative limit within which form appears. It was Nietzsche's view that tragedy illuminated the background implications of mythical disclosure as such. Dionysian wisdom "educated" the Olympian world by announcing the meaning of appearance to the old myths. That is to say, the tendency to reify myths, to see them as a kind of historical foundation (what Nietzsche called a "juvenile history") was checked in favor of a more genuine mythical sense of creative appearance. In other words, tragedy explicates the appearance-character of myth by rejecting the idea of "foundation" and promoting the notion of arrival out of a mystery as well as the continuing *priority* of a formless mystery.

The tragic outlook perceives truth to be a formless negativity and a formed world to be an appearance. Both the form and content of tragedy suggest the plausibility of such a generalization; that is to say, the tragic mode of presentation is essentially aesthetic and creative, and the theme of tragedy entails the priority of a destructive fate. We can recap our treatment of tragic myth by briefly summarizing the form and content of Greek drama.

Although it was our aim earlier to penetrate the underlying meaning of epic myth, suffice it to say that epic poetry was generally perceived to be a kind of historical account which described sacred events in the past. Drama, however, is more akin to ritual in that the myth coincides with a present enactment. Drama *embodies* the myth as opposed to being a report of the past. But drama has departed from both a literal identity with the past and an experience of identification in the present which characterized primitive rituals. Even though the audience could become wrapped up in the dramatic event, religious identification was now modified because the drama as such was recognized as a performance and hence not a strict identity. In other words drama introduced a kind of transparency to mythical disclosure. The play both *is* the myth (its presentation in time and space) and *is not* the myth (since it is an acknowledged departure from identity and "literalness").[39]

In a clear way the mask phenomenon best illuminates the perception of drama. The mask incarnates a mythical form; at the same time it is recognized as a creative addition to the scene. The drama is likewise neither literally true nor is it on that account "false" since it continues to establish cultural meaning. Dramatic truth, therefore, is truth-as-appearance, neither objective facts nor mythical literalness. For this reason Nietzsche proposed that tragic drama discovered the *essence* of mythical disclosure (and, for him, the essence of reality itself)—the emergence of form in the midst of a formless process, where form presents meaning without "substance."

If we recall the sacred-profane distinction, the masklike character of drama in a way consciously explicates the mythical sense of the sacred. The drama reveals a sacred meaning, and at the same time it is *known* to be a deliberate departure from ordinary (profane) experience and from any kind of literalness. Thus it could be said that through tragic drama, myth comes to *see itself* as myth in the way we have been trying to describe it, namely, as a "sacred appearance," neither a subjective fiction nor an objective fact (even in the religious fundamentalist sense of seeing a myth as a record of actual events).

Tragic drama, therefore, uncovers the essence of mythical disclosure and the mythical sense of the world—nonsubstantial appearances of existential meaning in the midst of a sacred mystery. Of course, later intellectual developments considered such an outlook objectionable and inadequate to reality, but this would result from new criteria based upon what could be called rational or empirical "realism." Perhaps it was the overt "phenomenalism" of drama that set the stage for criticism of mythical disclosure. If one were looking forward to philosophical realism one might declare that drama anticipated rational truth by showing the "fictional" character of myth. But one could just as well look *back* from tragedy and see in drama a most sophisticated culmination of mythical disclosure which uncovers the significance and underlying *sense* of a mythical world.

So much for the form of tragedy. As far as its content is concerned, the thematic priority of destructive fate further suggests the notion of appearance. Though tragedy celebrates and presents human form and meaning (the Apollonian), culture is nevertheless inevitably an appearance in that it is dismantled by a fatal negativity (the Dionysian). The key theme of tragedy seems to be unavoidable self-destruction which plays out the extrahuman forces of fate. When Aeschylus issues the classic tragic proposition that "wisdom comes alone through suffering" (*Agamemnon*, 177–178), we must be clear about its specific, Greek meaning. What is learned through suffering? I have tried to show that it cannot be a "moral" insight; the hero is subject to fate and is not at fault. It cannot be something comparable to Christian salvation since there is no reward for suffering (not even the social compensations of epic poetry). Tragic wisdom entails the insight that life is nonsubstantial and that limitation and negation are indigenous to the world. There is no ultimate solution to the human condition in tragedy. Therefore human aspirations are irrevocably checked by a negative limit and hence can be called an appearance. In sum, then, the form and content of tragedy mirror each other with respect to a certain phenomenalism. Neither the mythical imagery nor the structures of human culture have any ultimate "foundation."

I would like to close this chapter with some summary reflections about the contribution that a Nietzschean analysis has made to our overall study. We have proposed that tragedy reveals the meaning of myth, namely that form is appearance, in the sense of being nonfoundational but also in the positive sense of appearing, emerging. Consequently the *truth* of mythical disclosure is a *process* (unconcealment) which involves extraconscious forces, the variability of lived immediacy, and arrivals out of a mystery. In other words, form is not a fixed substance but a metamorphic occurrence essentially in the midst of an "other." Tragedy crystallizes mythical truth by recognizing the limit of form and emphasizing a "yield" to that limit.

As a result we can draw the following conclusion. Since mythical truth is *not* factuality (the profane) and *not* rational order through abstract, common ideas fixed in the conscious mind, then the typical critique of myth (i.e., that mythical forms are not facts, are not evident in ordinary sense experience, or are not universal principles which can order a plurality) is a *rigged* critique. When myth comes to be seen as appearance in the negative sense (i.e., unreal, fictional, untrue), this is not the discovery of truth but a *new* sense of truth, a new set of assumptions which will shape the world in a different way. From such an external standpoint myth cannot be judged a mistake because the conditions of mythical disclosure cannot be measured by empirical facts or rational principles. When myth is said to fall short of these criteria and is thus judged to be mistaken, its "failure" actually constitutes its success, its "error" is in fact its truth. There is a certain incommensurability between myth and various perspectives which seek to correct it. Hence such criticism is really a frame-up. As an analogy, consider a critique of science on the grounds that it ignores God. Science would not *be* science if it were founded on religious matters. Just as this critique is rigged, so too is a rational or empirical critique of myth.

The culmination of myth in tragedy shows the following understanding of the world: Form has a certain transparency in that it yields to its own limit, and "facts" yield to the sacred. Mythical truth displays an existential fluidity and the nonsubstantiality of form. Rational and empirical truth entails a reduction of lived experience to some fixed form in terms of unified, general ideas or objective data isolated from existential meaning. When, on rational or empirical grounds, a myth is said to resist verification or uniformity and generally lack substance, this is not a successful critique but rather a confirmation of mythical *truth*. The point of this study has been to survey the changes in Greek culture with respect to how and why philosophy came to displace myth. This development was not an exchange of error for truth but a competition between different forms of truth. It is simply wrong to think that myth was or can be replaced by philosophy. First of all we will see how philosophy grew *out of myth* and retained certain elements of mythical tradition. Secondly, whatever *is* distinctive about philosophy should be taken as being *added* to our understanding of the world rather than being the "proper" understanding of the world.

Nietzsche's position (often misunderstood) was not a rejection of rationality but rather its exclusivity, reductionism, and optimism which came at the expense of other forms of disclosure and a tragic view of the world he took to be inescapable. According to Nietzsche, reason and science are perspectival appearances (no less than myth), but a guiding assumption on the part of philosophers was that reason could penetrate "the truth" and overcome the uncertainties of life. Consequently philosophy was at odds with the nature of mythical disclosure. Nietzsche took issue with philosophy's *justification* for its proposed status. His notorious argument was that the philosophical claim to absolute truth was based on *contingencies* like utilitarian advantages or psychological need (e.g., security). Nietzsche focused on two important historical developments, Greek rationalism and Christian otherworldliness, claiming that their essential feature was the attempt to correct and overcome the negativity of the world process through either abstract ideas or spiritual transcendence. He traced this attempt to a human quality, a kind of weakness in the face of tragic negativity, rather than to some ultimate truth. It is no surprise that both Greek rationalism and Christianity found themselves at war with pagan mythology, because of the nonoptimistic, tragic elements of myth which seemed to require what Nietzsche called strength in the face of negativity. Perhaps, he suggested, the early Greek tradition tells us something about the world which need not be corrected.

Because he detected an esoteric psychology behind the "objective" claims of philosophy, Nietzsche refused to accept the proposed foundations of philosophical thought and its subsequent criticisms of myth. There are nonabsolute, nonobjective (and hence mythical?) predispositions hidden within the philosophical discovery of "reality." It is important to realize that Nietzsche saw nothing wrong with the advent of reason or individual self-consciousness. Rather, he opposed rational*ism* and individual*ism*, namely, the assumption that *reality* as a whole is rational or that the *essence* of human experience is located within the boundary of individual self-consciousness. When reason and individuation are *opposed* to the mythical matrix as we have described it, then an unwarranted split ensues which exiles mythical meaning or at least demotes it. When "reason" or "the individual" come to be identified with "reality," then mythical disclosure (which entailed a sense of mystery and an extra-individual complex) is *now* judged to be a fiction. But Nietzsche insisted that myth remains a significant form of disclosure, and he especially regretted that rational optimism covers over (or cannot withstand) an insight perfected in tragic poetry—the only ultimate "truth" is the loss or limit of form (an insight he considered consistent with a world of change and becoming).

The rational individualism which characterized later developments of philosophy in Greece in various ways deliberately opposed the tragic notion of a pervasive limit in favor of a substantiation of form (e.g., unchanging ideas, the immortality of the soul). According to Nietzsche, such developments represented the *isolation* of Apollonian individuation from its tragic correlation with the Dionysian to the point where form, measure, and structure became opaque to process and took on the character of "substance." But it is only this *opposition* to change, variability, and mystery that generated Nietzsche's critique of philosophy, not the advent of reason as such. In fact, Nietzsche advocated a perspectival pluralism where the world can take a meaning in various ways and where art and reason can coexist—witness his call for an "artistic Socrates."[40] So the enemy is not reason but rather exclusivity and uniformity. Our study is aimed at uncovering the historical roots of this problem in terms of the following guiding theme: Along with the benefits and positive elements of rationality there is shown in its historical emergence a clear *resistance* to certain defensible elements of mythical disclosure and the way the world is shown therein. It is the questionable character of this resistance which will open the door to a kind of pluralism.

# VI

# The Advent of Philosophy

With the emergence of philosophy in Greek culture there occurs the first recognizable shift away from the patterns of mythical tradition. The situation is complicated and resists easy classifications or strict distinctions, however. It seems evident that early philosophical developments show sufficient connections with mythical forms so that philosophy can be said in some respects to have grown *out of* myth.[1] Our analysis of the meaning and structure of mythical disclosure will serve us well in clarifying the complicated relationship between myth and philosophy. Although philosophy distinguishes itself by developing conceptual abstraction and logical reasoning, a division of philosophical "rationality" and mythical "irrationality" is unwarranted because of our elucidation of mythical sense. And although the *method* of philosophy shows a clear departure from myth, its underlying comprehension of the world appears in certain mythical prefigurations. In addition we will pay particular attention to various thematic correlations between myth (especially tragedy) and early philosophical developments.

The so-called Greek enlightenment began in the sixth century B.C. and came to a head in the fifth century B.C. with the Sophists. During this period the phenomenon of philosophy began to undermine traditional religious beliefs, practices, and customs.[2] It must be remembered, however, that the first philosophers were isolated figures, some of whom were even persecuted for their beliefs. It took a long time for their ideas to gain currency and become established as cultural ideals. (Such resistance was due less to obstinate ignorance or malevolence and more to the traumas of a paradigm clash; the emergence of philosophy was more like a political revolution than an obvious correction of a deluded past.) In any case let us briefly survey some basic characteristics of this period of intellectual development in Greece, characteristics which are recognizably related to each other in an overall complex.

**1.** The validity of divination, inspiration, and ritual began to be questioned. Mythical meaning was being displaced by abstract reasoning within the confines of the conscious mind and in the context of ordinary experience. We could say that such developments represented a switch of priorities with respect to the sacred and profane, where the sacred was losing its cultural status. In fact, during this period there were various attempts to offer profane explanations for religious myths and traditional deities: mistaken judgments about the world because of the powerful effects of natural phenomena (Democritus); human gratitude for beneficial natural phenomena (Prodicus); a human device for social control (Critias).[3]

**2.** Consequently, the sense of "givenness" and subsequent atmosphere of unquestioned authority which characterized mythical culture gave way to something previously absent as a cultural force—skepticism. It became a mark of philosophy to question and doubt the validity of myths, a disposition which on the one hand freed the mind for new discoveries, but which on the other hand introduced an element of rebellion which threatened the cohesion of cultural authority in general. A significant example in this regard is the *nomos-physis* distinction which took shape in some of the later Sophists. *Nomos* meant "custom" or "law," while *physis* generally came to mean "nature." This distinction was primarily used in reference to social, political, and moral issues and had various applications to different situations.[4] In such contexts the *nomos-physis* distinction reflected the belief that social and cultural structures were not intrinsic to the world but rather conventions imposed upon a natural order. In effect this distinction ruptured certain correlations which characterized mythical disclosure, especially the language-world and nature-culture correlations. If it is thought that what we say does not always match the "world" and that human cultural forms do not match "nature," then such distinctions entail an implicit measurement of language and culture against a separable criterion. From this there follows a simultaneous gain and loss: a spirit of criticism is encouraged which can lead to innovative thinking and cultural renovation but which can also lead to general disenchantment with cultural authority and alienation from the social order.

**3.** We have already seen how Greek myth portrayed the interplay between culture and nature, where subcultural, dark forces were acknowledged and woven into a mythical complex; and how nature was understood in terms of sacred meanings. Mythical disclosure cannot be understood as something separable from nature, and nature cannot be understood apart from the cultural presentations of myth. The *nomos-physis* distinction initiates a model of understanding which permits a number of unprecedented dichotomies. In general this distinction is the beginning of a division between humanity and world, in that human cultural concerns are set over against a nonhuman order of nature. Furthermore, the spirit of skepticism which grew out of this distinction suggests the beginning of a division between mind and world, where thought and reality no longer have a correlative fit. Specifically in this regard the *nomos-physis* distinction permits the development of a common model for the understanding of myth, namely, that myth is a (mistaken) projection upon nature. A central feature, therefore, of this period in Greek history is a separating of myth and nature, either for the purpose of skeptical criticism of myth or for the promotion of philosophical naturalism.

Though the *nomos-physis* distinction might seem to contain an explication of the mythical sense of nonsubstantiality we outlined previously (i.e., that cultural forms have no "foundation"), it nevertheless departs from mythical meaning because it *divides* culture from nature in a way not possible previously (witness the unprecedented developments of skepticism and relativism generated by the *nomos-physis* distinction). Moreover, the growing emphasis on nature indicates that culture is being *measured* according to a kind of natural standard. For this reason myth can begin to take on the character of appearance in the negative sense. The nonsubstantiality of myth had a positive meaning in that reality was shaped *as* appearance, but the *nomos-physis* distinction allows an unprecedented distinction between reality and appearance, where culture (or myth) no longer fits the world. With regard to the meaning of *physis*, it should be pointed out that its more naturalistic sense can be distinguished from a meaning more in line with the mythical sense of appearance. *Physis* is derived from the verb *phyein* which means "to bring forth, grow, or arise." Consequently the connotations of "nature" can be quite problematic when measuring a mythical world in terms of the emergence of natural philosophy. The notion of *physis*, therefore, need not suggest the correction of myth by a more realistic standard but rather a re-formation of reality according to an altered meaning of *physis* (from a sacred to a more profane meaning).

4. During this period we also witness a gradual depersonalization of the divine. God became less and less an object of worship and more an abstract cosmic principle which was understood in terms of rational

ideas rather than personal interaction. In the light of our analysis such a development should not be understood as simply a rejection of anthropomorphic interpretations of the divine (as if this were the actual foundation of myth) but rather as the diminution of the *existential* meaning of the sacred (i.e., as the eclipse of a lived world in favor of abstraction). But the fact that the divine continued to be a concern of philosophers indicates a link with the past. Although the method of philosophical understanding will be quite different, the maintenance of certain mythical *meanings* will be apparent, especially the retention of an axiological atmosphere with respect to the divine.[5]

5. Concurrent with all these developments is the crystallization of self-consciousness. The contextual, social self which characterized a mythical world shifted to an individual self beginning to exhibit the features of unity, interiority, and autonomy. It is important to realize how much the intellectual innovations of the time were matched by and related to the contours of self-consciousness: The departure from mythical disclosure requires the withdrawal of extraconscious disruptions; the detachment from lived experience and plurality which allows conceptual abstraction requires the unity and interiority of self-consciousness; and autonomous selfhood supports both moral and intellectual developments in that the individual gains a critical distance from tradition, custom, and social dependence. Clearly related to these matters is the changing attitude toward the affective dimension of human experience. Many moral reforms and philosophical methods revolved around a view of the passions which held them to be a controllable force rather than an overwhelming visitation. The distance from lived experience through the conscious mind's capacity for rational abstraction became the focus for this reformation of affective influences.

# The Beginnings: Hesiod and Thales

Hesiod's *Theogony* remains in most respects a mythical work, but certain elements of the poem clearly anticipate later philosophical aims and assumptions. For one thing, mythical pluralism is counteracted by Hesiod's underlying interest in the wholeness of reality. Rather than simply presenting the sacred meaning of various events or the origins of particular cultural phenomena, Hesiod seeks the origin and structure of the world order as a whole through his account of the primal beginning of the divine constellation. In this regard Hesiod's notion of an original separation of heaven and earth suggests, even if it does not explicate, a primordial, undifferentiated unity prior to the initial demarcation. Moreover, if we consider the nature of the gods in the poem, we find a comparable tendency toward unification and order. Hesiod's gods are clearly more abstract than Homeric deities. There are few signs of personality or existential manner; rather, the gods are more like conceptual generalities which denote certain values, principles, or natural phenomena without any animated idiosyncrasies. And, finally, the notion of related opposites in the *Theogony* together with the idea of regionalized placement in an overall configuration anticipates a prevalent theme in later Greek philosophy—justice as an ordered balance of differences.

With regard to Hesiod's *Works and Days*, Versenyi has given an illuminating account of the embryonic philosophical aspects taking shape there.[6] We notice a marked departure from mythical particulars to conceptual universals. Specific plurals like *ethea* (customs) have gravitated to singular universals like *ethos* (custom as such). The meaning of *aretē* is no longer expressed in terms of unique personal exemplars (e.g., Achilles) but rather in terms of abstract, generalized ideals (e.g., justice and work). And the relative confusion of the Homeric world in which there persisted a competitive conflict of divine powers is replaced by the overarching rule of Zeus as the embodiment of justice. Furthermore, certain formal and structural elements in *Works and Days* reveal the seeds of conceptual thinking. For instance, there is a kind of organic unity and a sense of growth through time which are missing in Homeric poetry.

As far as style is concerned, Homer's lofty poetry has given way to Hesiod's clearly more prosaic atmosphere with its emphasis on everyday concerns and matter-of-fact accounts of peasant life. Again we notice a shift from the sacred to the profane. A prosaic atmosphere is here not simply a matter of style; it indicates new priorities and forms of understanding which prefer the analysis of ordinary experience to the extraordinary advents of unique, mythical images. Hesiod is not simply presenting a sheer description of empirical events; he is describing things in terms of common properties and human life in terms of a regulation of the social order. His prosaic style is therefore indicative of a philosophical impulse which exchanges a mythical sense of the world for a concern with the general features of experience which can gather a plurality into an abstract order.

Hesiod's poetry may anticipate philosophy, but we now want to examine some distinctive features of philosophy as such. We can do so by discussing a figure whom the Greeks traditionally considered to be the first philosopher: Thales (640–546 B.C.). There is not a great deal known about Thales, and it is uncertain whether he ever wrote any works. Most of what we know of his philosophical views comes from Aristotle's commentaries, and we cannot be sure if Aristotle is presenting a dependable account of Thales's position. But for our purposes this is really beside the point. We can examine a doctrine attributed to Thales and simply explore the ways in which it departs from myth, thereby gaining a starting point for the differentiation of mythical and philosophical disclosure.

According to Aristotle, Thales was the first of the "natural philosophers" who sought to explain the world by reducing its various aspects to a common natural element. Thales is said to have proposed that everything can be reduced to water. The validity of such a proposition is also irrelevant for our purposes; we only want to dissect its meaning in order to ascertain a number of basic assumptions that lie behind a philosophical departure from myth. What can be drawn from Thales's apparently simple proposition? First of all, his attempt to reduce everything to a common element reveals a dismissal of mythical pluralism in favor of a unified explanation. The various mythical presentations of unique meanings have given way to a concern for a common element running through the whole cosmos as such.

Secondly, Thales reveals a kind of naturalism. The common element of the world is explained in terms of an observable, natural phenomenon: water. No longer is the world presented in terms of sacred imagery but rather a phenomenon available to ordinary experience; again, a shift from a sacred to a profane standard. Although the element of water is available to ordinary experience, however, Thales's general proposition as such is not. There may be an empirical component in his claim, but the conclusion is not strictly empirical. It might be something like an inductive generalization; by observing the predominance of water in the natural order, and the fundamental necessity of water and moisture for the maintenance of life, one might generalize beyond the evidence (not everything seems waterlike) and propose water as the essential component of all things. If he had confidence in his generalized conclusion, Thales might explain its meta-evidential aspect in terms of a distinction between reality and appearance; that is, though much of the world appears not to be waterlike, in reality its water-essence is hidden within various apparent forms or different configurations of water.

The final implication of Thales's proposition is perhaps the most significant. Something like induction shows a clear departure from mythical disclosure in that extraconscious arrivals and disruptions have completely withdrawn. The poets (even Hesiod) indicated a dependence on special sacred forces. We notice, therefore, that Thales's turn to ordinary experience of the natural world also implies a new psychology; the conscious mind has become the province of understanding. Unlike the poets, Thales's claim arises from the *unaided* human mind generalizing from the ordinary experience of natural phenomena. Although his proposition goes beyond immediate experience, it does so by abstracting from that experience via the reflective distance of self-consciousness, the ability to compare and generalize about experiences from the standpoint of an interior constancy. The profane is modified but still within the realm of profane experience, and no longer by sacred invasions. By generalizing profane experience, the mind locates its *own* capacity for understanding, and the sacred-profane interplay which characterized a mythical self has been condensed into a new shape.

Perhaps we can understand the mind's departure from the sacred by considering induction as a method. We have seen that one feature of mythical disclosure is its sense of "givenness," in that the self passively and uncritically "receives" its understanding of the world. Philosophy, however, is usually distinguished by its use of a method; that is to say, *prior* to its understanding of experience the mind devises certain assumptions which will determine *how* experience is to be interpreted and which reveal the active role of the mind. (In Greek, the prephilosophical meaning of *methodos* is "pursuit" or "a following after.") Both induction and deduction go beyond immediate experience, and it is the conscious mind's distance from experience which permits a methodological disposition. So, in philosophy the conscious mind shapes the form of inquiry (e.g., first observe, then generalize), while in mythical disclosure the mind passively receives the shape of the world (and therefore does not have a method at all).

To sum up, we have found the following characteristics of philosophy contained in its first historical moments: The search for a unified explanation; an emphasis upon profane experience as opposed to sacred imagery; the active role of the unaided conscious mind, free of sacred interruptions; and a distinction between appearance and reality.

In general we can say that Thales discovers what has come to be called an objective view of the world, a view which screens out the affective, existential, and sacred aspects of the world. But we cannot equate objectivity with "truth." It is, rather, a *new* criterion which *disengages* itself from the context of myth. When Anaxagoras, for example, proclaimed that the sun is not a god but an incandescent stone, he was not unveiling the "real" sun but rather a different way of understanding the sun.

# The First Philosophers

Although philosophy represented a departure from mythical disclosure, the relationship between early philosophy and myth is far from black and white. As we have seen, many philosophical developments grew out of a mythical background; the mythical tradition itself gradually cultivated views of the world and human selfhood which were preconditions for philosophical inquiry; and many of the first philosophers developed images and themes that clearly had mythical origins. In fact, as we will see, some philosophers simply conceptualized certain fundamental themes of Greek mythical culture. In other words, although philosophy introduced methodological or formal innovations which displaced the specific narrations of myth, nevertheless in many respects early philosophy shows a thematic continuity with mythical disclosure, at least with regard to the underlying *meaning* of a mythical world.

Let us begin by considering an example of the continuity between myth and philosophy, namely, an enduring interest in the divine as well as a perpetuation of the related notion that humanity runs up against a certain limit. Snell has pointed out that throughout Greek thought, from Homer to Aristotle, a distinction between the human and divine was maintained, at least with respect to the notion that human knowledge is limited and divine knowledge surpasses it.[7] Various thinkers interpreted differently the nature of divine knowledge, the extent and form of human limitation, and the possibility of human participation in divine knowledge. We will examine this in more detail as we proceed through the chapter, but we can begin by briefly restating the movement from Homer to Hesiod in terms of Snell's suggestion.

In Homer, knowledge is primarily visual. Humans are limited because they can only see so much. If they are to have extensive knowledge of the world, they need the gods or the muses, whose experience is wider. For Hesiod, knowledge entails the order of the whole rather than mere perceptual presentations. The gods and muses bestow this knowledge upon human beings. We have seen how Hesiod's gods develop an abstract, almost conceptual, nature, which leads to the point at hand. In Greek philosophy the notion of the divine shifted from the existential immediacy and living images of myth to the realm of thought and abstract ideas (which will become evident when we come to Xenophanes).[8] But notice what is significant here. The philosophers did not simply turn to thought alone; they presented thought as something *divine*. In my view it would be wrong to suggest that the relationship between god and thought in Greek philosophy was nothing more than nominal in nature, or·that it was a mere formality based on custom, or a strategy meant to placate and hence disarm opponents. I think our analysis of early Greek culture will help us detect a kind of internal coherence with respect to the transition from myth to philosophy. The first philosophers did not exactly abandon the past as much as they reshaped it.

Perhaps we can elaborate in the following way. The mythical distinction between the sacred and the profane can be analogically compared to the philosophical distinction between thought and experience (the conceptual and the empirical). Such a comparison might help us comprehend the enduring association between thought and divinity among Greek philosophers. We recall how in myth the sacred transforms ordinary profane experience, the simply "there." In philosophy, the simply "there" (immediate empirical perception) is now transformed by conceptual abstraction rather than sacred imagery. Of course the reason why the thought-experience distinction is only an analogue of the sacred-profane distinction is evident from previous discussions. Philosophy represents a switch of priorities and displacement of the *mythical* meaning of the sacred. What is analogically "sacred" to philosophy is derived from and remains within profane experience (e.g., the isolated *regularity* of the profane as such). But if Greek philosophers seriously identified thought with the divine, we might draw the following conclusion: The (mythical) meaning of the sacred may have changed (no longer an existential interruption of the profane but abstraction from and within profane experience), but the *sense* of a transcendence of immediacy remains, thereby making a divine designation still natural.[9]

In sum, even though philosophy's emphasis on abstract ideas displaced traditional sacred imagery and began to break away from the existential immediacy of a lived world which characterized mythical disclosure, nevertheless a certain sense of continuity between myth and philosophy can be demonstrated. The evidence, which should unfold as we proceed, is as follows: (1) The continuing association of thought with the divine; (2) philosophical doctrines which echo mythical themes or conceptualize a mythical sense of the world; and (3) a concern with and expression of the *existential meaning* of philosophical thought in a cultural context (e.g., Plato's view of philosophy as a means to moral transformation, political reform, and even personal salvation). Since philosophy, for the Greeks, was fundamentally a way of life and not simply intellectual reflection, it retained an existential meaning, even though it radically altered the mythical sense of an existential world. Now we turn to some of the important early philosophers with the aim of comprehending to what degree each thinker departs from mythical tradition and yet also remains connected with that tradition.

## XENOPHANES (560–475 B.C.)

In many respects Xenophanes represents a clear departure from myth, especially because he specifically criticizes the poets and at least prepares the contours of a rational alternative to a mythical world. He does, however, maintain a distinction between human and divine knowledge and suggests an inevitable limit to human knowledge.

> No man knows, or will ever know, the truth about the gods and about everything I speak of; for even if one chanced to say the complete truth, yet oneself knows it not; but seeming [*dokos*] is wrought over all things. (fr. 34) (189)[10]

It would seem, then, that Xenophanes considers human knowledge to be appearance and divine knowledge to be truth. Furthermore, divine knowledge seems to be a nonempirical truth, a realm of thought which is different in kind (and not degree, as in Homer) from human knowledge. Thus, the notion of "seeming" departs from the mythical sense of appearance and approaches a negative meaning, because it is measured against a qualitatively different form of knowledge. But the idea of a human limit shows a connection with tradition, and the previous fragment also suggests a kind of inevitable hiddenness. Although Xenophanes anticipates later intellectual developments, in general he does not clearly spell out criteria for truth. In a way, then, he is closer to the mythical sense of mystery than the later disposition toward rational certainty. Nevertheless we find in Xenophanes certain preparations for the future. For example, even though human knowledge faces a limit, one fragment suggests the possibility of improvement:

> Yet the gods have not revealed all things to men from the beginning;
> but by seeking men find out better in time. (fr. 18) (191)

Also, the reference to seeking (*epheuriskousin*) indicates that human knowledge is no longer subject to mythical inspiration because it is actively self-generated.

The most significant development in Xenophanes's thought is his revolutionary view of god. Although the fragments do contain references to a plurality of gods, nevertheless Xenophanes proposes a divine nature which transcends the pluralism and imagery of mythical deities. While retaining the mythical notion of the divine, Xenophanes transforms it by introducing nonmythical qualities of unity, imagelessness, and thought.

> One god, greatest among gods and men, in no way similar to mortals either in body or in thought. (fr. 23) (173)

> Always he remains in the same, moving not at all; nor is it fitting for him to go to different places at different times, but without toil he shakes all things by the thought of his mind. (fr. 26+25) (174)

On the basis of such a view Xenophanes attacks the poets for portraying the divine in ways which reflect the turmoil of life and "immoral" behavior. Hence he shows himself to be rejecting the existential immediacy and negativity which formerly characterized the sacred in favor of a moral transcendence above lived experience, which will have great significance in later intellectual developments.

> Homer and Hesiod have attributed to the gods everything that is a shame and reproach among men, stealing and committing adultery and deceiving each other. (fr. 11) (169)

Since the sacred is no longer a presentation of *all* important events, both beneficial and harmful, but rather a unified transcendence above the lived matrix, then an explanation for why the poets characterized the gods in the way that they did can no longer be found in the meaning of the sacred (as we have described it previously). For Xenophanes the nature of traditional gods is not an expression of something sacred but merely a projection of human nature. In other words, Xenophanes proposes a new interpretation of traditional myth—anthropomorphism.

> The Ethiopians say that their gods are snub-nosed and black, the Thracians that theirs have light blue eyes and red hair. (fr. 16) (171)

> But if cattle and horses or lions had hands, or were able to draw with their hands and do the works that men can do, horses would draw the forms of the gods like horses, and cattle like cattle, and they would make their bodies such as they each had themselves. (fr. 15) (172)

We notice in Xenophanes, therefore, the advent of new assumptions which will revolutionize human understanding of the world, principles of unity and abstraction which can counteract the variability, negativity, and uncertainty of the existential matrix. But, of course, since the traditional meaning of the sacred was precisely the *sense* of that matrix, then Xenophanes's polemic against the poets on account of their existential imagery represents less a correction and more a rejection of one kind of sense for another.

## ANAXIMANDER (611–547 B.C.)

The thought of Anaximander is extremely important for our purposes. We find there a conceptual account of the world which nevertheless mirrors certain fundamental themes in Greek myth. Mythical deities as well as Xenophanes's conception of god are missing in Anaximander's cosmology. Like Thales, he describes the world in terms of general conceptual principles related to natural elements and processes; but Anaximander seems quite different from so-called natural philosophers who attempt to reduce the world to a common natural substance. According to Anaximander, the essence of reality is the *apeiron*, meaning "indefinite," "unlimited." A single important fragment survives, third hand, in Simplicius's version of Theophrastus's account of Anaximander's first principle:

> He says that it is neither water nor any other of the so-called elements, but some other indefinite nature [*physin apeiron*], from which come into being all the heavens and the worlds in them. And the source of coming-to-be [*genesis*] for existing things is that into which destruction, too, happens "according to necessity [*kata to chreōn*]; for they pay penalty [*dikēn*, i.e., give justice] and retribution to each other for their injustice [*adikias*] according to the assessment of Time," as he

describes it in these rather poetical terms. (Simplicius, *Phys.* 24, 13) (103a)

I think this passage can be interpreted in the light of certain meanings which characterized the sacred in Greek myth, especially in tragedy. I would read here a conceptual account of the formlessness, mystery, and fatal negativity which constituted the background of mythical disclosure. First of all, the *apeiron* cannot be taken to mean some kind of substance or material element or spatial infinite. Rather, the *apeiron* would be better rendered the formless origin of form, that source of beings which accordingly cannot possess the form of any being and which is therefore without form. In Anaximander's cosmology, the emergence of entities out of this origin takes place according to the separation of two pairs of opposites (hot-cold and moist-dry) out of the *apeiron*. (These opposites were later to be characterized by Empedocles as the original elements: fire and air, water and earth.[11]) The elemental opposites, and hence all the various entities which are composed of elemental combinations, have their origin in the *apeiron* and return to it through annihilation. Anaximander therefore understands the world in terms of a process, a continuous flow of entities out of and back to the *apeiron*, from formlessness to form to formlessness.

We can hear a number of mythical reverberations in Anaximander's cosmology. First of all, the separation of opposites reminds us of the primal separation in Hesiod's *Theogony*. Furthermore, the *apeiron* would seem to explicate the unity prior to separation which was implicit in Hesiod's account. Also, even though Anaximander's world contains no gods, he is said to have called the *apeiron* divine.[12] Although the *apeiron* is not a personal god or divine mind directing the course of the world, it can be seen to reflect certain elements of the sacred which provided a hidden background to mythical disclosure: namely, mystery, formlessness, and a negative fate. Anaximander's distinction between the *apeiron* and entities mirrors the mythical sacred-profane distinction, though sacred forms have withdrawn and what remains is the background meaning of the sacred, conceived in terms of a formless origin. If we keep in mind the underlying *meaning* of the sacred (i.e., extraordinariness, mystery, power, efficacy, origins), then the "divine" aspect of the *apeiron* becomes intelligible. Furthermore, as a result we can see that Anaximander's thought is *both* innovative and traditional (as a conceptual explication of traditional themes). The inherent mystery of the *apeiron* would certainly distinguish it from the "profane" tendencies in a reductive naturalism, for example.

I think that Anaximander's philosophy also echoes the priority of negative fate and the positive fatalism which characterized tragic myth. For Anaximander, entities or forms are not substantial; they *appear* out of a formless origin and are destined to return there through annihilation. Such a movement happens according to "necessity," the Greek term being *chreōn*, which can also mean "fate." Let us examine Anaximander's cosmology more closely and see whether we can clarify the connection with tragedy.

The emergence of the world order involves the separation of opposites out of the *apeiron* and the subsequent generation of individual entities out these elemental opposites. The dynamics of this generation is presented in terms of a justice-injustice scheme. The opposites coexist in a continual tension (hot lives at the expense of cold, for example). When one opposite predominates by asserting itself to the exclusion of the other, we have what Anaximander calls injustice; in other words, if one opposite were exclusively maintained, the result would be the extinction of the other opposites and hence collapse of the whole (conceived as a *totality* of opposites from a common origin).

Justice would therefore represent a kind of harmonization, a balancing process through which nature repays "transgression" (i.e., the assertion of one opposite) by negating it in favor of the other opposite. The overall process indicates that justice is a harmony of opposites. Moreover, it is the formless equipoise of the *apeiron* which serves as the origin of the opposites *and* the process of opposition-exchange that makes up the changing course of nature. The analogy of a pendulum can illustrate such a process. The apex of one swing cannot predominate and the pendulum is drawn toward the other extreme, and so on; but it is the balance-point at the middle of the arc which serves as the "draw" for such a movement (and which is never *evident* in the movement). So, too, the process of nature involves opposite states exchanging place with one another.

Within the primal emergence out of a formless origin, individual formed states emerge out of their opposites (hot from cold, and so forth). What it means to *be* an individual state is the temporary negation of an opposite state (the *meaning* of hot is negatively related to cold). No one form can predominate, that is to say, no one form is substantial in itself but is simply a moment in an ever-moving opposition process. Furthermore, the dynamics of the process cannot be found in any one of the opposites or even an overall combination of opposites but rather in something which negates form as such, namely, the formless equipoise of the *apeiron* (cf. the pendulum analogy). The *apeiron* represents the primordial negation which lies behind the self-negating movement of nature's opposition process. In this way Anaximander's cosmology conceptualizes and further explicates the tragic sense of the world where nature feeds on itself in an overall process through which form is subordinated to a primal negation.

Anaximander's scheme also helps us understand more clearly the notion of positive fatalism which lies at the heart of tragic myth. It is wrong to interpret Anaximander's notion of injustice as some kind of cosmic error or sin, as if individuation and form were somehow violating the *apeiron*. As Jaeger has pointed out, it was not part of the Greek spirit to see the world as a fall from some kind of state of perfection.[13] We should not think that Anaximander held the *apeiron* to be "reality" and individuated states to be "illusions." For the Greeks, reality would never be identified with sheer formlessness. I think the tragic *correlation* of the Apollonian and Dionysian is the model which corresponds to Anaximander's conception of the world. In tragic myth the world is a constellation of forms which are, however, nonsubstantial owing to a Dionysian background which limits, but thus defines, their *presence*. In a similar way, the *apeiron* is not separate or apart from entities; rather, it is that which founds the *process* of entities as a changing complex of *emerging* forms. If reality is to be more than a static, formless "nothingness," it must be individuated. But individuation must somehow be "marked off" from something. Thus, individuation alone cannot sufficiently account for the nature of reality. The origin of an individuated world must therefore be found in something other than individuation. The *apeiron* is this "other"; it is the primal negation which allows the demarcation of forms and empowers the process of opposition exchange (which shapes the emergence of forms in relation to each other). Consequently, forms are inseparable from the *apeiron*; but the *apeiron* is also inseparable from the forms of the world. An ancient source reports that Anaximander's cosmic process grounded in the *apeiron* is eternal, without beginning or end.[14] There never was a time when a formed world did not exist. And yet if the world process is to be sufficiently understood, what is required is a two-dimensional paradigm—the *apeiron* and forms, i.e., an indeterminate origin within the process of individuation.

For Anaximander, therefore, the *apeiron* is a principle the very *meaning* of which is the giving-forth of a world from a hidden background (i.e., unconcealment, or the primal meaning of *physis*, appearing). We must recognize, then, the *positive* element in Anaximander's cosmology—but there is also a clear connection with the *fatalism* of tragic myth. The generation of an entity involves its passage upon an opposition process; hence, *as* an existent it cannot endure forever or predominate over nonexistence; all entities must eventually yield to nonexistence or formlessness. So, Anaximander's world order conceptualizes the positive fatalism of tragic myth: Reality is a world of forms which are, however, not "substances." We can now draw some conclusions about the meaning of justice (*dikē*) in relation to the *apeiron*. Justice is not the correction of a cosmic flaw but rather the overall balanced *process* of nature. The very existence of a form entails *both* its assertion and its negation. The nature of things requires this paradoxical juxtaposition, which is consequently not a moral but a *tragic* conception. The presence of opposition and negation does not imply something wrong with the world; it is rather the *way* of the world order. And according to Cornford, the original meaning of *dikē* was "way."[15]

To sum up Anaximander's connection with tragedy: The traditional, tragic idea of a limit to individual forms is now conceptually generalized; form as such entails a limit (*peras*) shown against the background of a necessarily correlative negation (*a-peiron*) "outside" and hence defining that limit. The *apeiron*, therefore, brings forth the process of appearance (unconcealment). Anaximander also adds the formal mechanics of an opposition exchange to explicate a world *order*. In other words, appearance is not simply a single or random emergence from formlessness but an emergence from and passage to formlessness by means of relational opposition. I would say that Anaximander here conceptualizes the dramatic foreground of tragic myth—the struggle of related individuals serving to actualize a negative fate.

Finally, the notions of justice, injustice, retribution, repayment, and the like indicate a continuation of a mythical sense of the world, that is, an existential, axiological tone as opposed to a purely factual, objective, or mechanical account. We should not assume that Anaximander was simply being metaphorical, or projecting human values onto nature, an assumption held even by later Greek writers (e.g., Simplicius's editorial comment that Anaximander was describing "nature" in rather "poetical" terms). Anaximander's thought precedes the later development of a *nomos-physis* distinction which can permit such an assumption. For Anaximander, "cosmic justice" would be an inseparable phrase. It is not the case that social, evaluative, and existential meanings are only human concerns and that nature is essentially free of these meanings. Not unlike Homer, Anaximander still sees nature *as* an existential/social/mythical matrix. Human existence and nature still appear in the same light, not in terms of the subject-object dichotomy which will characterize later scientific developments. Anaximander's notions of cosmic justice and necessity should be read as a depersonalized conceptualization of sacred, fateful forces which animated Greek mythical tradition.[16] Of course, it is the element of depersonalization that distinguishes Anaximander from previous forms of mythical disclosure. His innovation is the introduction of a regulated cosmic order, an orderly balance which overcomes the more capricious effects of traditional personal gods, but within Anaximander's more reasoned and lawful natural order there still reside significant vestiges of mythical sense.

## HERACLITUS (544–484 B.C.)

In many ways the thought of Heraclitus is consistent with and in fact further specifies and develops the kind of world view contained in Anaximander's cosmology. Consequently we will also find in Heraclitus many parallels with mythical thought. As a philosopher, Heraclitus is concerned with a conceptual account of the world as well as a unified account of the whole of reality. Let us examine the challenging fragments of this remarkable thinker with the aim of comprehending the subtle mixture of innovation and tradition running through his thought.

Heraclitus clearly draws a distinction between human and divine knowledge (e.g., frs. 78, 83, 102). Generally speaking, human knowledge is the realm of ordinary common sense (the perception of individual entities as such) as well as certain abstract conceptions marked off from one another (e.g., hot and cold, life and death, one and many). Divine knowledge entails an obscure first principle, the *logos*, which resolves the limits of human knowledge. In a way, calling human knowledge "limited" is misleading, as if wisdom were merely an "extension of view" (as in Homer). For Heraclitus the limit of human knowledge is a kind of blindness, and so wisdom requires a radical *change* of view. In many respects Heraclitus's doctrine of the logos in relation to ordinary human knowledge displays a deep affinity with the underlying meaning of the mythical sacred-profane distinction.

Heraclitus seems more optimistic than Xenophanes with regard to the accessibility of divine wisdom. The logos is not something separated from the course of the world; it is immanent, though initially hidden from human understanding. Since the logos is "common to all" (frs. 2, 89), anyone has the potential to participate in its nature. In other words, human knowledge can be transformed into divine knowledge. The difference between the two does not reflect different realms of reality but rather different dimensions of understanding. In fact, although Heraclitus does not dissociate the human soul from the world, he does portray the philosophical journey in terms of the soul and its comprehension. In a way he mirrors Sophocles's technique of confronting cosmic forces within the contours of the human soul. Furthermore, Heraclitus is the first thinker to actually sketch a picture of the soul which anticipates the modern criteria for selfhood. We notice that the soul seems to be a unified whole and that knowledge is discovered within its regions. Moreover, images of interiority and depth take shape in Heraclitus's thought:

> You would not find out the boundaries of the soul, even by travelling along every path: so deep a measure [*logon*] does it have. (fr. 45) (235)

I would caution, however, that Heraclitus's conception of the human self is still quite different from the complex of unity, interiority, and autonomy which shapes the modern sense of individual self-consciousness. The Heraclitean meaning of self is in fact much closer to the mythical understanding of human experience, something which should become clear as we proceed. In one respect, however, Heraclitus clearly does reflect the crystallization of self-consciousness. Occasionally he speaks in the first person, and he seems to single himself out and set himself against tradition and his contemporaries. He claims to have a unique insight that raises him above traditional poets, prophets, and sages (e.g., fr. 40). And he expresses a kind of intellectual solitude, as well as the internal direction of his thought, in one terse fragment which mirrors the outlook of Oedipus: "I searched out myself." (fr. 101) (249)

We should not think that Heraclitus *measures* wisdom according to a standard of self-consciousness or self-contained rational methods. His philosophy has a decidedly oracular tone, as if sounding from hidden depths (cf. fr. 123) or Delphic revelations (fr. 93). Insight into the logos is more a kind of inspiration than a result of active methodology (e.g., the emphasis on "listening" in fr. 50). Moreover, Heraclitus recognizes the validity of divine inspiration (fr. 92). In fragments 5 and 14 he affirms the value of religious rituals, although he clearly opposes the tendency to miss the sacred meaning of a ritual when the devices and practices themselves become the sole concern. In other words, Heraclitus warns against a reduction of religious meaning to the (profane) elements of a ritual. He makes a specific reference to Dionysian rituals and confirms a point we made previously; the unusual practices of that cult are justified only in terms of a sacred, mythical meaning which the rituals are meant to serve:

> For if it were not to Dionysus that they made the procession and sung the hymn to the shameful parts, the deed would be most shameless. (fr. 15) (246)

Let us try to unravel the meaning of Heraclitus's thought by examining his view of the world in the light of the logos. As a philosopher, Heraclitus is concerned with something deeper than mythical imagery; the ultimate nature of the cosmos is eternal and was not made by gods or men (fr. 30). Consequently the logos is prior to mythical presentation as such. Furthermore the logos reveals a kind of conceptual order and pattern within the course of nature, permitting an overall comprehension of a world of variability, change, and flux. However, the order of the cosmos is neither apart from, nor does it "resolve," change and flux; the logos in a way *is* flux, but flux made intelligible. Logos is often translated as "law" or "reason," which is not inconsistent with later usage, but its meaning for Heraclitus is not captured by these designations. Rather than resolve change from an invariable standpoint, rather than propose a rational order or constancy distinct from the fluid, lived world, the logos simply reveals the *sense* of that world as such. Even though the logos is a conceptual account and not a myth, nevertheless its meaning can be understood as a depersonalized generalization of certain fundamental aspects of mythical sense. As we proceed we should keep in mind the notions of mystery, nonsubstantial appearance, the limit of form, process, sacred negativity, and positive fatalism, with the aim of comprehending Heraclitus's link with the past.

Although Heraclitus emphasizes change and flux, he never suggests that reality is nothing more than changing states. That is why the casual classification of Heraclitus as a proponent of change can be so misleading.

> Listening not to me but to the *logos* it is wise to agree that all things are one. (fr. 50) (199)

It is true that Heraclitus sees change, multiplicity, and negativity as constitutive of reality, but he also aims to uncover a unity within an overall process of change. In other words, a unified whole can be found *in* change and not in the negation of change favoring some notion of absolute rest or substance. As a result, Heraclitus's conception of the world breaks the boundaries of what would seem to be mutually exclusive distinctions (unity and multiplicity, change and unchangeability, being and nonbeing), which makes his philosophy so difficult to grasp by ordinary common sense and reasoning, and which earned him the epithet "the obscure."

Wisdom, for Heraclitus, entails an insight into something mysterious, something without a definite character or form. There is a unity within the course of things which, however, cannot be captured by any particular thing or idea. Wisdom is "set apart from all things" (fr. 108).[17] But paradoxically, unity is not separable from multiplicity; it "steers all things *through* all things" (fr. 41; my italics).[18] Consequently that which is one is not other than the many. It is no wonder that Heraclitus concludes the essence of reality is a coincidence of the nameable and unnameable (fr. 32). Language seems to reach its breaking point in trying to capture such a paradoxical notion.

But the situation is not entirely beyond comprehension. A world of changing phenomena reveals many entities and ideas in intelligible forms. If common sense or ordinary thinking *fixes* on these forms alone, however, the overall nature of reality is missed. Unity, for Heraclitus, is not an invariable idea or substance, but rather the overall *process* of change as such. In itself this movement is inherently ungraspable and elusive; the process of nature cannot be identified with any particular entity within that process. The logos is Heraclitus's attempt to present in language the overall process of the world. He is proposing a philosophical understanding of a changing world without trying to go beyond the "evidence," that is to say, without trying to supercede, resolve, or "correct" the variability and flux that constitute our lived experience.

When considering individual entities, forms, or ideas, Heraclitus insists upon the notion of impermanence; nothing abides, there are no substances, everything is temporary and finite. All entities flow from and to formlessness. Only the flow itself persists, not as a thing but *as* a flow. Hence Heraclitus opts for becoming rather than being (some constant presence behind change). But Heraclitean becoming is not simply one side of a being-becoming polarity; it does not simply mean "changing things"; it is more than that because it refers to the overall unified process of changing things. And yet the process is not other than entities in the world; it is the flow-of-changing-things, a unified world-process. The concentration on a flow of things which is itself nothing may require paradoxical linguistic juxtapositions (e.g., being and nonbeing), but this does not mean that some kind of intelligibility cannot be gained in this regard.

Heraclitus offers us some assistance when he introduces his famous river metaphor: "In the same river we both step and do not step, we are and we are not" (fr. 49a).[19] Here we have a natural analogue which helps elucidate the character of the Heraclitean world order. Reality shows a simultaneous sameness and nonsameness. The same river is never at any time the same. It is always moving, both one and many. Therefore the flux in the world becomes unified, not by negating change and variation in favor of pure stability or strict regularity, but by penetrating the negation of process as such within which particular forms come and go. The "essence" of reality, therefore, is not a form but a process.

We should, of course, here be reminded of Anaximander's formless origin which orchestrates the mutual exchange of forms. Heraclitus offers a rich explication of such a paradigm and specifically the notion of justice-in-opposition contained in Anaximander's cosmology. When opposite states negate each other there is justice in that the overall world order requires this continuing exchange and fluctuation. Justice is the way of the cosmos, the exchange of opposites, each appearing by compensating for the assertion of the other. Heraclitus shares Anaximander's view that every entity must be checked by a limit.

Sun will not overstep his measures; otherwise the Erinyes, ministers of Justice, will find him out. (fr. 94) (229)

As in Anaximander's thought, justice involves the necessary dynamics of a moving cosmos. "Injustice" is not a reprehensible violation but simply a momentary swing of the cosmic pendulum which is necessarily followed by a return swing. Heraclitus explicitly emphasizes this point, namely that the struggle between opposites, each living at the expense of the other in a moving complex, is necessary and desirable. The assertion of one opposite is its emergence; but a multifarious world requires multiple emergence, and thus an exchange, to counteract domination by a single one. Furthermore, the sense of what a particular entity *is*, its being, entails (specifically) a demarcation from opposite entities and (generally) the background of nonbeing to limit and thus define being. Thus negation, change, and exchange figure into the very nature of things. Heraclitus would equate staticness with nothingness (i.e., indefiniteness); being entails emergence from nonbeing and the mutual opposition among beings which executes this process.

Consequently, Heraclitus does more than describe opposition; he affirms it, which leads us to his notorious advocation of war and strife. He rebukes those who would prefer that strife vanish from the world.[20] They do not realize that in wishing so they opt for oblivion, because entities would lose the conditions of their very existence. Like a mixed drink that would separate if not stirred (fr. 125), the world process would disintegrate if not "stirred" by opposition.

War is the father of all and king of all. . . . (fr. 53) (215)

It is necessary to know that war is common and right [*dikēn*] is strife and that all things happen by strife and necessity [*chreōn*]. (fr. 80) (214)

Since the world order is a process requiring negation, if opposition were to cease, then the world order would cease to be.

Heraclitus is emphasizing a fundamental question of existential meaning, namely, our *response* to a world of negativity (compare this to the inherent negativity of a mythical existential matrix). Heraclitus gives more than a descriptive account; he wants to engage the *value* of existence. Humans are asked to transform their ordinary view of the world which reflects evaluations based on the *rejection* of opposition and negation. What we ordinarily consider just (individual preservation) and unjust (destruction) are actually correlated in an overall process without which there would be no individuation at all. Thus the negative aspects of the world are also just.

To god all things are beautiful and good and just, but men have supposed some things to be unjust, others just. (fr. 102) (209)

Justice, for Heraclitus, encompasses the complex of construction and destruction. Hence the sheer preservation of individual forms would violate the conditions of reality, which is a unified process of passing and emerging forms (remember the mythical meaning of appearance).

Again, Heraclitus does not simply describe the logos; humans are asked to attune their existential attitude according to its nature. The logos is often enough associated with the divine to indicate its *sacred* meaning. In other words, the presence of negation in the world is accorded a positive value (like the sacred meaning of a negative fate in Greek myth). Since negation and finitude have sacred meaning, it is not our prerogative to ignore these cosmic forces. The logos corresponds to a fate with which humans must integrate themselves. Heraclitus underscores the point by claiming that this world order has no cause outside itself; it was not created but always was and always will be (fr. 30). There is no alternative to the world process so described.

From the standpoint of the overall process it is clear that opposing states, which from the limited standpoint of each state seem mutually exclusive, are in fact related positively as a unified process of generation. Now we can understand what Heraclitus means by the identity of opposites.

> God is day night, winter summer, war peace, satiety hunger. (fr. 67) (207)

> The path up and down are one and the same. (fr. 60) (203)

The meaning of night entails the absence of day and vice versa. "Disease makes health pleasant and good, hunger satiety, weariness rest" (fr. 111) (204). To understand the meaning of anything we need the broader view of a complex in which what seems opposed is really a unified relation. "Opposition" therefore can be a misnomer, since the logos reflects mutual *inclusion,* the alternating tensions of an overall matrix. The negation of one state maintains the process. So, "transcending" the limits of particular states Heraclitus notices a harmony in opposition:

> That which is in opposition is in concert, and from things that differ comes the most beautiful harmony. (fr. 8)[21]

We can better understand the extent to which the harmony of opposites shapes Heraclitean thought by considering the proposed identity of life and death (e.g., frs. 48, 88), surely the most fundamental opposition. "We are and we are not" (fr. 49a); life *is* death and death *is* life. From the standpoint of logical classification, this is a contradiction. But the logos is not limited to logical classification; it signifies something beyond the boundaries of class and form. The identity of life and death does not mean that a living body is identical with a corpse. In that case we have the time frame of life followed by its absence *afterward*. The Heraclitean identity of life and death encompasses the awareness of death *during* life. We might easily recognize that the meaning of the term "life" cannot be dissociated from "death" (to be alive is to be not dead), but the conceptual correlation only hints at the real issue, the *existential* meaning of life in relation to the *awareness* of death. It is precisely the formlessness of death that illuminates the form of life. Human existence, then, is necessarily finite. If we were truly immortal and free from the limit of loss, the world would not *matter* to us as it does when we are aware of the transitory nature of life and its conditions. It is in this sense, I think, that Heraclitus proposes the identity of life and death; the value and meaning of life are inseparable from the perceived limit of death. Consequently, Heraclitus here gives explicit form to the sense of positive fatalism we have witnessed in the Greek tradition.

For Heraclitus, the individual exists as a being-in-the-midst-of-nonbeing (what Heidegger calls being-toward-death). If human existence is to be understood, then, we have to confront negation and integrate our experience with something beyond the limits of individual consciousness and form. From this existential perspective, the life-death identity is consonant with the Dionysian ecstatic communion with self-negation. Furthermore, since the Heraclitean notion of nonbeing is not equivalent to sheer nothingness but is rather the overall process out of which being emerges and into which it is reabsorbed, then the identification of life and death shows that the "end" of individual life (death) is also the continuation of the life process as such, the death of each life maintains the course of other lives. We are reminded of the Dionysian dialectic of an infinite life ($z\bar{o}\bar{e}$) beneath finite life-and-death (*bios*). In this and the other links with the mythical tradition, there resound echoes of the sacred in Heraclitus's philosophy.

We can now develop the sense in which Heraclitus's thought compares with mythical disclosure. We can begin by discussing the degree to which Heraclitean notions contrast with empirical and conceptual assumptions which shaped later philosophical movements. First of all we can see how an empirical standard—namely that a thing's nature is fully captured in its perceived form—would not be acceptable to Heraclitus because of the necessary relation to opposite forms and formlessness. Secondly, the identity of opposites undermines a fundamental aspect of later rational thought, namely, strict distinctions between concepts (definition) and especially the principle of noncontradiction formalized by Aristotle. According to that principle, something either is or it is not (put this way it becomes the law of excluded middle), but Heraclitus proposes that an entity both is and is not. Generally speaking, Heraclitus would oppose both empirical and conceptual models of substance, which attempt to *reduce* reality to some kind of empirical or conceptual form alone, thereby violating the priority of process.

The logos is Heraclitus's attempt to capture process in language. Because of its inherent elusiveness it may be an untranslatable term. The fragments reveal several metaphorical designations like "fire" and "war" which capture the sense of a dynamic process. I prefer to concentrate on the association between logos and physis in the fragments, as long as physis is understood in the primal sense of "appearing." The logos names the overall process of appearing, not simply any particular form that appears. Every appearance emerges out of a hiddenness and also entails the dis-appearance of other forms. Therefore the *whole* encompasses a correlation of form and formlessness. In other words, there is always concealment within and behind every revelation (hence unconcealment might well serve as a term for the whole). Within such a notion is an implicit critique of any attempt to formally or substantially "grasp" reality in a fixed designation.

Heraclitus often criticizes human beings for their ignorance with respect to the logos:

> Of the *logos* which is as I describe it men always prove to be uncomprehending, both before they have heard it and when once they have heard it. For although all things happen according to this *logos* men are like people of no experience. . . . (fr. 1) (197)

> The *logos:* though men associate with it most closely, yet they are separated from it. . . . (fr. 72)[22]

But it is not that ignorance here reflects some absence of facts or particular ideas; rather, ignorance of the logos stems from over-familiarity with the world, the facile tendency to equate reality with ordinary experiences and conceptions alone. In fact it may be inevitable that we should "miss" the logos, because it is fundamentally a kind of hiddenness. In other words, "comprehending" the logos involves acknowledging something that can *not* be comprehended. Within the world order there is something that hides; however, it is not waiting to be disclosed, rather it is the background of any disclosure. Hiddenness is *essential* to the process of appearing: "physis loves to hide" (*physis kryptesthai philei*) (fr. 123).

In this way Heraclitus explicates the background of mystery in mythical disclosure. He speaks to the sense of transparency in mythical presentations, namely, the idea that mythical images are not substantial or factual but appearances in the midst of a mystery. A myth shapes a world, but it has no "foundation." At one point Heraclitus directly addresses the correlation between a sacred appearance and mystery:

> One thing, the only truly wise [*hen to sophon*], does not and does consent to be called by the name of Zeus. (fr. 32) (231)

The logos is a process which entails a coincidence of the nameable and unnameable; sacred language presents the appearance of a world, but it can never capture the background which allows appearance. Therefore, with respect to reality as a whole, the forms of language are themselves "myths" in the sense of being nonsubstantial appearances. Language is thus halfway between formlessness and substantial form—it reveals a world and yet remains within concealment. The best that could be said of language is that it *shows* but does not explain (i.e., reduce reality to any form). Heraclitus would call it a kind of sign.

> The lord whose oracle is in Delphi neither speaks out [*legei*] nor conceals, but gives a sign. (fr. 93) (247)

This would not only apply to mythical language but to any language which attempts to describe the logos. Heraclitus himself must resort to metaphors like "fire" (fr. 30). In a way a metaphor is halfway between a myth and a concept in that it is not a sacred image but is also not a natural or conceptual explanation. Fire is not meant to designate a natural element but rather the force of a destructive and illuminating process; but at least fire is not fully abstract and detached from lived experience. The metaphor reveals and yet does not fully capture the logos. Since the logos is not an entity, the metaphor cannot be said to "stand for" anything; it is an irreducible presentation of something which cannot be presented as such. The link between Heraclitus's philosophy and mythical disclosure may be that *poetic* language is the only way he can shape the sense of his philosophical understanding.

In closing, it is clear that Heraclitus, like Anaximander, offers a conceptual extension and explication of the tragic sense of positive fatalism. Heraclitus calls for the affirmation of a world permeated by negativity and finite limits (he deems it good, beautiful, and just). What distinguishes Heraclitus from tragic poetry, however, is as follows. We were able to discover the affirmative atmosphere of positive fatalism as an implicit ideal running through the existential setting of tragic drama, but Heraclitus does not present such an ideal simply through heroic exemplars, noble bearing, and human attitudes. As a philosopher he presents a general account of the world which allows an *explication* of the underlying meaning of tragic mythical disclosure. That is to say, the ideal of positive fatalism is not simply a human attitude but an attitude in accordance with the nature of the *world*. Heraclitus illuminates the "ontological" status of positive fatalism by showing that an affirmative stance toward negativity is the only appropriate response to the world's *nature*. The conditions of the existential matrix and the lived world—process, change, variability, destruction, instability, uncertainty, and so forth—are not deficiencies but rather the very conditions for the *being* (appearing) of the world. The existential challenge of Heraclitean thought is at one and the same time an intellectual insight into the nature of reality. I find Heraclitus shaping something which was suggested as the implicit substructure of mythical sense, namely, an existential-ontological circle; i.e., the "lived" world and "reality" interpenetrate each other, as opposed to being separable regions of "human experience" and the "objective world."

## PARMENIDES (540–470 B.C.)

The thought of Parmenides is notoriously difficult to interpret, although it is often uncritically categorized according to neat philosophical polarities. One reason for the difficulty is the ambiguous mixture of innovation and tradition in the fragments. Another reason is the problem of translation, which we will examine shortly.

To begin with, Parmenides maintains the distinction between human and divine knowledge in the following way. Human knowledge is the realm of seeming and opinion, the ordinary knowledge of beings, gained from the senses or concepts drawn from sense perception. Divine knowledge is the realm of truth, which encompasses Being distinguished from beings alone. Such a scheme is analogous in some ways to that of Xenophanes, who is supposed to have been Parmenides's teacher, but the revolutionary aspect of Parmenides's thought is that divine knowledge is not an answer to any particular question and does not refer to any particular being (even god) but rather *any* being as such: Being. Being is the most abstract and all-encompassing term that can be conceived (even Heraclitus's sentences about the logos can take a form such as "the logos 'is' . . ."). Thus Parmenides's Being is the epitome of philosophical abstraction and unity.

The importance of Parmenides for later philosophical developments can also be recognized with respect to the type of method taking shape in the fragments. He is often acknowledged to be the first thinker who proposed a strict distinction and separation between sense experience and abstract reason or logical argument. He, along with other Eleatic philosophers, initiated what came to be called a deductive method, in which knowledge is generated through abstract ideas and logical relations *alone,* without initial regard for the senses.[23] Parmenides seems to reject empirical knowledge or inferences drawn from the senses in favor of conceptual knowledge and methods.

Parmenides distinguishes between two ways of apprehending reality, the way of truth and the way of opinion. The former proposes to separate the truth of Being from non-Being, while the latter investigates becoming, the interplay of beings and nonbeing. The way of truth is animated by a radically new process of logical deduction.

. . . the one way, that it *is* and cannot not-be, is the path of persuasion, for it attends upon truth; the other, that it *is-not* and needs must not-be, that I tell thee is a path altogether unthinkable. For thou couldst not know that which is-not (that is impossible) nor utter it; for the same thing can be thought as can be. (fr. 2) (344)

For never shall this be proved, that things that are not are; . . . (fr. 7) (346)

One way only is left to be spoken of, that it *is*; and on this way are full many signs that what *is* is uncreated and imperishable, for it is entire, immovable and without end. It *was* not in the past, nor *shall* it be, since it *is* now, all at once, one, continuous; . . .The decision on these matters rests here: it *is* or it is not. But it has surely been decided, as it must be, to leave alone the one way as unthinkable and nameless (for it is no true way), and that the other is real and true. How could what *is* thereafter perish? and how could it come into being? For if it came into being, it is not, nor if it is going to be in the future. So coming into being is extinguished and perishing unimaginable. (fr. 8) (347)

The logic here is relentless and simple, stemming from a purely conceptual analysis. The premise concerning the meaning of "is" leads to the conclusion that no negation of the "is" can possibly be thought. The ultimate consequence of the argument is a claim that Being must be unified, immovable, unchanging, and imperishable. That claim entails a rejection of "becoming," since its meaning forces us to think of an "is not," which cannot be thought. It would seem that Parmenides's conclusion commands a complete departure from lived experience and sense perception of the natural world, and also that the Heraclitean notions of becoming, change, and negation are rejected in favor of stability, uniformity, and rest.

Although it is evident that the Parmenidean method and its outcome involve reasoning alone, and that it no doubt had an enormous influence on the form and methods of later philosophical developments, nevertheless a careful reading of the fragments casts some doubt on the usual interpretations of Parmenides's thought. It is not at all clear that his method is purely rational in the modern sense of the term or that Parmenides banishes the kind of ideas found in Heraclitus. Let us look more closely and try to clarify this problem of interpretation.

To what extent was Parmenides a "philosopher" in the strict sense? Although his language is surely abstract and conceptual, it is presented in the form of a poem (hexameter verse). Moreover, the poem's prologue is far from abstract but indeed strongly mythical in character.

> The steeds that carry me took me as far as my heart [*thymos*] could desire, when once they had brought me and set me on the renowned way of the goddess [*daimonos*], who leads the man who knows through every town. On that way was I conveyed; for on it did the wise steeds convey me, drawing my chariot, and maidens led the way. . . . while the daughters of the Sun, hasting to convey me into the light, threw back the veils from off their faces and left the abode of night. There are the gates of the ways of Night and Day. . . . They themselves, high in the air, are closed by mighty doors, and avenging Justice (*Dikē*) controls the double bolts. Her did the maidens entreat with gentle words and cunningly persuade to unfasten them without demur the bolted bar from the gates. . . . Straight through them, on the broad way, did the maidens guide the horses and the car. And the goddess (*thea*) greeted me kindly, and took my right hand in hers, and

spoke to me these words: "Welcome, o youth, that comest to my abode on the car that bears thee, tended by immortal charioteers. It is no ill chance [*moira kakē*], but right and justice [*themis te dikē te*], that has sent thee forth to travel on this way. Far indeed does it lie from the beaten track of men. Meet it is [*chreō*] that thou shouldst learn all things, the unshaken heart of well-rounded truth [*alētheiēs*], as well as the opinions [*doxas*] of mortals in which is no true belief [*pistis alēthēs*] at all. . . . " (fr. 1) (342)

There are a number of things in this prologue that we want to consider carefully. First of all, truth is divine and seems qualitatively different from ordinary human knowledge. Not only is truth not derived from human knowledge, it is also not discovered within the confines of the conscious mind; rather, truth is the revealed gift of a goddess. According to Parmenides, the thoughts expressed in the poem do not come *from* him but *to* him. There seems to be an extraconscious origin for truth, and in fact much of the imagery in the prologue is reminiscent of a primitive shaman complex.[24] Of course, Parmenides is a fully self-conscious individual; he associates himself with divine knowledge and proudly sets himself apart from his deluded contemporaries and traditional wisdom. Nevertheless, truth is "granted," and the notion of arrival from beyond the self shows a certain connection with mythical tradition. What is new, however, is that the gift is not any kind of information or power or specific knowledge (of gods, humans, or nature) but rather insight into Being itself, the essence of any being as such. Parmenides is given the capacity to strip away particular appearances and discover the ultimate nature of all things divine, human, and natural.

Parmenides speaks of a revealed, and therefore not strictly deduced insight into Being; hardly what one would expect from a philosopher. Of course it could be that the prologue is simply a vestigial formality or a strategic device to attract listeners or ward off critics by disguising his philosophy in traditional language; but such explanations could also be nothing more than wishful thinking on the part of later interpreters. There is no indication in the poem that Parmenides is anything but serious and sincere with respect to the mythical atmosphere of the prologue. On the face of it we should assume that Parmenides is reporting a profound encounter with a sacred revelation *from which* the more recognizably philosophical aspects of his thought proceed. At least we can say that Parmenides did not portray his intellectual journey according to the expected model of rationality, that is, "human inquiry" armed with nothing more than a rational methodology, through which the conscious mind discovers in and for itself the nature of things. Parmenides's thought is eminently logical but only *subsequent* to a revealed beginning which is not proposed to have been derived from any method or principle normally known to human reason.

Next we should turn to the content of the poem and examine its meaning. The logic of Parmenides is evident enough, but the usual interpretations of his position turn the *content* of his argument into something more in line with later philosophical assumptions and methods and less indicative of Parmenides's connection with other early philosophers and mythical tradition, a connection which a plausible alternative reading of the poem can suggest.

The idea that Parmenides denies the possibility of change and nonbeing is not completely unwarranted. But the *way* in which the argument is interpreted and the translations chosen to render the original Greek can introduce philosophical problems which perhaps were never intended. One could surely criticize the denial of change and negation by pointing out that change is quite evident in the world and that we do think nonbeing all the time (negative predicates). Well, perhaps change and negation are illusions; but Parmenides attributes them to human opinion (fr. 8), which is a less drastic term than illusion. The real problem, however, is the strong claim in the way of truth that such ideas are impossible and unthinkable. This seems counterintuitive, as does the proposed conclusion that nothing in reality is changing. Furthermore, one wonders why Parmenides would even allow an extensive discussion of such ideas in the way of opinion.

I think the problem lies less with Parmenides and more with his interpreters, for two reasons. First, they assume the precedence of a formal deductive method and clearly established rules of logical classification, as if Parmenides were executing his thought in the same way as Plato and Aristotle, for example. Secondly, the translations of Parmenidean "Being" are too often derived from a reified sense of "entities" or "beings." The result is the usual picture of Parmenides' argument: Since the categories being and nonbeing exclude each other, then a being or an entity must always remain in being and cannot be thought to not be. Therefore nothing ever changes (i.e., loses certain states of being) or goes out of being. The difficulties of such a position prompted later philosophers to seek a restoration of change in the face of Parmenidean logic. But I think Parmenides might be having words he did not intend put in his mouth. The "problem" of change might be a pseudoproblem owing to a misapprehension of the meaning of Being in the poem. This shows itself when *einai* and other terms are translated as "it is" or "things that are" or "beings," renderings which seem more appropriate for the way of opinion (individual entities) than the way of truth. For Parmenides, Being itself is to be distinguished, I think, from any sense of particular being or entity. The overall poem makes much more sense if Being is freed from any connotations which suggest "things" or "objects." As a consequence we find Parmenides thinking the Being of beings rather than Being *as* beings (i.e., as simply a generalization of all things that exist).[25] Let me suggest a few alternative interpretations of the poem which can elucidate such a sense of Being, and also place Parmenides much closer to certain ideas he is supposed to have overcome or rejected.

One possibility would be a grammatical interpretation of the way of truth. Accordingly, Being would not refer to entities or beings but rather the grammatical function of the "is." In other words, Parmenides's argument might involve the ubiquity of the copula as opposed to the unchangeability of beings. Being would be distinguished from *a* being since Being in this respect is not a predicate (compare Kant's analysis). Being precedes predication because one cannot predicate without the "is" (at least implicitly). As a consequence, change need not be completely denied in the way of truth. One can say "the color *is* changing"; thus change is permitted but the copula (Being) is "immovable." So it might not be that Parmenides denies natural change or time, but simply that he sees every aspect of reality in relation to Being, that is in relation to some kind of assertion. Even negation can be restored in such an interpretation. We can say "the stone *is* not round." Accordingly, "not round" can still be a part of Being; the "not" is therefore not a negation of Being. Hence we find a way to sidestep a common interpretation of Parmenides—that the way of truth holds the "is not" to be an unthinkable contradiction.[26]

A grammatical interpretation has its limits. After all, the world is not simply a collection of nouns and verbs. The grammatical function of the "is" implies, it seems to me, the general notion of *disclosure*. I would read the way of truth in the following manner. Parmenides's objections to non-Being do not refer to a supposed correlation of entities and opposite states (beings and nonbeing). Rather, if Being means disclosure, then talking about non-Being would imply something that is impossible: disclosing something not disclosed. Even negative states (opposite relations among beings) must be disclosed *as such* in language and thought. Now we might be able to read some important Parmenidean sentences in a clearer light.

. . . for Being and thinking are the same [*to gar auto noein estin te kai einai*]. (fr. 3)

Being needs speaking and thinking [*chrē to legein te noein t'eon emmenai*]. (fr. 6)

. . . for you will not find thought without "is," in relation to which it is uttered; for there is not, nor shall be, anything else besides "is," since Fate [*Moira*] fettered it to be entire and immovable. (fr. 8) (352)

Parmenides, therefore, proposes that language (*legein*), thinking (*noein*), and Being (*einai*) are all connected by necessity (cf. *chreōn*). The relationship between Being and thinking, however, is nothing like metaphysical idealism, where reality is reduced to mind as opposed to matter. Rather, Being is *disclosure* (even "mind" has to be disclosed) and disclosure needs thought and language.[27] If Being means disclosure and disclosure means thought and language, then it is impossible to think or speak non-Being, i.e., nondisclosure, since any thinking or speaking is a mode of disclosure. Hence Being is everpresent, self-contained, unchangeable, in *this* sense. Such, I think, is a much more plausible reading of the way of truth. Being, therefore, is not something static but an all-encompassing process, more a verb (be-ing) than a noun (entity). Accordingly, the "truth" of Being mentioned in the prologue can be identified with disclosure as such (*a-lētheia*, unconcealment), and Being can be connected with the primal meaning of physis.

Perhaps now the two parts of Parmenides's poem can be more clearly integrated. The prologue mentions the gates of light and darkness, and Parmenides passes through *both* of them. This together with the image of unveiling (the goddesses lifting their veils) helps support the proposal that Being is a primal process of appearing, disclosing, emerging from hiddenness. The way of opinion refers to beings and opposite states of being. The mistake criticized there is the supposition that reality can be ultimately separated into opposite states or that Being can ever be negated. The resolution becomes evident if we realize that opposite states (being and nonbeing) are still maintained by an everpresent Being (disclosure). Even nonbeing (opposite states) must be disclosed in language. In other words, there is something more than positive and negative states which encompasses *any* disclosure. Such is

Being, which is one, uncreated, with nothing outside it (fr. 8). The unity of Being is not meant to deny change, differences, negation, and opposition; rather, within such designations which characterize the way of opinion there lies the truth of Being, understood as disclosure.

We should also remember that Heraclitus's position is certainly comparable in many ways. He too proposed a unity within change, the eternal, uncreated logos. Furthermore, both Heraclitus and Anaximander looked beyond sheer opposition. Behind apparent opposition lay a harmony based upon a primal unity. Generally speaking, Parmenides can be compared to Heraclitus and Anaximander in the sense that beings and opposite states of beings all require some fundamental, primal appearing out of hiddenness; Parmenides names it Being, which is more than and hence distinguished from being-states as such. For all the change and negation in the world, that is not sufficient to account for the ultimate nature of reality. Particular beings and their negations are embedded in Being, which is neither a being nor a negative state since it is the disclosure of any state.

I have tried to suggest ways in which Parmenides can be read without the supposed exclusion of change and becoming. Actually the greatest obstacle to that supposition is found in the prologue, where the goddess tells Parmenides that the realm of becoming (being and nonbeing) must be apprehended as well as the truth of Being.

> Yet none the less shalt thou learn these things also—how the things that seem, as they all pass through everything, must gain the semblance of Being (fr. 1) (342)

It seems that knowledge of becoming is also necessary if Parmenides is to learn the truth. If becoming were to be excluded, then such a requirement, as well as the extensive analysis of becoming in the way of opinion, would not make much sense. But we have already suggested that coming into being, negative states of being, and going out of being need not be judged false or unthinkable. They are simply particularized appearances within an overall process of appearing—Being. Parmenides's criticisms come when such appearances are the only focus of attention, when negations of beings are thought to be an absolute end, or sheer nothingness, rather than the perdurance of Being. It is not nonbeing that bothers Parmenides (Being is not a being) but rather non-Being, or absolute nothingness as a viable thought. (Recall too that the Heraclitean logos did not entail sheer nothingness but simply the process of reality that cannot be captured in any particular being or idea.) Therefore, nonbeing (something beyond beings as such) is certainly intelligible for Parmenides, which helps explain the proposed necessity of the way of opinion, since nonbeing there does not negate Being in the way of truth. It is not that Being is some kind of static substance from which any notion of change must be purged. Rather, throughout the appearing, changing, and disappearing of beings there persists the ontological process of disclosure (unconcealment) which reveals the course of beings as such.

It turns out that Parmenides compares well with other early philosophers who look beyond beings or forms alone in order to penetrate the whole of reality. Furthermore, Parmenides is not the opponent of Heraclitus because both seem to espouse a primal process of appearance behind particular appearances. Neither thinker denies the reality of change and becoming; they both see a unity within change—the process of disclosure.

It may be that the language of Heraclitus and Parmenides permitted the later philosophical distinctions and opposition between becoming and being, but I tend to think that their two positions represent different emphases within a relatively common viewpoint. Heraclitus speaks of a process that is a unity (emphasizing process), while Parmenides speaks of a unity that is a process (emphasizing unity). Both, in my view, propose a unified process of emergence, unconcealment. It may also be that Parmenides is simply much less willing than Heraclitus to engage the "negative" background of emergence (concealment), focusing instead on emergence, hence his concentration on Being. Even though Parmenides mentions light and dark together in the prologue, perhaps he insists upon *silence* with regard to concealment. Perhaps he is more the purist when he describes Being as a well-rounded sphere, held fast within a limit, and incapable of indefinite dispersal (fr. 8). Even though concealment lies within the disclosure process (Parmenides's sphere image shows that Being is partly shaped by an indefinite beyond), nevertheless the "limit" might refer to the limit of language. We can acknowledge an inaccessible mystery behind disclosure which, however, Parmenides refuses to put in language, since that too would be disclosure.

# Time and Process

Some of the first philosophers explicitly identify the world's essence with time. For example, Anaximander declares that the world order proceeds "according to the assessment of time" (*kata tēn tou chronou taxin*), and Heraclitus associates time with a "kingship" in fragment 52. Accordingly, time is not simply an aspect of reality; rather, it constitutes the nature of things. We can understand this by interpreting time as *process;* in other words, time in this sense is not simply the units of past, present, and future, or particular changing states, but rather the overall process of change and becoming as such—emergence, alteration, and disappearance of forms. Philosophers we have discussed emphasized process in this sense as opposed to some kind of substance, i.e., an enduring, eternal form free from change and negation; they maintained that the very definition of form is constituted by negation, both a primal indeterminacy (illuminating form as such) and the reciprocal negation of opposite states (showing the relational interdetermination of forms).

These early philosophers, therefore, saw the world as essentially temporal. This is not contradicted by the fact that Anaximander, Heraclitus, and Parmenides declared their first principles to be eternal and uncreated: The notion of "eternal" here does not mean nontemporal or outside time but rather without beginning or end. The world for them is a process which is not resolved in, superceded by, or a departure from some sort of timeless state. The world is an eternal process, or eternal time.

The emphasis on process can be connected with important elements in the Greek mythical tradition, especially Dionysian religion and tragic poetry. The philosophers, however, broadened their mythical heritage considerably. They were not interested in mythical accounts of a temporal beginning (rituals or cosmogonic stories) or a temporal end (prophecy) but in the temporal nature of the world as such. In a way the philosophical treatment of process can be connected with our previous analysis of the sacred. Within particular mythical presentations we noticed the arriving-withdrawing character of the sacred, the disruption of consciousness, the pluralized emergence and disappearance of forms, and the negativity of fate. We noticed too how tragic myth gathered the sense of all this into an atmosphere of positive fatalism and affirmed the nonsubstantiality of form. In my view the first philosophers conceptually generalized, likewise affirmed, and gave an overall order to, the tragic sense of the sacred, though independent of mythical imagery. The conceptual account of a temporal process can be read, I think, as an explication of the substructural meaning of mythical disclosure. Philosophy and myth, therefore, cannot in this respect be strictly separated. The tragic poets themselves often generalized dramatic themes and spoke philosophically. With regard to time, for example, listen to Sophocles:

*Strangely the long and countless drift of time*
*Brings all things forth from darkness into light,*
*Then covers them once more.* (Ajax, 645-47)

Another connection between philosophy and myth can be found in cosmic models of time. The early Greek thinkers who addressed cosmic time employed a cyclic paradigm, where world periods would rise and fall, followed by immediate recurrences in endless succession. Such a paradigm can be traced to primitive mythical prototypes which reflected recurring patterns in nature, periodic episodes in the lived world, and the repetition of primal beginnings in rituals. A cyclic paradigm also implies the constitutive nature of time. A linear model of time, crystallized in the later Christian tradition, has time running an irreversible and unrepeatable course from an absolute beginning to a final end. Such a notion implies the conviction that time is inferior to a timeless eternity which will eventually resolve the negativity of temporality by bringing time to an end. Cyclic time, on the other hand, is eternal temporality, where time is self-contained, nonexpendable, and therefore essential, never to be resolved in a timeless state.[28]

The ontological status of time will become a fundamental issue with respect to the transition from myth to mature philosophy in Greece. Especially in Plato we will witness both an existential and an intellectual resistance to the effects of time, finitude, negation, and change—the conditions of the lived world which constituted mythical sense. A key factor in comprehending and negotiating the paradigm clash between myth and later philosophy will be the response to and evaluation of temporality. We will find that myth and early philosophy were able to find sense in, and thus affirm, something later philosophers were not able to tolerate, namely, temporal negation.

# Early Philosophy and Myth

Greek mystery religions were animated by the possibility of transforming human knowledge into divine knowledge, where ordinary experience and ideas could be transfigured by the infusion of a previously hidden sacred presence.[29] In many ways early Greek philosophy maintained a distinction between human and divine knowledge, as we have seen. Generally speaking, the distinction was translated into one between appearances and a primal origin. In addition, the idea of transformation was maintained, in that philosophical wisdom entailed lifting a veil of ignorance or limitation which ordinarily alienated human thought from the world's essence.

The nature of philosophy was such that myths per se were displaced or ignored. In searching for that which is essential or ultimate, the philosopher was no longer interested in the gods or their history but rather, as Eliade puts it, "the 'primordial situation' preceding that history."[30] The "precedence" of the primordial situation is not historical but ontological, since it is ever-present and active in all phenomena at all times. At this point the meaning of the Greek term *arché* shifted from its mythical meaning of "beginning" to the philosophical sense of origin or principle. Consequently, the direction of thought also changed. Myth was "retrogressive" in the sense that it prompted a retrieval by "going back" to beginnings via ritual acts or poetic telling. Philosophy became "introgressive" by going "beneath" or "within" present phenomena by means of thought and insight. As I have tried to argue, however, the turn to philosophy may not actually entail the *rejection* of myth but rather the general conceptualization of the underlying meaning and structure of mythical disclosure.

Perhaps the most important link between myth and philosophy is the notion of a primal unity, which, though not explicated in myth, was implied in Hesiod's poetry as well as in the meaning of fate and the sacred. Furthermore, the way in which early philosophers came to see the world as a unified whole can be connected in some way to modes of mythical *disclosure.* That is to say, usually the notion of a unified whole was not a logical conclusion based upon a method of deduction or induction. The term "natural philosopher" is in some respects a misnomer for many early Greek thinkers. Their first principles did not follow from observation or experimentation or any kind of method at all, but rather from an underived insight which they simply *declared.* The disposition to take a first principle as a given might be comparable to the mythical sense of givenness. The first philosophers sound more like inspired oracles than natural scientists.

Cornford has suggested that the early philosophers emerged from and hence were an extension of the traditional prophet-poet-sage complex.[31] If so, it is impossible to characterize the birth of philosophy as an opposition between reason and science on the one hand and religion on the other. Many philosophers saw themselves or were seen as shamanlike. Parmenides and Pythagoras are notable examples, and of particular interest is the case of Empedocles (496–435 B.C.). He might seem to be a model natural philosopher in that he breaks the world down into four basic elements, often extols the senses, and even adopts a kind of inductive approach when he cites specific observations to support his conclusions (e.g., frs. 20, 21). But at the same time he accounts for natural construction and destruction by means of the principles love and strife, which carry the existential overtones of myth and for which a specific precedent can be found in Hesiod's *Theogony*. Moreover, he often refers to a muse and specifically speaks of divine inspiration:

> But, ye gods, avert from my tongue the madness of those men, and guide forth from my reverent lips a pure stream! I beseech thee also, much-wooed and white-armed maiden Muse, convey such knowledge as divine law allows us creatures of a day to hear, driving the well-harnessed car from piety! (fr. 3)

> . . . know this for certain, since you have the account from a divinity. (fr. 23)[32]

And listen to the following passages from the *Purifications*, which show a remarkable affinity with shamanistic attributes like soul-flight, charismatic authority, healing powers, and reincarnation:

> He boasts not a human head upon his body, two branches spring not from his shoulders, no feet has he, no swift knees, no shaggy parts; rather is he only a holy, unspeakable mind [*phrēn*], darting with swift thoughts over the whole world. (fr. 134) (467)

> . . . I go about among you like an immortal god, mortal no more, honored as is my due and crowned with garlands and verdant wreaths. Whenever I enter the prosperous townships with these my followers, men and women both, I am revered; they follow me in countless numbers, asking where lies the path to gain, some seeking prophecies, while others, for many a day stabbed by grievous pains, beg to hear the word that heals all manner of illness. (fr. 112) (478)

> For already have I once been a boy and a girl, a bush and a bird and a dumb sea fish. (fr. 117) (476)

We find in Empedocles a curious mixture of naturalism and sacred imagery, which speaks against the strict separation of philosophy and myth.

It was not uncommon for early philosophers to be called divine or to have miraculous powers ascribed to them. Even Aristotle took such ascriptions seriously.[33] This might not seem so unusual if we remember that for the Greeks, "divine" need not refer only to a god as such. From the standpoint of sacred meaning it could also refer to anything of extraordinary significance. With respect to knowledge, "divine" referred to inspiration or extraordinary insight beyond ordinary experience and thought.[34] The idea of wisdom as the province of special individuals with the "gift" of access to something not derived from ordinary experience was a mark of early Greek philosophy.

Of course philosophy was not completely continuous with myth. There did emerge a contest for authority between philosophy and traditional paradigms. But the contest was not a result of utterly alien forces clashing in the cultural arena; rather, it was the result of *distinctions* developing within the original prophet-poet-sage complex—the poet offered knowledge of the past, the prophet knowledge of the future, and the philosopher knowledge of the (ever-) present.[35] Accordingly, the poet and philosopher began to compete with respect to the meaning of *archē* ("beginning" versus "principle"). The philosophers moved away from the poet's personalization of the *archē*; they also moved from mythical plurality to a notion of unity. When philosophers spoke of god or *archē*, they meant a unified essence.

But connections with myth are still quite evident. For example, Nilsson speaks of an archaic, impersonal power diffused throughout nature (i.e., mana) from which the gods took shape.[36] Hesiod too spoke of something prior to the gods. And the meaning of fate in Greek myth suggests an anterior, impersonal force within the complex of sacred forms. Early philosophy could be considered a retrieval of this impersonal priority in the sense that it explicated the hidden background of mythical imagery.

In addition, the first philosophers shared with the prophets and poets a certain model of knowledge, namely, that ordinary experience and thought are grounded in something hidden but discernable through a *special* faculty; and, not being common, such comprehension is not subject to external verification. In the case of philosophy the special faculty is *nous,* which can be translated "intuitive insight."[37] Again, the transition from myths to philosophical first principles had little if anything to do with observation or generalized inferences. The early philosophers were not practicing even a preliminary form of natural science in the strict sense of the term. Their criteria and starting points were not grounded in observable data or material states. According to Cornford, much of the blame for that misconception can be aimed at Aristotle:

> Misled by Aristotle's habit of regarding his predecessors as more or less imperfectly anticipating one or more of his own four causes (material, formal, moving and final), the older historians of philosophy accepted his view that the early Ionians were concerned only with 'principles of a material kind,' such as water or air. Accordingly they were represented as putting to themselves the question: What is the one (material) substance of which all things consist? But if we look at the systems themselves, the question they answer is a different one: How did a manifold and ordered world arise out of a primitive state of things?[38]

Although the turn from myths to nature was surely a precondition for the advent of science, nevertheless early philosophy was animated by essentially nonscientific, mythical elements: emergence out of a primal unity; the separation and struggle of related opposites; a justice scheme; attraction and repulsion (e.g., the importance of *eros*). Philosophy differed from myth in its depersonalization of these meanings, leading to a paradigm consisting of a primal origin and element-relations. Early philosophy was not a rejection of mythical tradition but a conceptualized account of the subtextual *sense* of mythical disclosure. If we keep in mind the primal meaning of physis (arising, appearing), then we might better understand the meaning of "nature" in early philosophy. Physis would refer to a premechanical, prescientific, and prenaturalistic sense of activity and process: disclosure of a world of becoming out of a hidden origin.

So, despite the revolutionary aspects of philosophy, many of the first Greek thinkers presented a view of the world which was comparable to mythical disclosure. From a thematic standpoint we have seen this to be especially true with respect to tragedy. I have suggested that early philosophy can be considered the reflective counterpart of tragic myth. The most important thematic parallel is the fatalistic sense of a limit to human knowledge and individuated form. Philosophers were acknowledging an inevitable mystery at the heart of things, an essence which is not a form or a being. The mystery is such that it has no rational or empirical "foundation."

Consequently, we must recognize an important distinction between early and later philosophy in relation to myth. A typical later critique of myth charges the absence of rational or empirical foundations (such as regularity and evidence); but part of the *sense* of myth was its transparency with respect to the background mystery of the sacred. The absence of a foundation can spawn a successful critique of myth only from an external standpoint. Internally the lack of foundation would stir an insight into the sense of myth. Early philosophers explicated and generalized the sense of myth by giving a reflective account of the nonsubstantiality of form, thereby explicating the meaning of mythical disclosure above and beyond specific mythical presentations.

In a way there is a progressive relationship between myth and early philosophy. If the reader is convinced that our analysis of the underlying meaning of myth is not forced or inappropriate, then the philosophers show themselves to be *drawing out* that meaning and sense, even though they are ignoring particular myths. The reflective distance from myths and their immediacy allows a vantage point from which the phenomenon of myth, the nature of myth as such, can be disclosed. Philosophical reflection can comprehend myth *as* a nonsubstantial presentation in the midst of an indeterminate origin, something not *explicit* in prephilosophical, mythical language. We saw that myth entailed the emergence of imagery out of a nonconscious "otherness," the background mystery of the sacred. But archaic experience was immediately captivated by the panorama of mythical images and was immersed in the stories and their functions. Later forms of poetry, especially tragedy, began to emphasize the ephemeral, nonsubstantial character of mythical forms and of life in general against the background of a fatal negativity. In my view the philosophers consummated the explication of a sacred otherness behind the forms of life by concentrating on an indeterminate essence.

By way of summary we can say that early philosophy rose above the story-character of myth but *not* the mythical sense of the world. The discovery of the sacred background in itself, explicitly formulated in thought, weakened the authority of myths. Philosophers were more interested in general, conceptual accounts which could embrace the world as such, stripped of mythical imagery. The importance of demythification in this sense for later scientific and philosophical developments is, of course, obvious; but I suggest that the initial turn to the world and nature away from gods and stories was demythification only with respect to the *form* of presentation. Many sacred *meanings* persisted. Though the emphasis on the natural world might suggest a turn to the profane, the "transcendent" character of their first principles shows that the early philosophers were *not* naturalists, rationalists, or empiricists, and that a certain kind of sacred meaning was maintained.

Anaximander's *apeiron*, Heraclitus's *logos*, and Parmenides's *einai* could in a way be called "mythic concepts." We could say that for these thinkers the world as such is a great myth in that it conforms to the general sense of mythical disclosure—i.e., form is not its own essence, its limit or loss is "in order"; indeed, the world as such has no foundation and no designation can fully capture its essence. Later philosophy will turn to form as a foundation and usher in a new standard of truth, but the first philosophers reflected the traditional mythical notion of the world yielding to an "other," a notion especially evident in the tragic character of early Greek culture. Yet the philosophers depicted this "other" without an image, without any form (other than its presentation in language), and thus drew out the implicit negativity of the sacred. Hence they gathered the general meaning of mytho-poetic disclosure *without myths*. As long as we remember that mythical *imagery* need not be the only factor here, then the proposed connection between philosophy and myth may not seem so strained, and we can avoid the objection that perhaps we are weakening or even robbing the intellectual achievements of the first philosophers. We should remember that myths were not "irrational," that within mythical presentations were clear elements of sense. It was the implicit sense of myth that was passed on to and in fact drawn out by the first philosophers. As a result we can modify a phrase often used to depict this transition—i.e., *from* myth *to* philosophy—and offer the following correction: *through* myth to philosophy. The former phrase is too suggestive of an unwarranted separation.[39]

# Consciousness, Unity, and Philosophy

How did the philosophers arrive at their unified first principles? As a possible answer, I want to suggest a relationship between the following factors: the development of self-consciousness, a broadened response to the sacred, some kind of mystical experience, and a philosophical outlook. Subsequent to the growing emphasis on self-consciousness, the perception of the sacred was subject to modification. When self-consciousness became increasingly distinguished from the world, the sacred was capable of taking on a certain distance; that is to say, the self was no longer fully immersed in and captivated by the local immediacy of sacred forms. With this distance, consciousness could become aware of the sacred matrix as such and thus comprehend a "whole." But how did the awareness of a whole become the philosophical notion of a *unity* (as opposed to merely a generalized aggregate)? A sense of unity could have arisen in the context of the detachable reflectiveness of consciousness, namely, a unitary dimension of experience "held back" from a pluralized world. In a purely mythical world the self was immediately embedded in lived experience; the mythical sense of a contextual self accounts for neither unity nor wholeness being explicit *issues* in mythical thought. Consequently, the new model of self-consciousness became a decisive factor in the discovery of these ideas. It is possible that self-consciousness generated new experiences which disclosed a "mystical" sense of unity which subsequently animated the linguistic formulations at the heart of early philosophical thought.

The first philosophers were not engaged in purely active reasoning and analysis. The advent of self-consciousness and reasoning did not entirely abandon the idea of a sacred power—that is to say, some irresistible, extrahuman power which absorbs human attention in an immediate encounter—but the encounter with the sacred was *broadened* beyond particular mythical forms such that a new paradigm of a unitary origin and particular "appearances" took shape. Such an interpretation is not at all alien to the atmosphere of early philosophy, especially that of Heraclitus and Parmenides.[40] Could it be that the rise of philosophy, which overcame mythical imagery, was generated from a mystical encounter with a unity transcending all imagery? It would then be no surprise that some of the first philosophers displayed a kind of nonanalytical, almost oracular, quality. It *is* possible that they reached their unitary insights simply by abstract thought alone (speculation, hypothesis, inference), but I think it more likely that their revolutionary ideas were triggered by some profound new *awareness* of a preconceptual sort. The only evidence for this is the atmosphere of the fragments. The posture and disposition of the philosophers speak against a sense of speculation or hypothesis. They do not appear to be "constructing" their basic insights; rather, they appear uncritically, intuitively, and immediately certain of their ideas, as if they were inspired, as if impressed by some irresistible, experiential impact or arresting evidence. That many of them explicitly refer to modes of inspiration only reinforces the mystical option.

I have suggested that the detachment of self-consciousness was a crucial element in the discovery of a unified whole. Detachment could allow such a sense of wholeness from the vantage point of a unitary, internal experience which tends to subsist through time, which is different from and yet involved with the plurality of phenomena. (Unity could be disclosed either by going *within* self-consciousness as opposed to the plurality of outward experiences, or by the ecstatic, Dionysian-like *dispersal* of self-consciousness into a formless field.) However, it would be wrong to think of such developments as simply subjective in nature. At this point in Greek thought it was not possible to think of the self as something utterly separate from the world. In other words, the detachment of self-consciousness did not entail a strict dichotomy between mind and world, or pure contemplative detachment from experience, or a spiritual journey within the soul alone, all of which were to characterize later versions of mysticism. Early philosophy was able to detach the self from lived *immediacy*, but it retained, I think, a lived relation to the world. The first philosophers did not oppose their views to an experiential world; they simply wanted to understand that world. We have seen how their thought retained much of the lived sense and existential meaning of mythical disclosure. Whatever they may have experienced internally was seen to be matched in the world (e.g., in the way its patterns and relationships began to make sense with respect to a unitary notion). So it is not as if self-consciousness projected or invented unity; rather, its distance from plurality became the catalyst for the *discovery* of unitary aspects of the world.

Early Greek philosophy was not a denial of myth or the lived world but was rather a reflective account of the background of myth, mystery as such, hiddenness presented as an all-embracing origin (*apeiron, logos, einai*). Mythical disclosure may have implied such a mystery, but the mythical mind was not fully conscious of this. Philosophy allowed the Greek mind to become more conscious of (and less overwhelmed by) a world still animated by its traditional meanings. It is true that early philosophy's displacement of myths in favor of conceptual thought *made possible* a revolutionary alternative to mythical thinking, namely, human experience of the world alone (i.e., the profane) and modes of thought abstracted from mythical sense; in other words, early philosophy made possible "natural philosophy." But the first thinkers were not natural philosophers or protoscientists in any definitive sense. The absence of a rational or empirical reduction and the subsequent acknowledgment of an inevitable mystery speak to this point. In early philosophy an essential mystery displaces the gods, while in natural philosophy (profane) nature displaces or eliminates mystery by means of an empirical/conceptual reduction. The first philosophers could well be called "nature mystics." (In Greek the connection between *mystikos* and mystery is indicated in its derivation from the verb *myein,* meaning "to close the eyes" or "shut the mouth," suggesting a kind of ineffability.) They turned to nature because the gods were no longer *needed;* a unitary insight now disclosed the world's sense. But the turn from gods to nature need not suggest some kind of cleavage. Recall the worldliness of Greek religion; the gods were not above nature but its existential *meaning.* Our analysis of Greek myth allows us to conclude that early philosophy was not a turn *to* nature but rather *from* stories of the gods to the subnarrative meaning of nature implicit within mythical disclosure. Such developments (especially abstraction and depersonalization) did make possible later movements in natural philosophy, Platonic rationalism, and Aristotelian empiricism, but early philosophy was quite different from these movements in many important respects.

## Cultural Resistance to Philosophy

The degree to which Greek philosophy did eventually come to depart from mythical tradition in more decisive ways was indicated in the list of characteristics discussed at the beginning of this chapter. The extent to which a cultural dichotomy developed became tangibly evident in Greek society. With the advent of natural philosophy and the teaching of the Sophists there followed many occasions of stiff resistance and institutional reaction against philosophy and its proponents.[41] Even as late as the end of the fifth century, atheism and astronomy were considered crimes, and a number of trials were held in Athens. We know that Anaxagoras, Protagoras, perhaps Euripides, and of course Socrates were prosecuted.[42] Anaxagoras, for example, was an atheist who believed that mind controlled all things, a conviction that anticipated later rationalistic movements. And his claim that the sun is simply an incandescent stone indicated a naturalistic turn from the sacred to the profane. That such intellectual convictions, which seem so plausible to us, could precipitate condemnation and persecution in Athens has always been disquieting for modern Grecophiles. How could the civilized Greeks have exhibited such strong currents of anti-intellectualism and reactionism? Perhaps it was simply due to persistent strains of ignorance or the protection of political power. Perhaps.

I would never want to defend the trials and executions; as such they *were* motivated by all-too-human weaknesses and motives (as well as a dogmatic fixation on traditional views). But underneath social, political, and legal surfaces the resistance to philosophy was indicative of a cultural *defense* which, though liable to misplaced reactions and closed assumptions about truth, was nevertheless not entirely reprehensible. From the standpoint of our analysis, the sustained and seemingly sincere antagonism toward philosophy was not a situation in which "ignorance" was repressing "truth." We are in a better position to recognize a paradigm clash, different and competing forms of truth. The trials may have been reprehensible, but that such things occurred can be interpreted in terms of a deep-seated resistance to new paradigms, which was not entirely unjustified.

In view of our analysis, what were some of the consequences of philosophy which could be legitimate problems for Greek culture and which could therefore generate sincere antagonism? First of all we have come to see that the transition from myth to philosophy cannot be sufficiently understood by way of loaded terms like "enlightenment." Rather, there emerged new models of truth and meaning, the exclusivity of which would banish significant and intelligible aspects of culture. The tendency to demote myth would not necessarily entail progress. We have seen how important aspects of the world constituted the sense of mythical disclosure. It was not only political leaders and lesser minds of the time who criticized philosophers. Aristophanes considered the advent of philosophy to be a genuine cultural crisis in which important values were threatened; and Pindar criticized natural philosophers for "breaking off the withered fruits of wisdom."[43]

The claim, for example, that the sun is not a god but an incandescent stone need not be understood in the context of exchanging a poorer "explanation" of the sun for a better one. We have seen that a mythical image should be read as a pretheoretical expression of an existential complex in which self and world are correlated and nature is understood in terms of lived meanings. Accordingly, mythical experience is intimately integrated with the world. The advent of abstraction and naturalism tended to undermine the existential complex and sever the self-world correlation. The deepest sense in which we could understand the historical resistance to philosophy would therefore be as follows: If the sun is no longer sacred, then it is stripped of its existential meaning, and a sense of alienation from the world would ensue. In *this* sense, the early resistance to philosophy would not be entirely unrelated to modern attempts to preserve and defend moral, religious, and aesthetic values against scientific determinism and materialism.[44] Generally speaking, then, we can conclude: Viewed from such a perspective, the historical resistance to a profaning of culture and concern over the loss of sacred meaning would not necessarily denote ignorance.

Secondly, the liberation of the individual and the promotion of free, critical thinking was a two-edged sword. On the one hand it allowed new discoveries and innovations which furthered the course of Greek culture. But on the other hand the concurrent break with traditionalism and the deauthorization of social, political, and religious customs, which had previously enjoyed unquestioned allegiance, could lead to licentiousness in less responsible individuals. (This, I think, was one of the latent and legitimate fears surrounding the trial of Socrates; his promotion of intellectual freedom could be abused if it was seen by the young to justify selfish aims and uncivil tendencies.)

Finally, there was a growing problem with regard to the social fabric of Greek culture. Gradually intellectuals began to adopt a kind of privacy in which they set themselves against traditional authorities and the common citizenry. The traditional notion that wisdom had an automatic association with leadership was undermined by the philosopher's retreat. Great minds became disengaged from society, and the common people were in a sense left on their own. This, together with the absence of universal education, precipitated the development of many regressive forms of primitivism and magic.[45] Futhermore, the concurrent emphasis on the common man was instrumental in the development of democratic political values, but many saw democracy as a promotion of mediocrity and a chaotic mass of conflicting claims unmediated by wise and noble leadership.

The advent of philosophy was partially animated by the emergence of self-consciousness; but the subsequent emphasis on individuality inevitably led to the breakdown of the social cohesion indigenous to the traditional "social self." This is a simultaneous gain and loss with which we still live today. The cultural turmoil in Athens and the Greek reaction against philosophy were in part a response to the dangers of individual freedom. An overall picture of social and political developments in classical Athens can best be described as an attempt to negotiate between conflicting but nevertheless related cultural forces: an organization of society according to a rational system of justice; the protection of excellence against democratization; the preservation of social cohesion in the face of growing individualism. We notice here a mixture of tradition and innovation. And there were different responses to the inherent problems of such a cultural mix. Some were nostalgic for the old order. Others sought to create a new order. And the philosopher we turn to next, Plato, envisioned a new, rationalized order which nevertheless retained many traditional elements.

# VII

# Plato

The philosophy of Plato (429–347 B.C.) is usually thought to represent the genuine beginning of western intellectual history, and for obvious reasons. Platonic dialogues offer the first attempt at an overall philosophy and formulate rational paradigms which in various ways have continued to shape our intellectual life. The questions, methods, and conceptual language found in Plato's thought can clearly distinguish a rational from a mythical attitude, and the modern reader can certainly recognize familiar territory here. We will want to emphasize the ways in which Plato departs from preceding traditions. Among the most important Platonic developments: a clear distinction between mind and world; the crystallization of self-consciousness, with decisive psychological, moral, and intellectual consequences; and the subordination of process and negativity to conceptual constancy. Even though later philosophical developments did not always concur with Platonism, nevertheless western intellectual history would not have been possible without the atmosphere and certain basic assumptions established in Plato's thought.

In addition to Platonism serving well to illuminate the transition from myth to philosophy, our overall study allows us to make more than contrasting use of Plato. We will find that many aspects of Platonic philosophy are intimately related to certain traditional attitudes. A comparison with mythical tradition goes a long way toward illuminating the thought of *Plato* too. Anyone who has carefully and thoroughly read the dialogues realizes the severe limits of the usual interpretation of Plato. Quite often modern philosophical expectations are frustrated in various ways. Throughout the dialogues seemingly strange ideas and attitudes are found; and so many conflicting positions abound, often without resolution, that one might wonder about the philosophical merits of Platonism. But such doubts result from *our* limited understanding of Greek cultural history and Plato's position therein. Platonic rationality did not entirely abandon the mythical past.

We would want to distinguish, therefore, between the influence of Platonism and Platonic dialogues themselves. If certain puzzles or frustrations appear in a reading of Plato, this is most likely because we select modern rational elements as the only standard for interpretation. Enigmatic aspects of the dialogues can be clarified if we attend to certain traditional cultural attitudes discussed in previous chapters. We will find that Plato's thought is actually a surprising combination of rationalism and mysticism, logic and myth, conscious and extraconscious forces. That is why Plato is so difficult to interpret properly; he mixes paradigms which some would think are mutually exclusive. With a broad historical outlook, we need not be too puzzled. In fact, Plato's thought can represent something quite positive and unique: Rather than being simply the first instance or preparation of rational paradigms, it presents a provocative coexistence of rational and mythical paradigms. Accordingly, we will want to examine both the revolutionary and the traditional elements of Plato's philosophy.

In addition, some Plato scholars have challenged the conventional notion that key positions taken in the dialogues (e.g., soul-body dualism, immortality, the division of reality into two separate realms) represent literal expressions of a Platonic "doctrine." I take that challenge to have some merit, and we will address the issue in this chapter. My procedure will take the following course: When considering the "revolutionary" aspects of Plato's philosophy, the analysis will emphasize the more conventional picture of his thought, because it does at least express the contrast with and departure from preceding modes of thought which in some way *is* evident in Platonism. The overall aim, however, is to draw out the direction of that departure and not necessarily to offer a definitive interpretation of Plato's philosophical position. When considering the "traditional" aspects of Plato's philosophy in terms of connections with preceding modes of thought, I will suggest ways in which Plato's supposed doctrines might be interpreted beyond the bounds of the conventional picture.

# Revolutionary Elements in Platonism

### THE REFLECTIVE INDIVIDUAL

To examine the ways in which Plato offered Greek culture an innovative departure from traditional attitudes, we should begin with the charismatic influence of Socrates.[1] When Socrates was brought to trial for corrupting the youth and denying the gods, the Greeks were playing out a dramatic confrontation between old and new cultures. The essence of that confrontation can be gleaned from Plato's *Apology*, the dialogue which recounts Socrates's own defense before his accusers, not so much in Socrates's specific replies to the charges as in his general posture relative to tradition and the community. What kind of challenge did Socrates represent? He led no army, had no wealth, and held no political office. He simply spent his days asking generic questions about philosophical, moral, religious, and political topics (e.g., What is justice?). These generic questions, which aimed for general definitions subsuming particular uses, seem to have been unprecedented.[2] Some evidence for this can be found in the *Laches* (192a), where Socrates is asking for the general meaning of courage that can unify all particular types of courage. When Socrates asks Laches if he understands the point of the question (i.e., the unification of particulars), Laches replies that he does not! From a historical standpoint, then, we have here an innovation rather than attention to perennial issues. This might account for the frustration and perplexity exhibited by some of Socrates's listeners, which could breed a kind of antagonism. In addition to posing new types of questions, Socrates exhibited great skill in criticizing the answers proposed by authoritative figures—testing their arguments, revealing doubtful assumptions, and generally demonstrating the inconsistencies and weaknesses in their positions (in public!).

Although Socrates himself offered no definitive answers to these questions, there were methodological and epistemological commitments evident in his procedure which undermined traditional values. Even if truth remained hidden, the path to truth was clear: One's position had to be logically consistent and founded on general assumptions which were definable and which could pass a test of counterinstances. In other words, truth would no longer follow simply from custom, authority, power, utility, or mass opinion. The search for truth requires a kind of detachment from the contingency and variability of such standpoints and a critical examination from the standpoint of individual reflection. Traditional "givenness" is now subject to doubt, and the consequences of doubt promote a withdrawal from the "external" world-complex in favor of "internal" reflection. What emerges from this is the primary gift of Socratic philosophy: the ideal of intellectual autonomy, that one should think for oneself rather than passively depend on others.

No belief about the world could persuade Socrates of its truth unless it passed the test of critical examination. We will shortly analyze
the Platonic criteria animating such a test. For now we should simply
recognize in Socrates the fruition of a development, the growth of
which we witnessed in previous periods of Greek culture—the disengagement of individual, reflective consciousness from the kind of immediate immersion in cosmic and social matrixes which characterized
a mythical world.

Socrates indeed represented a profound and dramatic commitment
to this new ideal. The extent to which he valued critical reflection is
clearly shown in the *Apology*. His accusers were willing to drop the
charges if he would only agree to stop philosophizing (they were
rightly fearful of making him a martyr). But Socrates preferred the
death sentence to such an offer and gave his famous reply: "the unex-
amined life is not worth living" (*Apology*, 38a). The most important
thing in life, even more important than life itself, is the pursuit of truth
through philosophical inquiry. Such courage and commitment were an
inspiration to the students of Socrates. The most famous of these, Plato,
was moved to abandon his career as a dramatist and dedicate his life to
writing philosophical "dramas," the dialogues which were meant to
bear witness to and carry forth the Socratic search for truth.

## A NEW VIEW OF THE SOUL

Not unrelated to this revolutionary intellectual disposition is a new
conception of the soul (*psychē*) which took shape in Plato's thought
and which led the Greek development of self-consciousness in a radically new direction. In the *Apology* Socrates tells the Athenians his
mission—persuade them to live primarily for the soul and not the
body. In the *Phaedo* the soul is described as something separate from
the body and possibly destined for an immortal existence beyond the
physical world. Moreover, the philosopher is encouraged to live primarily for the soul's mental function and even to welcome the death of
the body. In the *Phaedrus* the soul is depicted in a less polarized way;
its structure and dynamics are described in terms of a classic Platonic
paradigm—the ascent of the soul through levels of knowledge, gradually transcending the conditions of the physical world and apprehending eternal truths.

The Platonic distinction between the soul and the body is coextensive with an intellectual revolution covering both moral and philo-

sophical developments, namely, a certain *detachment* of the soul/
mind from physical passion/sense experience. We have seen how the
emergence of self-consciousness, especially in terms of unity and interiority, was a necessary condition for the development of philosophical abstraction and reflection. Perhaps the reason why Plato perfected
and crystallized the philosophical enterprise can be found in his dramatic delimitation of the conscious mind, the detachment of the soul
from external worldly conditions. By doing so, however, Plato gathered
a number of elements which lay outside the mainstream of traditional
Greek culture. Thus before we analyze the nature of Plato's philosophy, we should first explore its background, namely, a profound alteration of the Greek notion of *psychē*.

Plato's view of the soul was in some ways an extension of Pythagorean and Orphic doctrines, which Dodds maintains grew from Greek
contact with shaman cultures, around the seventh century B.C.[3] The
Orphic and Pythagorean version of shamanism, however, began to connect extraconscious experiences (dreams, visions, soul-flight) with an
occult power in human nature itself, thus greatly concentrating the
meaning of "self" which was evolving and gathering around the term
*psychē*. In other words, Greek shamanism was collecting forces which
were previously thought to be a sacred transcendence of the "human"
but which now characterized the extraordinary dimensions of the
human self. We find here a complicated relationship between religious
experience, the growth of self-consciousness, and a growing distinction between consciousness and the external world. The mythical integration of self and world began to unravel when the self gathered
various forces within its own sphere.[4] Greek shamanism was intimately
related to intellectual developments which were undermining a mythical sense of the world; it was therefore related to the emergence of
philosophy.

We can approach this development by considering the changing relationship between soul and body. We have seen how the *psychē* was
coming to be known as a unified, internal faculty. We have also discussed the Homeric notions of *psychē* (life force) and *soma* (corpse).
When *psychē* shifted from "life force" to "soul," *soma* underwent a
comparable shift from "corpse" to "body." In Homer, soul and body
could not be separately identified (there was no general term for body,
and *psychē* after death was not a disembodied state, but a "shade"). But
as *psychē* came to mean the *unified* conscious mind (linked to *nous*),
the plurality of body parts and functions became distinguished *as* such

from *psychē*; hence the *psychē-soma* distinction shifted from life-corpse to one between self-consciousness and a generalized term for its pluralized "other," the body.

In Greek shamanism this distinction grew into an opposition, where soul and body were separate realities. The *psychē* came to be seen as divine, and so the Greek duality of god and man turned into a human duality of soul and body. Such a dualism was unprecedented in Greek culture, and it had a direct bearing on philosophical developments. The distinction between mind and the physical world (a crucial element in the emergence of philosophy) was greatly facilitated by a religious factor—Greek shamanism.

Pythagoreanism is a prime example of Greek shamanism. It offered a more individualized form of religious experience (as opposed to the collective, Dionysian type) and contributed to the shaping of a new soul-concept. Pythagoras was thought to be divine and to possess the powers of prophecy, bilocation, and magical healing. He formed a religious cult which practiced abstinence, contemplation, and secret rituals. That cult developed radically new beliefs about the soul and human life, which Dodds calls "puritan psychology."[5] Such a psychology extended primitive shamanistic beliefs in a new direction and generated moral, psychological, and intellectual paradigms which would strongly influence developments in and beyond Greek culture. Puritan psychology can be summarized as follows: The soul is our true nature; the body and the physical world are alien territory into which the soul has fallen as punishment for sin; the demands of the body should be rejected, and the soul should gradually achieve spiritual and intellectual detachment; the soul passes through numerous embodiments until it can free itself from physical constraints, thereby gaining a disembodied, immortal existence.

Dodds has shown on the one hand how puritan psychology may have grown out of primitive shamanism, but on the other hand how it was colored by specific developments in Greek culture, especially moral and intellectual self-consciousness.[6] The connection with primitive shamanism can be understood in the following way: Psychic excursion led to a differentiation between soul and body; the shaman's "retreat" led to the idea of gaining psychic power through abstinence; tales of the disappearance and reappearance of shamans led to a belief in an indestructible self; and the transfer of power from dead to living shamans led to a belief in reincarnation. But Dodds points out the connection between reincarnation and moral developments in Greek culture. Morality has a ready interest in overcoming the natural time limit of death; otherwise the effectiveness and security of its principles can be in jeopardy. With regard to moral transgression, one might conceive two possible solutions to the limit of death: either descendants will pay or a person will pay in another life. Reincarnation served to offer a foundation for individual moral responsibility, to explain and resolve the inequities of life, and to illuminate the guilt feelings concurrent with the rise of individuality in the archaic age.

In the context of such moral developments, puritanism expressed a disdain for the body as a focus for guilt feelings and a measure against which the soul's nature could be disclosed. Consequently the limitations and sufferings in the physical world were seen as a form of punishment and an obstacle to be overcome in favor of some disembodied, immortal existence. Purity replaced justice and asceticism replaced moral training.[7] Puritanism, therefore, originated in Greece (and not earlier in Judaism or later in Christianity) as a combination of shamanism and Greek developments of moral/intellectual self-consciousness; but we should emphasize that puritanism introduced certain elements which were not typical of earlier Greek culture and which even at the time were not predominant—the infusion of an Olympian-like immortality into human nature, and death seen as a passage from earthly existence to a superior realm of timeless, incorporeal perfection.[8]

Puritan psychology had a strong influence on Plato. Furthermore, a connection between puritanism and philosophy is demonstrated in Platonism with its inseparable combination of spiritual, moral, and rational elements. Although moral and intellectual principles need not be strictly puritanical, nevertheless one cannot completely separate something like puritanism from moral, rational, and even scientific attitudes. Why? Because of at least one common feature found in all of them. Moral, rational, and scientific thinking follow from the conscious mind adopting a comparable kind of detachment from and transcendence of immediate lived experience, the existential and relational contexts which characterized a mythical world. And Platonism, the first fully organized philosophy, without which later intellectual developments (including Aristotle's more scientific philosophy) would not have been possible, combined moral, religious, and rational transcendence in one complex.

With this in mind we can better understand, for example, Plato's attitude toward mathematics. In Platonism, as in Pythagoreanism, mathematics was primarily connected with spiritual goals, because it promoted contemplative detachment (through abstraction) from the natural world. For Plato, knowledge was not simply cognitive; it was also salvific in that it elevated the soul beyond the negativity of the lived world.

> . . . the man whose mind is truly fixed on eternal realities has no lei- sure to turn his eyes downward upon the petty affairs of men, and so engaging in strife with them to be filled with envy and hate, but he fixes his gaze upon the things of the eternal and unchanging order, and seeing that they neither wrong nor are wronged by one another, but all abide in harmony as reason bids, he will endeavor to imitate them and, as far as may be, to fashion himself in their likeness and as- similate himself to them. . . .
>
> Then the philosopher associating with the divine order will him- self become orderly and divine in the measure permitted to man. (*Re- public*, 500c-d).

Plato, of course, radically altered the mythical sense of the divine. Such an alteration was well served by mathematics since it is the purest form of abstraction. Yet one might still wonder why Plato would con- nect mathematics with divinity. Aside from the proposal of salvation in a realm of eternal truths, a telling reason might be the psychological value of certainty. The a priori character of mathematics, the fact that here the mind begins and ends in its own sphere, free from the fluctua- tions of experience, ensures a form of necessary knowledge from which deception and change can be purged and with which the mind can stabilize and demystify the world. The perceived benefits of such knowledge may account for the continued association with sacred no- tions, although again the traditional meaning of the sacred is now changed. In fact, the issue of certainty is perhaps the key distinction between myth and later philosophical developments. Abstraction from the sensuous, lived world allows the possibility of uniformity and be- comes the foundation of formal logic and thus demonstration. Mathe- matics, as the purest form of abstraction and most conclusive form of knowledge, naturally emerged as an effective truth-standard in many Greek intellectual developments.[9] Beyond the Greek period, of course, mathematics continued to serve as a criterion for truth.[10]

The contrast with mythical disclosure helps us comprehend a com- mon element in seemingly different intellectual movements. The phi- losophy of Plato, especially the new psychology therein, helps us specify this common element in terms of the conscious mind's detachment from the lived world. Mythical disclosure presented the immediacy of existential involvement. With the advent of philosophy the mythical correlation of self and world was displaced by the mind's pursuit of unified concepts which could organize and stabilize reality. Plato's philosophy gathered spiritual, moral, and rational developments which can all be seen as displacements of traditional myth. The common element in this displacement is, I think, the crystallization of consciousness and the response of self-consciousness to the plurality, negativity, and fatalism of a mythical world.

To elaborate, in the turn away from mythical immediacy, the conscious mind discovers three possible solutions to the ruptures, dissolutions and mysteries inherent in a mythical world:

1. A **spiritual** solution, where transcendence of the temporal world becomes a kind of salvation.
2. A **moral** solution, where transcendence of the emotions permits self-control, which overcomes human abuse and traditional sacred expressions of lewd behavior, overwhelming passion, and the power principle.
3. A **rational** solution, where transcendence of sensuous/affective immediacy permits an intellectual order which replaces myth as a way of understanding the world.

Evidently the common feature in these solutions is transcendence of a mythical sense of world. Of course, the first form is clearly otherworldly; but compared to mythical disclosure, the third form (even in the form of science) is not worldly either, since it must pull away from the lived world. Against the background of mythical disclosure perhaps now we can more readily understand the many subsequent historical instances in which the first and third form *overlap*: Platonic spiritualism and rationalism were intimately related in Christian thought; monotheistic religions share at least one disposition with rationalism and empiricism, namely, a rejection of "primitive" mythology. Furthermore, spiritual, rational, and scientific developments in a way share a moral element, namely, a devaluation of the passions (which impede both purity and an objective methodology). In general, then, all three movements share a transcendence of (and dissatisfaction with) the world as understood in mythical disclosure; the spiritual, moral, and rational solutions all represent a certain kind of demythification.

The underlying element in these forms of demythification is the ascendancy of the conscious mind. In general, mythical sense is displaced, and specifically, the mythical gods withdraw from the scene. The revolutionary Platonic view of the *psyche* clearly illustrates how the conscious self came to *replace* mythical configurations: In a spiritual sense (#1), the "soul" itself takes on a divine aspect; in moral reasoning (#2), the individual "self" discovers and benefits from abstract ethical principles; and in philosophy (#3), "mind" replaces the gods and poets with respect to disclosing the nature of reality.

## NEW INTELLECTUAL CRITERIA

The transcendence which characterizes Platonic psychology prepares and constitutes a revolutionary doctrine of truth. The unity and interiority of self-consciousness permits a new direction for thought, namely, an inward turn which concentrates on the mind's capacity for abstraction and which subsequently can overcome plurality, negativity, and change in favor of abiding principles. As a result the mythical atmosphere of mystery, limitation, and fatalism is exchanged for a more optimistic doctrine which proclaims the world "knowable." The advent of such a doctrine, however, with its criterion of constancy, introduces a tension between philosophical understanding and other forms of disclosure and experience. Plato's thought clearly shows the tension. Let us briefly examine the nature and consequences of his intellectual innovations with respect to philosophy and morality.

**Philosophy.** A most concise presentation of Plato's philosophical outlook can be found in Books VI and VII of the *Republic*. Book VII contains the famous cave allegory which dramatizes the nature of philosophical knowledge outlined in Book VI (the divided line). We are asked to imagine a cave in which prisoners are chained to a bench facing a wall. They can only look forward and see a series of shadows passing along the wall. One of the prisoners is set free and turns around to find a ramp, along which figures are being passed, illuminated by a fire behind the ramp. At first his eyes are pained by the light, but after acclimating himself he realizes that what he had previously assumed to be real was only a shadow of something else. He then notices a bright light coming from the cave opening, and he makes a difficult climb to reach it. There he experiences for the first time the light of day and the natural objects outside the cave. Again his eyes are pained, so at first he can only perceive the objects through reflections in pools of water. Eventually he is able to witness these things in all their splendor, illuminated by the great light of the sun. Enthralled by the warmth and beauty of the scene, he nevertheless is compelled to return to the dark cave. He is moved to tell the other prisoners of his discovery: What they assume to be real is only a dim reflection of real things. But they cannot understand him, and the pain they feel from turning their sight around prompts great resistance. In fact, we are told that if they could get their hands on him they would kill him (517a). The reference, of course, is to the fate of Socrates.

The meaning of this allegory for "enlightenment" is prepared by a discussion of the divided line, where Plato outlines the levels of reality and corresponding levels of knowledge. The shadows symbolize faint reflections of natural objects which constitute the realm of conjecture. The figures on the ramp represent natural objects apprehended through the senses, designated as mere belief. The pool reflections stand for mathematical understanding. The real things symbolize Plato's notion of Forms, apprehended by *nous*. The sun represents the highest principle of the Good, which illuminates all the levels of reality and knowledge. According to this scheme, each level is a mere image of a higher level, leading all the way to the Forms and the Good. What distinguishes the higher from the lower levels is the degree of unity and unchangeability. Our initial encounter with the world is fraught with difficulties—change, deception, and variation. If we are to overcome these obstacles and gain true knowledge (the reduction to some kind of stable standard), we must pass beyond the sensuous encounter with the natural world and pursue the inward dimension of the mind, where mathematical abstraction and finally comprehension of the pure Forms will provide the necessary unification and constancy.

Plato's approach can in some respects be understood as a discovery and explication of the a priori nature of concepts.[11] When we talk of "knowing" something we employ various concepts and principles which go beyond pure sense perception. For example, if two animals are both called horses, the common notion of "horse" cannot be identified with the perceived animals, because their size, shape, color, and other features are not the same. If a large brown animal and a small white animal can both be called horses, and if size and color can change over time, then sense perceptions as such cannot constitute "horseness." Consequently, when we know something as a horse, we must comprehend some notion which transcends the variability and changeability of corporeal examples. In the area of mathematical knowledge, when we use the notion of a triangle, for example, we realize that the pure form of its definition cannot be found in a physical embodiment because of the natural world's imperfections. So, if the mind is to truly know reality, it must pass beyond ordinary sense experience and apprehend pure Forms, such as the extraphysical idea of Triangle as such. Other Forms represent conceptual categories (e.g., unity and multiplicity, identity and difference) which permit the overall orchestration of a rational methodology and a systematic organization of various particular formulations. All of these Forms, according to Plato, must in some sense transcend the conditions of the changing natural world. Plato can thus combine philosophy with puritan psychology by proposing an intellectual journey which also allows the soul to engage an eternal, unchanging dimension which resolves the negativity and limitations of life.

Plato's first principle, the Good, is eternal and unchanging, and it provides the basis for the eternal, unchanging Forms which resolve and make intelligible the temporal conditions of the natural world. Platonism represents a dramatic extension of philosophical developments in Greek culture. The process of conceptual abstraction, where unification and order are gained through detachment from lived immediacy, prompts Plato to devise a kind of ontological segregation. Conceptual understanding must radically alter and even fight off the lived world. Plato deems that world to be a deceptive reflection of a truth which is ultimately nontemporal in nature. If we retrieve the issue of certainty we can perhaps understand the motivation behind such a scheme. Plato is trying to promote certainty by in some way separating the conditions of knowledge from the fluctuations of temporal experience.[12] To insure conceptual knowledge, Plato suggests a realm in which ideas are "entities" in themselves, thereby marked off from, and thus unchanged by, the sensuous world. In relation to mythical sense and the cosmologies of the first philosophers, however, we notice here a priority or criterion which had not been previously articulated or needed. Plato's standards of eternal form and constancy issue in *new* criteria which clearly depart from both mythical disclosure and early philosophy (which in different ways were seen to accommodate temporality, negativity and mystery).

**Morality.**    Plato initiated an ethical revolution which in various ways continued to animate moral ideals in western culture. We are well prepared to understand that revolution because it stems from two developments we saw crystallized in Plato's thought: (1) an internalized self;

and (2) an intellectual/spiritual principle of constancy which orders the flux and turmoil of the passions. To pursue the issue properly we should place it in historical perspective with the help of Snell's insightful treatment of the subject.[13] The notion of moral "virtue" as we understand the term is derived from a Platonic transformation of traditional Greek values. We can find in Homer a certain moral sense, namely the curbing of an agitated or wild state of mind, but it usually follows from divine intervention. Furthermore, the motive seems to be worldly advantage or profit. In other words, such values remain embedded in an extra-individual sacred or situational matrix, and thus remain "external," since the notion of internal happiness or an autonomous state independent of a world situation is not yet evident. Strictly speaking, there is no concept of "conscience," even though the avenging fates could be called an external prefiguration of such an idea.

Traditional Greek evaluative terms show an outward, situational meaning. Originally, *agathos* (good) meant useful or proficient; and we have already noted that *aretē* meant nobility, success, reputation, and military excellence. Moral values first represented an aristocratic ideal, the uncommon good of individual excellence as opposed to a common good. The importance of honor, however, shows that such values maintained a social, communal aspect. When aristocratic standards began to fade, the notion of a common good arose and hence the idea of justice—the affirmation and protection of common individual "rights," the prevention of abuse by way of renouncing the power principle (the assertion of exceptional individuals). Such was the background of Solon's political and moral revolution. Justice so defined was guaranteed by means of written laws, by a permanent, conceptual transcendence abstracting from and thus unifying different individuals, renouncing individual power and replacing it with the state's power to enforce laws.

However, justice is not equivalent to virtue as we have come to understand the term, namely, as moral character. Justice involves enforcement by the state, mutual protection, and a proportion due each individual. The external nature of justice is shown in practice where it is essentially prohibitive and still in a sense profitable (Solon himself saw the fruits of justice to be the preservation and productivity of society). Virtue, on the other hand, implies an internalization of moral values, a positive state of character (e.g., *being* just) and not simply negative prohibitions (threats against unjust acts). With the idea of virtue, the "curbing power" is no longer external but an internal faculty.

Platonic philosophy and psychology present the conditions for such a concept of virtue by means of an internalized, rationalized soul.[14]

The figure of Socrates in the dialogues represents, among other things, the search for and justification of virtue, meant to overcome a number of moral attitudes that Plato considered dangerous or limited. Those attitudes can be summarized as follows:

1. **The power principle**, best represented by Thrasymachus (*Republic*, I), who conceived justice to be the advantage of the stronger (might makes right).
2. **Utilitarian ethics**, where the good is defined according to external advantages such as profit or glory.
3. **Prohibitive ethics**, represented by Glaukon (*Republic*, II), who believed that no one would be good without the threat of punishment.
4. **Ethical relativism**, stemming from some of the Sophists who maintained that moral values have no absolute foundation but are simply a matter of convention or individual preference.

Plato argued that such moral attitudes are deficient for a number of important reasons. The power principle would perpetuate human abuse; utilitarian standards would threaten morality in the absence of external advantages; mere prohibition would likewise threaten morality in the absence of detection and would also subvert the noble ideal that man can *be* good by nature; and relativism would threaten the educational force and authority of moral values.

In response Plato engaged the search for an absolute good and its internal appropriation. Justice must be grounded in virtue, an internal commitment to the good which persists independent of worldly advantage or disadvantage. Socrates even goes so far as to say it is better to suffer an injustice than to commit one (to which his own life bore witness). In other words, virtue is its own standard and its own reward. Without an internalized psychology and a strictly internal form of insight, however, such a notion would make little sense at all. That is one reason why some of Socrates's interlocutors did not simply disagree with him; they did not see the *point* of his position. This also accounts for the inseparable relationship between Platonic ethics, psychology, and metaphysics. The search for virtue and goodness requires an internalized soul which apprehends a realm transcending the pluralized conditions of the outward, natural world. In this respect Plato does argue for a certain advantage adhering to such a concept of virtue, but that advantage has nothing to do with tangible, material benefits. It rather exemplifies or follows from Plato's overall philosophy: Virtue allows contentment with oneself, that is, it fulfills an inner standard of goodness and avoids *self*-condemnation stemming from guilt or conscience; moreover, virtue may lead to advantage in an afterlife (e.g., the judgment of souls described in the myth of Er at the end of the *Republic*); and Plato believed that the realization of virtue would animate a natural and unforced display of justice, thus creating the advantage of social harmony.

Since the Platonic idea of virtue is intimately connected with a transcendence of ordinary experiences and situations, it becomes notoriously difficult to grasp. The key to this difficulty is the nature of the Good, an ultimate unity which is so universal as to defy definitional limits; if *everything* depends on the Good, what could possibly describe it? Plato does not so much define virtue as establish the direction for its discovery, the possibility of an individual appropriation through some kind of inward intuition.

But despite these difficulties, the Platonic outlook can hold great appeal, for both intellectual and moral reasons. Transcendence of plurality offers enormous power to the mind; the confusing display of experience can be controlled, ordered, and negotiated by means of overarching principles, thus exchanging a sense of strangeness for a profound new familiarity. Furthermore, transcendence overcomes the deficiencies of the above-mentioned moral attitudes and can regulate the variability of worldly claims. Platonic unification thus has great power, but its internalized transcendence is inevitably at odds with lived experience. It is no surprise that Platonic transcendence generated a kind of dualistic demarcation of distinct realms, with one realm "correcting" the deficiencies of the other. In fact, Platonism clearly indicates the overall corrective attitude of philosophy in relation to mythical disclosure. Whether the question is human nature or the nature of the world, philosophical developments emerged in part as a reaction against a mythical world, which was already in place and thus had to be opposed. It is this *evaluative* aspect of philosophy that helps account for the inseparable relationship between rational and moral developments in Greek intellectual history. It was Nietzsche's contention that reason and morality are two sides of the same coin, the correction of (or dissatisfaction with) an existential world. Thus for him the emergence of philosophy was not strictly speaking the discovery of objective truth, since it was animated by many nonobjective, evaluative dispositions.[15]

Consequently, the moral elements of Platonism are coextensive with an overall philosophical transcendence of a mythical world. Just as rational, abstract transcendence overcomes the "chaos" of variable, immediate, and unique elements in mythical disclosure, so too the new morality overcomes the chaos of passion, inclination, and destructive tendencies by means of a moral self enacting a comparable transcendence. Platonism allows the moral self to overcome the dark influences of mythical daemons over which consciousness had no control. Centered in itself, the soul achieves freedom, control, clarity, and the security of knowledge as the ground of action.[16] The judgment scene in the myth of Er dramatizes the completed turn from Homeric psychology to the notion of responsibility and choice in the soul itself. Furthermore, a prominent word in Platonic and subsequent moral thought is *sōphrosynē*, meaning self-control and moderation of extremes; and the "extreme," the overwhelming abandonment of conscious control and limits, was precisely that which constituted the mythical sense of experience in so many instances.

The Platonic revolution certainly represents a profound contribution to human culture. Countless intellectual developments would not have been possible apart from certain criteria established by Plato—the ideal of intelligibility, the dynamics of conceptual abstraction and definition, the importance of criticism and argument, and a kind of systematic rationality. Moreover, our moral principles continue to be influenced by the Platonic sense of virtue (e.g., the ideal of civil disobedience, which even became a standard for legal judgment at Nuremberg) and by the meaning of the mind-body distinction (e.g., objections to racism or sexism simply extend the scope of the ancient notion that a person's worth should not be drawn from physical attributes alone).

Despite the doubtless importance of such an intellectual revolution, however, the purpose of our investigation is to examine its history, meaning, and presumed status. Many who would reject certain elements of Platonism would still deem it the first significant step toward the "truth" and away from prephilosophical "ignorance"; but the importance of philosophical developments is one thing, the presumption of truth another. We have seen how the presumably objective features of Platonism are inseparable from certain moral and psychological dispositions. Put another way, the positive elements of philosophy have a decidedly negative background—a reaction *against* certain traditional forms of meaning and disclosure which did and can still be seen to make sense. Much of what Plato saw to be wrong with the world was precisely positive in mythical disclosure. In fact, the designation of Platonic philosophy as a "revolution" is in one sense quite apt: Mythical tradition was not corrected, it was overthrown. The tension between myth and philosophy was more akin to a clash of political ideologies, each with its own sense of purpose. The evaluative features of Platonic philosophy undermine the presumption that either it or its descendants can lay claim to any kind of absolute or objective status.

In addition, the assumption that philosophy corrected mythical ignorance runs up against another obstacle. We have already seen how early philosophical developments were in many ways *positively* related to prior mythical traditions. The same can be said for Platonism. For all its revolutionary elements, Plato's philosophy exhibited and maintained several important links with traditional Greek culture.

# Traditional Elements in Platonism

## A CORRELATION BETWEEN KNOWING AND DOING

We have seen how Platonism rejected traditional and early philosophical definitions of virtue and how its revolutionary position was supported by an internalized self. Even though Platonic insights required a kind of internal, intellectual detachment, however, a careful reading of the dialogues does not reveal a *complete* separation of knowledge and selfhood from involvement with the world. With regard to virtue, at least, we find one interesting connection between Platonism and tradition, namely, a correlation between knowing and doing. Attention to this connection will help us clarify the meaning of certain problematic Socratic propositions, e.g., "knowledge is virtue" and "no one does evil knowingly." Without an historical perspective, such propositions would immediately seem suspect, since one can present countless instances in which people *know* what is wrong and yet still *do* wrong. The issue turns on what is meant by "knowledge" and "virtue." We have seen that *arete* originally meant excellence, or some kind of *achievement*. Moreover, both *epistēmē* (knowledge) and *sophia* (wisdom) have a prephilosophical meaning in Greek which entails ability, especially the practical mastery of a craft. For the Greeks, therefore, these terms would not be utterly separable from action in the world. "Knowing" in this sense would correspond to "knowing how." The above-mentioned Socratic propositions can not be properly understood if measured by a strictly theoretical model of knowledge, because they assume a practical standard as well. The precise meaning of "knowledge is virtue" is not that knowing the good is an end in itself, or that knowing it will automatically lead to good conduct; rather, if one does not *do* the good, then one cannot be truly said to *know* the good (just as a carpenter who cannot build anything does not really "know" the craft). Although Platonism surely involves a radical element of detachment, the question of virtue shows a certain connection with mythical tradition, if we recall the notions of lived world, an active, contextual self, and the coincidence of thought and action.

## THE SOCIAL SELF

In addition to modifying intellectual detachment by way of practical wisdom, Platonism also modifies internalization by retaining certain features of the traditional social self. The advent of critical reflection and skepticism did not entail, for Plato, a strict separation of the individual from social institutions, the notion that individual thought and conscience take complete precedence over group interests or political obligations. Plato would not condone a modern tendency to define the self as a kind of private, autonomous individual for whom social relations are accidental or secondary. Although Plato does champion the free-thinking, critical individual, he does not espouse individual*ism*.

But surely, does not the posture of Socrates in the *Apology* suggest the separation of the individual from society? In some sense, yes. But Socrates did not conceive his philosophical mission to be an individual affair but a contribution to Athens, the *polis*. The relationship between the individual and the *polis* is clearly stated in a subsequent dialogue, the *Crito*. There Socrates is offered an opportunity to escape Athens and his pending execution. To the surprise of his friend, Socrates refuses, explaining that he owes unconditional loyalty to the *polis*, even though he is a victim of political and legal injustice. He decries the consequences that would follow from measuring action according to a private standard (50b). The *polis* is said to have priority over individuals for many reasons (50d, ff.): It provides material benefits, legal protection, and educational support, without which Socrates could not have developed his form of life. In other words, the individual cannot attain human fulfillment apart from the social order.[17] Accordingly,

Socrates concludes that death is preferable to exile (52c), an attitude which is not entirely alien to the traditional Greek estimation of the *polis*. Socrates would not truly *be* himself apart from Athens.[18]

But why should Socrates remain loyal to a city which has unjustly condemned him to death? Because even if an individual suffers at the hands of the state, the *idea* of a state cannot be undermined by a purely individual standard. Of course, Plato does not recommend complete subservience to the state. We notice a balance of individual criticism and political authority which clarifies the meaning of "civil disobedience." The free-thinking individual should criticize bad laws or an unjust application of good laws, but if in doing so one cannot change the law through persuasion or example, and if one falls victim to the law, one must accept and suffer the consequences of punishment. The individual can criticize a law but cannot undermine the *idea* of a lawful society. Socratic individuality is not a form of individualism; the individual is not separable from and cannot take priority over the social matrix but must rather critically *participate* in its design.

## THE REJECTION OF SOPHISTIC RELATIVISM AND HUMANISM

Plato opposed many of the philosophical developments of his time, especially the teachings of the Sophists. That opposition, although not a throwback to tradition, did display an analogous relationship to certain traditional assumptions that were threatened by the emergence of Sophism. Who were the Sophists and what was their contribution to Greek culture? Jaeger offers an illuminating exposition of this question.[19] With the growth of the *polis*, the idea of education evolved into *political* education, namely, moral, physical, and intellectual training designed to serve the *polis*. Athens was developing an aristocracy of intellect as opposed to one of wealth or physical strength. The Sophists inherited, in a way, the educational function of the poets. They were not really philosophers in the strict sense but rather educators of political leaders. They taught oratory and rhetoric, the powers of persuasion needed to actualize leadership in a political setting. The Sophists, therefore, taught *aretē*, meaning in this case "political excellence." Here *aretē* and knowledge thereof were purely practical and not theoretical. Socrates's critique of Sophism can be traced to a different interpretation of *aretē*. Despite that difference, the Sophists were of great importance to Greek history. They invented intellectual culture and education toward that end, a crucial development without which the philosophy of Plato and Aristotle would not have been possible.

Sophism did not represent a monolithic doctrine; there were many different ideas emerging in that movement. In order to comprehend Plato's objections, we need to summarize a number of important issues which stem from the Sophists' teachings. First of all, with the invention of rhetoric a significant problem arose which troubled Plato and which is still with us in many ways, namely, the conflict between persuasion and truth, especially in the political arena. Although, as we have seen, Plato embraced a practical and political dimension, he decried a purely practical standard in politics (e.g., winning an argument at any cost). The goal of education should not be stylistic tricks of public persuasion but rather principles of thought which could establish a position through reason and not simply the impulses of an audience.

Secondly, the Sophists effectively initiated a conflict between religion and culture. This of course was characteristic of philosophy in general, but the Sophists took it beyond the cosmic musings of early philosophy and emphasized the social and political character of human beings. By rejecting traditional religious prescriptions with regard to the social order, the Sophists thus invented what has come to be known as humanism, i.e., culture interpreted as the cultivation of human nature. They retained the educational function of music and poetry, however no longer as an expression of sacred meanings but as a means for developing *human* nature (cf. our humanities).

In many respects Plato could applaud such a development, but he saw a number of problems in the development of humanism: The human realm was emphasized at the expense of the nonhuman world; the liberation of the self opened the door for an unbridled assertion of human inclinations; and the traditional notion that humans are checked by some kind of transcendent authority was undermined, leading to such things as hedonism, relativism, and individualism. So even though Plato embraced the human pursuit of truth, he feared the tendency toward humanism which threatened to measure truth solely according to human needs. Consequently, Plato was compelled to retain the notion of god, even though he radically altered the traditional meaning of divinity. It is no surprise that he specifically criticized Protagoras's famous proposition, "man is the measure of all things." Plato proclaims that *god* is the measure of all things (*Laws*, 716c). In addition, against the potentially licentious effects of humanism and the attitude of self-centeredness, we are told that the world is not made for humanity, but humanity for the world (*Laws*, 903c).

Thirdly, with the new ideal of humanistic culture the Sophists explored the relation between a person's given nature and learning. They proposed that learning can build upon one's nature, a notion which contested the old aristocratic idea that character is inherited, not acquired. Protagoras's belief that *aretē* can be taught reflected a new kind of optimism about our general educability and the power of culture to elevate human nature. The entrenched aristocracy opposed such a notion, and so did Socrates and Plato, but for different reasons as we shall see. In any case the Sophists offered the possibility of universal acquisition of character and hence a universal conception of human nature (as opposed to the qualitative differences in an aristocratic hierarchy). We should recognize that a generalized notion of "human nature" as such is not a natural or self-evident idea but a historical discovery of the Greek mind.[20] Still, the Sophistic ideal of education did create some problems. As the educated individual broke free from fixed assumptions about social station and human possibilities, the relation between the individual and society became contentious. Criticism of tradition and social structures engendered a good deal of social conflict. Plato was troubled by a number of dangerous consequences made possible by such an atmosphere.

One last point will help illuminate Plato's concerns. Not unrelated to the Sophistic ideal of education was the *nomos-physis* distinction, which we have already discussed. In an educational context the distinction speaks to the difference between something added and something left to itself. Beyond that context a number of thinkers proposed the general idea that culture and law are conventions which are superimposed upon, or even at odds with, what is given by nature. That conception shattered the traditional notion that principles of value are natural (i.e., intrinsic), that cultural ideals follow an overall world order (as depicted either in the old myths or in later conceptions of justice—compare Hesiod, Solon, and Anaximander). The *nomos-physis* distinction generated a profound cultural crisis. Values lost their traditional "givenness" and compelling authority, and took on a kind of contingency; they now represented an externally imposed order supported no longer by the sacred or something intrinsic to human nature but by laws which punish transgression. The idea of law thus seemed to be nothing more than a utilitarian arrangement, and compliance a hedonistic response (i.e., avoiding the pain of punishment).

Plato was fearful of the consequences. In the absence of punishment or detection, there would be no compulsion to be moral. Also, a sense of deauthorization encouraged criticism and rebellion (which in fact led to many revolutions in Greek politics). Furthermore, relativism and individualism were inevitable outcomes, threatening social cohesion and authority. In other words, along with the positive aspects in philosophy's departure from traditional myth there arose a number of threats to traditional *social* stability which Plato found dangerous. In a way, then, Platonism represents a *philosophical* retrieval of certain traditional meanings, although no longer in an archaic form. Such, I think, is the key to understanding Plato's conception of virtue. He attempted to reestablish an intrinsic foundation for morality, although now in terms of philosophical assumptions—an internalized soul apprehending the rational foundation of reality in pure Forms distinct from the material world. This, of course, led to the Platonic idea that the intrinsic nature of human beings is something extraphysical.

Platonism, therefore, represented a synthesis of old and new aspects of Greek culture. It aimed to establish an intrinsic foundation for morality in terms of rational absolutes. Platonic Forms overcame *both* the pluralism of myth *and* the relativism and individualism of Sophistic philosophy. The Forms bear an analogous relationship to traditional meanings in that they stand above and check the pursuits of human beings. But the discovery of the Forms requires an individual mind pursuing an internal, philosophical path to discover these principles which are fixed essences within all of reality. In relation to myth, Plato was a revolutionary; but in relation to Sophism, he was a traditionalist because he embraced the notion of a fixed authority, though now in a rationalized form. In the *Republic* we find a political vision which on the one hand shows the individual philosopher breaking free from society and immersion in the world to discover the Good, and which on the other hand establishes on that basis a social order which checks individualism. Plato's republic becomes a rational state which subordinates individuals; it therefore ironically both stems from and yet regulates the liberation of individual self-consciousness. The emergence of criticism which contested traditional forces generated an additional contest between divergent rational developments. In Sophism we find the rational individual threatening the authority of the state. Platonism proposed a rationalized order of the state to suppress individualism, even though rationality stems from the liberation of individual self-consciousness from traditional myth. The point is that Platonism represents a kind of dialectical relation between rational inquiry and traditional authority.

## ARISTOCRACY IN PLATONISM

The connection in Plato between the rational individual (e.g., Socrates) and political authority can be clarified further by examining another aspect of Platonism which retained a traditional feature, namely, aristocratic politics. We have discussed the concept of justice and its development in Greek culture. Between the eighth and fifth centuries B.C., many economic, social, and political forces contributed to the rise of the lower classes. The challenge to aristocratic authority and abuses led to a demand for written laws which could define and enforce a kind of equality among individuals. Justice became the "war-cry of the class-conflict,"[21] and defined *aretē* for a new age, replacing the epic ideal of warlike valor. Law became the objective expression of the *polis*, reflecting the transition from an aristocracy to the importance of the individual as such. Democratic developments in Athens assumed cultural as well as political dimensions. The *polis* embodied an ideal which organized human life and began to speak of "human nature" in the light of this ideal, as opposed to the old aristocracy which reserved cultural values for a special class. Although certain aristocratic elements survived (an intellectual elite, economic and social privilege, with legislation against *abuse* of privilege), nevertheless a new ideal was open to all citizens, at least in principle—the cultivation of the person, the education of mind, body, and spirit, aiming toward participation in civic affairs.

Democracy, however, did not go unchallenged, and objections did not stem simply from economic or political interests; there was a cultural challenge as well. Even though the old aristocracy was fading, certain poets championed aristocratic ideals in the face of growing egalitarianism. The old order was never reestablished, but aristocratic values survived through these poems and continued to effect Greek culture in different ways. We have already witnessed the aristocratic reaction of Pindar. Another poet, Theognis, also decried the *cultural* consequences of democracy.[22] Theognis advocated the ideal of noble character and self-discipline as opposed to a herd and mob mentality. Nobility need not mean privilege; it can also refer to strength of character, being self-directed rather than rule-bound, acting well by nature rather than from fear of punishment, choosing excellence rather than conformity. Theognis speaks to an important problem, the rarity of excellence and talent in conflict with democratic commonness. One might welcome political and legal democracy and yet fear a kind of cultural levelling tendency.

To Plato surely the problem of democracy was dramatically evident in the trial and death of Socrates. If the Athenian assembly could prosecute its noblest citizen, it is no wonder that Plato grew to reject democratic politics. He embraced the traditional aristocratic notion that only a select few are capable of excellence and that the best society would therefore be one in which the many are ruled by an excellent few (aristocracy in Greek literally means "rule by the best"). In the *Republic*, Plato outlines his vision of an aristocratic society. The key to its justification can be found in the cave allegory. We recall that the prisoner's journey was painful and difficult, requiring courage and perseverance. The liberation from ignorance to wisdom was repulsive to the other prisoners; they preferred the comfort and familiarity of the shadows. The move from common sense to intellectual forms involves abandoning customary notions and undergoing the rigor and pain of transformation. Philosophical insight is thus a rare and demanding phenomenon.

The vision of the Good and the Forms can be analogically compared to the archaic function of "special insight" (had by epic heroes, poets, prophets). Plato retained the traditional notion that individuals having special access to cultural foundations should hold a special social status over those who do not. The sacred justification for authority in mythical culture became an intellectual justification in Platonism. Access to the Good is not available to the crowd. Plato rejected democracy because it amounts to pooling the deficient opinions of the masses, governing society on the basis of ignorance, and permitting the legal persecution of excellence (Socrates). Platonism therefore represented a philosophical transformation and yet perpetuation of aristocratic elements in mythical culture.

Plato's republic is divided into three realms: the philosopher kings, the guardians (who correspond somewhat to the traditional heroic ideal), and the commoners. The political order matches the Platonic tripartite structure of the soul: reason (*logos*), spiritedness (*thymos*), and appetite (*epithymia*). Contrary to democracy, authority descends from the top down and only in that direction, from the philosophers to the guardians who rule the masses. Justice entails a balance of function in which each realm performs its proper task (legislation, defense, and commerce) without transgression from the others. Here the traditional idea of *limit* has evolved into an organized hierarchy of separated functions.[23]

The cave allegory prepares and justifies Plato's political aristocracy. Only the select few who can apprehend the Good should rule society. The Good is universal and illuminates the value of all things. Since the Good as such must cover and thus transcend all particulars, those who apprehend it must of necessity be detached from everyday concerns in the world. If society were run collectively, special interests would clash and the overall good of society would always be interpreted differently by each group. The philosopher is a disinterested individual who has the capacity to judge the respective value of all interests. Social harmony stems from the masses yielding authority to the benign dictatorship of philosopher kings.

Plato's aristocracy clarifies the ambivalent coexistence of a philosophical ideal (free-thinking individuals) and political control of individuals. Plato affirms individual rational inquiry; it liberates the mind from convention, custom, and ordinary pursuits, thereby leading from ignorance to truth. But philosophical inquiry is a special path with special demands; it requires transcendence and a *sacrifice* of worldly concerns. Not everyone is so inclined. If individual freedom were given to *all* individuals, this would lead to abuse because most people are not capable of philosophical transcendence and would make freedom serve their worldly inclinations. Plato's sense of rank is not a complete throwback to the old aristocracy. The ideal of wisdom and leadership is in principle open to anyone, but practice shows that not everyone is capable of achieving it (or perhaps it should be said that the other prisoners in the cave were simply *unwilling* to achieve it). Therefore, Plato's aristocracy is really a meritocracy. Rank is secure but it must be earned.

## INTUITION IN PLATONISM

If we turn to the question of how the philosopher apprehends truth, we confront the most important connection between Platonism and mythical tradition—an analogical relationship between philosophical insight and the archaic phenomenon of inspiration, that is, a kind of "givenness" from beyond ordinary consciousness. Clarification of this matter will facilitate a proper reading of the complex and seemingly incongruous amalgam of different elements in Platonic dialogues.

One reason why Plato is difficult to interpret is that the dialogues represent a mixture of certain archaic features and the aforementioned different types of conscious transcendence (spiritual, moral, and rational). Plato combined Pythagorean notions with Socratic rationality and thus completed the transformation of a shamanistic separable self (which was extraconscious) into a distinct conscious self. The result was a kind of "rationalized shaman." Dodds has enumerated the various shamanistic features which were retained or modified in Platonic philosophy: reincarnation; the exceptional individual as the agent of truth; the shaman's trance became mental withdrawal from sense experience; occult knowledge became metaphysical insight; remembrance of past lives became recollection of the Forms (the notion that since the Forms are not learned from sense experience, they must reside in the mind before sense experience, and "discovering" them means "recalling" them from some kind of prior access in an eternal realm).[24]

We should recognize that Plato embraced many nonrational, mythical paradigms. Moreover, analogous paradigms can be found even in his account of strictly philosophical knowledge. Plato certainly took great pains to distinguish the philosopher from poets and seers. Philosophical knowledge is superior in that it is based on rational grounds, traceable to underlying, common principles which define, organize, and justify a position. Philosophy allows demonstration, that is, a thread of ideas which can communicate (share) and show the reasons why a position is so. Accordingly, something unknown is made known on the basis of some discoverable foundation. The poets, on the other hand, are quite different. Their presentations stem from a kind of intuition, a form of knowledge the reasons for which are *not* known. The poet cannot describe how he receives his insight; he cannot trace it back to anything other than a sudden and uncontrollable inspiration, the source of which is hidden. Others cannot share his experience, and so both the origin and the process of discovery are essentially esoteric. We notice here the uncommon, mysterious character of the sacred. The *why* and *how* of mytho-poetic knowledge cannot be reduced to common, accessible experience or ideas, hence the peculiar nonfactual nature of sacred imagery. The poet and his audience only know *that* something is given. For Plato it is the strict "givenness" of mythical disclosure that distinguishes poetic intuition from the demonstrative method of philosophical reasoning. Plato did not denigrate sacred intuition, however. He saw it playing an important role in human life. Furthermore, the dialogues seem to show that in some respects and at a certain point even philosophical knowledge reveals a comparable intuitional background. Let us explore this issue further.

Although Plato did not accept the traditional status of mythical disclosure, he did acknowledge and frequently discuss the cultural function of an extraconscious givenness in poetry, prophecy, and religious experience (e.g., in the *Ion*, *Meno*, *Phaedrus*, and *Symposium*). He also supported the religious authority of the Delphic oracle (*Republic*, IV.427b-c; *Laws*, V.738b-c, VI.759c). We even find the figure of Socrates often associated with archaic mythical forces. Socrates apparently began his philosophical career upon hearing a Delphic proclamation that no one in Athens was wiser than he (*Apology*, 20e, ff.); for this reason he often described his life as a divine calling. Socrates also had a daemon, a voice that dissuaded him from certain actions (*Apology*, 31d). At the end of his life Socrates paid heed to a recurrent dream commanding him to compose poetry (*Phaedo*, 60d, ff.), and his last words referred to a ritual offering (*Phaedo*, 118). In the *Phaedrus*, a "possessed" Socrates delivers a hymn to Eros (237a, ff.), and we have already considered that dialogue's treatment of sacred madness, the different forms of possession that spontaneously arrive from beyond the conscious self. There Socrates says something seemingly uncharacteristic of a philosophical disposition:

> . . . let us not be disturbed by an argument that seeks to scare us into preferring the friendship of the sane to that of the passionate. . . . this sort of madness is a gift of the gods, fraught with the highest bliss. And our proof assuredly will prevail with the wise, though not with the learned (or clever). (245b-c)

No rationalistic interpretation of Plato can ignore or explain away these decidedly nonrational elements in the dialogues. The question arises: Why did Plato give so much attention to these phenomena, especially since he did prefer rational knowledge to poetry, prophecy, and religious experience? Why did he tolerate and even affirm them if they do not satisfy the conditions of being communicable and grounded in *forms* of knowledge accessible to the conscious mind? The answers to these questions will only further undermine the presumptuous *separation* of myth and philosophy, at least with respect to Plato.

First of all, Plato maintained that the nonrational was an inevitable part of reality. The soul has a nonrational component (notice the image of two horses in the *Phaedrus*, 246a, ff.); so too does the cosmos itself (as we shall see in the *Timaeus*). Secondly, there seem to be in Platonism certain nonrational and nondemonstrable features of philosophical knowledge as well. Although rational principles serve as a basis for demonstration, the *discovery* of a rational ground as such seems to involve a kind of nondemonstrable givenness and a certain form of *mania*. The Forms in a way "dawn" upon the mind. Moveover, the Forms themselves are illuminated by the Good, which itself therefore cannot be a form of knowledge. We are told that the Good is beyond knowledge and truth (*Republic*, VI.509a) and is not a form of being, *ouk ousias* (509b). The Good, therefore, might represent illumination as such (see the sun image, 508a, ff.), that out of which the Forms can "dawn." In other words, the *origin* of philosophical insights involves an illumination process *beyond* the conscious mind or *toward* the mind (comparable to the mythical sense of arrival).

Such a notion would fit in well with Plato's theory of recollection, which was meant to resolve certain perplexing problems about knowledge. The learning process involves a search for something not present in the mind; and yet if we know what we are searching for prior to finding it, and recognize it when we do find it, how can it be entirely absent from the mind? The recollection theory maintains that learning is not the transmission of something unknown in the strict sense but rather the discovery of something already possessed, though in a latent form. In a way, then, recollection represents a process which moves from a nonconscious potential to conscious actuality. Furthermore, the phenomenon of "sudden insight" in the learning process greatly impressed Plato. Certain fundamental elements of knowledge seem not to be "derived" from anything, but rather "leap" into the mind. In other words, the foundation of rationality itself is not discovered through a rational inference or a transfer of knowledge from one mind to another; *becoming* a philosopher requires a kind of intuition *out of which* subsequent rational inferences are launched.

The philosopher, at the moment of primal discovery, finds himself at the borderline of conscious knowledge and must embrace a process in which the conscious mind is open to something beyond itself. For this reason, Plato describes the philosopher as possessed by a kind of *mania*. Philosophy, then, entails a special form of madness or disruption of ordinary consciousness. Since the philosopher is driven beyond ordinary experience and knowledge, he maintains a likeness to the extraordinary departures of traditional poets, seers, and prophets. We can now understand Plato's preoccupation with these archaic models: They served as instructive analogues to illuminate the nature of philosophical insight. Of course, Plato insisted that the traditional phenomenon of *mania* must be controlled, channeled, and directed toward a new and deeper goal than hitherto achieved (see the *Phaedrus*).

In the *Meno*, Plato criticizes the Sophistic notion that virtue (*aretē*) can be taught. He concludes that it cannot be taught, or transferred from one mind to another as in the case of learning a skill. The bulk of the dialogue involves an illustration of recollection, where Socrates leads a slave boy to discover the answer to a geometry problem without being directly told. Socrates argues that the slave boy must have latently known the answer and only had to be led to the point of discovery. He was not "taught" the answer but simply guided to the dawning of an intuition (underived knowledge). At the end of the dialogue Socrates refers to those inspired types (e.g., poets and prophets) who have knowledge with "no conscious thought," who cannot account for their achievements and are therefore "under divine influence, inspired and possessed by the divinity" (99c-e). Socrates concludes that "virtue will be acquired neither by nature nor by teaching. Whoever has it gets it by divine dispensation without taking thought" (99e–100a). Many have interpreted this conclusion as an example of Socratic irony awaiting a more rational answer in another dialogue, but this is a highly presumptuous interpretation which fails to see the issue in relation to traditional assumptions and an obvious historical situation.

Socrates often said that he was on a divine mission. Moreover, Plato was struck by something for which there was no easy answer. Socrates was manifestly wise; yet few others were wise and most rejected his wisdom. Why was this so? It was evident to Plato that Socrates was unique and uncommon. Wisdom seemed inexplicable and untransferable. Socrates's position in relation to society inspired the Platonic view that wisdom requires an inward journey, both rare and difficult (as in the cave allegory), where truth dawns upon the mind in a mysterious way. Wisdom is comparable, therefore, to other forms of inspiration, although no longer associated directly with traditional models in which a particular god intervenes upon consciousness. The moment of inspiration occurs within the soul's own inward journey. Yet if we recall the underlying meanings of the sacred (mystery, arrival, uniqueness, and the like), we can understand why Plato would declare that wisdom is divine inspiration. Socrates was in many ways comparable to traditional figures who were granted special insight by sacred powers. That is why the Platonic soul is "divine." We notice a transformed extension of something prepared in Homer—knowledge of reality grounded in divinity and sacred arrivals. For Plato, however, "sacred" knowledge had become philosophical insight, fully internalized by way of the soul's interior journey.

The notion of a special, nontransferable insight which occurs as an inspired arrival *to* the conscious mind from a hidden source also helps us comprehend other important features of Platonism. So many dialogues raise questions without providing conclusive answers. Could it be that Platonic philosophy was not intended to be a set of clear answers but rather a *critique* of (Sophistic) knowledge claims, because of the intuitive features of wisdom? It might well be that Socratic wisdom (i.e., an acknowledged ignorance, knowing that you do not know, as in the *Apology*) shows itself throughout the dialogues because of the aforementioned atmosphere of philosophical insight.[25] From an existential and practical standpoint, Socrates *was* wise and lived wisely, but from a theoretical standpoint, he could not readily describe wisdom or account for its acquisition (much like an inspired poet).

We have also seen that Plato's first principle (the Good) was said to be beyond being, knowledge, and truth, and thus a kind of mystery. The elusive character of certain fundamental notions helps us understand another surprising aspect of Platonism—the frequent use of myth in the course of philosophical inquiry. If a myth is a nonfactual presentation which expresses but cannot fully capture something inherently ungraspable, then Plato's use of myth would be consistent with his philosophical vision. There comes a time when rational description reaches a point of frustration, whereupon the mind yields to imaginative stories which can "point" to something nondiscursive or nonobjective, and which may trigger an intuition or a sudden, immediate intimation. Myth, as I have argued, is by nature related to the *limit* of human understanding and a certain sense of mystery regarding important elements in the world. Plato's philosophy would indicate a natural need for myth of some sort.

The most conclusive evidence for the Platonic sense of mystery and intuition can be found in the *Seventh Letter*. There Plato confronts a number of issues: the attempts to describe his teachings; the limits of so describing them; the ineffable character of insight; the rarity of insight; and consequently an aristocratic sense of education.

One statement at any rate I can make in regard to all who have written or may write with a claim to knowledge of the subjects to which I devote myself—no matter how they pretend to have acquired it, whether from my instruction or from others or by their own discovery. Such writers can in my opinion have no real acquaintance with the subject. I certainly have composed no work in regard to it, nor shall I ever do so in the future, for there is no way of putting it into words like other studies. Acquaintance with it must come rather after a long period of attendance on instruction in the subject itself and of close companionship, when, suddenly, like a blaze kindled by a leaping spark, it is generated by the soul and at once becomes self-sustaining.

Besides, this at any rate I know, that if there were to be a treatise or a lecture on the subject, I could do it best. . . . I do not, however, think the attempt to tell mankind of these matters a good thing, except in the case of some few who are capable of discovering the truth for themselves with a little guidance. (341b-e)

According to Plato, therefore, the limit of understanding is not a defect or a sign of failure in philosophy but is rather part of the nature of philosophical inquiry. Platonism is surely quite different from mythical disclosure. Rational inquiry and instruction are necessary aspects of education, but Plato seems to combine rational and intuitive elements. Philosophical training and analysis *lead* to a point where intuition can occur (compare the divided line in the *Republic* and the levels of knowledge outlined in the *Seventh Letter*, 342b, ff.). Then, philosophical insight will animate the appropriate application of rational methods to lower orders of knowledge. But the highest insights share with mythical disclosure a kind of "givenness."

... after practicing detailed comparisons of names and definitions and visual and other sense perceptions, after scrutinizing them in benevolent disputation by the use of question and answer without jealousy, at last in a flash understanding of each blazes up, and the mind, as it exerts all its powers to the limit of human capacity, is flooded with light. (344b-c)

# Plato and Myth

Not only does Platonism show a connection with certain traditional paradigms, but the use of myth also plays a decisive role in Plato's philosophical investigations.[26] We will not pursue an extensive analysis of Platonic myths but rather focus on one dialogue, the *Timaeus*, which will serve our discussion well and gather together many themes of this and preceding chapters. Then we will confront the differences between Platonic and prephilosophical myth, and accordingly Plato's departure from traditional mytho-poetic sense. Finally, we will consider ways in which the general issue of mythical disclosure might serve to modify the conventional interpretation of Plato's thought.

## THE *TIMAEUS*

On the surface the *Timaeus* presents a cosmological analysis, describing the origin and structure of the cosmos and the relationship between the Forms and the sense world, but the frequent classification of this dialogue as a kind of physics is a retrospective and misleading interpretation. The cosmos is presented in terms of an expansive myth. Since we have already established the function and character of mythical disclosure, we are able to understand the mythical dimension of the dialogue. The *Timaeus* is not primarily an attempt at science but rather an account of transcendent principles within the world and a call for the soul to transform itself according to spiritual values. The dialogue emphasizes certain extrafactual, existential, and salvific values for which myths have always been appropriate.

Evidence for the nonscientific aims of the dialogue can be found in the distinction between necessary and divine cause (68e–69a). Necessary (*anankaion*) cause involves mechanical cause and effect in the natural order; divine (*theion*) cause reflects the Good, or the values and purposes of things. Necessary cause reveals the "how," divine cause the "why" of the cosmos. The former should always be subordinated to the latter (69a). The priority here is not scientific description but philosophical wisdom, "with a view to the blessed life," *heneka eudaimonos biou* (69a). Necessary causes should be understood in the light of divine causes, as manifestations of the Good—a kind of cosmic harmony. Moreover, harmony cannot be shown by an objective, factual description, but by transcending things as such and apprehending the Good. The purpose of this transcendent perspective is to attune the soul according to cosmic harmony. The *Timaeus* is primarily geared toward a transformation of the soul. Myth is appropriate in the dialogue because of the element of mystery. The transcendent realm is beyond all particular descriptions and accounts. Consequently a proper account would be one which does not pretend to be purely descriptive. Myth, as a nonfactual *story*, fulfills this requirement. Plato's self-conscious use of myth accomplishes a telling which acknowledges the limitations of any telling in fundamental matters. Let us now examine Plato's myth of the world in the *Timaeus*.

The account begins with an inquiry into being and becoming (27d). Being is unchangeable, while becoming indicates constant change and flux. The changing world must have a cause, a ground; becoming as such cannot ground or explain itself, since it can never be reduced to a stable reference. An explanation of the world requires an unchangeable, eternal ground. The cause of becoming is described as a creator who "looks to the unchangeable and fashions the form and nature of his work after an unchangeable pattern" (28a). Plato's creator is not equivalent to something like the Christian God, who creates *ex nihilo*. We recall that for the Greeks, the world is eternal; the Greek meaning of creation is more like artistic creation, giving form to an amorphous raw material. The creator bases his creation on an eternal, unchanging pattern. There is no explicit reference to the Forms, but surely they are meant here. There is an indirect reference to the Good, Plato's first principle supporting the Forms. If the world is to be fair and its creator the best of causes, creation must be based on something eternal and unchanging (29a). Here an equation is set up between goodness and unchangeability.

The ultimate criterion of explanation would itself not be subject to an explanation. Hence we are told that the origin of the world (the creator) is "past finding out [*eurein ergon*], and even if we found him, to tell of him to all men would be impossible" (28c). That is why a myth is appropriate rather than a pure description. The world of becoming is only a "likeness" to principles of being. Therefore, an account of the universe, of likenesses in relation to an "original," can only be a "probability" (29c), a likely story. With regard to origins, then, "we ought to accept the tale [*mythos*] which is probable and inquire no further" (29d).

At 30a we are told of that which "is in the truest sense the origin of creation and the world." The creator is good and without jealousy; he desires all things to be like him (i.e., good) as far as possible. Creation is described as bringing order out of disorder, because order is *better* than disorder. The Good, then, would be ontologically prior to the creator, who acts as an instrument for the manifestation of the Good (order) in the world. At 30b-c, intelligence, soul, and body are described (these are not yet human attributes but rather cosmic principles). Intelligence is also a manifestation of the Good and hence creation. Intelligence (*nous*) is *better* than nonintelligence; and there is no intelligence without soul. The creator put intelligence in soul and soul in body, to create the "fairest and best." The world then became "a living creature truly endowed with soul and intelligence." Later (34b) the world is described as a "blessed god" (*eudaimona theon*).

The components of corporeal nature are the elements air, fire, earth, and water. The act of creation, however, entails the "priority" of soul (34c) in that these elements are "harmonized by proportion" and receive the "spirit of friendship" (32c). Thus corporeal nature is said to be formed *within* the soul (36d); the two are joined "center to center" (36e). Soul, pervading the entire universe, "herself turning in herself, began a divine beginning of never-ceasing and rational life enduring throughout all time" (36e). We can conclude, then, that the form of the world emerges through the soul (cf. 37a-c, the soul's operation of the forms sameness and diversity, and the subsequent disclosure of rational knowledge and right opinion). The world-soul and the creator cannot really be distinguished in this account. We thus are given the realms of being (Forms) and becoming (sense world), and the creative intermediation between the two, namely, the soul's formation of order out of disorder.

At 37d–38c, Plato gives a description of time and eternity, which is the centerpiece of his cosmology. The created world is an image of eternal Forms. The creator sought to make the image "still more like the original." Since the original is eternal (*aidion*), he aimed to make the cosmos "eternal, so far as might be." Since eternity as such cannot pertain to a creature, he created a "moving image of eternity," time. This image is "eternal, but moving according to number," while eternity itself "rests in unity."

The world and time are coextensive; there was no time "before" the world was created. But therefore one cannot even speak of a "beginning" to time and creation. Since creation is the temporal image of eternity, and since creation entails time as such, there cannot be any absolute "before" or "after" bracketing the whole of temporal creation. In other words, Plato's concept of creation cannot refer to a moment in which the temporal world came into existence. Consequently time as such exhibits a kind of eternity. We notice, then, a double meaning of eternity in the *Timaeus*: a nontemporal principle upon which the world of time is modelled, and temporal succession without beginning or end; i.e., eternity understood on the one hand as "outside time" and on the other hand as "endless time." The form of being "exists from eternity," and the world of becoming "has been, and is, and will be, in all time" (38b).

After discussing the principle of intelligence (*nous*), Plato introduces a mysterious coprinciple, necessity (*anankē*). "The creation of this world is the combined work of *anankē* and *nous*" (47e). We are told that intelligence "persuades" necessity to bring about perfection in creation (48a). The notion of persuasion further demonstrates that creation is not *ex nihilo* but rather an "ordering." Creation brings order to disorder, establishing "in each thing in relation to itself, and in all things in relation to each other, all the measures and harmonies which they could possibly receive" (69b). Prior to creation, everything is an accident, and there are no names. Out of this chaos the creator shapes an ordered cosmos. The creator introduces order amidst a nonrational principle of necessity. Naturally Plato's concept of "necessity" has none of the connotations adhering to later philosophical usage (e.g., the rational necessity of law). For Plato, *anankē* means the errant or wandering cause, suggesting randomness, chance, and disorder (closer, in fact, to the mythical notion of fate). How are we to understand this relationship between rational intelligence and nonrational necessity?

Keeping in mind the notion of persuasion, we can say the following. Plato proposes an eternal coexistence of intelligence and necessity. It is not the case that the world *is* in order and that there is disorder merely because the mind in its ignorance fails to see order (or that once order is seen, disorder "vanishes"). Rather, order is a continuing formation of order *out of* disorder. Disorder is not eliminated; it is the field (or, in Plato's term, the receptacle) in which order is shaped. Surely the Platonic cosmos is orderly; but it is so as a *creation*, an ordering in the midst of disorder. In other words, order is an eternal *activity*, not a standing fact; it is introduced through the intercession of the soul and is not therefore objectively present. Intelligence, then, requires the coprinciple of necessity, as that which must be persuaded to receive order.

Up to this point Plato has described two basic classifications, the intelligible Forms and the generated images. Now a third element is introduced to reflect the principle of necessity—the receptacle (*hypodochē*), which is called the nurse of generation and whose nature is "difficult to explain and dimly seen" (*chalepon kai amydron eidos*, 49a). The receptacle seems to reflect the flow of changing elements in the natural world, "that in which the elements severally grow up, and appear and decay" (49e). The receptacle never assumes the form of what it receives, since it itself is the "natural recipient of all impressions" (50b), or that out of which forms take shape; it is a *flow* and not a thing as such. Yet it is not strictly "other" than natural forms, since it is the flow *of* changing forms; it is "stirred and informed by them, and appears different from time to time by reason of them" (50c).

We can now summarize the three basic aspects of the cosmos, taking note of personalized references in the text: The *father*, namely the intelligible source (Form), of which created images are a likeness; the *mother*, namely the receptacle, in which the generation of images takes place; and the *child*, namely the images produced in creation. There is an interesting and ambiguous relationship between the Forms and the receptacle (a relationship probably made clearer by the metaphor of family reproduction). That which is to receive the generated images of the Forms, namely, the receptacle, must itself be formless or else it would intrude itself upon the forms received (50e). Hence the receptacle cannot be described or given any form. However, a cryptic remark is added, stating that the receptacle "in some mysterious way partakes of the intelligible and is most incomprehensible" (51b).

Being is truth and is apprehended by reason. Becoming, the flux of images, is apprehended by sense and opinion. The receptacle, also called eternal space (52b), is apprehended not by reason or sense, but in a "spurious" way. The receptacle is eternal and uncreated; although it is not intelligible like the Forms, it seems to be a necessary "participant" in creation. Since a created image is "not self-existent" (52c), it must be seen in reference to something else. The ultimate reference is a model Form; but in the created world, since the image can "be" neither in itself nor as a pure Form, it requires another reference, namely the receptacle as a field of becoming in which images can take shape.

Plato is aiming to describe the creation of order in a temporal field. Prior to creation the receptacle is a random chaos, without order or balance. The receptacle, therefore, is not a void but a random formlessness which accounts for the power of becoming and which permits the shaping of *changing* images patterned after eternal Forms. Creation stems from the creator-soul giving "form and number" to this chaotic flux (53b). The world-soul shapes the cosmos according to the Good, "out of things which were not fair and good" (53b). The world is thus presented in terms of a relationship between the unchangeable Good and a counterprinciple of flux: The soul apprehends the Forms

which are grounded in the Good; each Form, thus animated by a principle of unchangeability, permits the introduction of order to disorder
(*kosmos* to *chaos*); the product of the soul's creation, however, remains a *changing* order because of the receptacle's power. The created
world is therefore neither pure form nor pure formlessness but the
continual forming of a formless field, the orderly comprehension of
flux on the basis of fixed paradigms. The following cosmic structure
can be organized from our reading of the *Timaeus*:

1. **The Good**: the source of intelligible Forms; the principle of
   unchangeability.
2. **The Forms**: particular principles of intelligibility, termed the
   *father.*
3. **World-Soul**: the agent of creation; the faculty of intelligence.
4. **The Receptacle**: random formlessness; the field of creation, termed
   the *mother.*
5. **Images**: generated forms in becoming; the product of creation,
   termed the *child.*

Creation thus entails the forming of images *in* the formless receptacle, *through* the agency of intelligence, *from* principles of intelligibility, *grounded* in the Good. In the context of creation, the receptacle is
not strictly separable from intelligence and intelligibility. Creation
produces finite, temporal images which therefore must *become* (come
and go). The formless power of necessity permits the creation of forms
that emerge and disappear. Apart from creation, the receptacle is a random, formless flux. With the "persuasion" of intelligence, necessity
permits a *formed* flux (i.e., temporal forms in a process of becoming).
Through becoming, necessity retains its influence and thus "cooper-
ates" in creation. Such, I think, is the meaning of Plato's remark that the
receptacle in some way "participates" in intelligence. Plato surely
maintains the priority of rational principles, but at the same time he
presents the world as a mingling of rational and nonrational elements.
Rationality is a *result*, a process which continually works on and with
the nonrational.

We can take a step back now and consider the *Timaeus* in relation to
certain developments in Greek culture which our study has heretofore
outlined. First of all, the dialogue highlights the revolutionary developments of philosophy—conceptual principles within the soul (36e)
which allow abstract transcendence of temporal experience, thereby
giving the world a stable, unified form. The *Timaeus* also exhibits a

clear connection with mythical tradition in a number of ways, however. We have already discussed the dialogue's own mythical form. Furthermore, the personifications of intelligibility and necessity (father and mother) suggest the traditional distinction between the masculine–Olympian–Apollonian realm and the feminine–Chthonic–Dionysian dimension. Moreover, the notion of intelligence "persuading" necessity is clearly reminiscent of the closing scene in Aeschylus's *Oresteia*. In other words, although Plato emphasizes the rational over the nonrational, form over formless negativity, nevertheless there is evidence that he maintained somewhat the Aeschylean notion that reason and form are necessarily correlated with nonrational and formless forces. At least with respect to the temporal world, Plato seems to understand rationality as a process of "arranging" chaos into a form, a notion quite in line with certain mythical patterns in Greek tradition.

Platonism, of course, still represents a clear departure from traditional myth and early philosophy. Even though temporality and formlessness are retained as necessary cosmic principles, they pertain to the natural order. The realm of the Good and the Forms stands above the natural order, beyond its temporal character. Some of the early philosophers had given a *primary* status to formlessness, becoming, and temporality. Plato, though retaining these ideas, demotes them to a *secondary* status. The Good, as the principle of unchangeability, becomes the ultimate measure of reality, truth, and meaning. Consequently, proper knowledge of reality requires the stability of rational Forms which administer the basic principle of unchangeability by resolving various aspects of temporal instability. Platonism, therefore, represents a cosmic complex of Being–Reason–Form "governing" a counter-complex of becoming-passion-formlessness, with the aim of reform (i.e., making an "errant" world "good").

Accordingly, the notion of "persuasion" in the *Timaeus* is not quite comparable to the meaning of persuasion in the *Oresteia*. In the latter, nonrational forces were persuaded to yield a province of power to reason, and yet they retained their cultural role. Reason and fatal negativity negotiated a kind of coexistence (the essence of tragedy's Apollonian–Dionysian synthesis). In contrast, the "cooperation" of necessity in the *Timaeus* seems more like a token vote in a rigged election. The persuasion of chaos appears to produce a complete abdication; the extent of participation is comparable to that of the passive interlocutors in many Platonic dialogues, the "yes men" who seem to do little more than wave at the passing train of Socratic logic. Formless flux contributes a field of becoming for changing forms, but it does not share the ontological priority of form.

Furthermore, the cosmological analysis in the *Timaeus* is subordinated to a larger aim, namely, the rediscovery of the soul's original nature hidden by temporality, and the subsequent deliverance of the soul to an eternal realm altogether free of temporality. Birth in the world "corrupts" the soul's divine nature (46b). As the soul pursues knowledge and apprehends the underlying structure of the cosmos, the temporal images of eternity "remind" the soul of its true character (90d), which sets the stage for deliverance to an extraphysical, supratemporal form, for the "flight from this world to the other" (*Theaetetus*, 176ab).

Although Plato acknowledges certain traditional forces and presents some interesting parallels with mythical paradigms, nevertheless the subordination of change and time to a principle of unchangeability represents the culmination of a rational victory over traditional myth. Platonic psychology and metaphysics spotlight the essence and design of that victory by building a world-view around the conscious self's *transcendence* of immediate experience and the lived world. Thus Platonism initiates a basic paradigm which in various ways guided the subsequent intellectual history of western thought but which represents an *inversion* of mythical sense, or specifically of what Nietzsche called "tragic wisdom." That paradigm declares the *primacy* of form and conscious knowledge over formlessness and mystery; it requires a unified, interiorized, and autonomous conscious mind to shape the distance from sheer temporality needed to resolve the negativity of lived experience. But since temporality constitutes our initial encounter with the world, Platonism had to acknowledge a kind of reform intrinsic to philosophy; his image of two worlds was an expression of the implicit antagonism between form and formlessness, structure and negation, certainty and mystery. That antagonism and the disposition of reform were carried forward in different ways by subsequent cultural and intellectual developments (religious transcendence, rationalism, moralism, scientism).

It was Nietzsche's contention that Platonism and various subsequent "isms" had no objective justification since they were based on an unwarranted "moral" judgment of temporality and negativity. The very qualities of experience Plato found objectionable and corrigible were in fact the *conditions* of mythical sense and meaning. Archaic form reflected an immediate lived encounter; it also yielded to and arose out of an extraconscious formlessness. Although Platonism displays an interesting connection with tradition in that the forms of knowledge themselves "arrive" in some sense from beyond consciousness, nevertheless this seems to pertain to the ultimate origin of philosophical insight. Subsequent to that insight the world is given a stable form from the standpoint of conscious knowledge. The rational self *actively* forms its experience according to transcendent principles fixed in conscious reflection. Despite all the connections between Platonism and tradition, then, it is no wonder that Plato vigorously criticized traditional myths. The motive and spirit of that critique are clearly expressed in the *Republic*, where Plato launches his celebrated attack on the poets, who stand to be banished from the ideal city.

## PLATO'S CRITICISM OF TRADITIONAL MYTH

In Book II of the *Republic*, Plato outlines an educational program for the guardians. Education should begin with gymnastics (for the body) and music (for the soul). Music, which includes poetry, is instructive because it teaches harmony, proportion, and balance to counteract the disruptive passions. But "false" poetry and intemperate music must be censored because they obstruct the educational goals of a rational state (377, ff.). Socrates presents a series of citations from Homer and Hesiod which portray gods and heroes in objectionable ways. The poets tell "false stories" (*pseudeis mythous*) when they say the gods commit unnatural and obscene acts (e.g., Kronos and Uranos), fight each other, cause evil and ruin, punish the innocent (e.g., tragedy), change form, disguise themselves, or lie. God, we are told, must be constituted by goodness, truth, and unchangeability.

Later, in the *Laws* (Book VII), Plato will specify the permissible uses of poetry and music (if they contribute to moderation, lawfulness, and a proper understanding of the gods). Religious rites, festivals, and temples can also be included in the ideal state.[27] Dionysian music and dance must be excluded, however, because of their wild, frenetic nature (815c, ff.). The same holds true for tragedy if it does not conform to rational goals. In fact, the gods themselves are explicitly subordinated to principles of knowledge, as shown in the reference to mathematical abstraction in relation to a proper understanding of divinity (818, ff.). In any case, traditional cultural forms need not be excluded if they can be redefined by reason; thus it is possible "to come to the aid of ancient custom with *logos*" (890d).

But in Book X of the *Republic*, Plato recounts what he calls the ancient quarrel (*diaphora*) between philosophy and poetry (607b). In effect he proceeds to offer a philosophical justification for the exclusion of artists and poets from the state. Plato assumes that art aims to imitate natural phenomena. Given, then, the Platonic notion that natural objects are images of pure Forms, art succeeds in producing only an image of an image. (Art might then correspond to the shadows in the cave and the lowest level of the divided line.) Moreover, if one considers the technical arts, one finds another dimension between fine art, nature, and Forms. For example, a craftsman creates a table out of natural material according to a design stemming from the pure Form of table; a painter, then, imitates that product in his picture of a table. If we follow the series from Form to natural object to craft to art, we realize that fine art is "three removes from reality [*ontos*]," and hence that far from truth (599a).

Artists are useless because they produce nothing of technical or practical value and contribute nothing to the function of government (599b, ff.). Furthermore, art perpetuates ignorance by imitating sense images which require reason for a true account. For example, painters recreate the visual perspective that assumes distant objects to be smaller than near objects, a mistake of the senses that can only be corrected by reason and calculation (602d-e). Poetry suffers from a comparable defect in that it imitates the "natural condition" of human beings in their immediate, sensuous state, falling prey to passions and emotions without the calming regulation of reason (603c, ff.). Specific mention is made of tragic poetry, which excites the feelings and inhibits self-control, thereby encouraging nonrational behavior and surrender to powerful affective forces. Tragic poetry may be charming, but it hides the truth.

> . . . poetry, and in general the mimetic art, produces a product that is far removed from truth in the accomplishment of its task, and associates with the part in us that is remote from intelligence, and is its companion and friend for no sound and true purpose. . . . art, then, is an inferior thing cohabiting with an inferior and engendering inferior offspring. (603b)

The closing section of the *Republic* reveals the fundamental motive behind Plato's criticism of mytho-poetic language. Poetry draws us to the immediate, lived world and intensifies its natural attractions. Plato, for many reasons, aims beyond the lived world and hence beyond the meanings expressed in traditional myth: Rational certainty requires a

ground above and beyond temporal plurality; personal salvation requires some notion of immortality to resolve tragic fatalism; justice requires an extratemporal reward as an incentive in the face of the
world's inequities and the frequent impunity of wickedness; and moral
responsibility requires an autonomous self to overcome the existential
immediacy of myth, where affective dimensions of experience appeared as overwhelming invasions of the conscious self. Accordingly,
Plato closes the dialogue with an argument for immortality and the
myth of Er, which describes the judgment of souls after death on the
basis of personal accountability for actions, followed by appropriate
rewards and punishments.

Plato offers us a clear picture of the tension between traditional
myth and philosophy as well as the motives and methods behind a rational critique of traditional Greek culture and thought. Let us now
pursue an examination and evaluation of Plato's critique against the
background of our previous analyses. First let us consider Plato's contention that art and poetry are three times removed from truth. This is
surely right from the standpoint of *Plato's* conception of truth, but we
have already discussed the problematic nature of truth and extramythical measurements of mythical sense. Mytho-poetic language was
seen to disclose important elements of cultural meaning and truth.
Plato indeed had to alter completely the traditional function of myth
and poetry to justify his critique of art. In effect he judged art to be inferior measured against rational, empirical, and practical criteria. Not
only does art fall short of the Forms, it is also a deficient copy of empirical objects and technical products. Within the realm of natural phenomena, then, Plato assumed a representational theory of art, namely,
that art reproduces empirical observations. We can surely say that Plato
here was mistaken about the function of traditional poetry and myth.
We recall that myth was never meant to reproduce or even explain empirical facts or natural objects but rather to disclose *sacred* meanings
within the empirical (profane) world. Accordingly, Plato's analysis of
tragic poetry is certainly off the mark. Tragedy was never meant simply
to reflect the passionate life of human beings in their natural condition
but to reveal the sacred meaning of an existential matrix and to integrate the self with an overall world order. Tragic poetry was a form of
cultural education, presenting values, ideals, and religious transformation, all of which gave sense to the lived world.

Plato's critique of poetry, therefore, created a "straw man." He accused poetry of failing to properly execute rational and empirical de-

signs, when traditional poetry never intended such things. Mythical disclosure was embedded in existential plurality and temporality, not rational abstraction and uniformity. Myth was not on that account simply immersed in empirical or natural facts, however; it disclosed and established prefactual *meanings* which shaped the world into a *culture*. Plato assumed that myth was simply an errant or childish attempt at philosophy, but we have shown that myth and rationality are not entirely commensurable; they present different kinds of sense which cannot necessarily measure the respective purposes of each. In order to judge myth, Plato had to assume extramythical criteria and even *distort* the meaning and function of traditional myth.

Regarding the analysis in the *Republic*, Plato *rightly* finds in traditional poetry the absence of certainty, salvation, autonomy, and universal justice. But his critique assumes that myth—in its expression of mystery, plurality, fatalism, negativity, and a receptive self—*hides* or *distorts* the truth, when these meanings in fact constituted the *nature* of truth in myth. The inappropriate and arbitrary character of Plato's analysis is revealed in his supposition of an "ancient" quarrel between philosophy and myth. He thereby suggests the timelessness of his criteria and naturally recognizes mistakes in poetry. But our historical study has shown that this was a relatively *new* quarrel, that prior to the advent of philosophy the world made legitimate sense in a different way.

We can now clarify Plato's ambiguous and ambivalent attitude toward myth. His philosophy showed at one and the same time an attack upon myth and a utilization of myth; but there is no inconsistency here, because we realize that Plato rejected the *traditional* meaning of myth and created new myths to serve and illuminate his own philosophical purposes.[28] We have noticed, however, some interesting connections between Platonic myth and traditional paradigms. His myths express the existential meaning of philosophy (e.g., liberation, self-control, optimism, and the value and desirability of knowledge). Furthermore, a certain sense of mystery seems to pervade the ultimate origins of philosophical insight; hence the myths in the *Republic*, *Phaedo*, *Timaeus*, and elsewhere can even be said to *support* Plato's philosophical program. We have employed the mythical sense of "givenness" to elucidate this matter. For Plato, ultimate principles themselves cannot be explained since they are not derived from anything that can be described (since the Good is beyond description). Hence the *origin* of insight involves these principles simply being given, which makes a myth the only appropriate account of the origin.

Of course, the difference between Platonism and traditional myth is that for Plato mythical givenness pertains to the origin of these principles, which then proceed to rationally explain (demystify) the rest of the world. In mythical disclosure, on the other hand, *everything* of cultural importance was "given" and thus ultimately groundless (i.e., the mystery of the sacred as such).

That pervasive groundlessness was a defect according to Plato, but we remember that the *context* of mythical disclosure did suggest that myths display a certain authenticity. The existential, lived world as such *does* present a kind of plurality, mystery, givenness, finitude, and the like. In other words, we can conclude that the defect Plato sought to correct was not really in myth itself but in the lived world. Plato's critique of traditional myth was, then, a critique of the immediate existential world. His judgment of myth is certainly intelligible, but *only* from the standpoint of his own framework which aims to correct the world of immediate engagement. Outside that framework, however, his critique is not justified. Mythical disclosure involved the *sense* of a world Plato found ultimately senseless. So Platonism introduced a paradigm shift rather than truth in place of error. Our study of early philosophy, especially Anaximander and Heraclitus, speaks to this point. We suggested that early philosophy explicated the implicit meaning of Greek myth, especially tragedy. An intelligible, conceptual structure was given to a world of temporality, process, and finitude. Accordingly, the lived world as such can display a kind of truth on its own terms. Since traditional mythical sense pertained to the lived world, Plato's critique can only reflect his refusal to accommodate that truth. The myths were not so much mistaken as they were repugnant to Plato. Consequently, one might agree with Nietzsche that Platonic philosophy was supported not by objective judgments but by a kind of *moral* disposition.

## MYTHICAL AND PHENOMENOLOGICAL ASPECTS OF PLATO'S PHILOSOPHY

A crucial issue in an interpretation of Plato concerns the extent to which key notions such as soul-body dualism and the two-worlds scheme were intended as a literal doctrine in the dialogues. When considering the revolutionary nature of Plato's philosophy we focused on these notions as such because they served to illuminate the contrast between Plato's aims and the tradition which preceded him. When considering traditional aspects of Plato's philosophy, especially the role of intuition and myth, we noticed ways in which Plato's thought might involve something other than a literal, describable doctrine. From the vantage point of a phenomenological treatment of mythical disclosure, we can attempt to coordinate the two approaches to Plato taken in this chapter and to confront the question concerning the status of certain "doctrines" proposed in the dialogues.

As I indicated earlier, the idea that Plato's thought is less dogmatic and less conclusive than conventional interpretations of the dialogues has some merit. At the same time, when considering Plato's departure from traditional thought, I do not think we should underestimate the importance of certain doctrines for expressing and shaping that departure. We will focus on the common supposition that Plato proposed a number of dualistic doctrines: a kind of separation between soul and body, the Forms and the sense world, reason and passion, philosophy and poetry. When we consider the dialogues, many elements can cast doubt on the supposition that Plato was pursuing a defense of such notions in a literal sense. Since these notions do seem to figure prominently in the dialogues, however, then dispensing with a literal interpretation creates the following problem: If Plato did not espouse such doctrines, why were they proposed? Did he hold a different view? If so, what view? Were the doctrines to be understood in a special way? If so, in what way?

My own attitude is that Plato's thought *is* more open than the conventional interpretation would have it, but I also think that the dualistic doctrines do figure in Plato's thought in some way. Perhaps, as was indicated in the discussion of intuition, the open aspect involves the *limits* on the way in which such doctrines can be demonstrated or understood discursively.[29] After all, we do see certain priorities and commitments in Plato's writings. In some way or other the soul is preferable to the body, as is eternity to time, being to becoming, reason to passion, philosophy to art. Perhaps it is wrong to completely dualize Plato's position, but the priorities expressed there do present a significant departure from traditional modes of thought, and the dualistic tone in much of the dialogues at least shapes the direction of that departure.

I think that the phenomenological/mythical perspective taken in this study might help coordinate the competing aspects here, that is to say, it might permit an interpretation of Plato which is more open and less dogmatic but which also pays heed to the clear commitments that

are evident in the dialogues. We can begin by asking a phenomenological question: What elements, in addition to certain philosophical positions, are *shown* in the dialogues? We notice the following:
The presentation of philosophy in a dramatic form, i.e., as conversa-
tions between different characters; a certain inconclusive atmosphere;
myths, and positions related to or expressed in a mythical form; the existential setting of philosophy; philosophy as a way of life; the value of
a philosophical life; philosophy in competition with other forms of
life, thinking, and culture. A consideration of these elements can be related in a number of ways to the general phenomenon of mythical disclosure analyzed in this study, especially if the elements are gathered
around the form of presentation in Platonic dialogues.

That Plato deliberately chose to portray philosophy in a dramatic
context can be used to challenge the notion that he intended to declare
a strict doctrine.[30] The dialogue form can be seen to reflect some of the
features evident in mythical disclosure and traditional Greek culture.
In a sense Plato was sustaining the importance of drama in Greek tradition, and in doing so, he also sustained a number of mythical aspects,
especially the atmosphere of an existential setting and a sense of mystery, of a limit to explanation.

The philosophical drama of a Platonic dialogue explicitly focuses
on an existential, lived setting in terms of specific characters immersed
in specific situations at specific times.[31] A proper interpretation of a dialogue would therefore have to involve a consideration of the dramatic
context, namely, attention to the dialogue as a whole, as a literary work
of art, where specific characters, situations, events, and intentions all
figure into the philosophical meaning of the work.[32] The literary aspects of a dialogue indicate that its interpretation cannot be confined
to any specific statement; the deliberate design of the larger context requires a constant reading between the lines, which can suggest a modified or more tentative reading of any particular position declared in the
dialogue. If a philosophical issue is extracted from the dramatic setting, an essential feature of Plato's intention is eliminated. Too often
the supposition about a conclusive Platonic doctrine stems from such
an extraction. A dramatic perspective can show that particular philosophical positions in the dialogues are contextual and consequently
more open than conventional interpretations would suggest.[33]

The dialogues present multiple speeches, which is expressive of a
pedagogical assumption announced in the *Phaedrus* (271ff.), namely,
that philosophical speech must accommodate the type of listener and

his level of understanding.[34] So we witness many different types of speeches from different angles, which means that a decisive interpretation of Plato's own position becomes problematic. It could be said that Plato's use of a dialogue form shows that he was less interested in a decisive answer and more interested in engaging the listener or reader to philosophize and appropriate the issue at hand.[35] Individual appropriation suggests that a philosophical position cannot be divorced from the way in which the inner self strives to develop an insight. Consequently, an external, public, conclusive formulation would not match the full intentions of a dialogical approach to philosophy.[36] Finally, Socrates's speech in the *Phaedrus* (275ff.), which declares the limited value of writing, can clearly be related to Plato's form of presentation. The dramatic and contextual aspects of a dialogue can be said to reflect the limits of a written text and the need to pursue philosophy in one's life.[37] By way of summary, then, the dialogue form suggests that Plato's thought is more related to an existential setting, to the way in which philosophy *emerges* in life, than it is to a philosophical treatise or conclusive doctrine.[38]

The inconclusive aspects of Plato's dialogues, together with his deliberate use of myth, suggest that Plato's thought may be considered mythical in many ways. This term is to be taken in the positive sense established in our analysis, as a fundamental disclosure of truth and meaning which pertains to a lived setting and not an objective or fixed foundation. But at the same time we must also heed the ways in which Plato's thought is different from myth (especially traditional Greek myth) and consequently how Plato's view of philosophy is different from myth.[39] Accordingly one could develop a phenomenological interpretation of Plato's philosophy in terms of how it shows the emergence of a kind of thinking in human life that is different from and frequently at odds with *purely* mythical disclosure. The basic point I want to make is as follows: A phenomenological analysis can show Plato's thought to be more "mythical" than "doctrinal"; but compared to *traditional* myth, something quite different is happening in Plato. That difference must be kept clear; and its importance can be understood in phenomenological terms. But from the standpoint of our overall study, what remains problematic in Plato is his opposition to and corrective attitude toward traditional, prephilosophical myth. A mythical/phenomenological interpretation of the dialogues does not, I think, change this basic dichotomy evident in Plato's thinking.

A phenomenological analysis of Platonic "dualities" would concentrate less on the notion of ontological separation and more on the value and function of certain tensions established in Plato's thought. We have already discussed ways in which the duality of soul and body, reason and passion, can figure in the shaping of certain moral, social, and political values. In general, many benefits follow from a "distancing" of the person from purely physical and passionate forces (e.g., self-control, integrity in the face of material losses, appreciation of a person's worth beyond physical attributes and material possessions, suspension of the power principle). The *practice* of such distancing could be called the phenomenological meaning of the notion of a "soul."[40] The supposed two-worlds doctrine could likewise be seen to serve the function of distancing rational inquiry from complete immersion in the sense world and everyday life. Certain kinds of understanding require a step back from immediate engagement (e.g., searching for definitions, clarifying vaguely understood practices and beliefs, proposing an ideal, distinguishing truth from rhetorical persuasion).

From a phenomenological standpoint, then, the dualistic tone in Platonic dialogues can be understood not as a form of ontological dualism (separate realities) but as a form of *practical* and *functional* dualism, that is to say, the real contest that emerges when rational inquiry and certain values run up against competing forces in human life.[41] The dualistic images can be called presentational myths which shape the boundaries and tensions of this contest and express its direction, meaning, and value. And there is *truth* in such a dualistic tone at those times when rational inquiry is important and preferable to other kinds of engagement.[42] Such a phenomenological approach would complement the notion that Plato's philosophy is more open and inconclusive and less a proposal of literal doctrines. This together with the use of myths in the dialogues suggests a kind of mythical element in Plato's "doctrines" in terms of their being a founding expression of the *meaning* of a philosophical life.

That being said, however, the positions expressed in Plato's writings are no less significant in what they *do* say.[43] We should pay particular attention to what is said in the dialogues regarding the relationship between mythical disclosure and philosophical reason, especially in terms of (1) frequent references to the secondary status of myths that are employed in the dialogues,[44] and (2) a clear departure in Plato's philosophy from *traditional* Greek myth and its view of the world. However mythical Plato's thought may be, there remain the problems addressed in this study regarding the kind of separation from *pre-*

philosophical myth that is evident in the dialogues. In other words, we notice a kind of dualism which *is* doctrinal in Plato when it comes to separating philosophy from traditional myth and poetry. No matter how open Plato's thought may be, I do not think it is open to the idea that traditional myth, on its own terms, can possess any kind of truth.

Given Plato's philosophical intentions and the authoritative status of myth in Greek culture, we should be careful not to miss the point and import of his attack on the poets. The censoring of poetry in the *Republic* reflected a separation which was helping to shape clear boundaries for a new sense of truth. Plato rightly saw in traditional poetry a threat to his philosophical aims. As I suggested earlier, his objections to Homer and tragedy were at least based on an accurate assessment of the way the world and human existence are portrayed there. Both the world view of traditional myth (e.g., the lived world) and certain psychological features exhibited in poetry (e.g., inspiration) represented conditions which *are* in conflict with rationality and certain values Plato advocated. Those who find the censorship in the *Republic* troubling, or who try to explain it in modified terms, miss the historical point that the poets were considered cultural authorities. Greek myth and poetry were not merely forms of "literature" or "art." They were originally a form of culture, a view of the world, a source of education. Plato's objections to traditional poetry seem heavy-handed to us only because it carries a different significance now. The extent of Plato's concern about poetry simply confirms our assumption about the cultural importance of myth in the Greek world. Plato was not "censoring the arts," he was engaged in a historical contest for a view of the world and truth.[45] Given the authoritative status of traditional forms of culture, then to whatever extent one appreciates Plato's philosophical aims, one should appreciate his critique of poetry.[46]

Plato took traditional Greek myth very seriously, and in a way just as seriously as I have in this study, except that he did not find any truth in it. His critique of poetry has to do not with the question of art but the question of truth. Would those who object to Plato's censorship want to defend traditional poetry in terms of its truth? And *not* in terms of "aesthetic" or "literary" truth, but truth about the world and human existence in the manner presented in early Greek myth, on its *own* terms? In the light of our study, *I* want to do that. But such a defense entails much more than simply finding a place for poetry in culture; it requires a complete revision of what *truth* means and of long-held assumptions about the nature and status of philosophy and rationality in relation to myth. If anyone objects to such a defense and revision, then it seems to me that something like Plato's response would be the right move. Even though I am challenging that response, this much can be said for Plato: He genuinely understood what was at stake in the historical contest between philosophy and myth. If traditional culture was not repudiated in some way, then the manner in which the world and human self were portrayed there could lay claim to truth.

Now I can offer some conclusions concerning the ambiguous relationship between the mythical elements in Plato and mythical disclosure. Plato's philosophy involves many important cultural and intellectual doctrines that can be said to have a mythical meaning; that is to say, they involve the *disclosure* of a way of life and a kind of thinking taking shape in the context of human culture, and the *meaning* of that emergence in relation to competing forces, rather than a fixed account of reality. In other words, the dualistic "doctrines" can be seen to reflect a form of practical dualism rather than ontological dualism. Even Plato's attack on the poets might have been historically necessary for shaping the contours of philosophy and rational inquiry. It should even be seen to have some justification if myth and poetry are taken to have *exclusive* possession of truth (witness the philosophers on trial) or if there are indeed instances of cultural arts so shallow or base as to lead people astray.

But the larger question is whether Greek myths of the traditional type can be said to possess *any* sense of truth. It seems evident that Plato would say no. I am not arguing that Plato repudiated myth and poetry (much of his thought was mythical and poetic), but that he repudiated *traditional* myth and poetry, and that such an exclusion cannot ultimately be justified. The mythical element in Plato relates to a more open interpretation of his *philosophy*, but his rejection of traditional myth involves certain assumptions about philosophy (however interpreted) in relation to *pre*philosophical disclosure.

Plato's thought could be called an exchange of one myth for another myth.[47] But the notion of a "mythical exchange" (i.e., a movement without an objective foundation) should call into question the exclusion of the kind of sense found in pre-Platonic myth. Platonic myth can be said to disclose something true, but so too can early Greek myth, on its own terms. This forces us to rethink Plato's (and our) assumptions about philosophy and rationality. No matter how mythical Plato may have been in his thinking, he still saw philosophy as a correction of a world view expressed in traditional myth and poetry. It is *this* attitude (taken up by philosophers after Plato) that is problematic. The proper approach to the mythical exchange represented in Plato's thought would be to sort out when his departure from myth is appropriate and when it is not.

# VIII

# Aristotle

It is not worthwhile to examine carefully the opinions of those who exercise their cleverness in the form of myths [*tōn mythikōs sophizomenōn*]. (*Metaphysics*, III.4.1000a18)[1]

The philosophy of Aristotle (384–322 B.C.) represents a decisive turning point in intellectual history. In various ways Aristotle clinched the demythification process by formalizing and completing the turn from mytho-poetic disclosure to conceptual reason. Since conceptual and mythical elements were both evident in previous philosophers, conceptual developments alone would not be sufficient to account for Aristotle's innovation. He deliberately *separated* conceptual reason from mythical tendencies; if we recall the sacred-profane distinction, this amounted to establishing conceptual criteria based upon *profane* elements. To understand this we need to consider the issue of consciousness and its connection with a new, empirical standard of knowledge. As in Platonism, Aristotle's analysis of the soul represented a departure from mythical selfhood in that an interiorized, autonomous, and unified self prepared and supported a rational account of reality. But Aristotelian psychology contained none of the shamanlike features exhibited in Plato's depiction of the soul, none of the puritan elements, extrasensory journeys, or inspired states. Knowledge, for Aristotle, was confined to the limits of individual consciousness, without any of the extraordinary, extraconscious elements that characterized both myth and Platonism.

In other words, knowledge was condensed to the context of ordinary experience and normal perceptions (i.e., the profane). Of course knowledge would not entail immediate experience alone but rather abstractions drawn from that experience. As opposed to mythical immediacy (the lived world), Aristotle represented a form of empiricism, that is to say, ordinary conscious experience organized by and subjected to conceptual abstraction. As a result Aristotle rejected both mythical imagery and the intuitional atmosphere of earlier philosophers; both were founded on a certain kind of extraordinary insight. An empirical method, however, would establish insights derived from analyses of ordinary experience, which is common to all and most tangible (i.e., common sense). For Aristotle, *analysis* of experience was a function of the conscious mind, and intersubjective *verification* replaced the traditional notion of special insight. The ascendancy of consciousness was thus enhanced in Aristotelian thought. Furthermore, an empirical method, with its tangibility and dependability, seemed to permit a kind of knowledge which could best secure a universal (i.e., common) standpoint and which could overcome the mysteries of myth and early philosophy, including the unanswered questions haunting Plato's dialogues.

In contrast to Plato, not only does Aristotle omit the use of myth in his presentation of philosophy, he also forgoes the dramatic, existential atmosphere of dialogues in favor of the straightforward method of a treatise. In view of previous observations concerning the significance of Plato's dialogical method for an understanding of his thought, the shift to a treatise is more than just a formal change; it is substantive in terms of how philosophical discourse is to be practiced and understood. Aristotle pursues a more objective, rational account, which is intended to produce a more settled, decisive, and unified response to philosophical questions. That represents a clear departure from the previously examined mythical elements exhibited in Platonic dialogues.[2] In some respects Aristotle can be called the founder of *scientific* philosophy, the spirit of which eventually came to shape the western mind. ("Science" for Aristotle is not confined to and in many ways is very different from the modern sense of the term.) Through his investigations, certain criteria were explicated and firmly established as the "proper" instruments for thinking about the world—an empirical standard, conceptual definition, classification, categorization, analysis, formal logic, and demonstration.

We recall that Plato in a way synthesized archaic and classical elements of Greek culture in that he blended mythical and rational tendencies which were naturally prone to coexist, given our evolutionary model of Greek intellectual history. The gradual ascendancy of consciousness and rational reflection over the elusive transcendence of myth was completed in the thought of Aristotle. His attitude toward tradition is shown in the critical surveys of past positions which preface many of his investigations (especially the *Physics* and *Metaphysics*). It becomes clear that his aim was to purge Greek thought of its mythical, metaphorical, and intuitive elements in order to rationally construct an objective account of reality.

In describing Aristotle's thought as "scientific philosophy" we recognize both a similarity and dissimilarity with respect to previous thinkers, especially Plato. In his pursuit of rational knowledge Aristotle inherited and maintained the Platonic criterion for "knowability," namely universals, unchanging principles of intelligibility through which the mind could order, ground, and explain the vicissitudes of experience.

> Scientific knowledge [*epistēmē*] is judgment about things that are universal and necessary, and the conclusions of demonstration, and all scientific knowledge, follow from first principles, for scientific knowledge involves apprehension of a rational ground. (*Nicomachean Ethics*, VI.6.1140b30-35)

Aristotle's scientific spirit initiated a decisive alteration of Platonic assumptions, however. The new methodology stipulated that knowledge be pursued within the context of empirical analysis, stemming from observations of the perceptible and *verifiable* realm of common experience. For Aristotle, only in this way could knowledge be definite, universal, and stable, by being demonstrable and readily traceable to shared perceptions. In other words Aristotle proposed an empirical con-sensus rather than the special insights and elusive intuitions which characterized Platonism. According to Plato the ground of knowledge and being was supposed to reside in transcendent Forms which were distinct from the sense-world of particulars and which were revealed only when the mind loosened its connection with sense experience. Aristotle also located the ground of knowledge and being in form, but a form discovered *in* the sense-world of particulars, a completely *immanent* principle of intelligibility which could only be disclosed by a conceptual organization of observations.

Aristotle's scientific philosophy, therefore, represented a departure from transcendent tendencies in religion and Platonism toward a kind of "natural philosophy" (a term which up until the end of the last century denoted what we now call natural science). Natural philosophy and empirical methods were *not* emblematic of early Greek thinkers, as we have seen. Aristotle gathered together many revolutionary developments which altered the aims and assumptions of philosophical inquiry. Before we present a general discussion of his thought, we should examine the historical background of his innovations. Aristotle himself did not invent an empirical, scientific methodology. There were many developments which preceded Aristotle's formulation of a generalized, universal application of empirical paradigms (i.e., their *philosophical* application). These preparatory developments were specific and did not originate primarily in the work of philosophers.

## The Origins of Natural Philosophy

The rudiments of natural philosophy and empirical science grew out of practical rather than theoretical soil. The source appears to be the Greek medical tradition, the work and writings of physicians.[3] In the fifth century B.C., Greek medicine was beginning to shift from magic to a practical art based on observation and experiment. The origin of a disease was no longer attributed to a hidden demon but to some kind of natural disorder, traceable to regularities in nature (rather than the extra-ordinary character of the sacred), which reveal a more predictable and hence treatable *cause*. The answer was not given in advance but rather followed from practice and observation: The physician might notice a similarity of symptoms among different cases; he would administer certain medicines or modify the patient's activity, and the rate of success or failure would guide the physician to a tangible and controllable cause of the disease, with great practical benefit.

Not surprisingly the physicians were antagonistic toward traditional magic and myth. They engaged in specific critiques but also voiced a general assessment of myth as such. In other words, *beyond* the frequent practical success of the new method, medical writers defended the "truth" of their account according to a generalized naturalism which would *in principle* exclude traditional views. For example, the author of *On the Sacred Disease* not only suggests a new interpretation of the disease (epilepsy), he also presumes that it, like any other disease, is of nature (*physis*) and has a definite cause (*prophasis*); and that traditional ritual treatments are fraudulent; and that a "sacred" designation stems from ignorance or simply serves to justify the ineffectiveness of traditional healers.[4]

The key element in this document is *not* primarily skepticism about ritual healers, or practical success, or a recognition of natural (profane) causes, since there is evidence that such conditions also exist to some extent in primitive, magical societies. What is significant in this document is the *exclusion* of ritual healing and any notion of divine intervention, that is, the proposed validity of natural causes and invalidity of mythical phenomena *in general*.[5] Furthermore, it is not simply the turn to nature that characterizes this approach. The *antagonism* toward myth indicates another issue, the "correction" of the sacred (the irregular) by means of a profane standard (the regular). It is not only visible nature that interests the author, but nature as a set of causes which exhibit *uniformity* and *regularity*.

One can question the exclusivity and reductionist assumptions within such a position. For all their skepticism and empirical methods, early medical writers themselves seemed dogmatic and arbitrary to some extent. First of all, ritual healers did often get results; and many "enlightened" minds did not entirely reject the idea of sacred intervention with respect to diseases;[6] and the empirical justification for some of the new theories was not always evident; and finally, the naturalistic assumption itself was seemingly taken for granted (and necessarily so, since no test could support the claim that *all* phenomena can be reduced to natural causes). As we have said many times, the corrective attitude of postmythical developments assumes the universal applicability of its criteria, when in fact it amounts to an *exclusion* of traditional meanings and a new framework for what counts as "true."[7] As such, the framework-shift itself cannot be justified. With respect to the above medical treatise, Lloyd suggests that

> what we are dealing with has some of the features of a paradigm switch: the author and his opponents disagree fundamentally on what sort of account to give of the 'sacred disease,' that is on what would count as an 'explanation' or 'cause' of this and other phenomena. Unlike the Zande skeptics described by Evans-Pritchard, the Hippocratic writer rejects the notion of supernatural intervention in natural phenomena *as a whole*, as what might even be called a category mistake. Even when we have to deal with the divine, the divine is in no sense *super*natural. We have, however, seen that, although appeals to observation and research are made, the empirical support for his own theories and explanations is often weak, and indeed many of his ideas could have been undermined by quite simple tests. Again, although he employs techniques of refutation to good effect, the key notion of the uniformity of nature is an assumption, not a proposition for which he explicitly argues.[8]

Put in modern terms, we could say that the physician's observation-statements were "theory-laden," which some have argued is true of *any* observation-statement.[9] In other words, his observations did not "discover the facts"; a naturalistic theory determined in advance what would *count* as a "fact."

Returning to historical considerations, if we put aside the *status* of an empirical method and simply attend to its features, we can conclude that the Greek medical tradition, with its explicit use of observations, hypothesis, and experiment, represents the birth of science far more properly than early philosophical developments.[10] It was medical writers who seem to have originated the explicit formulation and application of an inductive method.[11] Alcmaeon, a fifth century physician, probably was the originator of a naturalistic, experimental medical theory that came to influence later philosophy with respect to the importance of induction. He distinguished between animal knowledge (strict sensation) and human knowledge, which involves conjecture about things unseen after analyzing what can be seen (i.e., inductive generalizations about experience).[12]

Hippocrates (469–399 B.C.), considered to be the father of Greek medicine, presumably was the author of *On Ancient Medicine*, which begins by criticizing dogmatic (deductive) theories of medicine in favor of an empirical method:

> Hence I claim that it has no need of empty postulates such as are inevitable in dealing with insoluble problems beyond the reach of observation [*ta aphanea te kai aporeomena*], for example, what goes on in the sky and beneath the earth. If a man pronounces some opinion he has formed on how these things are, it cannot be clear either to himself or to his hearers whether what he says is true or not; for there is no test that can be applied so as to yield certain knowledge.[13]

The deductive tendencies of early philosophy would not readily suit the *practice* of medicine with all the variations of disease and the urgent need for effective treatment. The development of an inductive method, therefore, did not initially stem from theoretical speculation but rather from practical concerns. In the face of sickness, Hippocrates advocated neither magical cures based on mythical powers nor deductive theories such as the balance and alteration of natural elements. He recommended observation and experiment, such as modifying diet, behavior, or environment, from which one could draw conclusions and prompt successful treatment.[14]

There were also many extensions of empirical methodology beyond medical practice. For example, in *On Airs, Waters and Places*,

Hippocrates proposed a natural explanation for human character traits.[15] An aggressive or passive disposition is not due to some mysterious divine influence but rather to climatic or geographical conditions (e.g., temperate or intemperate seasons). In other words, the mythical tendency to express certain character traits as *unique* (e.g., an unusual surge of courage attributed to a special sacred power) is here replaced by a reduction of differences to an observable *constant* (i.e., differences stem from variations of regular natural causes). Courage is thus nothing inherently "special"; it is explained according to a uniform notion of environmental effects. In addition, historians such as Hecataeus and Herodotus adopted empirical methods and thereby transformed the way in which the past and cultural origins were to be ascertained. On the assumption that knowledge should be based on sense experience, they insisted that historical knowledge be grounded in eyewitness accounts (thereby undermining the kind of history told by poets).[16]

The tangible and decisive character of empirical methods, as well as certain degrees of success in practical applications, led to an expansion of the method into a general theory of knowledge. As we have observed, the mythical mind certainly recognized empirical (profane) elements but subordinated them to prefactual, sacred meanings. Indeed the mythical disclosure of sacred "irregularities" (the uncommon) would presuppose a comprehension of profane regularities and therefore even an implicit awareness of causal relations in the natural order. But the developments we are now discussing amounted to an isolation of profane experience and its adoption as the *standard* for comprehending the world.

The expansion of an empirical method into a general theory of knowledge was decisively completed in the philosophy of Aristotle. With regard to the influence of medicine, Aristotle was the son of a practicing physician and was himself a biologist. In the first chapter of the *Metaphysics*, he gives a medical example to illustrate his epistemology (981a5–25). Generalization upon experience gives a physician the ability to combine similar symptoms and treatments, resulting in *knowledge* about a disease and its effects on humans (rather than the mere empirical recognition of a particular man with particular symptoms). But his knowledge can be gained only *through* experience. Of course Aristotle was not simply interested in medical knowledge, but knowledge in general. The empirical method generated from the medical tradition evolved into a comprehensive epistemology applicable to all phenomena. Again, Aristotle developed a scientific *philosophy*. Accordingly, Plato's transcendent metaphysics and deductive epistemology were no longer tenable for Aristotle. Although both philosophers sought universals to ground experience, Aristotle repudiated Platonic universals, which were independent of sense individuals. For Aristotle, universals are *immanent* in sense experience, gathered from observation and generalization.

Aristotle's methodology also illustrates his departure from traditional psychology. Knowledge entails the discovery of principles formulated *in* the conscious mind as opposed to insights granted from some transcendent realm (compare Platonic recollection). The mind's capacity for memory and abstraction "builds" knowledge by gathering similarities and patterns in sense experience (*Posterior Analytics*, II.19). Knowledge, of course, is not equivalent to sense experience. An inductive, empirical method discovers "essences" in experience, conceptual generalizations which themselves become the "objects" of investigation. "Sense perception is common to all, and therefore easy and no mark of wisdom" (*Metaphysics*, I.2.982a12–13). Knowledge expands immediate experience by means of general, unified classifications which ground, explain, and organize what is immediately given.[17] While both Plato and Aristotle looked beyond immediate experience for knowledge, Aristotle insisted that knowledge be drawn from, referred back to, and thus always correlated with, sense experience.

# Aristotle's Philosophy

**GENERAL PRINCIPLES**

Aristotle's writings are not always easy to understand, partly because they come to us indirectly through lecture notes. But any westerner in one way or another has immediate access to Aristotelian philosophy because western thought in many ways presupposes categories, methods, and classifications set up by Aristotle. This is especially true for the scientific tradition. Biology was a major influence in the development of Aristotle's thinking, but he went further to formulate a scientific philosophy which aimed to understand the nature of reality in general from a scientific perspective. Although many of Aristotle's particular findings and beliefs have been rejected by modern science, nevertheless the history of science as such, and the presumption that scientific methods properly disclose the nature of things, would have been impossible apart from Aristotelian foundations.

As we have seen, the nature of Aristotle's thought can initially be understood as a reaction against Platonism. A pupil at Plato's Academy, Aristotle later came to establish his own school, the Lyceum. There he sought answers to Plato's philosophical questions, but in a more definite way than his famous teacher. Frustrated by the absence of strict definition, the pursuit of universals beyond concrete experience, and the subsequent requirement of spiritual transcendence, Aristotle pursued precise definitions on the basis of universals inherent in concrete observation. Truth was no longer transcendent and elusive but direct and concretely immanent. Accordingly, Greek thought was finally divorced from mythical and intuitive elements in favor of rational, conceptual, and empirical categories that came to characterize the "objective" mainstream of western philosophy.[18]

Aristotle's scientific orientation is well illustrated in the *Categories*. In answering the question "What is X?" Plato declared the "what" (the essence) to be "beyond" the particular thing in question. A thing is a mere image of a transcendent Form. For Aristotle, that which explains a thing, its essence, is discovered *in* the thing by observing it and classifying its different characteristics. Universals are not beyond the realm of ordinary experience; they are the common classes which disclose the essence of things but which must be gathered from experience and specifically elaborated. Aristotle did not exactly disagree with Plato's notion of "form," only with his method of discovery and ontological placement. For Plato, being entailed universal Forms beyond particular appearances. For Aristotle, being is always a particular thing, an instance of a universal form, expressed in *this* particular way. Consequently, this being and its form may be conceptually distinguishable (by means of abstraction) but never ontologically separable. The object of investigation is always an *individual* entity which alone reveals its essence and form.

Aristotle's scientific philosophy involved, therefore, a turn to particular individuals, the disclosure of ordinary experience (the profane) on its own terms, the search for knowledge within the field of observable, concrete perceptions. What is X? Aristotle saw no need for mythical paradigms or some intangible, extrasensory ground. One need only observe X and extract information and explanations according to the various ways X is situated, behaves, and reveals itself. What follows is a general scheme for such an investigation, the ten categories, or ten ways in which X can be said to *be*, a collection of explanations for what X *is*. The categories are:

1. **substance**, the "what"
2. **quality**, what sort of thing
3. **quantity**, how large or how much
4. **relation**
5. **place**
6. **time**
7. and 8. **position** and **state**, how situated
9. **action**, doing what
10. **affection**, being acted upon (*Categories*, IV.1b25–28).

The most important category is substance (*ousia*); the remaining categories are its attributes. There are many ways in which a thing may be said to "be," but all must be related to one central point (*Metaphysics*, IV.2.1003a33–35). That reference point is *ousia* or "fundamental reality," that which is self-contained, unified, and subsistent through changes and which supports all the various ways of being (*Categories*, V.2b15–20; 4b16–20). Not only is substance a unity, it is also always an *individual* substance (*Categories*, V.3b10), that is, not a transcendent universal but something concrete, *this* being. Contrary to Platonism, therefore, Aristotelian philosophy begins with the scientific analysis of individual things and their attributes according to an empirical method.

In the *Physics*, Aristotle analyzes physical nature (an investigation which sets up the construction of a metaphysics, as we shall see). We are told that things come to be in three ways: by nature (an *inherent* principle of motion and rest); by art or design (a principle external to the thing); or by chance (no principle). Aristotle presents what amounts to a revolutionary assumption—that things of nature have *within* them principles which explain why they are the way they are (*Physics*, II.1.192b10–15). On the one hand Aristotle here overcomes the opposition between *nomos* and *physis* which had been proposed by earlier philosophers. Law is not a conventional "superimposition" upon nature; a thing's *nature* reveals its principle; law and nature are intrinsically correlated. Secondly, Aristotle here establishes a fundamental assumption of science, which demonstrates its debt to him no matter how many of Aristotle's particular findings may be discredited. Science assumes there is something *inherent* in nature (i.e., *not* a myth or a transcendent principle) which *explains* the activity of things, which can be discovered by the unaided human mind, and which permits prediction of subsequent activity (i.e., this "something" is consistently present in all cases of a given investigation). These *conceptual* (i.e., nonempirical) assumptions supporting a scientific methodology may seem self-evident, but they have a history and are traced back to Aristotelian philosophy, which established the orientational *framework* of scientific thinking.[19]

For Aristotle, principles of explanation are induced (generalized from observation without proving every case), and then the instantiations of these principles are subsequently deduced once the explanation is sufficiently established. Moreover, an explanation always describes a *cause*, and Aristotle proceeds to induce four basic causes which inhere in a thing. These causes will offer an explanation for the primary category of substance and answer the question "why?" to supplement categorical answers (what, when, how, where). The four causes are outlined in the *Physics* (II.3):

1. **material** cause (physical substrate)
2. **formal** cause (shape or design)
3. **efficient** cause (antecedent cause)
4. **final** cause (completion or purpose)

Aristotle primarily uses artifacts to illustrate this causal complex. For example: The material cause of a table is wood, its formal cause is the table-shape, the efficient cause is the craftsman, and the final cause is the completed product and its purpose or use.[20] The four causes enable us to explain the nature of a particular thing, to define it, and to apprehend its *being* (what and why it *is*). And once the mind grasps the fourfold causal framework, it is methodologically prepared with a preobservational confidence; that is, it knows what to look for ahead of time.

Although the notion of substance always refers to a particular entity, the concept of substance as such and principles of explanation are not equivalent to empirical perception; they are universals, applicable to *any* particular being. Accordingly, Aristotle was moved to construct a metaphysics on the basis of his physics, to provide the conceptual completion of the findings induced from nature. Principles of explanation and the thought processes involved can be examined and projected in their capacity as universally applicable to any entity whatsoever. Metaphysics is "primary philosophy" because it concerns being as such and attempts to answer the question: What can be said of any being insofar as it is a being? In this way a general scheme of universals can be discovered which speaks to reality as such and not simply any particular aspect of reality. Such a universal scheme cannot be *separated* from particular things, however, since the principles of knowledge are nothing more than the common classes of ways in which individual entities reveal themselves. Aristotle's metaphysics is dependent upon his physics, because his metaphysical paradigms are drawn from the four causes induced from nature. General ontology, then, becomes a kind of grand induction from preliminary empirical investigations of particular beings.

The categories supply knowledge of an individual entity as it stands before us. The four causes examined in the *Physics* complete the picture by adding the "why" to the "what." The highest form of knowledge goes beyond particular causes to universal causal principles applicable to any form of being. Extending the inductive method, Aristotle concludes that all beings can be explained by a fundamental complex of material, formal, efficient, and final causes. In the *Metaphysics*, Aristotle concentrates on these principles as such, universalizing them and simplifying the causal complex. Final and efficient causes can be united under formal cause (the form of the development process and the form of the antecedent cause). Consequently we are left with two basic principles underlying all of reality—matter (*hylē*) and form (*eidos*). In other words, every being has a concrete, perceptible "housing" for the different forms it can take. Matter and form, then, together account for being as such. In this way Aristotle saw himself improving upon the strict materialism of pre-Socratic thought (*his* interpretation of early philosophy) and the strict formalism of Plato's separable Ideas (again, his interpretation) by accounting for *both* in a single hylomorphic theory.

Aristotle does lean toward form, however, and connects it with substance. Just as substance was the primary category, form takes priority over other principles with regard to the essence of things: "By form I mean the essence of each thing and its primary substance" (*Metaphysics*, VII.7.1032b2–3; also 1041b1–10). Since matter as such has no shape or determination until organized by a formal design, the essential principle of being is form. In general, then, the answer to the question "What is X?" becomes centered in an immanent, particular form-as-substance, the essential "this" of an individual entity that grounds and gathers all the various ways in which it can be apprehended and the different developments it will undergo.

The distinction between matter and form is primarily a static explanation. Aristotle wanted to accommodate change and activity so as to counteract the (presumed) inertia of Eleatic philosophy. Accordingly, matter and form were further translated into the dynamic paradigm of potency (*dynamis*) and act (*energeia*). Matter as such is an indeterminate potential for the various determinations actualized in form. The matter of stone, for example, though inseparable from the forms of stone, cannot be identified with the different forms stone can take. Both principles are needed to account for the innumerable instances of change, growth, variation, and development in nature.[21]

The influence of biology is quite evident in Aristotle's formulation of a matter-form, potency-act paradigm. In a seed, for example, there is a potency which "explains" its development into a plant. Moreover, in life forms, mere material components as such cannot explain the activity and organization of parts in a living organism. Aristotle in effect extends this biological model to all areas of knowledge and reality. In physics, as we have seen, matter-potency accounts for the material base of things; form-act, the different shapes and designs. In Aristotle's epistemology the mind gains knowledge by abstracting form from matter and gathering it into the forms of the intellect. In psychology, matter-potency is the body; form-act, the soul which activates and organizes the body. (There presumably must be such a distinction since a corpse and a living body are materially identical.) In ethics and politics, moral principles actualize *cultural* potentialities; on both an individual and collective level, animal existence is then given a cultural *form*.

With matter and form, Aristotle discovers the most universal principles of explanation for any entity whatsoever. In the *Metaphysics* he thinks out this explanatory paradigm in itself, as distinct from the things it explains. The result is the notion of "prime matter" (IX.7), or pure potency (i.e., the conceptual completion of the fact that matter supports every being) and the notion of primary form or pure act, the "unmoved mover." Prime matter is the stuff of the cosmos, distinct but never separable from form. Primary form, however, as pure actuality has to be separated from potency and matter; it persists as the substantial collection of cosmic forms and as the primary act and cause to which all causes can be traced. Such is Aristotle's concept of god, the prime mover, the conceptual completion of activity and form. God is the self-contained source of all the various forms which reveal essences (actual forms distinct from material potency). As pure form, therefore, god is a nonmaterial substance, namely, thought; and being self-contained, god is consequently described as "thought thinking itself" (XII.9).

In sum, then, Aristotle can be understood as having extended his biology and physics into a metaphysics. He discovered a universal ground for knowledge and reality by starting with principles of explanation induced from observation of nature, and then pushing these models to their conceptual limit in the metaphysical principles of matter and form, potency and actuality. We now want to explicate in a general way the underlying assumptions of Aristotelian philosophy, especially in terms of its innovative departure from traditional forms of disclosure.

## INDIVIDUATION AND DESACRALIZATION

Aristotle crystallized what could be called an *individuation* paradigm. That is to say, he developed an ontology based upon the ordinary experience of individual entities as such. Our historical analysis allows us to recognize the revolutionary nature of this paradigm. Myth, early philosophy, and even Platonism had been animated by various senses of the sacred, by a kind of transcendence of individual things as such (the profane). Whether it was the gods, mystery, process, or Platonic Forms, the common feature was that individual things in ordinary experience alone were not enough to account for the world's nature and meaning.[22]

Of course, Plato also represented a radical departure from the traditional sense of the sacred by renouncing its presentation of negation, mystery, formlessness, and the lived world in favor of constancy and fixed form. Aristotle simply gave an empirical slant to this kind of desacralization by defining form as an *individual* substance, the "this" of immediate experience—a form which is universal, stable, and subsistent, but which is shown in *this* particular entity. Both Plato and Aristotle identified being and form; they simply disagreed about the ontological location of form. If we recall the ruptures of individual form in myth, especially in tragedy and early philosophies of process, where form is immersed in and even constituted by negation, we can recognize the shift in Aristotle's individuation paradigm. (In Nietzschean terminology it represents a desacralization of thought because it isolates and insulates Apollonian individuation and form from Dionysian formlessness. Subsequently, form loses the sacred sense of "appearance" and takes on the postmythical sense of "reality.")

Aristotelian individuation and desacralization can be found in his understanding of both the mind and the world. With regard to mind we notice a complete departure from traditional models. In myth the conscious self exhibited a kind of transparency in that it was continually open to extraconscious arrivals. Even in Plato knowledge in some respects involved the arrival of formal principles *to* the conscious mind (as recollection). For Aristotle the self takes on a kind of opacity because knowledge is disclosed by forms *in* the conscious mind, by the capacity to abstract from sense experience.

With regard to the world, Aristotle's philosophy gathered together the common experience of individual things as such and found here its ultimate reference point. As a consequence Greek thought was divorced from its mythical tendencies, which were evident whenever things were understood in terms of some mysterious "other" and which accordingly would express the *limits* of profane "facts" in terms of nonfactual imagery or a sense of mystery. The implicit meaning of the sacred showed itself to be some kind of transcendence of profane individuation. Aristotle's philosophy, in effect, established a formal reduction to a profane criterion.[23] Although the essence of a thing is not equivalent to its merely perceived presence, that essence is shown by a conceptual analysis of the perceived thing; that is to say, its essence entails a *definition* which clearly marks the limits of a thing by including it in a class of similar phenomena and so distinguishing it from other phenomena. Aristotle thereby set up an equation between definition, essence, and being (cf. *Posterior Analytics*, II.3.90b25–35, 91a1; *Metaphysics*, VI.1.1025b). In this way, elements of the profane (commonness and individuation) prepared a new conception of reality. The sense of the sacred which emphasized something "outside" the limits of profane individuation was exchanged for a concentration *within* the limits of individuation. The sacred correlation of a thing with its own negation, as well as the correlative matrixes of traditional culture, were exchanged for a collection of individuated regions in which essence meant substantial form marked off from negation and other forms. Consequently the "outside" was seen to be either opposite to being (as in the case of negation) or accidental to a thing's essence (as in the case of relation).

In this respect the clearest illustration of Aristotle's individuation paradigm is his famous principle of noncontradiction (and its corollaries, the principle of identity and the law of excluded middle). In order to understand this principle in its historical context we must first retrieve the process paradigm which characterized much of early Greek philosophy. Heraclitus had proposed a philosophy of becoming and temporality. With regard to individual beings, two basic conclusions follow. First, there is an essential correlation between being and non-being, because the *archē* is a unified process. Form emerges from formlessness, is constantly changing, and then returns to formlessness. Thus individuation is an appearing and not an ultimate reality in and of itself. Secondly, there is an essential correlation between beings, since the dynamics of the process is an opposition exchange. Such mutual negation not only serves the underlying process, it also defines each form in relation to its opposite. So the nature of being itself is defined in relation to nonbeing, and the nature of particular beings is defined in relation to other beings.

There were historical developments which resisted this (tragic) view of the world in favor of some kind of substance. But if the tendency toward substantial form and the conceptual preservation of individuation was to succeed in displacing a process paradigm, it had to overthrow in principle the essential correlation of form and formlessness and of opposite forms. Such a revolution was consummated in Aristotle's principle of noncontradiction.

> It is impossible for anything at the same time to be and not to be, and by this means have shown that this is the most indisputable of all principles. (*Metaphysics*, IV.4.1006a3–6)

In contrast to Heraclitus, who is specifically mentioned in the text (IV.3.1005b25), this principle is called an "ultimate belief" (*eschatēn doxan*) and the "starting-point" (*archē*) for all other principles (IV.3.1005b30–35). Without such a principle there would be no stable, positive reference point for an analysis or demonstrative proof.

If one were to defend Heraclitus's position, one would not do so by rejecting the principle of noncontradiction out of hand. It is certainly not a false statement, and it has a legitimate use: *This* tree is not *that* tree; a tree is not a stone; I am not another person; something empirically present is not absent. We remarked in an earlier chapter that avoiding contradiction is a precondition for communication in any form of language, primitive or otherwise. But the principle of noncontradiction can nevertheless be said to have a *limited* use. As applied to individuated beings as such, it shows validity, but in the light of early Greek philosophy, it becomes questionable to propose this principle as the fundamental starting-point for apprehending what a being finally is. Certainly for Heraclitus, a being is what it is; but it is also constituted by its relation to opposite states and the background formlessness of process in the midst of which it emerges, changes, and disappears. The nature (*physis*) of a thing cannot be isolated within the boundaries of individuation. Such a fixation may be possible in the mind or common sense, but not in reality. Nature does not display constant presences, and the demarcation of natural forms is more nominal than real. For example, there is no strict boundary between "seed," "plant," "fruit," "rot," and "compost" other than the linguistic and conceptual frames built in the midst of a single process. Reality cannot be sufficiently understood within the limits of individuation; the mind must be open to negation. Things "are" in the midst of formlessness and an interrelated process.

The apparent stalemate between Aristotle and Heraclitus is not difficult to resolve. It is not the case that Heraclitus was violating logic or undermining rationality.[24] Heraclitus and Aristotle were making sense in different ways. Our treatment of mythical sense and early philosophy has shown that certain rational principles and common sense assumptions can be "violated" without being liable to the charge of irrationality or nonsense. With regard to uniting contraries, Heraclitus was simply saying *more* than Aristotle wanted to say, finding sense beyond the parameters of Aristotelian logic.

Heraclitus would not disagree with the principle of noncontradiction, to a certain extent. The best way to understand this is to emphasize once again the sacred-profane distinction. Herein is contained a two-dimensional world. The principle of noncontradiction can hold true as a one-dimensional form of consistency: A tree is a tree; Zeus is Zeus; Achilles is Achilles (if he were to say in normal circumstances, "I am not Achilles," that would be a lie). But since the sacred often violates the rules of the profane, certain "irregular" statements can hold true for the sacred. In effect, as we have suggested, Heraclitus's logos represented a comparable distinction between the sacred and the profane. Normal statements about individual beings would require empirical and conceptual consistency. But in relation to the logos underlying all beings, such statements would not suffice. Aristotle's principle assumes a profane standard of empirical form and individuation. Heraclitean "contradiction" aims *beyond* a profane standard and therefore does not violate the principle. Hence there is a two-dimensional resolution of the problem here: From the standpoint of the profane, a being is what it is; from the standpoint of the (sacred) logos, a being is constituted by what it (as profane) is *not*.[25] The problem with Aristotle's principle of noncontradiction, therefore, is not its sense but its *exclusive* definition of sense. The apprehension of reality and truth solely in terms of individuated form and conceptual definition necessarily passes over and cannot adequately express something equally true about reality, namely *process*.[26] With respect to the issue of process and temporality, we should next consider Aristotle's analysis of time.

## ARISTOTLE'S CONCEPTION OF TIME

The principle of noncontradiction states that it is impossible for something to be and not be "at the same time" (*hama*). Aristotle was able to say this because his analysis of time exhibited a kind of individuation and fragmentation comparable to his conception of form. That analysis emphasized profane time and issued in a desacralization of temporality as understood by Heraclitus, for example. Let us examine Aristotle's conception of time, which is found for the most part in the *Physics* (IV.10–14).

Time is defined as the measure of motion with respect to before and after (219b1–2). At the center of this conception is the "now," the present moment which *defines* before and after, future and past, as not-yet-now and no-longer-now. Although time does not exist without change or motion (218b20–25), it is not motion as such but motion *measured* according to now-units (219b1-5). Aristotle's definition is the foundation of the moment-view of time, which conceives time to be a series of units following one another, each identified as a "now," unless they are approaching or have passed, at which point they are identified as not-yet- or no-longer-now. Such a reification of time into units is the precondition for something like clock-time, which might have been the aim of Aristotle's emphasis on measurement.

The definition of time according to now-moments is indeed familiar and intelligible, but the historical perspective of our study raises certain questions about how well the meaning of time is served by Aristotle's approach, which can easily be seen as a departure from a more original meaning of temporality found in previous thinkers and mythical disclosure. There the very origin and nature of things were illuminated by a temporal paradigm (process). Aristotle, however, in analyzing time was not considering anything like an origin; he presumed the existence of individual beings and considered time solely within the context of succeeding states of being, each designated by a "now."

Thus the individuation of being prepared the individuation of time into now-moments. The same questions raised about Aristotle's ontology pertain, therefore, to his theory of time as well. Although Aristotle disclosed much about time that is important, his scientific form of thinking inevitably led him to overlook a more primordial meaning of time as disclosed in prescientific forms of thinking. For the purpose of clarity, let us designate primordial time as "temporality" and subsequently discuss the limitations of Aristotle's position.[27]

The moment-view of time cannot accommodate temporality as an overall process of emergence and disappearance, that is, finitude itself as opposed to finite beings, change itself as opposed to changing states of being. Since it involves appearing, temporality has to do with origins, whereas Aristotelian time simply measures the localized motion of a being. That which time measures is the movement "from something to something" (219a10) as opposed to the nonbeing-being correlation in temporality. Moreover, since moment-time is the measure *of* a changing process, and temporality is process as such, then we notice that Aristotelian time is derived from original temporality.

At one point (222b30) Aristotle does attend to flux when he names time as the condition for destruction, but destruction rather than coming-to-be. Therefore, time is simply the movement of a thing toward its destruction. Temporality, however, encompasses both destruction *and* coming-to-be, not only passing-away but the emergence of being from hiddenness. Temporality is more than a thing's moments "in time"; as a whole it is a correlative presence-and-absence (accounting for Heraclitean-like paradoxes which Aristotle would find contradictory). Moment-time is therefore a reification of temporality on the side of presence, which consequently misses the *positive*, that is, the generative and disclosive dimension in temporal negativity.

Measured time also cannot accommodate temporality as "lived time" in which the process-character of existence is apprehended in nondiscrete and nonquantitative ways. Consider the vague stretches of time we considered in the first chapter (e.g., "I have no time," good times, a time of peace). Consider also activities in which the measurement of time (due to conscious attention) is distorted or even lost (e.g., an hour which seems like minutes or vice versa, or "Where did the time go?"). Lived time is also intentional (as in a time for planting). Surely such experiences and conditions are temporal, and yet they are not *defined* by measuredness. Aristotelian time cannot address them since it must "stand off" from experience in order to measure. More-

over, the intentionality of lived time indicates in another way the derivative nature of measured time: Whenever we *use* a clock, we do not aim
simply to break time up into numerical units but to arrange activities
into publicly shareable spans and reference points; minutes and hours
arrange a time to begin and end activities, to meet for them and depart
for others; days and years permit the organization of a historical record,
which is not simply a record for its own sake but the servant of cultural
purposes.

The emphasis on now-moments also creates a conceptual frame
which leads to many discrepancies when considering lived time. The
"now" forces us to picture past, present, and future as discrete regions,
since past and future are *not* now. Such distinctions are certainly intelligible to some extent, but they are inappropriate for existential time
in which past and future are clearly part of the present. The past and future have a kind of presence in that I am now recalling and anticipating. The present is a continuing concern about the past and future; I
can never truly isolate present actions from past conditions and future
aims.[28]

The most fundamental aspect of lived time is also missing from
Aristotle's account, namely, the existential meaning of temporality as
such, dwelling in a world of negation and destruction (the primary
theme of tragedy). We can approach this point by considering something Aristotle says at 221a5–10: that "to be in time" is the same for all
things. This is certainly true from the standpoint of all things being
measurable in time, but what about human beings, who do the measuring? If time is measurement, then a being which measures would seem
to have a special access to time.[29] Once again the nature of temporality
must be considered. A tree can have a time, but is it a temporal being?
To *exist* in time is surely not the same for all beings. All things change,
but are all *aware* of change as such? All life forms die, but are all aware
of death as such? It appears that only humans are aware of death, the ultimate finitude of temporality. Other beings are subject to finitude and
change, but it is not an issue for them. It seems that Aristotle projects a
characteristic of time (measure) upon all things, overlooking that it
can be so projected only by human beings, for whom a temporal world
*as such* is disclosed. We are aware of time not simply because we measure time but because we are aware of that which is measured, namely,
change; and we are aware of change because we are aware of temporality as such, coming-to-be and passing-away. And temporal finitude accounts for the unique human access to the meaning of being itself. The

being (appearing) of things is recognized against the background of nonbeing. Other beings, unaware of death, finitude, temporality as such, are not aware that things "are." The meaning of temporality is that all things appear (are) in flux. We are temporal in this special sense even when we are not measuring time. *Before* things can be measured, they must be disclosed, and this by means of temporal appearing. So the issue of time cannot be reduced to beings and their measured moments; there is *more* to time than this, and such a transcendence was expressed by various sacred notions in prescientific thinking (e.g., Dionysus, *logos*, *apeiron*, and such).

The difference between Aristotelian time and temporality is the difference between reification and process. Individuation and the "now" are clearly correlated in the principle of noncontradiction (being and nonbeing cannot be at the same time). The now is the reification of temporality from the standpoint of individuation isolated from a past-present-future complex (including emergence from and passage to formlessness) and disconnected from other beings (other nows). Moment-time is a fragmentation of temporality, which for Heraclitus was a unified process underlying all moments. Temporality as such "transcends" moments and unifies them, so that Heraclitus could quite rightly say something Aristotle would find nonsensical: "we are and we are not" in the *same* time (temporality).

Time, for Heraclitus, had to do with temporal origins and not simply present beings. Aristotle turned from this "archaeological" model to a logical and scientific analysis of time. Even Plato had connected time with origins in his notion of a "moving image of eternity." For Aristotle, time was simply an *aspect* of reality, of an already existing world, simply the measure of motion. It was no accident that Aristotle discussed time in the *Physics* rather than the *Metaphysics*. Since time was not connected with origins for Aristotle, when he did consider an ontological foundation, he saw it as something nontemporal. Since reality was no longer illuminated by a temporal paradigm, he was bound to opt for a *timeless* paradigm—pure form, which was Aristotle's prime mover, or god.

In effect it was Aristotle's individuated fragmentation of temporality that forced him in this direction. With time split up into parts, it could no longer be associated with any notion of a whole. For this reason the positive characteristics of temporality exhibited in Heraclitean philosophy (unity, *archē*) were automatically missed. If time is the momentary reification of becoming (now-points), then time is

something that passes (a now from a not-yet to a no-longer). But an
*arché* cannot be said to "pass." Consequently, Aristotle had to separate
the notion of *arché* from time. For Heraclitus, temporality (the logos)
does not pass; we are *and* we are not, in the same time-process. With
such a process-paradigm, the temporal negation of individuation is an
*arché* and it continually defines the nature of being. Since Aristotle defined being as an individuated substance, temporality was not only a
form of negation, it was an ontological *privation* which could not be
connected with an essence.

Despite his disagreements with Plato, Aristotle likewise demanded
a nontemporal ground of being to compensate for temporal negativity
(note the connection between knowledge, necessity, and eternity in
the *Metaphysics*, VI.3.1139b15–25). Furthermore he followed Plato
in connecting the idea of a ground with a transformed sense of divinity, namely, a god who is no longer simply immortal (unending) but
nontemporal in nature, detached from time and the vicissitudes of experience. Even though Aristotle was a more worldly philosopher than
Plato (and apparently did not consider the soul to be immortal or destined for a timeless existence), and even though Aristotle affirmed a
world of time and acknowledged temporal conditions as part of a
thing's being, nevertheless he considered time to be simply the passing instances of fixed forms. Unlike Plato, he did not think of temporal forms as approximations of eternal forms but as their direct
embodiments; still, they embody forms which have a fixed, nontemporal nature. The divine mind, the unmoved mover, represented
the unchanging reference for all the changing instantiations in a
world of time.

Although Aristotle's scientific philosophy rebuffed the transcendent flights of Platonism, he too felt the need to resolve the negativity of
a world constituted by temporality. The common factor in Aristotle and
Plato is the turn from existential immediacy to conceptual abstraction
(whether scientific or otherwise). The conditions of a temporal world
are such that Aristotle's conceptual aims quite naturally demanded a
supratemporal ground. In the *Physics* (VIII.6), he argues that the eternal motion of the cosmos requires an eternal mover which itself is not
moved. The different causes in the world themselves must have a cause
which itself is not caused. Without an unmoved mover or an uncaused
cause, reality would suffer an infinite dispersal and the mind would not
be able to "grasp" the world as a whole. Aristotle's insistence that a
thing must have a cause (i.e., an explanatory ground) could not rest

with scientific analysis. The cosmos as a whole must have a grounding explanation. Aristotle would not tolerate any ontological mysteries.

The path to Aristotle's supratemporal, divine ground can be understood by way of the following proposition: "actuality is prior to potentiality" (*Metaphysics*, XII.6.1072a9). Actualized form must be ontologically prior to the indeterminacy of potentiality (*not yet* being) if reality is to be sufficiently grounded, explained, and free of negation. Furthermore, since potentiality for Aristotle is the realm of matter, then such a ground must be pure form, the nonmaterial realm of *thought*. The mind of god, which contains all the forms of the cosmos, satisfies the conditions of an ultimate ground and cause. Even though for an object in the natural world its potentiality is temporally prior to the actualization of that potential, from a metaphysical standpoint, that which its potential is aiming *toward* is always actual in the mind of god. So even before an acorn becomes an oak tree, the form of the tree *is* in the divine mind. In this way, the "negativity" of potentiality is kept from being a primal condition. The world is thereby saved from the unacceptable notion that it arises out of nonbeing, or, as myth might say, "night" (1072a20). We notice here a reversal of traditional paradigms (both philosophical and mythical).

Aristotle also completed the transition from a mythical sense of divinity to a philosophical conception of god. According to Aristotle, god is one (1074a35–40); a plurality of forces is "not good" and should be reduced to one (1076a1–5).[30] God is also essentially good and outside time (1072b25–30). Finally, god is pure thought and self-contained as thought thinking itself: "its thinking is a thinking on thinking" (1074b34). Here Aristotle's theology completes the conceptual transformation of the traditional sense of divinity by being purely cognitive and detached from the temporal world (thought thinking *itself* and *not* the world), thereby overcoming even the Platonic notion of "participation." Aristotle's retention of the divine exhibits a vestige of myth, but it seems little more than nominally related to the mythical sense of the sacred. Conceptual detachment from the lived world seems to reach a point of consummation in Aristotelian theology.

In general, then, Aristotle's departure from tradition and the way reality is shaped in his thought are clearly the result of a paradigm shift (and not a correction of the past). A temporal paradigm had previously disclosed sense and meaning in the context of temporal negativity, that which did not make sense for Aristotle, who therefore opted for a new criterion of sense. It is that criterion (substantial form, a fixed ground), and not therefore temporality itself, which prompted Aristotle to prefer unity over multiplicity, substance over process, explanatory grounds over appearance and hiddenness, eternity over time. It is only the *presumption* of an individuation paradigm that produces the "incoherence" of temporal conditions; the tragic paradigm of myth and early philosophy was able to find coherence in the same conditions. If reification and substantial determinations are the presumed standard, then it is inevitable that the lived world and existential temporality will appear flawed. Since the world *is* temporal, the construction of individuated conceptual "frames" will be frustrated and the world appears to be a set of *passing* substances, and therefore an ontological privation. Consequently the ground of reality quite naturally will require placement outside this field of passing forms. It is no accident that so much of philosophy was and continued to be interested in eternal absolutes and metaphysical conceptions of god. It is also no wonder that philosophy took a corrective attitude toward temporal negation and the features of the lived world which resisted substantiation and certainty. But, since these features of the lived world can and did exhibit a sense of coherence (in myth and early philosophy), and since a temporal paradigm can find these conditions fully adequate to reality, then the corrective posture of Plato and Aristotle was a frameup. The fact that philosophy disclosed a *different* kind of sense is both true and important; however, the *reduction* of sense to its criteria is problematic. What philosophy found to be "real" and "apparent" was fully determined by its paradigms and not by the nature of reality.

## Aristotle's Revolution

The philosophy of Aristotle established revolutionary criteria for truth—a rational, scientific methodology, the self-containment of conscious experience and thought, an emphasis on common assumptions, and the concentration of reality within individuated form (both empirical and conceptual). Accordingly, the conditions of mythical disclosure could no longer count as "true." It is not that Aristotle utterly rejected myth; he recognized many important insights contained in poetry and ancient tales. He did, however, *demote* myth to a lower order of culture because rationality was to be the sole arbiter of whatever could count as true, in myth or anything else. Aristotle accepted a good deal of traditional culture but subjected it to a new order of interpretation.[31]

Aristotle has often been called the philosopher of common sense. His investigations seem only to clarify and organize that which is obvious in human experience. He constantly appeals to what is "commonly understood." Of course Aristotle's thought is more than just common sense; it is a philosophical system of *universals*, principles of thought derived from common sense. But we are rarely startled by his findings. Looking back at Greek intellectual history we usually declare Aristotle to be a more "realistic" thinker. Then one *should* be startled by something: How could Aristotle's insights have been missed before? The reason is simple: Aristotle created a new interpretation; his philosophy seems obvious because he fashioned paradigms which historically helped to shape *our* vision of the world. In effect, he identified the "real" with the "obvious." The sacred-profane distinction shows that previous periods of culture could have easily recognized Aristotle's "data" (the profane); however, that was not then the criterion for "reality." The obvious was always subordinated to something uncommon, and objectivity had not yet displaced existential meaning. Pre-Aristotelian culture was not a dark age waiting to be enlightened. If it seems so, it was *made* dark in retrospect by a new form of illumination. (No one in those earlier times would have said: "We live in darkness. We do not understand our world. When will someone deliver us from ignorance?")

Aristotle's innovation lay in his identification of reality and truth with individuated form and empirical methods, that is, with a scientific rationalism (replacing "tragic wisdom" and sacred meanings). The concept of "being" was delivered from Parmenidean mysteries and identified with particular beings perceived by the senses. Even the culmination of Aristotle's metaphysics, the positing of a suprasensible unmoved mover, was itself a consequence of the thought processes at work in the apprehension of particular being, since a first cause was seen to follow from the observed fact that every being has a cause (*Physics*, VIII.6). Furthermore, the positing of an unmoved mover as pure act and thought was the completion of the cognitive processes which constituted knowledge of the world, the positing of the phenomenon of thought as such (thought thinking itself). Even though the divine unmoved mover shows an element of sacred transcendence and therefore is more mythical than scientific, it still represented for Aristotle a natural extension of the analytical thinking of particular being that characterized his inquiry. The unmoved mover was his attempt to gather the entire range of thought processes and principles of being into *one thought*. That is what made Aristotle's thinking metaphysical as well as scientific.

Even though metaphysics is out of fashion today, historically speaking, I think that it was precisely the *metaphysical* dimension of Aristotle's thought that nurtured and supported both the disposition of certainty about scientific rationality and the impression that something like Aristotle's approach is so much more "realistic" than other world views. The Aristotelian perspective had to fight off various other elements in Greek culture. Metaphysical principles were the ultimate weapon in that fight because they served to ground the new enterprise and establish a reference point from which traditional views could be judged deficient. From the standpoint of our study, the importance of Aristotle lies not simply in his focus on empirical perception (since that can be found in any form of thinking) but rather in the *universalization* of common experience of particular beings, the derivation of universals from such experience, and the construction of a metaphysical ground to secure that perspective and identify it with a bedrock truth. The historical development of western science and the philosophical trends tied to scientific thinking might have been impossible, or at least might have withered from inertia, without a certain metaphysical foundation which could establish the confidence and certainty that this mode of thinking reaches all the way to the ultimate nature of things and which could therefore fight off doubt or antagonism. Even though dogmatism is rejected in principle by science, nevertheless the disposition of certainty about scientific *methods* stems from a concealed or forgotten metaphysics, a historical legacy which became so implicit as to go unnoticed. The absence of a metaphysical outlook may be no more than the historical victory of a viewpoint which no longer has to justify itself. Metaphysics was far from a dispensable quirk in the history of thought; it was the groundwork without which even so-called antimetaphysical developments (e.g., empiricism) might never have been historically established.[32]

It was indeed Aristotle's metaphysical universalization of objective experience, individuated being, and empirical methods that allowed scientific thinking to pursue its course with assurance and zeal, justified by the philosophical conviction that it was the proper method for discovering truth. Furthermore, it was Aristotle's release of scientific thinking and its eventual predominance that allowed his empirical individuation paradigm—with its sense of objectivity and clarity freed from anything elusive or mythical—to become so ingrained in consciousness as to eventually appear "realistic." But the so-called self-evidency of individuated form and empirical/conceptual truth is a historical development. Aristotle constructed a sense of truth around ordinary objective experience and conscious knowledge to replace the extraordinary, nonfactual transcendence of myth and early philosophy. His metaphysical extension universalized and thus secured conscious experience, the cool clarity of "nature as such," stripped of myth and mystery. What is problematic here is a simultaneous gain and loss: On the one hand there came the positive disclosure of and access to nature; on the other hand a reductive tendency issued in the foreclosure of mythical sense. Aristotle's metaphysical extension accomplished such a reduction by shaping reality according to an abstract detachment of conscious thought from the flux of lived experience. His conceptual methods proposed a universalization of only a certain kind of thought and experience. Accordingly, conscious knowledge was held to be sufficient for a grasp of reality, and consequently the highest value was given to a mode of apprehension which in fact was *limited* to consciousness, abstraction, and individuated form.

The whole of early Greek culture was founded upon extraconscious mythical forces. It is not the specific myths themselves that need to be defended but the subtextual sense of mythical disclosure. The integration of consciousness with something nonconscious speaks to the origins of disclosure as such. The notion of existential transcendence illuminates important meanings in appropriate ways. Tragic wisdom offers an accommodation with a world constituted by temporal negation. Finally, the mythical sense of mystery speaks to the limit of explanation which at a certain point is evident in *any* form of thinking. We found these insights to be implicit in myth and explicit to some extent in early philosophy. We can go further and suggest the inherence of a mythical dimension in all cultural and intellectual pursuits. If one were to argue for the mythical dimension of thought in any form, this would not infect thought with falsehood but only transform (and pluralize) the meaning of truth. Aristotle's philosophy is problematic only in the extent to which it arbitrarily exiled significant forms of sense that preceded it. Truth is not at issue here, only the reductive imperialism of a certain kind of truth.

Aristotle's efforts in this regard can best be illustrated by his "sacralization" of rationality. His rational paradigm was so exclusive and universal as to appear divine, thereby altering traditional models of virtue, human nature, and religious sensibility. The essence and aim of human life was identified with reason.

> So if among virtuous actions political and military actions are distinguished by nobility and greatness, and these are unleisurely and aim at an end and are not desirable for their own sake, but the activity of reason [*nous*], which is contemplative [*theōrētikē*], seems to be both superior in serious worth and to aim at no end beyond itself, and to have its pleasure proper to itself (and this augments the activity), and the self-sufficiency, leisureliness, unweariedness (so far as this is possible for man), and all the other attributes ascribed to the supremely happy man are evidently those connected with this activity, it follows that this will be the complete happiness [*eudaimonia*] of man. . . .
>
> But such a life would be too high for man; for it is not in so far as he is man that he will live so, but in so far as something divine is present in him; and by so much as this is superior to our composite nature is its activity superior to that which is the exercise of the other kind of virtue. If reason is divine, then, in comparison with man, the life according to it is divine in comparison with human life. . . . This would seem, too, to be each man himself, since it is the authoritative and better part of him. It would be strange, then, if he were to choose not the life of his self but that of something else. And what we said before will apply now; that which is proper to each thing is by nature best and most pleasant for each thing; for man, therefore, the life according to reason is best and pleasantest, since reason more than anything else *is* man. This life therefore is also the happiest. (*Nicomachean Ethics*, X.7.1177b15–1178a10)

This passage alone is sufficient to highlight the way in which Aristotle transformed the ideals of the early Greek world. We should close the chapter, however, by taking note of certain connections between Aristotelian thought and traditional elements in Greek culture.

# Traditional Elements in Aristotle's Thought

Despite his innovations, Aristotle still retained the legacy of his past in several respects, some of which would distinguish his philosophy from certain modern assumptions about human nature and the world.[33] Let us briefly outline a number of important examples.

## THE SOUL

According to Aristotle the soul is the form of the body. Such a notion compares favorably with the Homeric idea of *psychē* as life force, at least in contrast to Orphic and Pythagorean dualistic conceptions of the soul as separable from and in fact imprisoned in the body. For Aristotle the soul seems to represent the organized animation of a living body. Consequently, with the body's demise, the soul would also cease to be. There does not seem to be any sense of immortality in Aristotle's psychology, which of course shows a link with pre-Platonic viewpoints. Aristotle seemed, however, to sidestep the existential implications of finitude which inspired the tragic dimension of early Greek thought. In fact, rather than yield to mortality as such, Aristotle opted for the compensation of contemplation. Even though humans do not survive death and cannot enjoy the pure eternity of god (*Metaphysics*, XII.7.1072b15), nevertheless their rational nature participates in the divine eternity of thought, and contemplation gives humanity access in this life to immortal dimensions.

> If reason is divine, then, in comparison with man, the life according to it is divine in comparison with human life. But we must not follow those who advise us, being men, to think of human things, and, being mortal, of mortal things, but must, so far as we can, make ourselves immortal [*eph'hoson endechetai athanatizein*], and strain every nerve to live in accordance with the best thing in us; for even if it be small in bulk, much more does it in power and worth surpass everything. (*Nicomachean Ethics*, X.7.1177b30–1178a2)

## THE SOCIAL SELF

Aristotle retained the traditional notion of a social self and therefore would not connect the meaning of "human" with the modern notion of an isolated, private individual. Man is *physei politikon*, by *nature* a social being (*Nicomachean Ethics*, I.7.1097b12; the term *zōon* is added in the *Politics*, I.2.1253a2, thus "political animal"). Social and political relations are not second-order aspects of human nature; rather, they constitute the very meaning and fulfillment of humanity.

> He who by nature and not by mere accident is without a *polis*, is either a bad man or above humanity; he is like the "tribeless, lawless, hearthless one" whom Homer denounces (*Iliad*, IX.63); the natural outcast is forthwith a lover of war; he may be compared to an isolated piece at draughts. (*Politics*, I.2.1253a2–10)

## VIRTUE

The guiding principle in Aristotle's conception of virtue is the notion of a mean between extremes (*Nicomachean Ethics*, II.6). As we saw previously, the virtue of courage is the mean between cowardice and foolhardiness. We notice here a certain connection with the ancient idea of a balance of opposites (in Hesiod, Anaximander, and others). Aristotle's conception of virtue also reflected many traditional social values evident in early Greek culture. For example, moral goodness stems from inner excellence (*aretē*), i.e., character as opposed to rule-obeyance or fear of punishment. Virtue reflects the actualization of the human potential for goodness, and it is "aristocratic" to the extent that the measure of the good is the good man from whom goodness follows *naturally* after cultivation and habituation (see *Nicomachean Ethics*, IX.8). In addition, Aristotle's catalogue of virtues suggests a well-rounded natural life which would not entirely suit the Greek puritan and later Christian standards of virtue. The basic virtues include prudence, justice, moderation, and courage (the last of which Christian writers found perplexing). Aristotle's view of the good life also affirmed a number of elements found in Homeric social values: pleasure, wealth, honor, and even pride (*Nicomachean Ethics*, IV.3). Of course, he added intellectual virtues and deemed them superior to all others. The pursuit of philosophical wisdom was seen to be the epitome of human *aretē*.[34]

## TELEOLOGY

For Aristotle, *telos* (the end, purpose, or completion of a thing) is a *cause* of activity, not only in human production but in nature as well (*Physics*, II.7–8). In fact the very nature of a thing is identified with its *telos* (*Politics*, I.2.1252b30–35). *Telos* is also identified with goodness (*Metaphysics*, V.2.1013b25–30) and finally with the ultimate principle of the unmoved mover (XII.7–9).[35] Aristotle's teleology represents one of the basic differences between his and later forms of natural science. Indeed, such a contrast shows that Aristotelian science to some extent reflected certain prescientific viewpoints. For Aristotle, evaluative notions such as goodness and beauty were a part of nature and hence would not violate "objectivity." Furthermore, the idea that a goal is a *cause* of motion and is inherent in a thing's nature suggests a connection with mythical sense, namely, that something "more" than empirical immediacy accounts for the nature of things.[36] Finally, a certain natural pluralism follows from Aristotle's teleology since different purposes produce different natures and different causes of motion.[37]

The meaning of all this can be understood in terms of the reaction against Aristotle by proponents of the new science during the Enlightenment period. The modern conceptions of "empirical fact" and "natural causality" were born out of a rejection of Aristotelian final cause. States of completion were no longer causes but effects; purposes were no longer a part of nature; they were reduced to human interpretations of natural processes. What remained was a principle of causality limited to *antecedent* causes (in line with what Aristotle called efficient cause). The idea of a "future cause" did not suit the stricter empiricism of the new age. The result was a purely mechanical picture of the world, where purposes and values were not necessary in an account of nature. Finally, causality was interpreted according to a paradigm of *uniformity*. Aristotle had proposed that different things move in different ways because of their different natures (e.g., it is the nature of heavenly bodies to move in a circle). Newtonian physics introduced a uniform law of motion which accounts for all kinds of motion in terms of a single principle (every body left to itself moves in a straight line at a uniform speed; interferences with this standard state account for different motions). Mathematics became the primary tool of scientific thinking since perceived phenomena alone could not suffice for such a paradigm. The conceptual tendency toward uniformity was finally maximized, quite beyond anything intended by Aristotle.[38]

## INTUITION

For all his emphasis on demonstration, explanation, and definition, Aristotle did not ignore the role of intuition, or underived insight, in the process of knowledge. Although he did not share Plato's belief that intellectual intuition was the privilege of the select few, he did recognize that the *foundations* of rational knowledge are themselves underived and in a sense given.

> Scientific knowledge [*epistēmē*] is judgment about things that are universal and necessary, and the conclusions of demonstration, and all scientific knowledge, follow from first principles (for scientific knowledge involves apprehension of a rational ground). This being so, the first principles from which what is scientifically known follows cannot be an object of scientific knowledge, of art, or of practical wisdom; for that which can be scientifically known can be

demonstrated, and art and practical wisdom deal with things that are variable. Nor are these first principles the objects of philosophic wisdom, for it is the mark of the philosopher to have *demonstration* about some things. . . . The remaining alternative is that it is intuitive reason [*nous*] that grasps the first principles. (*Nicomachean Ethics*, VI.6)

Aristotle here acknowledges something widely recognized in the history of philosophy: First principles ground our knowledge of the world, but they themselves are not demonstrable. They are simply self-evident to the intellect as the fundamental starting point. We notice here something which spotlights a key question in our investigation. Aristotle did not find the "underived" character of first principles to be a problem or worthy of question as such. One reason for this is simple: Like many philosophers after him, he proposed a *metaphysical* ground for first principles in the form of a divine mind, a kind of resolution which in effect intercepts and disarms the problem. This, however, only *extends* the problem of underivability beyond the human mind and of course creates additional problems for philosophy (the knowledge of god). But even in nontheological and nonmetaphysical developments in western thought, the "self-evidency" of certain basic principles continued to be unproblematic. Self-evidency meant much more than simply something exhibiting itself (many things exhibit themselves and yet are problematic); it meant self-justifying and thus "beyond question." Although they are underived, first principles were unproblematic because the conceptual aims of philosophy *demanded* them. Our historical investigation shows the way here. The philosophers rejected mythical disclosure in favor of conceptual universals which could resolve the vicissitudes, uncertainties, and temporality of the lived world. First principles were beyond question because of *those* aims and not because they were inherently unquestionable. Indeed, the history of Greek culture shows alternative forms of sense, which makes the self-evidency of rational principles *highly* problematic (not to the extent that they are disclosed, i.e., evident to the human mind, but to the extent that they become the measure of *any* form of disclosure).

Accordingly we can close this chapter with some questions which will prepare the conclusion of our investigation. If rational principles are themselves underived, should this not then raise legitimate questions as to how they are disclosed, questions which take us *outside* rational paradigms? Would it not be the case that an underivable *disclosing* of rational principles takes precedence over rationality, and that consequently emphasizing a *process* of disclosure as such makes mysterious any paradigmatic *product* of disclosure (since any explanation would itself also have to be disclosed)? If rational principles are ultimately underived, on what grounds can they be used to judge other forms of disclosure which exhibit sense without them? If rationality is underived and simply given, is it not as such comparable in some way to a myth (i.e., something meaningful but without a foundation)? Keep in mind that such questions are not meant to attack the importance or function of reason, or to suggest that scientific methods, for example, are no different from mythical accounts, or that mythical accounts could somehow replace or match scientific explanations. We simply notice a *pluralistic* model of truth which retains much of the sense of myth. Scientific and rational paradigms, from the standpoint of their *establishment*, are no more "justified" than the deities of Greek myth.

# IX

# The Relationship between Philosophy and Myth

## Summary Conclusions and Reflections

On the basis of our analysis, a number of conclusions emerge which go beyond the historical treatment and raise important questions regarding philosophy and rationality in general.

1. The historical development of rationality at the expense of myth did not represent the discovery of truth to replace the ignorance or fictions of the past but rather a *different* view of the world based upon different and *selective* assumptions.

2. The idea of mythical *sense*, together with the selectivity of philosophy, suggest that myth too is a form of truth. A defense of myth is not intended to cast doubt on rationality as such, however, but only on a strictly rational or uniform conception of truth.

3. There is a certain incommensurability between mythical language and rational/scientific language; neither form can be meaningfully translated into the other without subverting their appropriate aims. Incommensurability, however, is not a problem if a pluralistic model of truth is adopted.

4. Both the lived world and much of human thought show meaningful echoes of mythical disclosure. The emphasis, however, should not be put on specific mythical images but on the implicit *meanings* analyzed in our study.

5. At a certain point, rationality and even science show something comparable to the nonfactual and existential elements of myth.

6. Finally, therefore, the idea of rationality *versus* myth is both misleading and at times simply wrong because rationality and myth can overlap, and even when they do not overlap it is not an either-or situation. Our historical study has shown that rationality and myth *have* coexisted, *can* coexist and, I would suggest, *should* coexist.[1]

## PLATONIC PHILOSOPHY

Philosophy as it was embodied in Platonism can be understood in two senses: (1) the nature and importance of philosophical issues, insights, and methods which came to shape the course of intellectual history; and (2) the emergence of philosophy as a reaction against and dissatisfaction with a previous form of culture embodied in myth and poetry. This investigation is *not* taking issue with the first point (how could it, since it is a philosophical analysis?); the critique of philosophy involves the second point. Since mythical disclosure can be seen to be coherent on its own terms, questions arise regarding the judgment of myth; or regarding the justification for seeing philosophy as a displacement of myth (rather than as an *added* dimension of thought).

Nietzsche is famous for trying to undermine Plato's judgment of myth by tracing the emergence of philosophy to certain psychological factors such as an inability or refusal to accept the lived world (which is constituted by becoming, negativity, and uncertainty). If rationality can be traced to "all too human" dispositions, then the "objective" support for philosophy disappears. But we need not psychologize philosophy in order to question its status in relation to myth. If we attend to philosophy as a historical phenomenon and acknowledge the forms of sense that preceded it (i.e., a coherent world *without* philosophy), then the following question arises: On what grounds could the advent of philosophical insights and methods be called a correction of the past or a form of progress?

One could never deny that the emergence of rationality and scientific thinking was an event of monumental importance. The question is: How can it be said that such developments brought us "closer to the truth" or at least the proper method for its discovery? To argue that philosophy brought about progress because myth and poetry did not understand the world rationally or empirically would, of course, beg the question. It seems to me that the only successful argument for progress in the strict sense would require some kind of suprahistorical or supracultural vantage point from which one could measure such a development. Furthermore, one would have to account for the "ignorance" of the previous period. From a suprahistorical vantage point, one answer would be some notion of a fall (otherwise why would the truth go unheeded for so long?), but surely such an account sounds like a myth. Short of a fall, one might suppose that truth simply takes time, that it is progressively revealed out of a state of ignorance, that somehow we are initially immersed in a corrigible view of the world which requires a gradual resolution. But how do we know *this* is true? Where was truth before its discovery? Why did it remain hidden? What is reality like, such that this situation obtains? Would we not need access to truth independent of its historical discovery in order to equate rationality and truth, to account for progress? Something like a fall from truth might then seem more attractive to account for prior ignorance.

The point is that both notions of a suprahistorical truth and a fall *were* proposed by Plato (in the Forms and recollection). The problem, of course, is that these notions are more like myths than rational or empirical truths. Accordingly, modern thinking has come to distrust or reject such notions. However, even though western thought, especially in its scientific emphasis, has come to reject Plato's version of universals and the metaphysical dualism apparent in his philosophy, nevertheless it has *continued* in various ways to reflect certain Platonic assumptions with respect to the status of mytho-poetic disclosure and the lived world. A metaphysical myth has been replaced by a methodological one which is similar in spirit to Plato's cave allegory and which, I think, is historically linked to Platonism—namely, the idea that there is something wrong with or limited in the way we first encounter the world, especially in our affective life. For example, existential concerns tell us nothing about the world itself, only about human values which at best are neither true nor false but which accordingly must be screened out if objective truth is to be discovered.

Surely objectivity has its place and tells us much about the world; and with respect to the specific aims of science, certain forms of disclosure do indeed have to be screened out. But the shift to objective methods is one thing; the "correction" of preobjective disclosure, another thing entirely. The spirit of Platonism is evident in a kind of objective imperialism which judges other forms of disclosure and which, despite its rejection of Plato's *metaphysical* dualism, espouses a derivative (and equally suspect) *methodological* split. Even with respect to rational and empirical methods, where is it written that lived experience must be modified or corrected in order to find truth?

The long-standing antagonism between philosophy/science and the lived world of myth shows that modern rationality is still Platonic in certain respects. I believe it was no accident that Plato, the philosopher who first set the stage for conceptual reason, proposed a two-worlds scheme; western rationality in different ways has exhibited variations on a theme first sketched in Plato's allegory of the cave. Any doctrine of truth which screens out, suspends, or rejects other forms of disclosure that find a place in culture and which considers them outside the realm of truth, would have to be Platonic in some respects or else that doctrine would seem arbitrary. Plato's "suspicious" notions of eternal Forms and the fall of the soul should be taken very seriously because without them the *justification* for his rejection of traditional myth would be lost. A transcendent viewpoint which hovers above time and culture would seem to be required if other forms of culture are to be measured. The equivalence of rationality and truth has become so established that its historical dependence on Platonic transcendence has faded from view. But accordingly, if Platonic transcendence seems indeed mythical to the modern mind, then it might follow that the justification for the rationality-truth equation and the idea of "progress" from myth to philosophy are themselves myths. This would not make them false (especially considering the possibility that such ideas may have been historically necessary for the *establishment* of philosophy in the midst of already established and well entrenched forms of culture). A mythical interpretation of such ideas would simply refer to the way in which they should be understood and also to the absence of an ultimate foundation by means of which other forms of disclosure could be excluded from the realm of truth. The mythical element would allow us to conclude that with respect to truth we are not always bound by categories and methods of philosophy and science, which categories and methods have remained in principle unchanged from the start regarding the "demotion" of myth, poetry, and the lived world. We are free to say that the world can be legitimately disclosed in ways other than established rational methods and principles.

## PHILOSOPHY AND EXISTENTIAL MEANING

Plato's philosophy was indeed very important and decisive for western intellectual history; but side by side with his rational discourse we found a mythical dimension. The myths about the fall of the soul, recollection, and eternal Forms, were not simply an incidental embellishment of philosophical issues. Platonic myths express the *tension* between rational inquiry and the lived world. In this way Platonism was more revealing than modern apologists who might say that the two-worlds doctrine merely symbolizes elements in the rational enterprise, and who thereby fail to acknowledge that there *is* a tension, a battle, a moral element. For Plato, philosophy was desirable and preferable to the world which was celebrated in myth. Furthermore, for Plato as *innovator*, it was more evident that philosophy has to "fight off" the lived world. Platonic myths can be read in terms of the existential significance of his philosophical endeavor, namely, moral, aesthetic, transformative, edificatory, and even salvific aims. Philosophy for Plato elevates and improves the human condition; it stabilizes human understanding in a chaotic world, resolves negativity, and overcomes fatalism. In other words, Platonic myths speak directly to certain nonobjective features of philosophy. Rationality has an existential dimension, a level of meaning which is correlated with human existence and concerns, and which is therefore not *purely* objective.

The issue of existential meaning can illuminate the connection between philosophy and myth, a connection which was quite explicit in Platonism and yet which can be implicitly evident in any form of thinking. As was said earlier, even science has to matter to human beings; one would be hard pressed to strictly separate this existential element from the overall process of scientific inquiry. Furthermore, evaluative judgments and even aesthetic sensibilities are never entirely absent from science (e.g., ideals of honesty and unbiased research; the preference for order and simplicity; motivations for theory-choice; the elegance of a mathematical proof).[2]

Our previous discussion of justification fits in here as well. Uniformity, conformity, universality, regularity, and predictability are all essential components of conceptual, empirical, and scientific thinking; and yet these components themselves cannot be justified (being the *conditions* for justification). At this paradigmatic level, an attempt at justification leads to an infinite regress. A type of ground might be located in certain consequences, such as pragmatic or psychological benefits (e.g., regularity permitting control of the environment, or the edifying effects of certainty and familiarity), but in the face of such human contingencies, an *objective* ground seems lacking, and the best that can be said is: "We are simply better off being rational; the alternative is unacceptable." Fine, but what, then, is truth? Where is it written that predictability, for example, is a necessary condition for truth, that something unpredictable is not yet properly known? The *value* of predictability may be the only recourse, but this is surely contingent and nonobjective (since it seems human-dependent and thus would tell us nothing about the world itself).

The point here is not to dismiss reason, empirical facts, prediction, and science, or to label them "subjective." We only want to unmask the

pretense of strict objectivity and subvert the exclusive identification of
these components with truth (i.e., the "isms" that extend knowledge
into a kind of metaphysics: rationalism, empiricism, positivism, and
the like). We have seen that existential meaning in a mythical world
need not be called subjective. The situation here is the same. Empirical
facts and conceptual order do disclose elements of the world, but that
disclosure is not entirely separable from existential meanings. Two
related conclusions follow: (1) The existential connection ruins the
presumption of strict objectivity and necessity. (2) Other forms of disclosure which exhibit existential meaning can no longer be judged deficient on that score.

We have seen how mythical sense can disclose much that is true
about the world, important elements of meaning and culture which rational and scientific models cannot or do not properly disclose. Now
we notice a certain existential dimension in rationality as well. It
would then follow that no form of thought is thoroughly objective or
"value free." Existential conditions certainly exclude any notion of an
absolute, fixed standpoint (compare the sense of plurality and appearance in mythical disclosure); but not only is absolute truth in question,
so too is the absolute status of any particular *approach* to truth (which
need not possess the truth to think itself the proper *method*). Would
this not make truth relative or subjective? Not so, since relativism and
subjectivism are simply *inversions* of absolutism and objectivism,
which if rejected at the start would render their inversions moot. Our
position does not rob rationality of truth; it only indicates that the
world can be disclosed in many ways, leading to a pluralistic notion of
truth(s). The existential element does not relativize or subjectify truth
but rather opens it up. Truth can now embrace many forms of disclosure rather than be measured by one particular form of disclosure.

Rationality makes possible a form of truth in which things can be
traced to conceptual or empirical warrants. In many contexts this
works quite well and tells us much about the world. But rationality *itself* has no objective foundation. We can understand this from a logical
standpoint (the attempt to find a reason for rationality leads to an infinite regress), a historical standpoint (rationality emerged as a cultural
"contestant"), or an existential standpoint (the evaluative background). If rationality as such lacks an objective foundation, then in
this respect it is analogically *mythical* in character, either in terms of
the absence of justification (thereby sharing the mythical sense of appearance) or in terms of the existential element, or both. This does not

make a particular rational account of things the same as a mythical account; the analogy refers to the *establishment* of rationality, which is paradigmatically prior to its execution.

After Plato, philosophy tried to strip away the mythical elements which accompanied its inception. Aristotle called for a greater degree of objectivity, less imagery and story-telling; and his dismissal of Plato's images of transcendence signaled a turn from the sacred to the profane. But one need not take Plato's myths literally to defend the meaning of his mythical presentations. Perhaps Plato had more insight regarding the existential aspects of philosophy (and the nonobjective background of its historical establishment). Later developments took Plato's gift and yet assumed the need for greater and greater precision and objectivity, thereby pushing the existential elements aside. Plato's myths need not be read as mistaken attempts at objective explanation but as an expression of the nonobjective meanings pervading philosophical inquiry (i.e., its benefits, its "contentious" relation to other forms of disclosure, its moral and psychological implications, the elusive advent of philosophical insight).

Aristotle's mistake was not in promoting and polishing rational inquiry but in presuming that philosophy was utterly different from mythical disclosure; the groundlessness of rationality and its existential background make that presumption highly questionable. There are indeed important differences between philosophy and myth, but at certain levels there are striking similarities. The problem with philosophy is not that it moved away from mythical imagery but simply that it took itself to be *nothing like* myth.[3] Existential and mythical elements are not sufficient conditions for philosophical and scientific inquiry, but I would say they are necessary conditions. Consequently, any account of philosophy and science which excludes existential and mythical elements is likewise not sufficient.[4]

Philosophy disclosed important elements of thought but erred in tending toward a metaphysical *reduction* of thought to those elements, to the exclusion of other important elements. In other words, it reduced the *process* of disclosure to a particular *product* of disclosure. Reason is one thing, rationalism another; empirical facts one thing, empiricism or empirical realism another; logic and concepts one thing, uniformity another; philosophy one thing, metaphysics another. The former in each set are legitimate phenomena: they are not simply subjective but are ways in which the world is disclosed. The latter in each set, however, can be traced to the *human* concern for certainty, the desire to ward off plurality and negativity in favor of a reduction to form (as opposed to the "groundlessness" of form in disclosure as a sheer appearing, a correlation of form and formlessness). The former in each set can reflect the nonsubjective self-world correlation that was characteristic of mythical disclosure. The latter, however, reflect a reduction to human consciousness and human concerns, and it is here that the existential element goes beyond mythical disclosure (compare tragic fatalism). The latter "isms" polarize truth and can be criticized accordingly; *they* can be deemed subjective and dispensable. For example, an empirical method is a form of truth; but the claim that empirical facts alone count for truth (empiricism) can be traced to all too human contingencies. Only the latter "isms," and not the former phenomena, are properly susceptible to Nietzsche's psychological critique in that the former tell us much about the world while the latter tell us what the human subject *wants* the world to be. The tendency to resist or reject negativity and mystery in the world was a key element in the development from myth to philosophy in Greece. *That* tendency betrays the supposition that philosophy was a liberation from error to truth (rather than a different form of truth). *That* tendency pushed philosophy beyond its form of disclosure to something unwarranted—the "isms" which reduce truth to their form of disclosure and which reflect human dispositions rather than the world.

Plato's eternal Forms and Aristotle's eternal god above time were not accidental or incidental. Those thinkers found the immediate lived world to be an obstacle for knowledge. Conceptual reason seemed to demand some kind of separation from the lived world. But one can certainly question this separation and its dispositional background. Philosophy can be seen in a new light wherein it is integrated with the lived world and thereby closer to myth. This does not threaten philosophical truth; it only revises it. Philosophy (especially in its inception) shows itself to have much in common with myth. The philosophical "isms," however, are characterized by the mistaken assumption that they are nonmythical, that their forms of disclosure reveal an objective, fixed reference point for truth, and are therefore nothing like the conditions of myth. In relation to mythical disclosure and meaning, that assumption can be criticized as a reduction of truth to a human interest in certainty, as the reduction of disclosure to a particular product of disclosure, and as the reduction of the world to conceptual forms in the conscious mind. In this respect we realize that the historical emergence of human self-consciousness was a two-edged sword. On the one hand it allowed the development of rationality; on the other hand it produced an overemphasis on rationality and the conscious subject which ushered in a rupture with myth and a highly questionable polarization of truth.

## CONSCIOUSNESS

Our study has shown that "human nature" has not always been limited to the conscious self. The idea that consciousness is influenced by nonconscious forces has, of course, been recognized in modern thought, most notably in the work of Freud. Freud's revolutionary discovery was simply a rediscovery of something ancient, however (and it was prefigured in many ways in the work of Schopenhauer and Nietzsche). But the crucial point is that we cannot confine this discovery to psychological matters. Most of the assumptions of philosophical thinking and the developments of modern thought stem from consciousness or a fixation on the contents of the conscious mind. The obvious example is Descartes's isolation of the *cogito* as the fundamental starting point for thought. Philosophical objections to Cartesian rationalism do not change the fact that Descartes crystallized an assumption at work in *all* forms of rationality beginning with Plato: namely, disclosure of the world in terms of "ideas" (rationalists and empiricists disagree only with respect to the *origin* of ideas and the proper methodology). Ideas are mental formulations which abstract from experience by means of the reflective "distance" of consciousness from the lived world, whereby the conscious mind as detached "subject" renders the world an "object." Kant explicated this common element in philosophical thinking by showing that knowledge of the world cannot be understood apart from the activity of the mind. But our study has shown that the "conscious mind" is not a timeless paradigm. We have seen that the development of rationality was indeed matched by self-conscious individuation; but as a *historical* phenomenon, the coincidence of consciousness and rationality raises questions about the absolute status of that form of disclosure.[5]

The transition from myth to rationality was made possible by the ascendancy of consciousness. In mythical disclosure the self was contextual and passive, in that it was embedded in a field of meanings and was a "receiver" of existential imagery. Rationality emerged through the isolation of the receiver from its field, the independence of consciousness from the lived, sensuous imagery of myth, and the detachment of consciousness which generated its own peculiar form of disclosure, namely, abstraction. Mythical disclosure was neither factual nor objective nor fixed; it was more an aesthetic process, a form-ing and ordering in the midst of an existential field (in which formlessness and disorder still persist). In mythical disclosure its form was determined by its (existential) content. Rationality and logic represented the liberation of form and order from any particular content, with the result being the determination of content by principles of form and order. Disclosure was no longer a process of appearing in the midst of negativity but rather a discovery of fixed forms and orderly patterns— hence the first philosophers' objections to myths with their mysteries, existential plurality, and fatalism. But that revolutionary development was animated by the crystallization of self-consciousness, because it was the new paradigmatic complex of interiority, unity, and autonomy that permitted *detachment* from the lived world and the process of appearing.

The connection between self-consciousness, abstraction, and rationality helps illuminate the historical coexistence of distinct but correlated developments in the course of western thought, a coexistence which accordingly can be understood as anything but accidental or coincidental. Those developments include:

1. the **mind conceived as an active power** (initiating its activity and "working on" its objects)
2. the encouragement of **free inquiry and criticism** over against the forces of tradition and religious revelation
3. the emergence of **individualism** in various forms over against the forces of social control
4. political revolutions based upon the rejection of aristocratic and authoritarian rule in favor of **democratic values** such as common **individual rights**, **individual liberty**, and **individual freedom of thought**
5. the **abstract ordering of nature** in the sciences
6. the extension of **abstract principles** to their own realm of generality in metaphysics
7. an interest in theology because of the need to ground rational ideas in a **divine mind**
8. a concern for the **preservation of consciousness** in a religious doctrine of immortality

9. the **rational control of the disruptive passions**, a priority shared to a certain degree by religion, philosophy, and science.

Although these developments have not all always been coordinated (especially in our age), nevertheless the Enlightenment period of the seventeenth and eighteenth centuries did represent a fabric of concerns which included them all. The overlapping interests of philosophers such as Descartes (science, metaphysics, theology), Locke (science, psychology, democratic politics), and Kant (science, moral theory, religious belief) as well as the overall complex of interests in their period of history can, I think, be understood at least partly in terms of the correlation between self-consciousness and abstraction. Furthermore, that correlation shows itself to be a departure from the lived world which characterized the sense of mythical disclosure.

Our study of the Greeks has also prepared an answer to another important question. The *historical* nature of self-consciousness and rationality (as well as the connections with myth exhibited in the historical transition from myth to reason) undermine the presumption of their absolute priority or status. Accordingly we can better understand why, despite the influence and progress of rationality, an interest in myth has never disappeared. Even when reason came to demote myths, they maintained an influence in the form of allegory or symbolism. The lasting importance of art is nothing less than the vestiges of a mythical heritage.

But more than that, it would no longer be such a surprise that the history of culture exhibits the continuing presence of mythical and nonrational elements. A rationalist should no longer be shocked about the apparent paradox of our own age: The growth of science, technology, and rationality coming to meet stiff resistance from some quarters; and even the serious resurgence of many nonrational attitudes. Religious and nonscientific beliefs are as strong as ever in our century. Anti-individual and anti-intellectual forces have asserted themselves in political movements and religious cults. The lure of the "irrational" has not been stemmed. There is a fascination with primitive cultures, and that fascination has found expression in many of the arts. The question, of course, is: Why should such things happen in an age of science and reason? This is a "problem" only because of the intellectual fixation on paradigms established in the Enlightenment. The so-called crisis of the early twentieth century was defined according to the Enlightenment belief in rational progress, which was threatened by shocking wars of destruction, among other things. Nonscientific attitudes are a problem only from the standpoint of positivistic paradigms. The "threat" from nonconscious and extra-individual forces is such only from the standpoint of a consciousness paradigm.

I hasten to add that an abandonment of rationality is an undesirable and dangerous thing. Much of what philosophy has given us is a great blessing. But one should not be shocked or surprised by the continuing presence and influence of counter-rational forces in human culture. Beyond certain social and political dangers (which we *ought* to oppose), the threats to rationality and the Enlightenment paradigms need not be regarded as a lapse into ignorance or a form of cultural regression but rather as the continuation of the cultural contest which was exhibited in Greek history and which reveals the historical, situational, and therefore *limited* status of rational paradigms with respect to disclosure of the world. There is something important in various challenges to rationality; their persistence in history and culture is no threat to truth. There is no crisis here, only a pluralization of truth.

# Myth and Nonobjective Aspects of Thought

## MYTH, FACT, AND MYSTERY

In common usage a myth is something that is not grounded in fact and on that account false. In the background, of course, is the assumption that factuality is the measure of truth. A fact is said to be fixed and certain by means of a reduction to some stable standard (either empirical or conceptual), and on that account "objectively true." Our investigation, however, has aimed to establish the following: Much that is important and true is nonobjective and not grounded in facts, including the assumption of factual objectivity itself. To say, for example, that facts give us truth and that myths do not, is not itself a factual statement. It requires some metafactual vantage point which identifies facts with reality. To say that a myth is not a factual claim is clear enough indeed (even consistent with the meaning of mythical disclosure), but to say that a myth is not on that account true, is not only to say that facts are facts but that facts equal truth; and *this* goes beyond the facts, in much the same way, I would suggest, as a myth does. But if factuality itself must transcend facts, then the nonfactual nature of myth is no absolute argument against its truth. We have established that the truth of mythical disclosure involves prefactual and preobjective meanings. Such a designation reflects two essential components: (1) *the absence of an objective foundation* (cf. the mythical sense of appearance, mystery, and givenness); and (2) *existential significance*. If we look behind mythical imagery to such background meanings we find a way to connect myth with supposedly nonmythical forms of thought.

We have discussed Aristotle's insight concerning the indemonstrability of philosophical first principles.

> . . . not all knowledge is demonstrative: on the contrary, knowledge of the immediate premises is independent of demonstration. The necessity of this is obvious; for since we must know the prior premises from which the demonstration is drawn, and since the regress must end in immediate truths, those truths must be indemonstrable. (*Posterior Analytics*, I.3.19–23)

Philosophers since Aristotle have recognized the indemonstrability of first principles; they cannot themselves be justified since they are the conditions for justification. The philosophers, however, were tied to these principles as fixed conditions for truth, and hence they did not find the issue of indemonstrability *as such* problematic or worthy of thought. For instance, in the above remarks Aristotle simply declares that the regress *must* end. Since he is interested in conceptual certainty, demonstration, and grounding, he is not troubled that these principles have no foundation. Rather than see them as "groundless," he declares them to be "self-evidently true."

But in a way, Aristotle *was* aware of the problematic nature of indemonstrability; that can be inferred from his appeal to a divine mind meant to ground first principles and represent a kind of source or first cause. This, of course, only extends the problem by graduating it to another level, but it should be pointed out that philosophers for a long time continued such a reduction to a divine mind, which might reflect their uneasiness about indemonstrability. At least they were implicitly acknowledging a problem, even though their solution might be questioned. The same could not be said for post-theological doctrines which uncritically employ rational paradigms without sensing a kind of abyss beyond their borders. The point is this: Short of a theological solution, even rational and scientific paradigms run up against a mystery, which stated positively just means the givenness of fundamental assumptions, the origin of which simply cannot be disclosed on rational or scientific grounds. One might say they simply *are* disclosed, or *appear*; one might have recourse to the existential meaningfulness of such paradigms. Either way, the mythical sense of existential givenness has not been completely abandoned.

Aristotle himself referred to the existential element in knowledge when in the very first sentence of the *Metaphysics* he declares that "all men by nature desire to know." Here it is not knowledge that comes first but desire. In other words, knowledge must first matter to human beings. But why should knowledge matter? A host of answers might surface: it aids in survival; it satisfies a need for certainty and familiarity; it overcomes a sense of fear and anxiety in the face of the unknown; it speaks to the adventure of the quest and the sheer joy of discovery. None of these, of course, is an "objective" answer, but they are not on that account "subjective" either. Phenomenologically speaking, human beings do not first find themselves "projecting" such values onto a neutral world. The world is first *disclosed* in such an existential context, an intimate correlation which precedes any demarcation into subjective and objective spheres.

The indemonstrability of rational paradigms has led us to an existential element and a kind of mystery. Why do human beings desire to know? That question cannot be answered since no answer (knowledge) would exhaust the question. The issue of circularity has always been a problem in philosophy; but at a certain point it should no longer be a problem, but rather a "virtuous" circle. Paradigms turn back upon themselves and run up against something ungraspable. From the standpoint of justification, that would make any paradigm itself groundless. On *that* score, rational paradigms are no better than mythical paradigms and cannot claim any privileged status. But the circularity of paradigms would not make them any less true either, as long as truth can be understood in an expanded, extraparadigmatic way, namely, a kind of existential givenness, the origin of which is a mystery.

In other words, at a certain point one can find a mythical element in all forms of thought, in terms of mystery, appearance, givenness, and existential meaning. Not all forms of thought employ mythical imagery, but the background sense of mythical disclosure analyzed in this investigation allows us to see a connection. Rationality and science exhibit elements of preobjective and existential meaning which disclose the world in an analogously mythical way. Mythical *imagery* can be understood as a concrete expression of existential givenness in that living sacred forces are seen to embody and grant those elements of meaning which simply appear to consciousness as given. In fact, the sacred transcendence of mythical imagery only highlights the extrahuman sense of these elements, i.e., that they constitute the *world* and are not just a human construction. By way of summarizing the relationship between myth and other forms of knowledge, it would not be entirely nonsensical to talk of science, for example, as a "gift of the gods" or account for its origin with some adventure tale. Such talk would not in any way affect the way science works and would actually express much of its meaningfulness as well as the "virtuousness" of the paradigmatic circle.

Our study allows us to talk of a mythical background of science because the truth of myth refers to existential meaning, something which is bound to emerge when we ask the question: Why science? Such a question forbids any scientific or objective answer. Again, certain meanings might well come to mind: the adventure of inquiry and discovery, with its inherent joys and satisfactions; the automatic human drive to know; the need to master the earth through technology; the practical benefits that follow from science. None of these factors is strictly objective since they seem human-dependent. But since these meanings also seem inseparable from the practice of science, one would not want to segregate them from science by proposing a subjective sphere in some way parallel to the objective sphere. The relationship seems much too intimate for that. At the same time, one would not want to "anthropologize" science either, because of the way science works and is practiced: Science sees itself responding *to* and guided *by* events in the *world*; and the world responds *back* to scientific inquiry, displaying a decidedly extrahuman confirmation. Such a phenomenological view of science makes the notion of a human "superimposition" entirely inappropriate.

Now, an effective way of expressing the existential meaning of science without a subjective/humanistic slant would be a myth, namely, an existential, nonobjective image which tells the "story" of science and at the same time expresses its extrahuman aspect by way of sacred imagery above and beyond humanity as such, an image of a granting which speaks to the issue of paradigmatic givenness. One might resist such a suggestion, but I would say that a myth at least is *no worse* than any other attempt to express such matters.[6]

## SUBJECTIVITY, OBJECTIVITY, AND PLURALISM

We have seen that the Greek mythical world was essentially pluralistic as opposed to the tendencies in philosophy toward uniformity and reductionism. Whatever motivations supported those tendencies, it was only on *that* account that mythical disclosure was exiled from the realm of truth. Our historical analysis of philosophy and the question of paradigmatic circularity have weakened the presumptions of uniformity and reductionism, thereby suggesting a pluralized coexistence of different forms of disclosure. The notion of pluralism is not meant in any way to subjectify truth. In fact the distinction between objectivity and subjectivity—i.e., between truth and opinion, fact and value, the world in itself and the human response to the world—that distinction was a philosophical construction which was meant to overcome the variability and existential dimension of the lived world. Such a distinction *can* find a legitimate use but not as an absolute standard for truth. Myth can no longer be exiled from truth on the grounds of its nonobjective character. But a call for a pluralistic coexistence of truths does not in any way entail objectifying myth or subjectifying rationality. The subject-object distinction itself ought to be questioned, and for a number of reasons.

First, the subject-object distinction is a historical and circumstantial phenomenon which has no absolute foundation. The mythical sense of existential transcendence reflected a form of disclosure which could not be sufficiently understood by means of that distinction. The suggested relationship between myth and philosophy hints at a model of thinking which is at once nonobjective and nonsubjective. "Subject" and "object" polarize an original correlation of self and world which was evident in the beginnings of culture and which continued to be evident in the advent of philosophy. The subject-object model, then, is not one to which we need be bound.

Secondly, modern philosophy has shown that the strict distinction between subject and object may be unwarranted because of the inseparability and correlative nature of the components. What we call "objective" may actually be constituted by subjectivity. From an epistemological standpoint, this has been an animating insight ever since Descartes and Kant. But there the subject was still a ground of knowledge, a kind of objective reference (rational faculties) to be distinguished from existential subjectivity (i.e., emotions, values, and such). Existential philosophers have argued against the separation of values from knowledge, however, and claimed that what is called objective is nothing more than an unwarranted detachment from existential concerns which can never be separated from our knowledge of the world.

Thirdly, although we might well fear that defending the truth-value of existential concerns or mythical disclosure might subjectify truth, that fear is dependent upon the subject-object distinction holding sway. To defend nonobjective modes of disclosure, and indeed propose the nonobjective element in all forms of disclosure, is not to subjectify but pluralize truth. If it were not for the connotations of "objectivity," one might propose the term "objective pluralism" to indicate the *legitimacy* of different though coexisting modes of disclosure (i.e., science, myth, art, and values); but in order to do this, the subject-object distinction must be suspended. If one were to limit the truth of rationality and science, for example, the last thing one would want to do is subjectify truth, because this would simply continue a segregation which a phenomenological view of knowledge would not permit. In the same way that myth is not subjective, science is certainly not a mere human projection but a disclosure of the *world* (more accurately, *part* of the world).

What is implied here is the collapse of the fact-value distinction. The disclosure of scientific facts is inseparable from certain values, and the dismissal of values from the realm of truth can seem counterintuitive (is my aversion to torture merely a matter of opinion?). Some have tried to propose an objective foundation for values (a hard task indeed). Another strategy, however, is to argue against strict objectivity in *any* form of thought. Then the nonobjective feature of values would not be a fatal problem; nor would "facts" be threatened. The way in which we *understand* them would simply change. The categories "objective" and "subjective" would no longer be sufficient. A fact would no longer stand for pure objectivity, and a value need no longer be called "merely" subjective.

The tendency to subjectify knowledge is often irresistible when an "absolute" standard is found lacking, but that tendency simply continues a highly dubious separation of mind and world, and tends to cast doubt on the authority of the knowledge in question. What follows are such things as epistemological and ethical relativism and phenomenalism. But such developments are a kind of perversion which stems from a dishonest intellectual revelry, an insincere display of mental gymnastics which in fact demonstrates the limitations of the subject-object distinction. Phenomenologically speaking, no one who *prac-

*tices* science or *holds* ethical values or *responds* to beauty or *engages* in philosophical inquiry ever perceives such activity to be a subjective projection upon a neutral or unknowable world. The direction is decidedly *from* the world, no matter how much the activity requires the participation of the subject. The tendency toward subjectivism is simply an unbridled application of the distinction between mind and world which characterized the emergence of philosophy. We did not find such a distinction in mythical disclosure, where the mind was decidedly passive, uncritical, and *receptive* to sacred meanings. Philosophy was animated by a critical demarcation between mind and world, between individual inquiry and tradition. That demarcation permitted the kind of doubt and questioning spirit necessary for philosophy and science. On the other hand, mythical disclosure offers a valuable counterweight to subjectivism, which really amounts to *excessive* doubt, to the point where disclosure is separated from the *world*.

In science and philosophy a critical spirit is necessary and valuable (here a subject-object distinction might find a legitimate use), but criticism oversteps its limits when something like skepticism is proposed, where one doubts the existence of the external world or other minds or the validity of knowledge in general. Here the skeptic must ignore or suspend practical certainties about the world (as does Hume), contradict his intention to communicate, or indeed undermine the legitimacy of his own inquiry and conclusions. The critical spirit also gets into trouble when it questions the truth claims of moral and aesthetic values, when such values so decisively *claim* us in important ways. We will shortly develop this issue further, but at this point I only mean to say that the fear of subjectivism is unnecessary even if strict objectivity is abandoned. Such things as subjectivism, relativism, and skepticism are in fact pseudoproblems perpetuated by certain philosophical constructions. Philosophy did not discover these problems, it *created* them as a result of a mind-world, subject-object distinction which was set up only *after* the inception of philosophy.[7]

## MYTH, SCIENCE, AND EXPLANATION

The historical development from myth to scientific thinking has been characterized in our study as a movement from the sacred to the profane; that is to say, from uncommon, existential meanings to common, objective regularities. But one would have to resist a strict separation of such modes of disclosure. We have seen that a mythical view of the world acknowledged both sacred and profane elements, with the latter subordinated to the former. Science, therefore, came to emphasize something that was *not absent* in a mythical world. The problem is a tendency toward a one-sided abandonment of the sacred, where the profane becomes the only standard of intelligibility. The difference between science and myth is a different *emphasis* on certain elements of the world which are evident in *any* phase of human history and thought. Myth and science do not represent two different worlds or a competition for the proper account of the world but rather different ways of properly disclosing a single, multidimensional world.

It is true that science as such did not exist in mythical disclosure, but the sacred-profane distinction allows us to say that a rudimentary *potential* for science did exist. The emergence of science drew out that potential. Concurrently there developed a tendency to segregate certain aspects of culture or judge sacred elements according to profane standards. That, as I have argued, cannot be justified. The development of science was not the gradual discovery of truth but the gradual discovery of *science*. But any attempt to defend myth against positivism or scientism (the limiting of truth to science) must also heed the potential for science in prescientific disclosure and thus avoid the naive, romantic notion that science is some kind of unwarranted intrusion upon the world or even simply a human invention. The *world* has (profane) elements that are properly disclosed by science.

Snell has offered an interesting treatment of this matter from a linguistic standpoint.[8] He tries to show how rational and scientific concepts grew gradually and directly out of the Greek language, which would indicate the derivative character of all subsequent scientific terminology. In this development the definite article played an important role in that it allowed abstract nouns to be formed from other parts of speech (e.g., *to agathon*, the good). The use of the definite article creating noun substantives brought about a complex of functions necessary for scientific thinking, namely a *specific focus* upon abstract principles meant to order and explain phenomena. "The tree" as a scientific concept is not merely an individual tree nor simply the class of empirical trees; it is Tree, tree-ness, everything that makes up tree. Furthermore, with the definite article this abstraction is individualized, statements can be made about it, the abstract is turned into a concrete (linguistic) individual, an object of thought to which the mind can specifically attend. Rational/logical/scientific thought arises in a movement of reflection where substantives (including verbal and adjectival substantives) turn statements into objects of statements.

The generic use of the definite article simply fulfills a potential for abstraction found even in primitive language. Greeks in the fifth century B.C. took great delight in formulating generic nouns out of adjectives and verbs. But then verbal dynamism began to surrender to the clarity and precision of the noun, which grew to dominate more and more (e.g., from "he came to proclaim" to "he came to issue a proclamation"). All this led to the ascendancy of the concept and conceptual methods (and the shift from process to substance).

Such an analysis shows that rationality is potentially present in language as such. That potential emerged gradually as the predicate function of the collective noun was developed through the use of the definite article, which came to particularize the universal. One can say that rationality is always implicit in language—"this is a tree" already implies the rational framework of a particular-universal relationship—but by isolating and explicitly focusing on properties implicit in language, the mind loops back on itself and thus becomes self-reflective. In this way, the logical/rational function of grammatical properties was slowly uncovered. At first the causal function of the conjunction "because" was simply a matter of grammatical coordination, but the implicit prerequisites of logical principles and conceptual causal relations can be found in grammatical coordinations and connections such as a copula linking subjects and predicates, prepositions linking parts of sentences, and conjunctions linking sentences. At first a logical function was implicitly understood in the context of sentences, then certain words came to reflect more than their grammatical function by expressing a latent logical function. Logic became explicit and itself an object of reflection. Sentences were formed to express the form of sentences, so that form was now separated from the ordinary context of speech. Such a separation gave birth to rational/logical/scientific thinking.

Reason and science, therefore, did not emerge "out of the blue" but rather out of a potentiality in language. Nonetheless that emergence was not effortless; it was a struggle, because language contains *other* elements which resist logical and scientific tendencies. That is why, as we have seen, the development of reason and science was also an evaluation (and devaluation) of other elements in language (e.g., myth, poetry, common sense). In science such a conflict is well illustrated in the thought of Democritus, who dismissed the fluctuation and contingency of sense experience in favor of mathematical, quantitative measurement (a geometrical combination of irreducible atoms in a void). Ever since, science has tended toward a reduction of experience to some form of mathematical measurement (in which abstraction becomes complete).

But we have seen how the seeds of scientific thinking were harbored in ordinary language. Science can be understood as an isolated emphasis on certain features of language. Science, however, becomes problematic when such an emphasis devalues or excludes other elements of language. A study of the Greek language helps us speak to this problem. There we realize the *correlation* between concepts and ordinary speech. The Greek language unearthed scientific concepts from preconceptual soil. For us the concepts are *at the start* distant from other forms of language because the Greeks achieved this distance and passed it on to us, but a historical study more clearly reveals the connection between science and nonscientific language. If science and other forms of disclosure have a common linguistic environment, then the tendency to displace or demote nonscientific disclosure loses its absolute or unquestioned justification.[9]

The problem at hand has nothing to do with science as such but rather with an unwarranted judgment upon or exclusion of nonscientific thinking, or at least with a questionable hierarchy of knowledge. Keeping in mind our previous discussions of myth, the sacred, and the profane, we can say the following: Science illuminates the profane as such (e.g., common regularities, natural causes, abstract measurement), and on that account is valid and important as a presentation of certain aspects of the world. Moreover, science *can* pursue a correction of myth *if* a myth is intended as an alternative or competing explanation for certain phenomena, as it might be for some (e.g., a god "causes" plants to grow, or astrological configurations "cause" events or character traits). But if science stretches over into scientism by identifying scientific findings with truth per se, and subsequently screens out or explains away certain *meanings* which animate mythical disclosure, many problems follow.

Such problems can be traced to a kind of hyperprofanization of thought which offers a metaphysical reduction to profane criteria: e.g., materialism, naturalism, or positivism which, when unable to verify certain ideas or meanings, rejects them or exiles them from the province of truth. For example: Since "mind" or "soul" or "god" cannot be observed and measured, then they do not exist; if nature is determined by causal laws, then human freedom is impossible; since values cannot be objectively verified or standardized, then either they do not exist (nihilism) or they express nothing more than subjective preferences (emotivism).

In such developments existential *meanings* which were expressed in mythical imagery (e.g., a sacred force in nature, which gives voice to wonder, beauty, benevolence, and gratitude) came to be seen as subjective, merely human qualities, rather than (if we consider our internal analysis of myth) as meaningful aspects of the world; aspects the very nature of which are not meant to be susceptible to naturalistic, objective (i.e., profane) requirements of uniformity, regularity, and constancy. Such requirements led to an assumption that a thing's "being" could only be guaranteed by empirical, intersubjective verification, and that certain intangibles like mind, god, freedom, or values cannot be said to truly "be" in themselves. But since such intangibles *are* disclosed in human culture, there we have a selective interpretation of the meaning of "being." The naturalist would conclude that such intangibles are subjective occasions or fictions or inventions, or perhaps myths—but our analysis of myth allows us to defend the *truth* of such phenomena, on the basis of a nonobjective, nonreified notion of "being" (appearing).

Here we might find a way to resolve certain perennial philosophical problems (e.g., mind-body, freedom-determinism, fact-value) on the basis of a positive interpretation of myth and a pluralistic model of truth, both of which can retrieve the legitimacy of nonobjective, nonreifiable phenomena. Pluralism involves the suspension of a strict separation between objectivity and subjectivity (a separation which is at a certain level inappropriate for any form of knowledge); it also permits the coexistence of different modes of disclosure and the restoration of certain elements whose exile has always aroused objections and counterintuitions. Witness the following forms of banishment: "You may *feel* 'free' but you're *really* not." "Your 'ideas' are *really* only brain states." "That sunset is not *really* 'beautiful,' you're only projecting beauty onto it." One can defend the truth of such phenomena, not by searching for or trying to accommodate objective explanations, but rather by showing the limits of objectivity as a truth standard.

We should reserve the term "explanation" for the legitimate but selective realm of profane elements where a phenomenon is traced to some grounding framework (e.g., empirical causes or conceptual principles), where a phenomenon is understood in terms of something *else*, an operation which moves from something lesser known (the original phenomenon) to something more generally and more certainly known (the framework) which renders the phenomenon ordered, regular, and predictable. The growth of plants, for example, can be explained by natural laws and causal relations.

To some, a myth might seem to be an explanation, but our study has aimed to cast serious doubt on such a supposition. To those who would think that a myth is a good explanation (e.g., "fundamentalists"), or a bad explanation (e.g., positivists), one should reply that a myth is not *meant* to be an explanation in the strict sense. The primitive mind knew quite well what we mean by explaining; it recognized in some respects profane regularities and ordinary causal "tracings." Myths were a response to phenomena that could *not* be explained. But science too is a response to something that cannot (initially) be explained. On that account many would quite naturally assume science to be doing a better job; but an internal analysis of mythical disclosure shows that myths were not trying to explain phenomena in the strict sense of the term (where according to conceptual and empirical standards they could be seen as *bad* explanations). Rather, mythical imagery (the sacred) is *marked* by a transcendence of (profane) regularity and causal reductions—that is to say, some unusual, unexpected, unpredictable, mysterious, but nevertheless important phenomenon or meaning. It could be said that a myth presents a kind of answer, but examined internally it would be better to say that a myth does not explain but rather presents the inexplicable *as such*, through the use of sacred imagery (i.e., a positive response to the inexplicable).

If science can explain phenomena that myth has presented in its way, science should do so; and indeed, if a myth is intended as an explanation, then science properly stands to correct it. But this does not mean that myth as a whole can or should be so corrected. Our investigation has stressed the background *meaning* of mythical disclosure. That meaning might still well apply to certain issues that continue to (and, I submit, always will) resist explanation (e.g., ultimate origins, beauty, purpose, values, existential significance), issues which therefore will continue to be mythical in a positive sense.[10]

The mythical mind was capable of explanation in terms of natural classifications and modes of thought categorizing profane patterns (see Levi-Strauss, *The Primitive Mind*). Moreover, explanatory operations were often displayed in myths themselves or in aspects of myth. In other words, one cannot say that myths never had anything to do with profane matters or with explanations of a sort; but we can still say that the mystery and meaning of the sacred are the *essence* of myth, that which would still persist even if mythical forms of explanation were challenged. The point is that science can correct myth when it comes to explanatory matters. Indeed, rational forms of explanation can be seen as the *improvement* of explanatory abilities that are exhibited at *any* stage of human history (when it comes to the profane). So, some elements of mythical understanding can and should be exchanged for newer, more objective discoveries. But in myth, mixed in with and prior to profane interests are sacred matters of preobjective meaning which cannot be reduced to an explanation. The sacred-profane distinction, therefore, allows us to draw two important conclusions: (1) Rationality is a cultivation of profane elements found in mythical culture. We see, then, some continuity between myth and rationality, as well as the *progress* that reason can represent with respect to explanation. (2) Myth is an expression of nonobjective meanings which cannot be reduced to explanations. Rationality does not represent progress in *all* matters. The only questionable feature in the historical development from myth to rationality is the assumption of *exclusivity* on the part of philosophers.

A continuing interest in and defense of myth can be supported as long as myth is understood as something other than an explanation, indeed as the very presentation of the inexplicable; and as long as certain elements of the world continue essentially to resist explanation. Of course, some might envision or hope for complete explication of things, but a number of questions come to mind: Would we really want the search for knowledge to end (recall Lessing's choice of an eternal quest over the possession of truth)? Even if we did know all the facts, would there not still be an "other" beyond the limits of the known world? What about the *meaning* of all known facts? What about the origin of the cosmos? Of culture? What about the uniqueness and unpredictability of the human person? What about beauty and other values that elude settlement? There seem to be many elements of existence which by their very nature resist objective explanation. That includes, as we have seen, the circularity of explanatory paradigms themselves. Even rationality and science run up against a limit to explanation, and at that point myth, or something akin to mythical meaning, offers a positive appropriation and expression of that limit.[11]

# Myth, Truth, and Certainty

One guiding assumption in the history of philosophy ever since Plato has been the requirement that truth entail a kind of certainty. If knowledge is to be "certain" it must reduce the world to a fixed standard, free of negation, change, and variation. As we have seen, mythical disclosure was embedded in the lived world, the *uncertain* character of which was precisely the meaning of much of mythical sense. That, of course, is why philosophers were prone to reject myth and banish it from the realm of truth. Any attempt to retrieve mythical truth must not simply raise the banner of myth but show the inherent limitations and shortcomings of the certainty requirement with respect to truth.

Toward that end a number of strategies are possible. The first involves attention to the essentially *historical* nature of philosophical paradigms, wherein their status is far from absolute or necessary. Our study has suggested that we can be anything but certain about the status of certainty, since the prephilosophical world was shown to make sense in quite different ways. Mythical disclosure was a presentation of various existential uncertainties, and was not corrected but rather *rejected* by philosophers, a cultural selection animated by anything but objective reasons.

That suggests a second strategy, namely the *psychological* critique mastered by Nietzsche. Accordingly, the certainty requirement can be traced to all-too-human dispositions and motives, especially a *resistance* to the finitude, negativity, and uncertainty of the lived world. The modern philosopher who consummated the disposition toward certainty was Descartes. His inquiry was prepared by a premethodological interest in certitude and an explicit declaration of *strict* certainty as the goal of thinking. The Cartesian method led to the discovery of the *cogito* as the ground of certainty and the separation of self-conscious cognition from sense experience and the lived world. Descartes also had a concomitant interest in a perfect god and the immortality of the soul as the ultimate reference points for intellectual and existential concerns. According to Nietzsche, such developments stem from a psychological need to overcome the limitations of the lived world and represent both a theoretical and practical form of "salvation." In response to Cartesian truth claims, Nietzsche insists that we recognize behind them a *type* of human being, someone unwilling or unable to accept negativity, finitude, and uncertainty, someone who wants security and interprets the world accordingly. Another type of human being might just as easily accept what Descartes did not (compare tragic wisdom). Consequently, when faced with certain philosophical problems posed by Cartesian thought (e.g., the mind-body problem, subject-object dualism, and skepticism), what should stand out as most *problematic* is the original insistence on certainty. The surest way to a resolution of those problems is the suspension of certainty as a truth standard. Perhaps the certainty-truth equation is itself a kind of myth, a form of disclosure with no absolute foundation or objective justification.

That leads to a third strategy, namely a *phenomenological* analysis of truth, something which occupied the thought of Heidegger. Ever since Descartes and the subsequent exchanges between rationalism and empiricism, modern philosophy has tended to confine the notion of truth to two basic types: conceptual truth and empirical truth. Conceptual truth involves propositions which are known a priori, that is to say, true by reason alone without any appeal to experience. That includes mathematics ($2+2=4$), definitions (bachelors are unmarried males), and logical principles (identity and noncontradiction). The denial of a conceptual truth is said to be logically impossible, so that here truth is necessary and permits the highest kind of certainty. Empirical truth involves propositions which are synthetic and known a posteriori, that is to say, true by observation of sense data. That includes ordinary facts of experience (the cat is on the mat) and scientific explanations (sunlight causes plants to grow). Empirical truths are said to be contingent and not necessary since their denial is not logically impossible. For that reason they do not permit indubitable certainty, and yet they possess another kind of certainty, namely, tangible settlement of particular cases by observation and verification, or absent refutation.

Modern philosophy has moved from attempts to choose between conceptual and empirical conditions as the ground of truth (i.e., strict rationalism and empiricism) to various forms of negotiation between them (e.g., Kant's synthetic a priori). In any case there has developed the conviction that if something is to be "true" it must satisfy at least one of the conditions; that if something is neither conceptually nor empirically true, then it is either not true or at best neither true nor false, and therefore outside the realm of intelligibility. That is because no degree of *certainty* can be achieved outside the standards of logical necessity or empirical verification. Hence: "A god is more than a man" is conceptually true; "The early Greeks believed that the world was controlled by gods" is empirically true; but "The world is controlled by gods" is neither conceptually nor empirically true. The same analysis has been applied to other kinds of claims too: "A painting is a work of art" (conceptually true); "Mary thinks the painting is beautiful" (empirically true); "The painting is beautiful" (neither conceptually nor empirically true).

Important questions arise regarding such selective and exclusive determinations of truth, however. How do we know that the claim "For any claim to be true it must satisfy conceptual or empirical criteria" is *itself* true? That claim cannot be justified by either conceptual or empirical criteria (the stipulated conditions for truth). It is neither conceptually true (since a denial is not logically impossible) nor empirically true (since it cannot be verified by experience). It appears that such a truth standard is itself groundless since we have no way of knowing whether it is true. Faced with this problem, the history of philosophy exhibits a number of proposed solutions wherein such criteria can be traced further to and grounded in some prior determination—e.g., conceptual principles traced to a divine mind or a human faculty of intellectual intuition; empirical principles traced to free-standing conditions or facts in the world (realism).

However, such solutions do not really resolve as much as extend further the problem of paradigmatic circularity and groundlessness. How do we know the proposed foundations themselves are justified? Intellectual intuition cannot itself be "conceived" since it is the precondition for any conception. Free-standing factuality cannot itself be verified, since it is the precondition for verification. We seem forced to conclude that a truth standard simply is there, evident, it is simply given, simply *disclosed* without any prior justification. Any attempt to trace such a process of disclosure to the mind or to the world runs up against the following problem: From both a historical and a phenomenological standpoint the nature of the human mind, its role in knowledge, and the notion of a "world" are themselves already *disclosed* in the process, *before* we attempt to reduce the process to any such conditions. Traditional philosophy finds its innermost explanatory urges frustrated when it appears that we can never get behind or ground a truth standard.

Heidegger's analysis of truth (*a-lētheia*) as un-concealment (disclosure out of hiddenness) is meant to draw a *positive* conclusion from what seems a deficiency according to traditional standards of truth. One can sidestep the philosophical problems inherent in theoretical justification or the epistemological choices between subject and object by *acknowledging* truth standards as groundless, i.e., as emerging in a process of disclosure which itself can never be grounded. That would not threaten the possibility of truth (or the practice of knowledge) but rather revise what is *meant* by truth, leading to a pre-paradigmatic sense of truth which reflects not simply *what* is true according to some paradigm but also *that* a certain paradigm is disclosed as such; i.e., truth as a *process* of unconcealing certain paradigms which subsequently measure the world in certain ways. Truth in the most fundamental sense can never be disclosed, if it is meant as disclosure pure and simple. It could never be disclosed how we are disclosing beings (any answer would presuppose the act of disclosing). Moreover, the historical nature of human self-disclosure and of our disclosure of the world forbids the reduction of truth in this sense to either human faculties or facts in the world. But the lack of a ground does not rob knowledge of truth; it rather speaks to the way in which knowledge comes to be disclosed (out of concealment) and relinquishes the traditional requirement that truth stem from an ultimate foundation.

In other words, the groundlessness of a conceptual or empirical standard does not render conceptual or empirical claims "untrue." It simply shows that the question of truth must address something "other" than the claims themselves or any paradigm as such. Truth is broadened to include a primal, irreducible process of unconcealment (*alētheia*). *What* is disclosed stems from paradigmatic settings for disclosing the world (such as empirical, moral, and religious frameworks which set the stage for thinking), which are particular forms of truth; *their* truth can be described simply in terms of their historical or phenomenological emergence—*that* they are disclosed. In this way, the notion of "aletheic" truth permits a positive response to paradigmatic circularity (making it a "virtuous" circle), as opposed to limiting the question of truth to some kind of standard (in which case paradigmatic circularity appears "vicious").

By way of recapitulation, it is the traditional requirement that truth be certain and uniform which must be overcome if the problems of paradigmatic circularity and competing forms of disclosure are to be resolved. Indeed, such problems *become* problems only as a consequence of that requirement. The certainty requirement amounts to an attempt to reduce the *process* of disclosure (aletheic truth) to a particular *product* of disclosure (a form of truth). Truth as disclosure, where various paradigmatic settings emerge out of concealment, permits the coexistence of different forms of disclosure, a pluralized model of truth. If truth is a preparadigmatic process of disclosure as such, then none of its paradigmatic products can be grounded so as to stand as a measurement for truth or other products of the process. The paradigmatic settings could well be called myths in that they lack any ultimate foundation. Traditional foundations or grounds such as mind, consciousness, objects, even god, all have to be disclosed as such. Therefore what is "prior" is an essentially ungraspable process of disclosure which can only be characterized (phenomenologically) as emergence out of hiddenness. That would clarify the perennial problem of foundations in the history of philosophy (e.g., circularity and the endless competition between various results of disclosure) as well as the aptness of the proposed mythical solution to the problem, namely, that what lies behind knowledge is not a foundation or ground but rather a mystery, and that no form of thought can ultimately satisfy the requirements of certainty, demonstration, or proof. Rationality, therefore, at a certain point is much closer to myth than the expectations of traditional philosophy would have ever allowed.[12]

Recalling our treatment of mythical truth, the proposal that all thought is in a sense mythical would not be a threat. But what, then, can "support" our knowledge of the world? From *within* certain frameworks, that is accomplished by a guiding paradigm. For example, scientific findings are supported by scientific assumptions and methodological criteria. But what supports science as such or other guiding paradigms? In a way, *nothing*! But might this lead to the conclusion that ultimately nothing is true or knowable? No, because again something like radical skepticism, phenomenalism, or nihilism is in fact a consequence of insisting on the certainty requirement and then "negating" knowledge when that requirement fails. But might it be, then, that *anything* could count as true? Again, no, but this question calls for some particular attention.

There are different forms of disclosure that cannot be ultimately justified. They can, however, be seen as true in the following way: They simply *are* disclosed and their importance is evident and established. Certain forms of disclosure have emerged in history and found a cultural and linguistic place, for which justification is not only unnecessary but somewhat comical considering the unobstructed operation and success of cultural paradigms. That need not imply a situation in which "anything goes." It is not the case that *anything* can be thought true. The *world* determines certain limits on what can be thought. The mind can imagine or devise some things which nevertheless can be rejected. One can say that the world is properly disclosed in *many* ways, however, as this study has aimed to show, but it is important to understand *how* different forms of disclosure respond to the world and to clarify their meaning and limits. And doing so permits us to make certain judgments. If science, for example, tries to exile myth or replace its cultural role, that can be called wrong. If mythical thinking tries to reject science or replace its role, that too can be corrected. A plurality of truths allows both external coexistence and internal correction if the bounds of any particular form are overstepped. Different forms of sense permit occasions in which unwarranted invasions can be called nonsense.

The point is that the rejection of a uniform truth and ultimate justification need not entail chaos, unintelligibility, or the absence of any kind of judgment. Some things *can* be judged or isolated from the realm of truth. But without a uniform, objective, or absolute standard, how can that be done? Well, for one thing, it *is* done. I think a successful delimitation of truth would stem not from some eternal, fixed, and invariable standpoint but from a *result*, namely, a form of disclosure which simply finds a place in history and culture. Moreover, an essential mark of that placement would be some form of agreement, a necessary (but not sufficient) condition for distinguishing something true from something purely subjective. I leave open the question of how much agreement would be needed, except to say that a principle of *uniform* or *complete* agreement (i.e., the notion of pure objectivity) is not only unnecessary but contrary to the meaning of truth. As we have seen, mythical disclosure is certainly different from scientific disclosure in many ways. Science and myth do not always "agree." And yet myth presented a form of sense in which a community of persons could come to some kind of agreement, suggesting that important elements of the *world* were at issue, as opposed to mere opinions or subjective superimpositions or arbitrary violations of what is given in the world.

To address a modern philosophical problem, it is surely the case that values reflect different viewpoints and much disagreement, but that need not make values subjective. Someone who sees beauty or goodness in certain things, although someone else disagrees, is not considered deranged or irrational, for one thing. And phenomenologically speaking, there is always a sense of *response* rather than "opinion," and a certain amount of agreement can be found in the community. If I declare a sunset to *be* beautiful, surely I will not be the only one to so think. A group of admirers who share my view and consider it true might be confronted with someone who simply does not agree or who even finds the scene repugnant for some reason; or with a nihilist who insists that there are "really" no values in the world; or with an empiricist for whom the scene is "really" a set of neutral sense data upon which the human subject "projects" a value. None of this will cause the group to cave in, or doubt its view, or seek psychiatric help, or readily admit a mistake (as though a snake in the bush were shown to really be a rope). The group will not be dissuaded from its contention that the sunset *is* (truly) beautiful.

But how can one and the same scene be viewed differently and yet truly "possess" a certain quality? Why doesn't *everyone* view the scene in the same way? Surely one should not take these questions lightly. But another question comes to mind: Why should it *have* to be viewed identically by everyone in order for it to be deemed true? Once again it is the traditional requirement that truth be certain and uniform which in fact creates the problem of truth with respect to values. If one and the same object is perceived differently by two persons (e.g., a sincere disagreement about the aesthetic quality of an art work), then it would seem natural to assume that the different claims are not grounded in the object but in the perception of the subject. Such an interpretation is natural, however, only with respect to a background assumption that truth must be uniform and invariable. The very same situation would not be such a problem if one were to assume that one and the same "object" could be properly disclosed in different ways, *to* which "subjects" *respond*. Rather than beauty being in the eye of the beholder, one could say that beauty is in the *world* of the beholder (and that the same world can also truly be ugly). I admit that such a notion is neither self-evident nor without controversy. I only mean to say that the alternative view is suspect for a number of reasons: A subjective model for values seems inappropriate and counterintuitive from a phenomenological viewpoint; it also cannot properly account for agreement; and it implies the highly questionable assumption that *total* agreement or uniformity is the measure of truth.

I think that a historical and phenomenological analysis forbids the idea that *any* form of knowledge involves (or can involve) total agreement. In other words, the notion of "pure objectivity" is an unwarranted assumption. Our investigation has aimed to elucidate nonobjective elements in everything from myth to science. Scientific disclosure is anything but automatic, self-evident, and uncontested, considering its historical nature and the contest with nonscientific disclosure which made sense of the world in other ways. Even *within* science the idea of total agreement is unwarranted, considering its own history, revolutionary paradigm shifts, theory-laden observation, continuing controversies, and finally the ongoing openness of science to new ideas and methods, which so far shows no sign of ever coming to a head in some fixed standpoint. Even the most "objective" forms of thought have never displayed anything resembling complete consensus (even with respect to methodology), although we often assume (or want) such a consensus.

All forms of meaningful disclosure have to rise above pure subjectivity in order to attain truth, one mark of which is agreement, or a response to the *world* due to something being impressed upon us in an extrasubjective way. But total agreement is an inappropriate requirement for truth. Perhaps the difference between scientific and other forms of disclosure is that science aims for and permits more agreement, especially by screening out *less* agreeable elements (e.g,. the lived world). But that does not make science purely objective or fixed in complete agreement; nor does that make science completely different or separate from nonscience; nor does that make other forms of disclosure less significant, especially considering their cultural importance and degrees of agreement.

If the various paradigmatic settings for disclosure are to be more than mere arbitrary conventions, then agreement cannot be the only mark of truth. What we say must also be in some way a *response* to the world and have some degree of coherence; but in the light of our analysis such additional marks must be more modest than traditional requirements would have it. That being said, other marks of truth are as follows: **appropriateness**, in that what we say is "fitting" for phenomena, where there is a sense of appropriate showing, where the world responds back to our saying (but this has nothing to do with objectivism); **reliability**, in that what we say has a kind of continuity, we can "go on" with it, rather than being utterly unstable or instantaneous or "only once" (but this has nothing to do with eternal truth or strict certainty or constant universals); **workability**, in that what we say is effective, it permits us to engage the world and the world permits that engagement; **sense**, in that what we say gathers experience into a shape that gives a coherence to particulars (but this has nothing to do with rigid, systematic structure or an inviolable order).

These marks round out the picture of truth and reflect how various forms of disclosure have become settled and accepted in cultural history. In the light of these marks we can talk about truth without metaphysical guarantees or the certainty requirement. Accordingly, though, there are *limits* to what can be said and to the effectiveness of paradigmatic settings, but such limit conditions are appropriate to the overall atmosphere of our study. There are aletheic aspects of truth which express the limits of disclosure and which consequently permit judgments when a form of disclosure fails to respect those limits. Truth requires that we renounce foundationalism and acknowledge a mystery at the deepest levels of thinking. Truth also requires that we renounce reductionism and embrace pluralism and inclusiveness; no one setting can stand as the measure for other settings.

We can conclude that a form of disclosure shows truth if it finds an appropriate cultural and linguistic place, if it permits a significant degree of agreement, and if it does not pretend to certainty or aim for exclusivity. The absence of an *ultimate* justification or indubitable guarantee need not be a threat to truth. It is only a threat to certain metaphysical commitments which began with Plato but which in many ways are simply alienated from the history and practice of thought. History presents various paradigmatic settings which simply "appeared" and took shape, guiding and affecting our lives in important ways, without our having to settle the question of ultimate justification. There is something profound in artists refusing to consider the ultimate meaning of art, or practicing scientists uninterested in metaphysical guarantees for induction, or religious persons unmoved by failed proofs for the existence of God, or people putting their lives on the line for values without universal settlement. There is something revealing in philosophical skeptics moving confidently through their surroundings, or materialists who permit us to use mental language despite their contention that minds do not exist, or determinists who continue to employ praise and blame language. The point is that many forms of understanding simply *are* an important part of our language and practice, the denial of which ignores our form of life, and for which the lack of justification is inconsequential.

Some things can be excluded from truth, but not by means of rational justification or an absolute standard. A form of disclosure is "authorized" by its historical and cultural placement, which from a phenomenological viewpoint is in the end simply "given." With respect to cultural and intellectual paradigms and the lack of ultimate justification, at a certain point *we must be just as receptive and unskeptical as mythical thought was concerning the sacred.* The absence of strict certainty and uniformity is far from a deficiency in our thinking. It points back to our prerational origins and retrieves a pluralistic openness which the active history of thought has always exhibited but which certain metaphysical interpretations of thought have always resisted.

In sum, then, the preceding critique of certainty and uniformity highlights the basic contention of this chapter, namely, that rationality cannot be strictly separated from myth because of the thematic links between them. In one way or another the underlying characteristics of mythical disclosure prepared in the first chapter have resounded in our treatment of rational thought: The question of origins leading to a kind of **mystery**; the priority of disclosure out of hiddenness echoing the mythical sense of **appearance**; the priority of **process** over substantial foundations; an inevitable **pluralism** to replace metaphysical reductionism; the nonobjective **existential element of thought**, and the nonsubjective **transcendence** in that element, which overcomes subject-object dualism and restores the **self-world correlation** reflected in the lived world; the **givenness** of paradigms resulting from the absence of justification; the unskeptical attitude of **receptivity** as a positive response to givenness; and the renunciation of certainty and metaphysical absolutes, which echoes the mythical sense of **limits** and **finitude**.

Accordingly, the overlapping relationship between myth and rationality at this level recalls two things which lie at the heart of this investigation: (1) A specifically mythical account of the world cannot be exiled from the realm of truth. (2) A rational account of the world *retains* the background meaning of mythical disclosure (and in fact is able to *explicate* that meaning). The point is not only to protect myth from various forms of rational-ism but also to acknowledge the links between myth and reason, which can go a long way toward resolving perennial philosophical problems which had been *created* by rationalistic, metaphysical, and reductionistic assumptions in the first place. Therefore it is not only mythical truth that needs protection but philosophy as well. If the *nature* of philosophy shows a connection with myth, then the traditional antagonism of philosophy toward myth not only represents an unwarranted judgment of myth, it also betrays a kind of self-alienation and self-distortion *within* philosophy.

In the end, if philosophy gazes beyond the lived world and its mythical element, it runs the risk of losing its way and stumbling into darkness, as Thales did when he fell into the well. What philosophy should fear is not the derision of the servant-girl; philosophy will always seem strange to many people, and yet it will always be more important than common sense and ordinary knowledge. The servant-girl did not herself understand the profound implications of Thales's "absent-mindedness." Only philosophy can do that, by *comprehending* what is gained and what is lost through rationality; in other words, by engaging in self-criticism and self-correction. Therefore, what philosophy should fear about the fall into the well is its own incapacitation and injury, which prevents it from walking more attentively through the terrain it had previously overlooked.

# NOTES

## INTRODUCTION

1. Translation from G. S. Kirk and J. E. Raven, *The Presocratic Philosophers* (Cambridge University Press, 1966), p. 78.
2. The term "existential" is ambiguous and easily open to misunderstanding because of the contemporary label "existentialism." I can only say at the outset that I am drawing from the thought of Nietzsche and Heidegger, two philosophers who have been categorized as existentialists, but neither of whom ever called themselves or could be called such, if that label reflects certain assumptions of thinkers like Kierkegaard or Sartre.
3. Translated by John Macquarrie and Edward Robinson (New York: Harper and Row, 1962).
4. See "On the Essence of Truth," in *Basic Writings*, ed. David Krell (New York: Harper and Row, 1977).
5. By way of Heidegger, I will employ another term that is current in contemporary thought, namely a "phenomenological" approach. Like existentialism, phenomenology is a classification that can cause confusion. Heidegger distinguished his approach from that of the school of phenomenology which grew from Husserl's investigations. In my treatment a phenomenon is any entity, event, meaning, or situation that shows itself in the world. A phenomenological analysis is one that attempts to let a phenomenon show itself in the way that it shows itself, that is to say, without reducing it to something else or importing certain theoretical presuppositions or assumptions that would be inappropriate for the phenomenon in question and violate its meaning. For example, a phenomenological approach would not permit reducing an

emotion to something like a glandular secretion, or an idea to a neural firing, or, as we shall see, interpreting myth as a primitive form of scientific explanation.

6. For a helpful summary of the scholarly issues surrounding Heidegger's interpretation, see Robert Bernasconi, *The Question of Language in Heidegger's History of Being* (New Jersey: Humanities Press, 1985), pp. 15–27.

7. *On Time and Being*, trans. Joan Stambaugh (New York: Harper and Row, 1972), p. 8.

8. See "Letter on Humanism," in *Basic Writings*, and *On the Way to Language*, trans. Peter D. Hertz (New York: Harper and Row, 1971), and *Poetry, Language, Thought*, trans. Albert Hofstadter (New York: Harper and Row, 1971).

9. Hermann Fränkel, *Early Greek Poetry and Philosophy*, trans. Moses Hadas and James Willis (New York: Harcourt Brace Jovanovich, 1975), p. 4. On language as the important reference for studying myth, see Walter Burkert, *Structure and History in Greek Mythology and Ritual* (Berkeley and Los Angeles: University of California Press, 1979), pp. 2–3.

10. Heidegger and Wittgenstein, for all their differences, share one interesting point of view. They believe that many philosophical problems cannot be solved because they are "pseudo-problems." In other words, philosophy may have to criticize *itself* in certain respects. For these thinkers, the *way* philosophical problems are posed and the assumptions behind them are flawed. If this is true, and I believe it is, then it would seem right to be very interested in the historical emergence of philosophy as such. If we can reasonably sketch the form of prephilosophical culture, then we will be in a much better position to know how and why certain philosophical problems and assumptions arose, and whether they exhibit any shortcomings. But such an excavation has more than historical value. Perhaps then we will learn to think more clearly about philosophical questions, and we may also discover a wealth of clues that will lead to certain answers.

## CHAPTER I

1. For a brief account of so-called recurrent themes in myth, see C. Kluckhorn, "Recurrent Themes in Myth and Mythmaking," in *Myth and Mythmaking*, ed. Henry A. Murray (Boston: Beacon Press, 1968), chapter 2. For an introduction to various theories of religion, see Brian Morris, *Anthropological Studies of Religion* (Cambridge University

Press, 1987). For a summary of theories of myth and Greek myth in particular, see Jean-Pierre Vernant, *Myth and Society in Ancient Greece*, trans. Janet Lloyd (Atlantic Highlands, N.J.: Humanities Press, 1980), pp. 207–233.

2. G. S. Kirk, *The Nature of Greek Myths* (New York: Penguin Books, 1974), p. 27. For his critique of various theories of myth, see chapters 3 and 4.

3. Ibid., pp. 27–28. See also pp. 33–34 for a helpful distinction between myth and folktale.

4. See Burkert, *Structure and History in Greek Mythology and Ritual*, p. 4ff.

5. Mircea Eliade, *Myth and Reality*, trans. Willard R. Trask (New York: Harper and Row, 1968), pp. 5–6.

6. Jane Ellen Harrison, *Themis* (New York: University Books, 1962), pp. 328–331.

7. C. Kerenyi, *The Religion of the Greeks and Romans*, trans. Christopher Holme (Westport Connecticut: Greenwood Press, 1977), pp. 29, 61.

8. Walter F. Otto, *Dionysus: Myth and Cult*, trans. Robert B. Palmer (Bloomington: Indiana University Press, 1965), p. 17.

9. See Kirk, *The Nature of Greek Myths*, pp. 66–68; and a qualified version of the myth-ritual correlation, p. 225.

10. Burkert claims that the character of myth can be found in the use to which it is put (*Structure and History in Greek Mythology and Ritual*, pp. 22–23).

11. See Otto, *Dionysus: Myth and Cult*, pp. 18–22.

12. Ibid., p. 33.

13. See ibid., pp. 29–30.

14. Ernst Cassirer, *The Philosophy of Symbolic Forms*, vol. 2: *Mythical Thought*, trans. Ralph Manheim (New Haven: Yale University Press, 1955), pp. 77–79 et passim. Although Cassirer gives an insightful analysis of myth and considers it to be a legitimate form of thought, he adopts the "progressive" view that rationality is superior to myth. See Hans Blumenberg, *Work on Myth*, trans. Robert M. Wallace (Cambridge, Mass.: MIT Press, 1985), pp. 167–68. For Heidegger's response to Cassirer's book, see *The Piety of Thinking*, trans. James G. Hart and John C. Maraldo (Bloomington: Indiana University Press, 1976), pp. 32–45. This collection also contains some helpful commentaries on the subject of myth.

15. Ernst Cassirer, *Language and Myth*, trans. Susan K. Langer (New York: Dover Publications, 1953), p. 66.

16. Cf. Wittgenstein's remark: "the characteristic feature of the awakening mind of man is precisely that a phenomenon comes to have meaning for him." This is found in "Remarks on Frazer's *Golden Bough*," trans. John Beversluis, in *Wittgenstein: Sources and Perspectives*, ed. C. G. Luckhardt (Ithaca, New York: Cornell University Press, 1979), p. 67.

17. For an analysis of Hesiod's Prometheus myth in terms of concealing and limits, see Vernant, *Myth and Society in Ancient Greece*, pp. 168–185.

18. For example see R. Horton's piece on African traditional thought in *Rationality*, ed. B. R. Wilson (New York: Harper and Row, 1971), p. 142. See also G. E. R. Lloyd, *Magic, Reason and Experience* (Cambridge University Press, 1979), pp. 37–58. This is a very impressive study of the relationship and differences between magic and science in the Greek world, with extensive documentation. See also Jean-Pierre Vernant, *Myth and Thought Among the Greeks* (Routledge and Kegan Paul, 1983), who discusses Babylonian astronomy—with its careful observations and quantitative formulas that had predictive power—which was nevertheless motivated by and based on the belief that planets were divine and connected with human fortunes (p. 177). For a detailed discussion of classificatory and causal thinking in primitive culture, see Claude Levi-Strauss, *The Primitive Mind* (Chicago: University of Chicago Press, 1966), especially chapters 2, 5, and 6.

19. Alan M. Olson gives an insightful analysis of the connection between myth and limits in terms of Jaspers's notion of "boundary situation," in *Myth, Symbol and Reality*, ed. Alan M. Olson (South Bend: University of Notre Dame Press, 1980), ch. 7, p. 106ff.

20. See Cassirer, *The Philosophy of Symbolic Forms*, vol. 2, p. 200.

21. Cassirer gives an interesting example. In ancient Persia, Mithra was not originally a sun god, that is, he was not at first literally identified with the sun but was the spirit of heavenly light appearing on the horizon *before* the sun itself actually appears. The sun is therefore the manifestation of Mithra (*Language and Myth*, p. 14). The suggestion is that light is prior to objects, a preobjective meaning of light that is phenomenologically intelligible.

22. Cassirer speaks to this issue of the precedence of meaning over objectivity when he claims that in primitive language naming is not a process of identifying external similarities (objectivity) but functional similarities (meaning). He gives the example of an Indian tribe with the same word for dancing and working because of the importance of dancing for farming (*Language and Myth*, p. 40).

23. See Cassirer, *The Philosophy of Symbolic Forms*, vol. 2, pp. 192, 199; and *Language and Myth*, pp. 10–11. Again, we *can* learn much about myth by means of structural, social, psychological, symbolic, and functional analyses as long as these models are not reductive or exclusive. But I think that the notions of lived world, existential meaning, and the sacred give us our best shot at what is "universal" across mythical cultures or varieties of myth, although this will *not* give us anything like common details or a uniform structure or a universal world-view or a single truth within all the different traditions.

24. H. and H. A. Frankfort, *Before Philosophy* (Baltimore: Penguin Books, 1949), pp. 12–14.

25. Again, see Wittgenstein's critique of Frazer in "Remarks in Frazer's *Golden Bough*." For example:

> Frazer's account of the magical and religious views of mankind is unsatisfactory: it makes these views look like *errors*. . . . The very idea of wanting to explain a practise—for example, the killing of the priest-king—seems wrong to me. All that Frazer does is to make them plausible to people who think as he does. It is very remarkable that in the final analysis all these practises are presented as, so to speak, pieces of stupidity.
> But it will never be plausible to say that mankind does all that out of sheer stupidity. (p. 61)
> . . .
> And the explanation isn't what satisfies us here at all. When Frazer begins by telling us the story of the King of the Wood of Nemi, he does this in a tone which shows that he feels, and wants us to feel, that something strange and dreadful is happening. But the question "why does this happen?" is properly answered by saying: Because it is dreadful. That is, the same thing that accounts for the fact that this incident strikes us as dreadful, magnificent, horrible, tragic, etc., as anything but trivial and insignificant, it is *that* which has called this incident to life.
> Here one can only *describe* and say: this is what human life is like. (p. 63)
> . . .
> Frazer is much more savage than most of his savages, for they are not as far removed from the understanding of a spiritual matter as a twentieth-century Englishman. *His* explanations of primitive practises are much cruder than the meaning of these practises themselves. (pp. 68–69)
> . . .
> One could say "every view has its charm," but that would be false. The correct thing to say is that every view is significant for the one who sees it as significant (but that does not mean, sees it other than it is). Indeed, in this sense, every view is equally significant. (p. 71)

See also the introduction to Lloyd, *Magic, Reason and Experience*, especially pp. 2–3. For example:

> Any attempt to contrast magic as a whole directly with science is now seen to be liable to distort the nature and aims of the former.

Magic, so it has forcefully and in part, at least, surely rightly argued, should be seen less as attempting to be efficacious, than as affective, expressive or symbolic. The criteria that are relevant to judging magical behavior are not whether it achieves practical results but whether it has been carried out appropriately or not.

26. H. and H. A. Frankfort, *Before Philosophy*, p. 17.
27. For a discussion of mythical cause vs. causal regularity, see Lloyd, *Magic, Reason and Experience*, pp. 52–53.
28. See ibid., p. 66, for more examples.
29. For a discussion of this question see the essays in *Rationality*, especially Peter Winch, "Understanding a Primitive Society," pp. 78–111, and Steven Lukes, "Some Problems About Rationality," pp. 194–213.
30. *Mythos* and *logos* were not originally opposed in meaning, since both terms were associated with formulated speech; *mythos* could be called *hieros logos*, sacred speech (Vernant, *Myth and Society in Ancient Greece*, pp. 186–87). It was only when *logos* evolved to the sense of logical reasoning that *mythos* became problematic. *Mythos* came to be seen not as a relevant presentation of the world but as simply a story which has an emotional effect on listeners and thus not a decisive account (*logos*). See Walter Burkert, *Greek Religion*, trans. John Raffan (Cambridge, Mass.: Harvard University Press, 1985), p. 312. If there is a logic in myth, then unlike the logic of reason, it is, as Vernant says, "a logic of the ambiguous, the equivocal, a logic of polarity" (p. 239).
31. Bruno Snell, *The Discovery of the Mind*, trans. T. G. Rosenmeyer (New York: Harper and Row, 1960), p. 5.
32. Cassirer, *The Philosophy of Symbolic Forms*, vol. 2, p. 49. Even for us the *meaning* of a loved one's death is not expressed in terms of biological laws.
33. For a discussion of the differences between myth and dogmatic monotheism, see Blumenberg, *Work on Myth*, pp. 215–262.
34. Generally speaking, the question of language acquisition can also serve as an example of preobjective meaning. For a long time empiricist assumptions have muddied our understanding of language. In most cases, and especially with children, language is not learned by "attaching" words to sense data but rather by first learning meanings, functions, environmental situations, and so forth.
35. Cassirer, *The Philosophy of Symbolic Forms*, vol. 2, pp. 53–55.
36. Ibid., p. 58.
37. See ibid., pp. 181–84.
38. Snell, *The Discovery of the Mind*, p. 225.
39. Ibid., p. 224.

40. See Cassirer, *Language and Myth*, pp. 59–61.

41. See ibid., pp. 56–58.

42. As St. John's "In the beginning was the Word." Examples from India, Egypt, and elsewhere can be found in *Language and Myth*, pp. 45–48.

43. For example, the Egyptian goddess Isis, who, persuading Ra to disclose his name, gained power over him and all other gods. See ibid., pp. 48–49.

44. For example, a person's name is often like a physical possession or one's very spirit or a spiritual double; taking or taking on someone's name brings in that person's soul; new stages of life require new names; the dead can be invoked by speaking their names. See ibid., pp. 49–53.

45. The validity of the representational view of language has, of course, been criticized by many contemporary philosophers, most notably Heidegger and the later Wittgenstein.

46. See Vernant, *Myth and Society in Ancient Greece*, pp. 94–95.

47. Snell, *The Discovery of the Mind*, p. 213, and ch. 9 in general.

48. Burkert, *Greek Religion*, p. 247. See Kirk, *The Nature of Greek Myths*, ch. 12. This last chapter does a good job of undermining the strict separation of myth and logic but gives little if any help for an understanding of what differences there *are*.

49. Cassirer, *The Philosophy of Symbolic Forms*, vol. 2, pp. 83–118.

50. Ibid., pp. 103–104. Such a form of space is quite comprehensible since our lives are filled with existential spatial designations: home, property, work places, holy places, dangerous places, and the like. See Heidegger's evocative analysis in "Building, Dwelling, Thinking," in *Basic Writings*.

51. See Fränkel, *Early Greek Poetry and Philosophy*, pp. 133–34.

52. Cassirer, *The Philosophy of Symbolic Forms*, vol. 2, p. 109.

53. Ibid., p. 111.

54. See Heidegger's treatment in *Being and Time*, sections 78–81.

55. In other words, there is no such thing as "knowledge for its own sake." Whenever something like that is said, it is best interpreted as a response to some situation, such as when the search for knowledge is at odds with utilitarian interests or established assumptions. This would not show that knowledge was utterly detached from some existential meaning. We should remember that when such things were first said historically (e.g., by the Stoics), contemplative detachment was seen as a *value*, as salvific, even divine.

56. See Cassirer, *The Philosophy of Symbolic Forms*, vol. 2, pp. 185–86. "Life" is not divided into strict distinctions of human, animal, and plant, hence the many forms of man-animal identifications (e.g., totemism), and the "personal" animistic relationships which seem so odd to us. For example, the previously mentioned Sakkudei pray to plants and ask a pig's forgiveness when it is to be sacrificed.

57. *The Philosophy of Symbolic Forms*, vol. 2, pp. 155–56.
58. In addition to studies by Snell and Dodds that develop this point, I will occasionally refer to the controversial thesis of Julian Jaynes, who combines a linguistic approach with brain physiology to argue for the absence of self-consciousness in ancient man. Jaynes also explores a physiological model of altered experience based on brain lateralization to argue that such phenomena as inspiration, possession, prophecy, hearing voices, and seeing visions, which characterize much of early literature, were in fact genuine experiences in early civilizations. See *The Origin of Consciousness in the Breakdown of the Bicameral Mind* (Boston: Houghton Mifflin Co., 1976).
59. See Cassirer, *The Philosophy of Symbolic Forms*, vol. 2, p. 175.
60. Ibid., p. 179.
61. Ibid., pp. 162–65.
62. In fact, if we give phenomenological consideration to certain experiences of existential importance, the mythical idea of divine intervention, for example, can display a more appropriate form than reflective or objective explanations. Are there not mythical reverberations in the phrase "falling in love"? Even we moderns talk of the self being "overwhelmed," even "lost." Are these nothing more than figures of speech? Could we not say that when the Greeks attributed love to divine intervention, such a form is phenomenologically more apt than attributing it to a part of the self (i.e., emotions or drives) or physiology (glands and chemistry), which seem irrelevant to the *overwhelming* character of love, which profane it, so to speak? If I break my arm, I *will* think of my bones and muscles. But if my heart is broken or I fall in love, I will *never* think of my glands, and in fact my conventional self will feel strangely lost.
63. On this question see Heidegger's "The Origin of the Work of Art," in *Poetry, Language, Thought*.

## CHAPTER II

1. Kerenyi, *The Religion of the Greeks and Romans*, p. 51. An excellent overall source is Burkert, *Greek Religion*.
2. Vernant, *Myth and Thought among the Greeks*, p. 330.
3. Otto, *Dionysus: Myth and Cult*, p. 29.
4. Walter F. Otto, *The Homeric Gods*, trans. Moses Hadas (New York: Octagon Books, 1978), p. 287.
5. See Fränkel, *Early Greek Poetry and Philosophy*, p. 61.
6. Otto, *The Homeric Gods*, p. 11.

7. See Fränkel, *Early Greek Poetry and Philosophy*, p. 59, and Vernant, *Myth and Society in Ancient Greece*, pp. 95–98.
8. Otto, *The Homeric Gods*, p. 169. This work is an evocative and vivid interpretation of the meaning and spirit of the major Greek deities. See also Burkert, *Greek Religion*, pp. 125–170.
9. Burkert, *Greek Religion*, pp. 271–72.
10. Vernant, *Myth and Society in Ancient Greece*, pp. 98–99.
11. See Burkert, *Greek Religion*, p. 189.
12. Ibid., p. 248; see also p. 216.
13. Ibid., pp. 95–98, 119–120.
14. There are some exceptions. In the *Odyssey*, Menelaus is said to go to the Elysian Fields. Some heroic figures, such as Heracles, are transformed into immortals. And in later periods, Orphic and other mystery cults developed hopes for some kind of immortal existence. See ibid., pp. 194–99.
15. Kerenyi, *The Religion of the Greeks and Romans*, pp. 269–270.
16. Vernant gives a specific analysis of Greek stone figures meant to represent the dead, an analysis which complements Kerenyi's point (*Myth and Thought among the Greeks*, pp. 305–320).
17. Vernant gives an analysis of Hesiod's Prometheus myth in this regard (*Myth and Society in Ancient Greece*, pp. 168–185).
18. There were, of course, scientific and philosophical developments in India and China, but these cultures did not experience the kind of deliberate attempt at emancipation from traditional religion which marked the truly revolutionary nature of science and philosophy in Greece and which prefigured the criteria of scientific thinking accepted throughout the world today. For an interpretation of the relationship between Greek science and the sociopolitical atmosphere of argumentation, see Lloyd, *Magic, Reason and Experience*, ch. 4. See also Vernant, *Myth and Society in Ancient Greece*, for a discussion of the links between an agonistic spirit and politics (pp. 19–44) and a comparison-contrast analysis of ancient Chinese and Greek intellectual developments (pp. 71–91).
19. See Kerenyi, *The Religion of the Greeks and Romans*, pp. 192–200.
20. According to Nietzsche, the absence of laughter was a central flaw of the New Testament. In a later period in Greek culture, Plato will rebuke Homer for describing the gods as giving way to unquenchable laughter (*Republic*, III, 388e).
21. The term "festive" is Kerenyi's choice and is nicely sketched in *The Religion of the Greeks and Romans*, pp. 49–70.
22. See Fränkel, *Early Greek Poetry and Philosophy*, p. 84.
23. Kerenyi, *The Religion of the Greeks and Romans*, p. 153.
24. Ibid., pp. 111–14.
25. Burkert, *Greek Religion*, pp. 199–203.

26. Dodds, *The Greeks and the Irrational* (Berkeley: University of California Press, 1968), chapters 3 and 4. See also Burkert, *Greek Religion*, pp. 109–118.

27. For an interesting study of Greek culture and ideas of madness, see Bennett Simon, *Mind and Madness in Ancient Greece* (Ithaca: Cornell University Press, 1978).

28. Julian Jaynes proposes that prophetic "advents" stem from lateralized brain function. Also, he cites experiments which indicate that women are less lateralized as far as speech is concerned than men. Since speech is spread through both hemispheres more so in women, this would make them biologically more susceptible to something like prophecy. See *The Origin of Consciousness in the Breakdown of the Bicameral Mind*, pp. 343–44.

29. See ibid., pp. 353–360 on this point, and also p. 324 for a helpful summation of a prophetic paradigm.

30. See the *Laws*, 791a, and the *Politics*, 1342a7ff., and Dodds, *The Greeks and the Irrational*, pp. 75–80 for a more detailed account of such rites.

31. Jaynes offers some interesting observations about poetry and its ancient connection with music and musical patterns such as rhythm, repetition, and alliteration, along with brain functions associated with such things, to give a physiological reference for the auditory experiences of ancient poets. See *The Origin of Consciousness in the Breakdown of the Bicameral Mind*, pp. 361–378.

32. See Dodds, *The Greeks and the Irrational*, ch. 4, for a more detailed discussion of this question.

33. Mircea Eliade, *Yoga: Immortality and Freedom*, trans. Willard R. Trask (Princeton: Princeton University Press, 1969), p. 320.

34. F. M. Cornford, *Principium Sapientiae* (Gloucester, Mass.: Peter Smith, 1971), pp. 93–105.

35. For a discussion of the relation between Hesiod's poetry, foreign influences, and more ancient sources, see Albin Lesky, *A History of Greek Literature*, trans. James Willis and Cornelis de Heer (New York: Thomas Y. Crowell Co., 1966), pp. 91–96.

36. *Hesiod*, trans. H. G. Evelyn-White (Cambridge: Harvard University Press, 1914).

37. See Mitchell H. Miller, "The Implicit Logic of Hesiod's Cosmogony: An Examination of *Theogony*, 116–133," *Independent Journal of Philosophy*, 4, 1980, pp. 131–142.

38. Fränkel, *Early Greek Poetry and Philosophy*, p. 101.

39. For a discussion of the Heracles myth as a paradigm of this relationship, see Kirk, *The Nature of Greek Myths*, ch. 8, and Burkert, *Structure and History in Greek Mythology and Ritual*, pp. 78–98.

**CHAPTER III**

1. I am using Richmond Lattimore's translation, *The Iliad of Homer* (Chicago: University of Chicago Press, 1951).
2. For discussions of the Homeric question see Fränkel, *Early Greek Poetry and Philosophy*, pp. 6–8, and Lesky, *A History of Greek Literature*, pp. 14–41.
3. See Snell, *The Discovery of the Mind*, ch. 1, especially pp. 21–22, and Burkert, *Greek Religion*, pp. 182–89.
4. Laszlo Versenyi, *Man's Measure* (Albany: SUNY Press, 1974), p. 26.
5. Fränkel, *Early Greek Poetry and Philosophy*, pp. 56–57.
6. Ibid.
7. Cf. the *Iliad*, XVI.443ff., and for a general discussion, see Otto, *The Homeric Gods*, pp. 263–65.
8. See Versenyi, *Man's Measure*, pp. 7–9.
9. For an analysis of Sarpedon's speech and the nature of heroic action, see Pietro Pucci, "Banter and Banquets for Heroic Death," in *Post-Structuralist Classics*, ed. Andrew Benjamin (London: Routledge, 1988), pp. 132–159.
10. If we remember that glory is the chief criterion for heroic values, rather than an egalitarian sense of justice, we can better understand the so-called immoral attitudes of the heroes (e.g., brutality, aggressiveness, pride, and a strong sense of rank) as a *different* set of values which fits a different set of circumstances. Furthermore, we can better understand the typical heroic respect for the enemy, because one's opponent can also embody glory, and *as* an opponent he supplies the opportunity for one's own glory.
11. Werner Jaeger, *Paideia: The Ideals of Greek Culture*, vol. 1, trans. Gilbert Highet (New York: Oxford University Press, 1945), p. 57.
12. The religious life of the common person was of a much more ceremonial and dependent form than that of the Homeric heroes. For a brief sketch of the religious life of the common people in ancient Greece, see H. J. Rose, *Religion in Greece and Rome* (New York: Harper and Row, 1959), pp. 18–46.
13. See Snell, *The Discovery of the Mind*, pp. 4–7.
14. See ibid., pp. 8–22 for a full discussion of this question and numerous textual references.
15. Snell also shows how these functions are not absolutely separated and often overlap: ibid., pp. 12-14.
16. Ibid., p. 19.
17. For a dissenting opinion on this question, see David Claus, *Toward the Soul* (New Haven: Yale University Press, 1981), which traces the meaning of *psyche* from Homer to Plato. Claus tries to argue for the notion of "life force" as

an implicit unity and hence against the notion of a disparate personality in Homer (see especially pp. 47 and 97). It may be that there is an implicit unity in Homer, but as I have said, I am not sure how much we can make of that or whether it could overcome plurality in any significant way. I think he assumes a physical interpretation of the organs. If these Homeric words refer to a plurality of existential function and not physical organs, then Claus's belief that *psyche* is needed to reflect nonphysical states would be unnecessary. Furthermore, I was not convinced by his argument that a unified life force is at work in Homer, or even necessary for that matter. Life as lived experience need not imply a unity. It seems to me that tracing the different Homeric functions back to some unified life force is a retrospective generalization not evident in the *Iliad*.

18. See *The Greeks and the Irrational*, pp. 2–11.

19. Ibid., pp. 11–12.

20. There are many examples of possession and auditory and visual hallucinations in modern experience too. Of course, for us, such experiences are a form of psychosis. There are some parallels between the epic self and modern psychosis, but the crucial difference is that in the epic world these events are considered culturally important and therefore "in order." And, as previously mentioned, the degree of cultural support diminishes the dysfunctional, pathological consequences of such experiences. On this point, see Simon, *Mind and Madness in Ancient Greece*, ch. 4, especially p. 64.

21. Fränkel, *Early Greek Poetry and Philosophy*, p. 80.

22. Versenyi, *Man's Measure*, p. 11.

23. An exception is a remark by Achilles: "I detest that man, who hides one thing in the depths of his heart, and speaks forth another" (IX.312–13).

24. Versenyi, *Man's Measure*, p. 12.

25. Simon, *Mind and Madness in Ancient Greece*, p. 284.

26. Versenyi, *Man's Measure*, p. 16. The Greek experience of the divine was generally not a one-to-one, singular, solitary "personal" relationship, but one continually caught up in a social setting. See Vernant, *Myth and Thought among the Greeks*, p. 323ff.

27. Otto, *The Homeric Gods*, p. 177.

28. See Vernant, *Myth and Society in Ancient Greece*, p. 106.

29. For a discussion of the differences between the *Iliad* and the *Odyssey* in this context, see Fränkel, *Early Greek Poetry and Philosophy*, pp. 85–93.

30. Instead of a despairing reaction to catastrophe stemming from *expected* support (cf. Why have you forsaken us?), Menelaus and Achilles say simply "Zeus, no god is more destructive than you" (*Iliad*, III.365 and XXII.15). See Burkert, *Greek Religion*, p. 274.

31. Versenyi, *Man's Measure*, p. 20.

32. Apollo's maxim "Know Thyself" was not a call for individual self-discovery but a reminder to know one's limits, to know that one is not a god. As Burkert remarks, the maxim is more pessimistic than progressive (*Greek Religion*, p. 148).

33. See Jaynes, *The Origin of Consciousness in the Breakdown of the Bicameral Mind*, p. 79.

34. For an account of epic poetry in the context of an oral culture, as well as comparative findings from other oral traditions, see Fränkel, *Early Greek Poetry and Philosophy*, pp. 6–44.

35. Simon, *Mind and Madness in Ancient Greece*, p. 85.

36. Versenyi, *Man's Measure*, pp. 41–42. See also Vernant, *Myth and Society in Ancient Greece*, pp. 187–190.

37. Some other effects: With an oral *mythos*, the power, drama, and impact of language is essential, since it is *enacted* by a human speaker; so writing permits another kind of abstraction: a distance from the affective aspect of a live presentation (cf. the difference between reading a play and seeing one performed). Also, the later "demonstrative" form of arguments in philosophy was modelled after mathematical reasoning with numbers and geometrical figures, something requiring graphics. On these points, see Vernant, op. cit. However, we must not go too far in dividing cultural developments along the lines of writing (see Lloyd, *Magic, Reason and Experience*, pp. 239–240). We have to remember that the mode of oral transmission continued to be a basic element in Greek culture and education up until the time of Plato. The most notable example is Socrates, who practiced oral dialogue rather than written composition.

38. For an analysis see Vernant, *Myth and Thought among the Greeks*, pp. 3–72.

39. Versenyi, *Man's Measure*, p. 45.

40. Ibid., pp. 45–46.

41. One influence here was the advent of the *polis*. When warfare was incorporated into the *polis'* overall function, there developed the notion of a citizen-warrior, and hence a breakdown of a strict hierarchy and separation between warriors and the common man which was characteristic of the epic age. Consequently, distinct warrior values were blended into a wider picture of human ideals. See Vernant, *Myth and Society in Ancient Greece*, p. 28.

42. See Vernant, *Myth and Thought among the Greeks*, chs. 14 and 15.

**CHAPTER IV**

1. Jaynes gives an interesting analysis of such a situation, though referring to a much earlier period in which consciousness first emerged and before

which, he claims, there was no self-consciousness at all. See *The Origin of Consciousness in the Breakdown of the Bicameral Mind*, pp. 204–222.

2. Dodds notes (*The Greeks and the Irrational*, p. 44) that we should not go so far as to declare a historical discontinuity between the epic and archaic periods. The two ages might be better seen as "selections" of warrior and peasant values respectively. Surely we could imagine the archaic attitude among peasants of Homer's time or the epic attitude among warriors in a later age. Therefore, to speak strictly of evolution or discontinuity would be misleading. We can say that *culture* was developing and that the cultural ideals of the two periods might be to some extent discontinuous. Since we cannot penetrate first hand the experience of human beings in these times, cultural documents are our only form of access. Therefore we are on safer ground if we talk of cultural transformations rather than the experiences of all human beings. But such cultural documents are indeed a window through which we can see general features of human experience prevailing at that time. As I have said, it would be equally wrong to claim that these cultural documents are not a true reflection of human life but simply a poetic embellishment.

3. Ibid., ch. 2.

4. *Greek Lyrics*, trans. Richmond Lattimore (Chicago: University of Chicago Press, 1960), p. 44.

5. *The Oxford Book of Greek Verse in Translation*, ed. T. F. Higham and C. M. Bowra (London: Oxford University Press, 1938), p. 203.

6. Some of what follows is drawn from Snell, *The Discovery of the Mind*, ch. 3.

7. *Greek Lyrics*, p. 40.

8. *The Oxford Book of Greek Verse in Translation*, p. 210.

9. *Greek Lyrics*, p. 40.

10. *The Oxford Book of Greek Verse in Translation*, p. 211.

11. Versenyi, *Man's Measure*, p. 73.

12. Snell, *The Discovery of the Mind*, p. 49.

13. *The Oxford Book of Greek Verse in Translation*, p. 211.

14. Snell, *The Discovery of the Mind*, p. 57.

15. Jaynes points out that Sappho uses a word in fragment 15, *synoida*, which can be rendered "know-together" and which anticipates the later latinization con-scious (*The Origin of Consciousness*, p. 285). Here we can see that the etymology of "conscious" itself reveals the sense of a unification of experience. But since "conscious" in common usage can also mean simple awareness (e.g., awake), I chose "self-consciousness" to express the features of unity, interiority, and autonomy. As we proceed, however, the term "consciousness" will often be used in this regard, and

the reader is asked to keep in mind its special meaning, as opposed to mere awareness.

16. Ibid., p. 282.
17. See ibid., p. 286.
18. Fragment 8. See Fränkel, *Early Greek Poetry and Philosophy*, p. 229. A similar thought is expressed by Zeus in the *Odyssey*, I.32–34.
19. Fragment 24. See Fränkel, *Early Greek Poetry and Philosophy*, p. 226. Vernant discusses the relationship between sociopolitical developments and abstraction in such actions as defining law, the allocation of duties, and the principles of citizenship, in terms of common features divorced from things like ancestry and profession (*Myth and Thought among the Greeks*, p. 359ff.).
20. Fragment 3. See Jaeger, *Paideia*, vol. 1, p. 141.
21. We cannot be sure of the accuracy of this attribution, but that anyone said it is significant enough. For a more extended study of Solon's thought, see Fränkel, *Early Greek Poetry and Philosophy*, pp. 217-237, and Jaeger, *Paideia*, vol. 1, pp. 136–149. As we have seen previously, Apollo's version of this maxim has a very different atmosphere.
22. Snell, *The Discovery of the Mind*, pp. 69–70.
23. See Jaeger, *Paideia*, vol. 1, p. 117.
24. I would say the same for us, because in my view the idea of privacy, in any form, is comprehensible only in relation to publicity. In other words, interiority may be a mark of selfhood, but this does not entail pure privacy. The idea of an atomic, insulated self might certainly be a temptation when we consider distinctions between public disclosure and secrecy, for example. But the notion of a private self as such, with the implication that human selfhood can be strictly marked off from the world and other selves, is only an intellectual invention which does nothing more than create pseudoproblems like the existence of other minds, solipsism, and skepticism. Modern philosophers such as Hegel, Marx, Heidegger, and Wittgenstein, among others, have all tried to show, from admittedly different standpoints, the untenability of a private self.
25. See Jaeger, *Paideia*, vol. 1, pp. 121–27.
26. For a general discussion of Pindar's poetry, see ibid., pp. 205–222; Fränkel, *Early Greek Poetry and Philosophy*, pp. 425–504; and Snell, *The Discovery of the Mind*, ch. 4.
27. *Sixth Nemean Ode*, trans. Lattimore in *The Portable Greek Reader*, ed. W. H. Auden (New York: Viking Press, 1948), p. 247.
28. *Greek Lyrics*, p. 61. Despite Pindar's traditionalism, the immediate content of traditional tales was for him usually a paradigm for a particular value he was promoting. Indeed, he often rejected certain features of tales he found unworthy (e.g., cannibalism). See Vernant, *Myth and Society in Ancient Greece*, pp. 194–95.

29. *Tenth Pythian Ode*, trans. Lattimore in *The Portable Greek Reader*, p. 244. For a general discussion of these issues, see my essay "The Greeks and the Meaning of Athletics," in *Rethinking College Athletics*, ed. Judith Andre and David James (Philadelphia: Temple University Press, forthcoming).

30. The word *athlos*, meaning "contest" or "struggle", is thus connected with the agonistic spirit of Greek myth.

31. *Sixth Nemean Ode*, Fränkel, *Early Greek Poetry and Philosophy*, p. 472.

32. *Eighth Pythian Ode*, 88–100, ibid., p. 499.

## CHAPTER V

1. Arthur Schopenhauer, *The World as Will and Representation*, trans. E. F. J. Payne (New York: Dover, 1966), p. 433.

2. Ibid., pp. 434–35.

3. The best translation is found in *Basic Writings of Nietzsche*, trans. Walter Kaufmann (New York: Modern Library, 1968). An excellent secondary work is M. S. Silk and J. P. Stern, *Nietzsche on Tragedy* (Cambridge University Press, 1981). There one can find a treatment of other interpretations of tragedy as well as a thorough evaluation and clarification of Nietzsche's position from the standpoint of Greek scholarship. For a general account of Nietzsche's philosophy in the context of his views on the Greeks, see my *Nietzsche and Eternal Recurrence: The Redemption of Time and Becoming* (University Press of America, 1978).

4. Much of the following is taken from Kerenyi's extensive treatment of Dionysian myth and religion, *Dionysos*, trans. Ralph Manheim (Princeton: Princeton University Press, 1976).

5. Ibid., pp. 139–141.

6. See ibid., pp. 52–125.

7. Ibid., pp. xxxi–xxxvii.

8. Ibid., p. 183.

9. Dionysus himself is a god who displays certain feminine characteristics (e.g., his feminine demeanor and appearance described in *The Bacchae*). Also, certain Dionysian practices (e.g., boiling goat pieces in milk) suggest the notion of returning to the Mother (Kerenyi, *Dionysos*, p. 256). For a discussion of the feminine and the Dionysian in relation to Nietzsche's philosophy, see my article "Nietzsche on Woman," *Southern Journal of Philosophy*, vol. XIX, no. 3, pp. 333–345.

10. For an account of Dionysian cult activities, see Kerenyi, *Dionysos*, pp. 199–204, W. K. C. Guthrie, *The Greeks and Their Gods* (Boston: Beacon

Press, 1950), pp. 147–152, and J. G. Frazer, *The Golden Bough* (New York: Macmillan, 1963), pp. 448–456.

11. Otto's *Dionysus: Myth and Cult* offers a vivid study of Dionysus which emphasizes the manic element.

12. For a discussion of maenadism and other comparable religious practices, see Dodds, *The Greeks and the Irrational*, pp. 270–282.

13. We know today that the complete repression of violence can lead to terrible outbreaks of violence and that too much rationality can even lead to psychosis. See Simon, *Mind and Madness in Ancient Greece*, p. 149.

14. See Kerenyi, *Dionysos*, pp. 189–198.

15. Versenyi, *Man's Measure*, p. 114.

16. See Kerenyi, *Dionysos*, pp. 330–348.

17. For a related discussion, see my "Laughter in Nietzsche's Thought: A Philosophical Tragicomedy," *International Studies in Philosophy*, vol. XX, no. 2, 1988.

18. There *is* a kind of infinity suggested by the Dionysian life force, but it is really a formless infinity. If there is any sense of immortality in Dionysian religion it should be seen as the ongoing process of life which persists through the destruction of individual life forms. Thus we cannot infer a doctrine of personal immortality from early Dionysian worship; rather, Dionysus himself seems to represent a formless process which gives and takes all form. It was only in later developments that the religion adopted notions of an afterlife and dualistic distinctions between this world and a hereafter; beliefs which, however, did not seem to characterize the original version. See Kerenyi, *Dionysos*, pp. 364 and 381, and in general pp. 349–388. See also Burkert, *Greek Religion*, pp. 290–95.

19. Versenyi, *Man's Measure*, p. 122.

20. Kerenyi points out certain historical and mythical references which support Nietzsche's contention that Apollo was seen by the Greeks to be connected with Dionysus in various ways. For example, Apollo and Dionysus both had related cults at Delphi (*Dionysos*, p. 213); one tradition held Apollo's mother to be a Dionysian woman (p. 214); another maintained that Apollo rescued Dionysus by gathering his broken pieces (p. 231); and Apollo's oracle received its messages from subterranean, and hence Dionysian, regions (p. 232).

21. Snell, *The Discovery of the Mind*, p. 103.

22. Ibid., p. 108.

23. Ibid., pp. 103–104.

24. When a hero goes mad, however, it is still because of divine intervention (Simon, *Mind and Madness in Ancient Greece*, p. 93); furthermore,

extraconscious forces continue to be a factor in tragic poetry since the seer often plays an important role (e.g., Cassandra and Teiresias).

25. This and other translations are taken from *The Complete Greek Tragedies*, ed. David Grene and Richmond Lattimore (Chicago: University of Chicago Press, 1959).

26. See Jaeger, *Paideia*, vol. 1, pp. 253–54.

27. For this reason Shakespearean tragedy in most cases cannot be compared to Greek tragedy, since the dilemma in the former can usually be traced to human motives or character flaws, giving it a kind of subjunctive resolvability.

28. There is an ambiguity in the Greek that permits translating this line: "in the end he comes to nothing." See Versenyi, *Man's Measure*, p. 212.

29. See ibid., pp. 212–15.

30. Ibid., pp. 231–32.

31. For a treatment of Aristophanes in this regard, see Snell, *The Discovery of the Mind*, ch. 6.

32. Some references for a critical attitude toward traditional myths in the plays: *Heracles*, 1307f., 1341–46; *Iphigenia at Taurus*, 386–91; *Trojan Women*, 983–89.

33. *The Birth of Tragedy*, sections 10–14.

34. The failure to recognize such a distinction prevents Walter Kaufmann from fully understanding Nietzsche's critique when he tries to defend Euripides as the most tragic of the three poets: *Tragedy and Philosophy* (Garden City, N.Y.: Anchor Books, 1968), pp. 283–301.

35. The implication is that the human self is becoming its own god. Burkert cites the following fragment of Euripides: "The *nous* in each one is god for men" (*Greek Religion*, p. 319).

36. See Snell, *The Discovery of the Mind*, p. 119.

37. Nietzsche, *The Birth of Tragedy*, section 10.

38. For an analysis in this regard see David Halliburton, "Concealing Revealing: A Perspective on Greek Tragedy," in *Post-Structuralist Classics*, pp. 245–267. The essay also considers the temporality intrinsic to tragedy and the role of tragedy in education.

39. See Snell, *The Discovery of the Mind*, pp. 97–98. What is called the suspension of disbelief, or being caught up in a dramatic performance as though it were real and yet implicitly knowing it is not real—this zone in between the real and the apparent can serve as an analogy for the possibility of *living* a myth without being tied to its literalness, i.e., an outlook which is neither fundamentalist nor allegorist (the myth seen as a dispensable image of some deeper truth).

40. Nietzsche, *The Birth of Tragedy*, section 14. Among other things I try to develop this important aspect of Nietzsche's philosophy in chapters 3 and 5 of *Nietzsche and Eternal Recurrence*.

## CHAPTER VI

1. See *The Discovery of the Mind*, pp. 131–32, where Snell suggests a developmental relationship between epic poetry and history, theogony/cosmogony and natural philosophy, lyric poetry and value inquiry, tragedy and moral philosophy. See also Burkert, *Greek Religion,* pp. 305–337.

2. Vernant discusses the connection between the emergence of philosophy, science, and abstract thinking and sociopolitical developments, where secularization, commonality, debate among equals, and writing were changing the status of traditional mythical forces (*Myth and Thought among the Greeks,* pp. 176–189).

3. Lloyd, *Magic, Reason and Experience,* pp. 14–15.

4. See Dodds, *The Greeks and the Irrational,* pp. 182–83.

5. In general, even after they turned to philosophy the Greeks did not always abandon traditional myths, because they frequently saw the narrative stories as compatible with reason—e.g., as an indirect, symbolic, or allegorical representation of a rational truth. See Paul Veyne, *Did the Greeks Believe in their Myths?,* trans. Paula Wissing (Chicago: University of Chicago Press, 1988), especially pp. 1–18, and Vernant, *Myth and Society in Ancient Greece,* p. 202ff.

6. Versenyi, *Man's Measure,* pp. 58–69.

7. Snell, *The Discovery of the Mind,* ch. 7.

8. With regard to the Homeric connection between knowing, seeing, and divinity, Kerenyi discusses the vestiges of this complex in later Greek philosophy despite the turn to abstraction (*The Religion of the Greeks and Romans,* pp. 147–151). Knowing and seeing maintained a correlation in Greek thought, if only through the visual metaphors that persisted in Greek (and our) intellectual language (e.g., "seeing" the point, a "bright" mind, and so forth). Such a connection can be historically traced to the mythical sense of a god's knowing-as-seeing.

9. Moreover, the analogy between conceptual thought and the sacred will also help us understand the continued insistence on the part of some later Greek philosophers that although the human mind actively executes the principles of knowledge, these principles are not simply the products of the human mind; they have an extrahuman origin to which the mind must conform.

10. Translations in this chapter, unless noted otherwise, are taken from G. S. Kirk and J. E. Raven, *The Presocratic Philosophers* (Cambridge University Press, 1966). The numbers following fragment numbers indicate the boldface notation sequence in that work. I should add that the dates I give for these philosophers are not certain.

11. Kirk and Raven, *The Presocratic Philosophers,* p. 119.

12. Ibid., p. 114.
13. Jaeger, *Paideia,* vol. 1, p. 159.
14. Hippolytus, *Ref.* I.6.2., Diels and Kranz, *Die Fragmente der Vorsok-ritiker,* 12A11.
15. F. M. Cornford, *From Religion to Philosophy* (New York: Harper and Row, 1957), pp. 172–74.
16. In this regard see Charles H. Kahn, "Anaximander's Fragment: The Universe Governed by Law," in *The Pre-Socratics,* ed. A. P. D. Mourelatos (Garden City, N.Y.: Anchor Books, 1974), pp. 99–117. This collection contains many useful articles on pre-Socratic philosophy. For some of Heidegger's interpretations, see *Early Greek Thinking,* trans. David F. Krell and Frank A. Capuzzi (New York: Harper and Row, 1975).
17. Kathleen Freeman, *Ancilla to the Pre-Socratic Philosophers* (Cambridge: Harvard University Press, 1966), p. 32.
18. Ibid., p. 27.
19. Ibid., p. 28.
20. Aristotle reports this criticism in reference to a line from the *Iliad.* See Kirk and Raven, *The Presocratic Philosophers,* p. 196, #216.
21. Freeman, *Ancilla to the Pre-Socratic Philosophers,* p. 25.
22. Ibid., p. 29.
23. Lloyd, *Magic, Reason and Experience,* pp. 71 and 78.
24. Cornford, *Principium Sapientiae,* pp. 118–120.
25. Heidegger tries to rework the translation of Parmenides for such purposes. Among other works, see *What Is Called Thinking?* trans. Fred D. Wieck and J. Glenn Gray (New York: Harper and Row, 1968), specifically Lecture X.
26. One can connect this point with Aristotle's remark that privation (*sterēsis*) can still be a kind of *eidos* or form (*Physics,* 193b19–20).
27. Parmenides, or any Greek for that matter, would have been incapable of metaphysical idealism as we know it, because the *separation* of mind and world, subject and object, which is a precondition for the turn toward idealism, was not truly established until Descartes. Parmenides's *noein-legein-einai* complex is not unrelated to the mythical correlation of self and world, or language and world.
28. For a brief discussion of this point, see my *Nietzsche and Eternal Recurrence,* pp. 120–27.
29. For a summary discussion of the mystery cults, see Burkert, *Greek Religion,* pp. 276–304.
30. Eliade, *Myth and Reality,* p. 111.
31. Cornford, *Principium Sapientiae,* ch. 7.
32. Freeman, *Ancilla to the Pre-Socratic Philosophers,* pp. 51, 55.
33. Cornford, *Principium Sapientiae,* p. 108.
34. Ibid.

35. See ibid., ch. 8.
36. M. P. Nilsson, *History of Greek Religion* (Oxford, 1949), ch. 4.
37. But as Vernant points out, the philosophers did not match the shaman's connection with secret, esoteric doctrines, as in the mystery cults. They became teachers, with followers, and they willingly revealed their insights for public discussion, to all who would listen. See *Myth and Thought among the Greeks*, pp. 352–57.
38. Cornford, *Principium Sapientiae*, p. 159. See also Fränkel, *Early Greek Poetry and Philosophy*, p. 261ff.
39. Drew Hyland, in *The Origins of Philosophy* (New York: Capricorn Books, G. P. Putnam's Sons, 1973), also argues against a strict separation of Greek myth and philosophy. He discounts the notion that early philosophy represented a turn away from myth toward a kind of scientific materialism (p. 97). Rather, early philosophy and myth represent different ways of characterizing similar issues (p. 21); one can find "philosophical" themes, e.g., finitude, mystery, opposition, and becoming, in Greek myth and poetry (p. 30ff.). Of course, I agree. My only reservation is that we should not forget that the *mode* of presentation is different in myth and philosophy. That difference has important implications. These "philosophical" themes emerge as such through reflection *on* the myths and their implicit meanings. These themes were not explicitly expressed as such in early myth and poetry. This is what philosophy offers that is not found in myth per se. In this sense, myths are not philosophical. Hyland says that the poets were philosophical because they wondered about things and raised questions (p. 47). I have some trouble with this. In retrospect, *we* can sense the issues and questions implied in myth and poetry. But did myth really take a "questioning" attitude? Is such an attitude evident in the language of myth and poetry? My analysis of receptivity, givenness, and inspiration tends to cast doubt on such a notion. I am not even sure many of the first *philosophers* really took a questioning attitude, if that implies reflective distance and a starting point in human inquiry as such. Much of early philosophy, at least in the language we have, seems more oracular than inquisitive. It is with Socrates that a questioning attitude clearly emerges; and this, as we shall see, implies significant changes from earlier attitudes. In a related point, another reason why Hyland objects to a strict separation of myth and philosophy stems from his contention that both arise out of human nature. I see two problems here. First, such a contention tends to cover up significant differences between myth and philosophy. Secondly, much of my analysis is meant to challenge any anthropological reduction of myth to "human nature." In retrospect perhaps we are prone to think this way, but a phenomenological analysis shows that the modern conception of human nature is not fully evident as such in prephilosophical myth and is

not a timeless notion that could be proposed as the *basis* of myth. If there *is* something constant in the history of culture, the existential setting of the lived world would be the best candidate. But such a setting in mythical culture does not exhibit the clear markings of human nature that have emerged as a *discrete* complex only *since* the advent of philosophy. Aside from these reservations, I find Hyland's study to be an insightful entry into the subject of Greek myth and philosophy.

40. For an account of the mystical as opposed to the logical elements of Parmenides's philosophy, see Fränkel, *Early Greek Poetry and Philosophy,* pp. 366–370.

41. See Dodds, *The Greeks and the Irrational,* ch. 6, and Burkert, *Greek Religion,* pp. 311–17.

42. Dodds, *The Greeks and the Irrational,* p. 189.

43. Fragment 209, translated in Fränkel, *Early Greek Poetry and Philosophy,* p. 479.

44. Kant's critique of theoretical reason is a notable example. There is, however, an important difference. Such modern attempts leave nature to science and maintain existential meaning within the human sphere, which leads to the troublesome fact-value distinction. Mythical disclosure, on the other hand, understood the *world* in terms of such existential meanings.

45. See Dodds, *The Greeks and the Irrational,* pp. 192–95.

**CHAPTER VII**

1. In referring to Plato and Platonism, I am including the influence of Socrates (469–399 B.C.). I will consider Plato and Socrates a kind of intellectual complex and will not strictly distinguish between them. Although an important question concerns the degree to which the dialogues are Socratic or Platonic, it need not be answered in such a study as this. I am not sure the question can be clearly resolved in any case. Most of what we know of Socrates comes from Plato's works, since Socrates never wrote anything; and the voice of Socrates continues to be the main character throughout most of the dialogues. As a result we may never be sure where Socrates leaves off and Plato begins. (Two interesting traditional elements are shown here—the oral aspect of Socratic philosophy and the absence of self-reference on Plato's part.) Even though there is some truth to the distinction between so-called early Socratic and later Platonic dialogues, nevertheless many features of both can be ascertained in the different periods. Translations in this chapter are taken from

*The Collected Dialogues of Plato*, edited by Edith Hamilton and Huntington Cairns (Princeton: Princeton University Press, 1961).

2. Gottfried Martin, *An Introduction to General Metaphysics*, trans. Eva Schaper and Ivor Leclerc (London: Allen and Unwin, 1961), p. 28.

3. Dodds, *The Greeks and the Irrational*, pp. 140–42, and ch. 5 in general.

4. Even when the Greeks did develop the notion of a self which is individual, internalized, unified, and different from the body, this did not approach the modern notion of a unique, individual "personality" essentially different from other selves and the rest of reality. See Vernant, *Myth and Thought among the Greeks*, pp. 334–35.

5. Dodds, *The Greeks and the Irrational*, p. 149. The term "puritan" is, of course, to be distinguished from later more specific uses referring to a particular group or attitude.

6. Ibid., pp. 149–156.

7. Ibid., p. 154.

8. According to Vernant, in *Myth and Thought among the Greeks*, when such views of the soul emerged, the negative images previously associated with Hades, as a hateful kind of oblivion, became associated with earthly life (pp. 82–83). With the idea of an immortal soul delivered from the temporal world after the death of the body, there occurred a "reversal of attitude," where "life becomes charged with the mythical values attached to death, and death acquires those hitherto associated with life" (p. 118).

9. For a discussion of the relationship in Greek thought between mathematics, demonstration, philosophy, and science, see Lloyd, *Magic, Reason and Experience*, pp. 115–125. Stanley Rosen, in *The Quarrel Between Philosophy and Poetry* (New York: Routledge, 1988), shows in various ways how Plato's thought is not reducible to a mathematical model.

10. Augustine and Descartes, for example, maintained an association between mathematics and divine truth. Mathematics was essential to the development of mechanics and classical physics and has continued to be so in modern science. For example, water is not *essentially* its sense qualities or even its material elements (hydrogen and oxygen) but a certain *ratio* of elements ($H_2O$) since a different ratio gives a different entity ($H_2O_2$ = peroxide). And mathematics is the centerpiece of our knowledge about atomic structure. Modern science thus represents an interesting echo of the Pythagorean belief that reality is essentially made up of numbers. The difference would be that for the Pythagoreans number was not simply quantitative but qualitative in meaning. Knowledge of harmony and proportion was the goal of mathematical training. The Greeks continued this tradition by maintaining the role of mathematics and music in education. On this point, see Jaeger, *Paideia*, vol. I, pp. 162–65. For a general discussion of the mathematical and modern sci-

ence, see Martin Heidegger, *What is a Thing?* trans. W. B. Barton, Jr., and Vera Deutsch (Chicago: Henry Regnery Co., 1967), pp. 65–108.

11. Platonic Forms cannot simply be identified with concepts, however, because they also represent the notion of ideals, with moral and even aesthetic dimensions.

12. See the *Philebus*, 59a-d, for the connection between permanence and truth, and the impossibility of finding precision, exactitude, and certainty in temporal conditions. But Plato adds (62b-d) that a human life must mix exact with less exact sciences. See Rosen, *The Quarrel between Philosophy and Poetry*, pp. 56–57.

13. Snell, *The Discovery of the Mind*, ch. 8.

14. The early Platonic position has the rational soul curbing the physical body; a later position has the rational part of the soul curbing the irrational part of the soul.

15. The advent of rationality can also be connected with social developments. Lloyd maintains that rational methods can be historically correlated with Greek political forces, namely, the democratic assembly and the need for persuasion leading to the development of critical skills. See *Magic, Reason and Experience*, pp. 240–264.

16. See Cassirer, *The Philosophy of Symbolic Forms*, vol. 2, p. 172.

17. Such is the meaning of Aristotle's proposition that man is a "political animal," a notion which receives a radical reformulation and extension centuries later in Hegel and Marx.

18. In another context Plato offers a reflexive model of human experience, when in a discussion of love, the lover is said to be a "mirror" in which the beloved "beholds himself" (*Phaedrus*, 255c, ff.).

19. See *Paideia*, vol. 1, pp. 286–331.

20. Ibid., p. 307.

21. Ibid., p. 102.

22. See ibid., pp. 187–204.

23. Such a division of labor was even prefigured in Homer:

> *Because the god has granted you the actions of warfare*
> *therefore you wish in counsel also to be wise beyond others.*
> *But you cannot choose to have all gifts given to you together.*
> *To one man the god has granted the actions of warfare,*
> *to one to be a dancer, to another the lyre and the singing,*
> *and in the breast of another Zeus of the wide brows establishes*
> *wisdom, a lordly thing, and many take profit beside him*
> *and he saves many, but the man's own thought surpasses all*
> *others.*
>
> (*Iliad*, XIII. 727–734)

24. Dodds, *The Greeks and the Irrational*, pp. 209–210.

25. In the *Symposium*, Socrates yields to the proclamations of a prophetess, Diotima, on the nature of *eros*. Love is described as a drive caused by the lack or absence of something. The love of wisdom (*philo-sophia*) is said to be in between ignorance and wisdom, and so the philosopher cannot be said to possess wisdom (202d–204b). See David F. Krell, "'Knowledge is Remembrance': Diotima's Instruction at *Symposium*, 207c8–208b6," in *Post-Structuralist Classics*, pp. 160–172.

26. See Julius A. Elias, *Plato's Defence of Poetry* (Albany: SUNY Press, 1984), Robert Zaslavsky, *Platonic Myth and Platonic Writing* (University Press of America, 1981), and Kent F. Moors, *Platonic Myth: An Introductory Study* (University Press of America, 1982).

27. For a summary discussion of Plato's integration of philosophy and religion in the *Laws*, in terms of the importance of religious customs and practices for generating social order and piety in the masses, see Burkert, *Greek Religion*, pp. 332–37.

28. Plato *did* use some myths from the tradition, but these were usually of the Orphic type which were not indicative of the mainstream. See Vernant, *Myth and Society in Ancient Greece*, p. 202.

29. See Stanley Rosen, *Plato's Symposium* (New Haven: Yale University Press, 1968), p. xv.

30. See, e.g., Hyland, *The Origins of Philosophy*, p. 344; and Jacob Klein, *A Commentary on Plato's Meno* (Chapel Hill: University of North Carolina Press, 1965), pp. 4–8.

31. Hyland, *The Origins of Philosophy*, p. 345.

32. Stanley Rosen, *Plato's Sophist* (New Haven: Yale University Press, 1983), p. 1. Rosen describes the setting of a dialogue as "dramatic phenomenology," which involves artistic reproduction of speeches and deeds to provide an indirect commentary on the significance of the speeches, all within the context of a unified statement about the good life or philosophical life (pp. 12–13).

33. Kenneth Dorter, in *Plato's Phaedo* (Toronto: University of Toronto Press, 1982), adopts a balanced approach by taking seriously both the dramatic aspects and the philosophical positions discussed in the dialogues (p. ix). He cautions that although an interpretation must consider the literary aspects of a dialogue, this should not be taken to mean that the arguments or philosophical positions are irrelevant or that an interpretation can be wide open (p. 4). Although Dorter argues against a strict soul-body dualism in Plato, he holds the view that there *is* a more fundamental ontological dualism concerning the eternal and the temporal (pp. 182–85).

34. Rosen, *Plato's Sophist*, p. 15.

35. See Hyland, *The Origins of Philosophy*, p. 344ff.; and Klein, *A Commentary on Plato's Meno*, p. 9. Klein also takes a balanced position by saying

that there *are* doctrines in Plato's thought, but not a clear and closed philosophical system.

36. Hyland maintains that the inconclusiveness of Platonic dialogues points to the limits of conclusive knowledge in philosophy (*The Origins of Philosophy*, p. 348). Consequently, Socratic wisdom (i.e., knowing the limits of one's knowledge) may be an essential feature of the dialogue form (p. 349). Rosen, in *Plato's Symposium*, maintains that every dialogue is a dialectic between intuition and reason in that the soul is open to the Ideas, but it also obscures them. The dialogue is thus a "third" element between the Ideas and our life in the world, a mediation which avoids the dualism of a "two-worlds" doctrine (p. 197–98).

37. Klein, *A Commentary on Plato's Meno*, pp. 10–17. Rosen calls a dialogue a perfect form of writing for expressing the limits of writing and doctrines (*Plato's Symposium*, p. xviii).

38. Rosen, *Plato's Symposium*, p. xxii.

39. Rosen states that every dialogue can be called a myth as long as the presence of *logos*, or reason, is also recognized (ibid., p. 1).

40. See Dorter, *Plato's Phaedo*, where Platonic images of an afterlife and soul-body separation are described as metaphors expressing how one should live in the present (pp. 81, 176ff.).

41. In *The Quarrel Between Philosophy and Poetry* (p. 114) Rosen points out those instances in the *Republic* where philosophy is described in terms of a battle, a war (470b4ff., 474b3–4, 496d4, 517a5, 534b8). In this way, the activity of philosophy fits in with the agonistic atmosphere of Greek culture. But I would add that this is not a battle meant to be "won" entirely, but rather an ongoing contest, a continuing tension with other forces meant for coexistence.

42. Such *practical* differentiations are essential to the enterprise of *teaching* philosophy, where we have to challenge the minds of our students, which usually come to us ruled by errors, biases, emotions, customs, other minds, laziness, confusion, and what not.

43. It seems to me that a less dogmatic interpretation of Plato cannot *ignore* references in the dialogues which seem to present a more literal kind of ontological dualism. We cannot be sure Plato did *not* intend such things, in some way. Concerning immortality, a kind of balance is evident in the *Phaedo*, where a myth of the *afterlife* is recounted (107c–115a), after which Socrates says that although it would be unreasonable to take the myth literally, something like it is fitting and worth risking for one who believes it.

44. A mythical element in Plato should be distinguished from the actual myths told in the dialogues. The myths often seem to be taken as a metaphorical supplement to reason, in their appeal to imagination and emotion, or to what is described in the *Phaedo* as "the child within us"

(77e). The poets do *not* as such engage a logos. See Dorter, *Plato's Phaedo*, pp. 6–8.

45. It is evident that Plato loved poetry, but his conception of truth was more important to him (*Republic*, X. 607b–608b). A helpful collection of essays concerning Plato's treatment of poetry and art is *Plato on Beauty, Wisdom and the Arts*, ed. Julius Moravcsik and Philip Temko (Totowa, NJ: Roman and Littlefield, 1982).

46. See Dorter, *Plato's Phaedo*, p. 203. For a modern analogy consider objections to "creation science." Or, would not a modern university want to "censor" someone who, let's say, insisted on teaching history from an astrological standpoint?

47. See Klein, *A Commentary on Plato's Meno*, p. 171.


**CHAPTER VIII**

1. Translation by Fränkel, *Early Greek Poetry and Philosophy*, p. 108n. Subsequent translations, unless otherwise indicated, are taken from *The Basic Works of Aristotle*, ed. Richard McKeon (New York: Random House, 1941). Again, I am not pretending to offer a definitive or nuanced analysis of Aristotle's thought. I want to emphasize those elements that contrast with the mythical tradition.

2. See Rosen, *Plato's Sophist*, p. 7.

3. Much of what follows is taken from Cornford, *Principium Sapientiae*, ch. 3, and especially from Lloyd, *Magic, Reason and Experience*.

4. Lloyd, *Magic, Reason and Experience*, pp. 15–16.

5. Ibid., pp. 18–25.

6. Ibid., p. 29.

7. We have already discussed the difference between myth and science with respect to their meaning and aims. In the case of death from disease, for example, science wants an explanation based on natural laws, which are nonspecific and repeatable. Our phenomenological analysis of myth, however, indicated qualitatively different concerns: existential involvement (the drama and import of death); immediate specificity (why *this* person died at *this* time). If a mythical account were nothing more than an attempt to explain the mechanics of death and disease, it could well be corrected. There may indeed be examples of pseudo-science in myth (e.g., the belief that a dance does cause rain), but that would not change the fact that there is much *more* to mythical disclosure which is not susceptible to scientific correction.

8. Lloyd *Magic, Reason and Experience*, pp. 26–27.

9. Ibid., p. 128.

10. For an extended discussion of medical dissection as an example of experimentation, see ibid., pp. 146-169.
11. Cornford, *Principium Sapientiae*, p. 32ff.
12. Snell, *The Discovery of the Mind*, pp. 146-47.
13. Quoted by Cornford in *Principium Sapientiae*, p. 32.
14. Again, Lloyd warns against simplistic or polarized interpretations of this historical period. The new medicine was not strictly empirical and was not always successful in treatment (*Magic, Reason and Experience*, pp. 54-57); in general, Greek science was not rigorously experimental, since "observations were more often employed to illustrate and support theories than to test them" (p. 200). A complete separation of magic and science is untenable since many scientific developments retained religious influences, and temple medicine often involved treatments which were comparable to Hippocratic medicine (pp. 40-41). For a helpful summary of the complicated picture regarding magic, religion, philosophy, and science in the Greek world, and thus the difficulty of separate classifications, see pp. 227-28 and 232-34.
15. *The Portable Greek Reader*, pp. 438-465.
16. Snell, *The Discovery of the Mind*, pp. 143-44. For a discussion of Thucydides in this regard, see Vernant, *Myth and Society in Ancient Greece*, pp. 190-93. Incidentally, Aristotle's philosophical interest in what is universal leads him to grade poetry higher than history; since poets deal with universal meanings, their work is more philosophical than history, which deals with particular events (*Poetics*, 9.1451b5-8).
17. Reason and science are constituted by such *general* objects of study; and that distinguishes reason and science from both purely empirical matters and the nonempirical, sacred regions of myth (specific *existential* meanings beyond the brute given). Such objectification of mental functions shows on the one hand the mind's discovery of *itself* and on the other hand how this discovery required an active *disengagement* from prerational modes of disclosure. See Snell, *The Discovery of the Mind*, ch. 10.
18. It is certainly true that Plato was an equally important influence on western intellectual history, but Aristotle succeeded in filtering out certain indecisive and archaic elements in Platonism. In other words, Aristotle helped determine how Plato would be *read*, what would be emphasized and what would not.
19. Even though modern science may refute certain findings in the history of science, we can still talk of different periods of "science" because of this shared framework, which is *not* a point of contention. However, assumptions about natural explanation, causality, prediction, and the like are "self-evident" only once science is in place; they themselves cannot be tested (being preconditions for a test) and are thus prescientific. That is

why Aristotelian thought is so important; we witness the way in which Aristotle *transformed* the meaning of reality and truth by establishing scientific assumptions at the expense of other modes of disclosure, a transformation which is not as such a scientific matter.

20. That the process of production seems to suit this causal complex best would undermine Aristotle's previous distinction between natural things and designed things. For a discussion of the production model implicit in the classical matter-form distinction and a phenomenological critique of the distinction's ontological status, see Martin Heidegger, *The Basic Problems of Phenomenology*, trans. Albert Hofstadter (Bloomington: Indiana University Press, 1982), section 11.

21. The distinction between matter and form could be said to represent Aristotle's version of a correlation between formlessness and form. Of course, the mythical and early philosophical correlation has been altered, because material "formlessness" remains inseparable from form and an empirical, tangible context. The notion of formlessness found in tragedy and early philosophy reflected an *existential* context of negation, death, and hiddenness in mythical "appearance," i.e., the *lived* process of emergence and disappearance, which is a different issue from the Aristotelian notion of a potential *substrate* for forms.

22. In the *Metaphysics* (I.9.991a10–30) Aristotle argues that Plato's transcendent Forms contribute no information and add nothing to our immediate knowledge of things and are thus redundant. This may be quite right. But as we saw in the *Timaeus*, the Forms were not equivalent to conceptual universals; they were primarily intended not to "inform" but to "transform," i.e., to harmonize the soul with extra-immediate moral and spiritual values.

23. For example, the mythical presentation of thunder as divine wrath is replaced by a strictly naturalistic explanation, i.e., "sound produced in the clouds" (*Metaphysics*, VII.17.1041a24–25).

24. Hegel devised an intelligible logic which subordinated the principle of noncontradiction to a dialectical model which gave a fundamental role to negation and relation.

25. For a comparable discussion of different kinds of sense in mystical language see my "Mysticism and Language," *International Philosophical Quarterly*, vol. XXII, no. 1, March 1982, pp. 51–64.

26. According to Nietzsche, Aristotle's principle represents a (moral) judgment upon negation and process, an inability to withstand the tragic sense of life. A rationalistic paradigm would not reflect truth but what it *wants* truth to be—an abiding constancy to insulate the mind from the terror of negation. See *The Will to Power*, trans. Walter Kaufmann and R. J. Hollingdale (New York: Vintage Books, 1967), section 516.

27. For a phenomenological critique of Aristotle's treatise on time, see

Heidegger, *Being and Time*, sections 78–83, and *The Basic Problems of Phenomenology*, section 19.

28. Augustine speaks to this point somewhat when he defines past and future in terms of present memories and anticipations (*Confessions*, XI, ch. 28).

29. At one point (223a20–30) Aristotle does acknowledge such an issue when he asks: Might it be that time, as measurement, is connected with the soul, such that there would not be time without the soul which measures? But the question is only raised parenthetically. It does not seem to influence his analysis in the *Physics*, which is more empirical than psychological. Augustine, in the *Confessions*, although he was influenced by Aristotle's analysis, took up this psychological question as fundamental to the meaning of time. For him there is no time apart from the soul (XI, ch. 28), which would mean that not all creatures are identically "in time."

30. Aristotle quotes a line from Homer: "Lordship for many is no good thing. Let there be one ruler, one king" (*Iliad*, II.204). Of course, Aristotle takes this thought beyond its mythical and social context.

31. For example, he accepted the possibility of prophetic dreams, but only in the context of verifying them according to rational methods. His general interpretation of dreams was that they are derived from prior presentations in sense experience. See Dodds, *The Greeks and the Irrational*, p. 120. Aristotle's overall view was that myths can have validity if they are stripped of their personified imagery and anthropomorphism (*Metaphysics*, 1074b, ff.). Myth can even be seen as a forerunner of philosophical reason, as a child's speech is to that of an adult. But myth can only be intelligible in terms of a rational "translation." In this way, Aristotle was engaged in "demythologizing" his tradition (cf. Bultmann). He allowed for truth in myth, but only after its (childish) mode of presentation was exchanged for its heretofore concealed rational meaning. See Vernant, *Myth and Society in Ancient Greece*, pp. 203–205. Subsequent to such a treatment, the particular mode of mytho-poetic disclosure shifts from its culture-forming role to a mere "facet" of culture, i.e., it becomes an art form understood in the light of aesthetics. Whatever truth there was in poetry is exchanged for the category of "beauty." See Snell, *The Discovery of the Mind*, p. 117.

32. The historical displacement of mythical disclosure by scientific rationalism was not based upon a difference of opinion but the belief that myth did not match reality. That is why many premethodological and extra-experimental assumptions were a necessary part of the history of science. For example, European philosophers and scientists in the Medieval and Enlightenment periods did not so much reject as transform theological assumptions; and Newtonian physics was backed up by the notions of absolute space and time.

33. For a Heideggerian reading of Aristotle which differs from customary assumptions, see Walter Brogan, "Is Aristotle a Metaphysician?" *Journal of the British Society for Phenomenology*, vol. 15, no. 3, Oct. 1984, pp. 249–261.

34. Also, Aristotle's analysis of moral action gathered the transition from a mythical sense of fatalism to notions of autonomy and freedom. Witness his account of voluntary action (*Nicomachean Ethics*, III.1–5), and his claim that virtue and vice are both in our power (III.5.1113b5–10) and that virtue is a result of deliberate choice (*Eudemian Ethics*, III.1.1228a23–24). It should be pointed out that with regard to ethics, Aristotle did not espouse a rigid, formulaic, or foundationalist approach to moral thinking. Necessary truths and uniform universals are not the province of ethics (or politics), which is more loose, contingent, and vague than precise. *Phronēsis*, or a kind of practical discretion, is the guide here rather than *epistēmē* (*Nicomachean Ethics*, 1139a, ff.). See H. G. Gadamer, *The Idea of the Good in Platonic–Aristotelian Philosophy*, trans. P. Christopher Smith (New Haven: Yale University Press, 1986).

35. Aristotle's teleology accounts for the ambiguity in the term "end" (i.e., a cessation and a goal). *Telos* originally meant nothing more than a spatial or temporal *limit*. Aristotle added the concept of completed development, independent of the possibility that a thing's development might be prematurely interrupted or ruined. In effect, the concept of a thing "turning out well" reflects Aristotle's alternative to tragic fatalism.

36. At least with regard to things in the natural world, Aristotle's insistence that a potential which is *not yet* present must be included in our understanding of a thing shows that being must in some way be correlated with nonbeing and understood in terms of temporal development. That makes Aristotle's thinking more embedded in the world of our experience; but as we have seen, his ultimate metaphysical commitments take him beyond negativity and temporality.

37. See also the *Eudemian Ethics*, 1217b, for a pluralized meaning of being and goodness, as opposed to their supposed uniform meaning in Platonism.

38. For a discussion of the differences between Aristotelian physics and modern science, see Heidegger, *What Is a Thing?*, pp. 66–108.

## CHAPTER IX

1. Blumenberg, in *Work on Myth*, argues that myth and scientific rationality are both indispensable and not incompatible. He also examines the uses of and challenges to Greek myth in post-Classical periods, in Chris-

tianity, and in various philosophical and literary figures (especially Goethe). Myth continued to flourish in European culture in various ways. And there was a comparable "enlightenment" tension beginning in the seventeenth century that in some ways rehearsed the Greek experience. I have not addressed post-Greek developments in this study, but not simply to preserve a manageable focus. The advent of rationality in Greece would have an effect on how myth would be understood thereafter. That complicates things quite a bit. So it is important to begin with a particular treatment of the nature of myth prior to and during the first emergence of rationality.

2. Contemporary philosophers of science have argued against the assumption that science is strictly objective and separable from social and political elements, metaphysical commitments, creative imagination, and selective observation, among other things. See, e.g., Stephen Toulmin, *Foresight and Understanding* (NY: Harper and Row, 1963); Thomas S. Kuhn, *The Structure of Scientific Revolutions* (Chicago: University of Chicago Press, 1970); Paul Feyerabend, *Against Method* (London: Verso, 1978); *Challenges to Empiricism*, ed. H. Morick (Hackett, 1980); Richard Bernstein, *Beyond Objectivity and Relativism* (Philadelphia: University of Pennsylvania Press, 1983); and W. H. Newton-Smith, *The Rationality of Science* (London: Routledge and Kegan Paul, 1981). For a Heideggerian angle, see Theodore Kisiel, "Heidegger and the New Images of Science," *Research in Phenomenology*, 7 (1977), pp. 162–181, and Joseph Rouse, "Kuhn, Heidegger and Scientific Realism," *Man and World*, 14 (1981), pp. 269–290.

3. Aristotle made a remark that might complicate things a bit here. After saying that philosophy begins in wonder, he notes that even a lover of myth is in a sense a lover of wisdom (*philo-sophia*) because myth is composed of wonders (*Metaphysics*, 982b18). If Aristotle is not equivocating here, we notice a link. The term for wonder (*thaumazein*) can mean a kind of astonishment and thereby connect with the sense of the extraordinary and mystery in myth. See John Llewelyn, "On the Saying that Philosophy Begins in Thaumazein," in *Post-Structuralist Classics*, pp. 173–191. But it seems to me that the explanatory tendencies in rationality show the difference. If philosophy *begins* with astonishment, the question is whether it can *end* there too, that is, seek not to eliminate astonishment but to sustain it in the sense of the limits of explanation and the sheer extraordinary marvel of the world. See Heidegger, "What is Metaphysics?" in *Basic Writings*.

4. According to Blumenberg the assumption that logos can put an end to myth is betrayed because such attempts are always cast in terms of metaphors of myth; in this sense myth never ends (*Work on Myth*, pp. 629–633).

5. Even beyond historical considerations, from a phenomenological stand-point only a fraction of our experience is truly self-conscious. More often than not we are absorbed in the world without standing back from our experience or activity. And yet modern philosophical models which aim to analyze *all* of existence follow from and depend upon the separation of self-conscious reflection from objects of experience. One example of the limitations inherent in such an approach is the so-called problem of skepticism. It is the subject-object, mind-world separation which is the *precondition* for such a problem. Such a problem can be taken seriously *only* from a reflective standpoint; we do not live or act as skeptics (i.e., doubt the existence of the external world, other minds, or the possibility of knowledge). In fact, many of the difficulties facing traditional philosophical attempts to understand human knowledge and experience can be traced to the following situation: Since the *practice* of philosophy requires reflective distance from the world, philosophers have been naturally prone to interpret human knowledge as a form of reflection which is distinct from the world (i.e., "ideas" and "things," "knowledge" and "reality"); such distinctions *create* the perennial epistemological problems (e.g., how are ideas properly related to things in the world?). But here philosophers may have been guilty of imposing a model of knowing which simply follows from the way *philosophers* think and which may be inadequate for expressing other forms of engagement. In other words, philosophical reflection *itself* may lead to inevitable distortions of human experience and its environment. That is one reason why Wittgenstein demanded a radical *limitation* of philosophical vocabulary, and why Heidegger attempted a radical existential *alteration* of philosophical language.

6. An appropriate myth for such a purpose might be the story of Prometheus, who stole fire from Zeus and gave it to the human race. Fire could express the light of knowledge which gives us the power to order and predict the course of things from an a priori, paradigmatic standpoint (the name Prometheus can be translated as "fore-knowledge"). Furthermore, the punishment of Prometheus could express a sacred check upon the power of knowledge, the gains of which must come to honor a certain limit. The implicit dangers of knowledge expressed in the myth are well illustrated in the modern age, where the consummation of scientific knowledge, nuclear physics, has led to the consummate danger of atomic weapons.

7. Many have argued that the persistence of these issues in modern philosophy is a direct result of Descartes's strict *separation* of mind and world, subject and object, idea and thing. Once that is done and accepted to any degree, the skeptic cannot be dissuaded from doubting a legitimate "connection" between what we know and what the world is like.

8. Snell, *The Discovery of the Mind*, chapter 10.

9. The tendency toward a displacement of myth by science is not a necessary condition for scientific thinking (a scientist might well acknowledge the limits of scientific inquiry and methods). That tendency is really a consequence of certain *metaphysical* urges in western thought since Plato wherein truth is assumed to be absolute or uniform. It is the assumption of uniformity that leads to reductionism, the *reinterpretation* of different forms of disclosure according to a single standard. Given a commitment to uniformity, when one is faced with different modes of thinking, one is compelled to *choose*. Or, if that choice runs up against objections or if exclusions seem unjustified, one might be compelled to question the very possibility of truth (i.e., skepticism or relativism). None of this follows from the various forms of disclosure themselves but rather from a metaphysical commitment to a highly questionable confinement of truth to a single form.

10. We might adopt a variation of Aristotle's insightful distinction: "It is the mark of an educated man to look for precision in each class of things just as far as the nature of the subject admits" (*Nicomachean Ethics*, I.3.1094b24–26).

11. A few remarks are in order concerning my treatment of science. For the most part I have been criticizing either one of two attitudes about scientific inquiry: (1) A positivistic confinement of truth to the scientific method, or (2) the standard view of science which at least assumes that the scientific method yields purely objective results. As previously noted, however, many developments in contemporary philosophy of science have aimed to discredit such attitudes and to loosen fixed assumptions about science. Many insights have challenged positivism and the standard view: The selectivity and active contribution of methodology with respect to results; the "theory-ladenness" of facts; the possible incommensurability of competing scientific paradigms; the importance of historical, social, political, and aesthetic elements in the practice of science; the role of creative imagination in scientific inquiry; an open-ended future for science without the assumption of fixed methodology or consummation of inquiry and findings. I have not pursued a detailed treatment of such developments. The main intention has been to loosen the situation *external* to science (i.e., the tendency to judge or devalue nonscientific forms of disclosure). The new philosophy of science, which loosens the situation *internal* to science, not only does not detract from this argument but extends it further and suggests a connection between certain mythical themes and science. In the light of the new philosophy of science, my critique of science creates a straw man. However, the positivistic and standard views *do* still persist in the minds of many.

12. The primal sense of truth as a process of disclosure, together with the overlapping of different forms of disclosure (e.g., myth and rationality), indicates that the term "pluralism" is not meant to denote a kind of atomistic separatism. Different forms of truth can be "referred" to something primal (different forms of *disclosure*), but that referral does not require a uniform reduction, a fixed standard, or even a hierarchy. In addition the overlap factor shows the difficulty of drawing clear boundary lines between different forms of disclosure. Pluralism is meant to express something like a "family" (to borrow a term from Wittgenstein) which is neither uniform nor strictly discontinuous. The same would apply to a pluralistic understanding *within* types of disclosure (i.e., the coexistence of different developments in philosophy, art, religion, or politics), which is something implicit in this investigation but not developed as such.

# SELECTED BIBLIOGRAPHY

Aristotle. *The Basic Works of Aristotle.* Edited by Richard McKeon. New York: Random House, 1941.

Benjamin, Andrew, ed. *Post-Structuralist Classics.* London: Routledge, 1988.

Blumenburg, Hans. *Work on Myth.* Translated by Robert M. Wallace. Cambridge: MIT Press, 1985.

Burkert, Walter. *Greek Religion.* Translated by John Raffan. Cambridge: Harvard University Press, 1985.

_____. *Structure and History in Greek Mythology and Ritual.* Berkeley: University of California Press, 1979.

Burnet, John. *Early Greek Philosophy.* New York: Meridian Books, 1957.

Campbell, Joseph. *The Masks of God.* New York: Viking Press, 1969.

_____. *The Hero with a Thousand Faces.* Princeton: Princeton University Press, 1949.

Cassirer, Ernst. *Language and Myth.* Translated by Susan K. Langer. New York: Dover Publications, 1953.

_____. *The Philosophy of Symbolic Forms.* Vol. 2: *Mythical Thought.* Translated by Ralph Manheim. New Haven: Yale University Press, 1955.

Cherniss, Harold. *Aristotle's Criticism of Plato and the Academy.* New York: Russell and Russell, 1962.

_____. *Aristotle's Criticism of Presocratic Philosophy.* New York: Octagon Books, 1976.

Claus, David B. *Toward the Soul.* New Haven: Yale University Press, 1981.

Cornford, F. M. *Principium Sapientiae.* Gloucester, Mass.: Peter Smith, 1971.

Dietrich, B. C. *The Origins of Greek Religion.* Berlin: Walter de Gruyter, 1974.

Dodds, E. R. *The Greeks and the Irrational.* Berkeley: University of California Press, 1968.

Dorter, Kenneth. *Plato's Phaedo.* Toronto: University of Toronto Press, 1982.

Easterling and Muir, eds. *Greek Religion and Society.* Cambridge University Press, 1985.

Edel, Abraham. *Aristotle and His Philosophy.* Chapel Hill: University of North Carolina Press, 1982.

Eliade, Mircea. *Cosmos and History: The Myth of the Eternal Return.* Translated by Willard R. Trask. New York: Harper and Row, 1959.

_____. *Myth and Reality.* Translated by Willard R. Trask. New York: Harper and Row, 1963.

_____. *Shamanism.* Translated by Willard R. Trask. Princeton: Princeton University Press, 1964.

_____. *Yoga: Immortality and Freedom*. Translated by Willard R. Trask. Princeton: Princeton University Press, 1969.

Elias, Julius A. *Plato's Defence of Poetry*. Albany: SUNY Press, 1984.

Ferrari, G. R. F. *Listening to the Cicadas: A Study of Plato's Phaedrus*. Cambridge University Press, 1987.

Feyerabend, Paul. *Against Method*. London: Verso, 1978.

Fränkel, Hermann. *Early Greek Poetry and Philosophy*. Translated by Moses Hadas and James Willis. New York: Harcourt Brace Jovanovich, 1975.

Frankfort, H., et al. *Before Philosophy*. Baltimore: Penguin Books, 1949.

Freeman, Kathleen, tr. *Ancilla to the Pre-Socratic Philosophers*. Cambridge: Harvard University Press, 1966.

Friedländer, Paul. *Plato*. Three Volumes. Translated by Hans Meyerhoff. Princeton: Princeton University Press, 1969.

Gadamar, Hans-George. *Truth and Method*. New York: The Seabury Press, 1975.

_____. *The Idea of the Good in Platonic-Aristotelian Philosophy*. Translated by P. Christopher Smith. New Haven: Yale University Press, 1986.

Griffin, Jasper. *Homer on Life and Death*. Oxford: Clarendon Press, 1980.

Grene, David, and Richmond Lattimore, eds. *The Complete Greek Tragedies*. Chicago: University of Chicago Press, 1959.

Graves, Robert. *The Greek Myths*. Baltimore: Penguin Books, 1955.

Guthrie, W. K. C. *The Greeks and Their Gods*. Boston: Beacon Press, 1950.

_____. *A History of Greek Philosophy*. Two Volumes. Cambridge University Press, 1962.

Harrison, Jane Ellen. *Epilegomena to the Study of Greek Religion* and *Themis*. New Hyde Park, N.Y.: University Books, 1962.

Hatab, Lawrence J. *Nietzsche and Eternal Recurrence: The Redemption of Time and Becoming*. University Press of America, 1978.

Havelock, Eric A. *Preface to Plato*. Cambridge: Harvard University Press, 1963.

Heidegger, Martin. *Being and Time*. Translated by John Macquarrie and Edward Robinson. New York: Harper and Row, 1962.

_____. *The Basic Problems of Phenomenology*. Translated by Albert Hofstadter. Bloomington: Indiana University Press, 1982.

_____. *Basic Writings*. Edited by David Krell. New York: Harper and Row, 1977.

_____. *On the Way to Language*. Translated by Peter D. Hertz. New York: Harper and Row, 1971.

_____. *On Time and Being*. Translated by Joan Stambaugh. New York: Harper and Row, 1972.

_____. *Poetry Language Thought*. Translated by Albert Hofstadter. New York: Harper and Row, 1971.

_____. *An Introduction to Metaphysics*. Translated by Ralph Manheim. New Haven: Yale University Press, 1959.

_____. *The Piety of Thinking*. Translated by James G. Hart and John C. Maraldo. Bloomington: Indiana University Press, 1976.

_____. *What Is Called Thinking?* Translated by Fred D. Wieck and J. Glenn Gray. New York: Harper and Row, 1968.

_____. *Early Greek Thinking.* Translated by David F. Krell and Frank A. Capuzzi. New York: Harper and Row, 1975.

_____. *Identity and Difference.* Translated by Joan Stambaugh. New York: Harper and Row, 1969.

_____. *What Is a Thing?* Translated by W. B. Barton Jr. and Vera Deutsch. Chicago: Henry Regnery Co., 1967.

Hesiod. *Hesiod.* Translated by H. G. Evelyn-White. Cambridge: Harvard University Press, 1914.

Homer. *The Iliad of Homer.* Translated by Richmond Lattimore. University of Chicago Press, 1951.

_____. *The Odyssey of Homer.* Translated by Richmond Lattimore. New York: Harper and Row, 1965.

Hyland, Drew. *The Origins of Philosophy.* New York: G. P. Putnam's Sons, 1973.

Jaeger, Werner. *Paideia: The Ideals of Greek Culture.* Translated by Gilbert Highet. New York: Oxford University Press, 1945.

_____. *Aristotle.* Translated by Richard Robinson. New York: Oxford University Press, 1962.

_____. *Theology of the Early Greek Philosophers.* Oxford: Clarendon Press, 1947.

Jaynes, Julian. *The Origin of Consciousness in the Breakdown of the Bicameral Mind.* Boston: Houghton Mifflin Co., 1976.

Kahn, Charles H. *The Art and Thought of Heracleitus.* Cambridge University Press, 1979.

_____. *Anaximander and the Origins of Greek Cosmology.* New York: Columbia University Press, 1960.

Kaufmann, Walter. *Tragedy and Philosophy.* New York: Anchor Books, 1968.

Kerenyi, C. *Dionysos.* Translated by Ralph Manheim. Princeton: Princeton University Press, 1976.

_____. *The Religion of the Greeks and Romans.* Translated by Christopher Holme. Westport, Conn.: Greenwood Press, 1973.

_____. *Eleusis.* Translated by Ralph Manheim. New York: Pantheon Books, 1967.

_____. *The Gods of the Greeks.* Translated by Norman Cameron. New York: Thames and Hudson, 1951.

_____. *The Heroes of the Greeks.* Translated by H. J. Rose. New York: Thames and Hudson, 1959.

Kirk, G. S. *The Nature of Greek Myths.* New York: Penguin Books, 1974.

_____. *Heracleitus: The Cosmic Fragments.* Cambridge University Press, 1962.

Kirk, G. S. and J. E. Raven. *The Presocratic Philosophers.* Cambridge University Press, 1966.

Klein, Jacob. *A Commentary on Plato's Meno.* Chapel Hill: University of North Carolina Press, 1965.

Kohanski, Alexander S. *The Greek Mode of Thought in Western Philosophy.* Associated University Presses, 1984.

Kuhn, Thomas S. *The Structure of Scientific Revolutions.* Chicago: University of Chicago Press, 1970.

Lattimore, Richmond, tr. *Greek Lyrics.* Chicago: University of Chicago Press, 1960.

Lear, Jonathan. *Aristotle: The Desire to Understand.* Cambridge University Press, 1988.

Lesky, Albin. *A History of Greek Literature.* Translated by James Willis and Cornelis de Heer. New York: Thomas Y. Crowell Co., 1966.

———. *Greek Tragic Poetry.* Translated by Matthew Dillon. New Haven: Yale University Press, 1983.

Levi-Strauss, Claude. *The Savage Mind.* Chicago: University of Chicago Press, 1966.

Lloyd, G. E. R. *Magic, Reason and Experience.* Cambridge University Press, 1979.

Moors, Kent F. *Platonic Myth: An Introductory Study.* University Press of America, 1982.

Moravcik, Julius, and Philip Temko, eds. *Plato on Beauty, Wisdom and the Arts.* Totowa, N.J.: Rowman and Littlefield, 1982.

Morick, Harold, ed. *Challenges to Empiricism.* Indianapolis: Hackett Publishing Co., 1980.

Morris, Brian. *Anthropological Studies of Religion.* Cambridge University Press, 1987.

Mourelatos, Alexander P. D. *The Route of Parmenides.* New Haven: Yale University Press, 1970.

———, ed. *The Pre-Socratics.* New York: Anchor Books, 1974.

Murray, Henry A., ed. *Myth and Mythmaking.* Boston: Beacon Press, 1968.

Nietzsche, Friedrich. *Basic Writings of Nietzsche.* Translated by Walter Kaufmann. New York: Modern Library, 1968.

———. *The Portable Nietzsche.* Translated by Walter Kaufmann. New York: Viking Press, 1968.

———. *The Will to Power.* Translated by Walter Kaufmann and R. J. Hollingdale. New York: Vintage Books, 1967.

Olson, Alan M., ed. *Myth, Symbol and Reality.* South Bend: University of Notre Dame Press, 1980.

Otto, Rudolph. *The Idea of the Holy.* Translated by J. W. Harvey. New York: Oxford University Press, 1923.

Otto, Walter F. *Dionysus: Myth and Cult.* Translated by Robert B. Palmer. Bloomington: Indiana University Press, 1965.

———. *The Homeric Gods.* Translated by Moses Hadas. New York: Octagon Books, 1978.

Pickard-Cambridge, A. W. *Dithyramb Tragedy and Comedy.* Second edition revised by T. B. L. Webster. New York: Oxford University Press, 1962.

Peters, F. E. *Greek Philosophical Terms*. New York: New York University Press, 1967.

Plato. *The Collected Dialogues of Plato*. Edited by Edith Hamilton and Huntington Cairns. Princeton: Princeton University Press, 1961.

Ricoeur, Paul. *The Symbolism of Evil*. Translated by E. Buchanan. New York: Harper and Row, 1967.

Rose, H. J. *Religion in Greece and Rome*. New York: Harper and Row, 1959.

Rosen, Stanley. *Plato's Sophist*. New Haven: Yale University Press, 1983.

———. *Plato's Symposium*. New Haven: Yale University Press, 1968.

———. *The Quarrel Between Philosophy and Poetry*. New York: Routledge, 1988.

Schlagel, Richard S. *From Myth to the Modern Mind*. Vol. I: *Animism to Archimedes*. New York: Peter Lang, 1985.

Sallis, John. *Being and Logos: The Way of Platonic Dialogue*. Pittsburgh: Duquesne University Press, 1975.

———, ed. *Philosophy and Archaic Experience*. Pittsburgh: Duquesne University Press, 1982.

Silk, M. S. and J. P. Stern. *Nietzsche on Tragedy*. Cambridge University Press, 1981.

Simon, Bennett. *Mind and Madness in Ancient Greece*. Ithaca: Cornell University Press, 1978.

Snell, Bruno. *The Discovery of the Mind*. Translated by T. G. Rosenmeyer. New York: Harper and Row, 1960.

Vernant, Jean-Pierre. *Myth and Thought among the Greeks*. London: Routledge and Kegan Paul, 1983.

———. *Myth and Society in Ancient Greece*. Translated by Janet Lloyd. Sussex: Harvester Press, 1980.

——— and Pierre Vidal-Naquet. *Myth and Tragedy in Ancient Greece*. Translated by Janet Lloyd. Atlantic Highlands, N.J.: Humanities Press, 1981.

Versenyi, Laszlo. *Man's Measure*. Albany: SUNY Press, 1974.

Veyne, Paul. *Did the Greeks Believe in Their Myths?* Translated by Paula Wissing. Chicago: University of Chicago Press, 1988.

Wilson, Brian R., ed. *Rationality*. New York: Harper and Row, 1970.

Zaslavsky, Robert. *Platonic Myth and Platonic Writing*. University Press of America, 1981.

# Index